Manston's
Europe '90

Also in the Travel Key Guide Series:

Manston's Italy

Manston's Travel Key Britain

Manston's Flea Markets, Antique Fairs,
and Auctions of Britain

Manston's Flea Markets, Antique Fairs,
and Auctions of France

Manston's Flea Markets, Antique Fairs,
and Auctions of Germany

*is for information.
Throughout Europe, the lower-case "i" is used
as the international symbol direct travelers to
information offices.*

Manston's Europe '90

How to Make a Phone Call, Do Your Laundry, Find a Toilet, and Much More

by
Peter B. Manston

A Travel Key Guide
Published by Travel Keys
Sacramento, California U.S.A.

Published by

Travel Keys
P. O. Box 160691
Sacramento, California 95816 U.S.A.
Telephone (916) 452-5200

Designed by Peter B. Manston
Editing by Robert C. Bynum
Type galleys by Lithographics
Printed and bound by Arcata Graphics
    (Kingsport)
Manufactured in the United States of America
First Printing January 1990

ISBN 0-931367-18-2 (pbk.)

ISSN 1048-4000

Contents

Acknowledgements

Between the day this book was just a gleam in my mind's eye and the day you get this book into your hands, dozens of people urged me on and generously helped. A few helped immeasurably by asking a single crucial question which significantly improved the final product. Others shared information and experiences. Some confirmed facts and processes by taking early and primitive drafts of some chapters with them, and testing them out all over Europe. Others shared their years of experience living there, checking the foreign language words and lending their knowledge. Some of the people who gave help of one sort or another are: Liz Brady, Duane Phillips, Joseph Magruder, Agnes Manston (my mother), Larry and Yvonne of the Rest Stop, Mel Green, Don Horel, Ed Mack, Larry Nelson, Jonellen Goddard, Armando Herra, Pavlos Kaltsas, Diane Keeney, Jacques and Ulda Crets-Clercxx, the California State Library staff, many officials of the various national tourist offices, U.S. State Department, and Canadian Ministry of External Affairs, European consulate staff, and the European staff of the United States Department of Commerce Foreign Commercial Service, and Ortrud Alderman and Bernadette Meauzé for translation assistance.

There are two people who deserve special thanks. Robert C. Bynum followed this project from its genesis, proving to be not only the book's godfather but also a perceptive and patient editor. Paula R. Mazuski provided encouragement and unstinting support when the work got hard and its completion kept receding into the distance like a mirage on a desert road.

My thanks to all.

Disclaimer of Responsibility

Don't forget that times change! In the everyday world, what we do today isn't necessarily what we'll have to do tomorrow. Prices go up, and very occasionally down. This guide will be updated in future editions as Europe changes.

This book is as complete and accurate as possible. Facts have been exhaustively checked and rechecked. Information had to be sifted and weighed. Therefore, though the information and prices are deemed to be accurate, they may not always be what you find. Neither the author nor the publisher can be responsible if you are inconvenienced by the information contained in the book.

The persons, companies, and institutions named in the book are believed to be reputable and engaged in the business or service they purport to. Any questions should be directed to them rather than the publisher. Inclusion or exclusion of mention of a firm or organization is not a reflection on the suitability of their services or product.

When you find differences, please let us know. Fill out the "Will You Help?" form section at the end of the book. What *you* find and suggest can make the next edition even more complete and more useful to those who follow your path.

Introduction
Why This Book, Too?

Simple things you take for granted at home can become incredibly difficult in a foreign country. How and where to buy a ticket for a bus or subway can be confusing and even frustrating. Once you have your ticket, what do you do next?

Doing the laundry (or having it done for you) is not always easy when you're abroad.

Using the telephone is so complex that many travelers won't even try.

The traveler simply needs help.

This book can eliminate many irritations and frustrations of travel, leaving you free to enjoy your vacation or concentrate on your business.

There are dozens of other guides to Europe. You can get them about theatres in London, cathedrals in any country, and dozens listing hotels and restaurants. "Manston's Europe," however, is a guide to *traveling* in Europe, emphasizing specific nuts-and-bolts information such as:

- how to keep clothes clean.
- how to find a toilet when you need it and what to expect when you do.
- how to find and use a telephone.
- how to mail a letter or postcard.
- how to use public transportation.
- how to get tax refunds of up to 33% on purchases of items you'll bring home.
- where to get help, including embassy and consulate locations, phone numbers, and what they can do for you.

This book, which will slip into your pocket or purse, provides this information and much, much more. A concise, instant reference, it is indexed by subjects as well as by countries.

You may not need all of this information at once—or some of it ever—but think about how essential it will be when you need it right away. You'll have instant access to facts not readily available elsewhere in a single easy-to-use form. You'll feel more secure.

It is to every traveler who, far from home, has felt uneasy facing the unknown that this book is dedicated.

Before You Go
Information Sources

You will probably gather information from many sources: libraries, bookstores, national tourism promotion offices, travel agents, Sunday travel sections, and friends and relatives. Some sources offer general information, while others offer quite specialized information. Some brochures, events calendars, guidebooks, and city maps will only be available when you get to your destination.

Libraries

Libraries will have the largest quantity of information but it is not always current. Most public libraries have the common travel books. Guides a few years old are still useful as a general reference, though not for making reservations or determining current prices.

Libraries also have books about European history, politics, and culture. To get a better idea of the variety of travel books, look at the "Books In Print" subject volumes for paperbacks and hardbacks.

A good library will have American, Canadian, and European magazines and newspapers. University and college libraries usually contain the most complete selections. Even if you can't read the language, the pictures and advertisements will give you some flavor of the country.

By using the library, you'll get lots of ideas to plan your trip. The only drawback to library books is that you can't take them with you, unless you're going on a short trip.

Bookstores

Current information is best found in the most recent books available in bookstores. By nature, however, most material on the shelves will be produced for the mass market. More specialized books listed in "Books in Print" (available for reference at most bookstores) can be special ordered either through the bookstore or (if the bookstore can't), directly from the publisher.

A few bookstores devoted to travel books, maps, guides, etc. offer greater depth. The following specialized bookstores all welcome mail and telephone orders and offer free catalogues:

Book Passage
51 Tamal Vista Blvd.
Corte Madera, Calif.
94925
Tel. (800) 321-9785
or (415) 927-0960

Easy Going
1400 Shattuck Ave.
Berkeley, Calif. 94709
Tel. (800) 233-3533 or
From California &
Canada (415) 843-3533

Gulliver's Travel
Book Shop
609 Bloor St. West
Toronto, Ont. M6G 1K5
Tel. (416) 537-7700
(Subject lists rather
than a catalogue.)

Complete Traveller
Bookstore
199 Madison Ave.
New York, N.Y. 10016
Tel. (212) 685-9007
($2 for first catalogue)

Forsyth Travel
Library
9154 W. 57th St.
P.O. Box 2975
Shawnee Mission,
Kansas 66201-1375
Tel. (913) 384-3440 or
(800) 367-7984
Fax (913) 384-3553

Le Travel Store
295 Horton Plaza
San Diego, Calif. 92101
Tel. (800) 854-6677
Calif.)
From California
(619) 544-0005

Librairie Ulysse
1208 St-Denis
Montréal, Québec
H2X 3J5 Canada
Tel. (514) 289-9875

The Literate Traveler
8306 Wilshire Blvd.,
Suite 591
Beverly Hills, Calif.
90211
Tel. (805) 373-6956

**Phileas Fogg's Books
& Maps for the
Traveler**
87 Stanford Shopping
Center
Palo Alto, Calif. 94304
Tel. (800) 233-FOGG
(California only)
or (800) 533-FOGG (U.S.
except Calif.)
From Canada
(415) 327-1754

Travel Genie
Map & Book Store
3714 Lincolnway
Ames, Iowa 50010
Tel. (515) 292-1070

Travellers Bookstore
75 Rockefeller Plaza
22 W. 52nd St.
New York, N.Y. 10019
Tel. (212) 664-0995

TravelBooks
1133 Corporation Road
Hyannis, Mass. 02601
Tel. (800) 869-3535
Fax (508) 772-3536

European Government Tourist Offices

Tourism is considered a nonpolluting national
resource to be carefully nurtured, and European
nations—except Albania—want you to come and
visit. Almost all—except Albania and East Germany and a few tiny countries—have government tourist offices in North America.

To encourage you to visit, they put out volumes
of material, mostly free for the asking. It ranges
from carefully designed books to lush, four-color
glossy brochures to typewritten hotel lists. All
entice you. Some nations shower you with more
information than others: Britain will send
volumes of free information, while some Eastern
countries have only a brochure or two. Italy and
Greece put out free books designed for
prospective tourists. East Germany's embassy
has been known to send out a free, several
hundred-page four-color book about the country
as well as tourist-oriented booklets

You'll get a rich harvest for the price of a few postcards or letters. If you have special interests, such as fishing, churches, or music festivals, be sure to mention them in your request for information.

You should remember that the information you receive isn't unbiased: no tourist office will allude to political or social problems, polluted beaches, slag heaps, or slums. Neither will they mention smog-eaten monuments, or, for that matter, monumental traffic jams. Further, the focus may be where the particular nation wants the tourists to go: for example, the free Italian book devotes an equal amount of space to every single region, interesting or not to the traveler.

A list of European national tourist offices in the United States and Canada is below. European nations also have offices in other European countries' capitals and other major cities. You can find these offices in phone books or any local tourist information office. These offices have much of the same literature and offer much the same advice. However, some of the brochures may only be available in the language of the country you're in.

European Government Tourist Offices in the United States

Andorra
Andorra Tourist Office
120 E. 55th St.
New York, NY 10022
Tel. (212) 688-8681

Austria

Austrian National
Tourist Office
500 N. Michigan Ave.
#544
Chicago, Illinois 60611
Tel. (312) 644-5556
Fax (312) 644-6526
Telex 230-254311

Austrian National
Tourist Office
4800 San Felipe St.
#500 Houston, Texas
77056
Tel. (713) 850-8888
Fax (713) 850-7857
Telex 230-765544

Austrian National
Tourist Office
11601 Wilshire Blvd.,
Suite 2480
Los Angeles, Calif.
90025-1760
Tel. (213) 477-3332
Fax (213) 477-5141
Telex 23-9720194

Austrian National
Tourist Office
500 Fifth Ave. #2009
New York, N.Y. 10110
Tel. (212) 944-6880
Fax (212) 730-4568
Telex 23-224254

Belgium
Belgian National Tourist
Office
745 Fifth Ave.
New York, N.Y. 10151
Tel. (212) 758-8130
Fax (212) 355-7675

Bulgaria
Balkan
Holidays/USA/Ltd.
161 E. 86th St.
New York, N.Y. 10028
Tel. (212) 722-1110   or
(800) 525-1110
Fax (212) 996-3316
Telex 429767

Czechoslovakia
Cedok Czechoslovak
Travel Bureau
10 E. 40th St.,   Suite
1902
New York, N.Y. 10016
Tel. (212) 689-9720
Fax (212) 481-0597

Denmark
Danish Tourist Board
655 Third Ave.
New York, N.Y. 10017
Tel. (212) 949-2333
Fax (212) 983-5260
Telex 520681 SCANDIA
NY   (Please also see
Scandinavia listing.)

Finland
Finnish Tourist Board
655 Third Ave.
New York, N.Y. 10017
Tel. (212) 370-5540

Finnish Tourist Board
1900 Ave. of the Stars
#1025
Los Angeles, Calif.
90067   Tel. (213)
277-5226

(Please also see Scandinavia listing.)

France
French Government
Tourist Office
9454 Wilshire Blvd.,
Suite 303
Beverly Hills, Calif.
90212
Tel. (213) 271-6665

French Government
Tourist Office
645 North Michigan
Ave., Suite 630
Chicago, Illinois 60611
Tel. (312) 337-6301 or
(312) 751-7800 (business)

French Government
Tourist Office
World Trade Center 103,
2050 Stemmons Freeway
P.O. Box 58610
Dallas, Texas 75258
Tel. (214) 742-7011

French Government
Tourist Office
One Hallidie Plaza #250
San Francisco, Calif.
94102
Tel. (415) 986-4161

French Government
Tourist Office
610 Fifth Ave.
New York, N.Y. 10020
Tel. (212) 757-1125

Germany, FRG (West)

German National
Tourist Office
444 S. Flower St.,
Suite 2230
Los Angeles, Calif.
90071
Tel. (213) 688-7332

German National
Tourist Office
747 Third Ave.
New York, N.Y. 10017
Tel. (212) 308-3300
Fax (212) 688-1322

Germany, GDR (East)

Embassy of the German
Democratic Republic
Consular Section
1717 Massachusetts
Ave., N.W.
Washington, D.C. 20036
Tel. (202) 232-3134

Great Britain

British Tourist
Authority
John Hancock Center
875 N. Michigan Ave.,
Suite 3320
Chicago, Illinois
60611-1977
Tel. (312) 787-0490

British Tourist
Authority
Cedar Maple Plaza
2305 Cedar Springs Rd.
Dallas, Texas
75201-1814
Tel. (214) 720-4040

British Tourist
Authority
World Trade Center
350 S. Figueroa St.,
Suite 450
Los Angeles, Calif.
90071-1203
Tel. (213) 628-3525

British Tourist
Authority
40 W. 57th St., 3rd
Floor
New York, N.Y. 10019
Tel. (212) 581-4700

Greece
Greek National Tourist
Organization
168 N. Michigan Ave.
Chicago, Illinois 60601
Tel. (312) 782-1084

Greek National Tourist
Organization
611 W. Sixth St., Suite
2198
Los Angeles, Calif.
90017
Tel. (213) 626-6696
Telex GRECTOUR LSA
686441

Greek National Tourist
Organization
645 Fifth Ave., Fifth Fl.
New York, N.Y. 10022
Tel. (212) 421-5777

Hungary
Hungarian Travel
Bureau (Ibusz)
One Parker Plaza, Suite
1104   Fort Lee, N.J.
07024 Tel. (212)
582-7412 and (201)
592-8585

Ireland
Irish Tourist Board
757 Third Ave.
New York, N.Y. 10017
Tel. (212) 418-0800

Italy
Italian Government
Tourist Office (E.N.I.T.)
500 N. Michigan Ave.
Chicago, Illinois 60611
Tel. (312) 644-0990

Italian Government
Tourist Office (E.N.I.T.)
630 Fifth Ave., Suite
1565
New York, N.Y. 10111
Tel. (212) 245-4961

Italian Government
Tourist Office (E.N.I.T.)
360 Post St., Suite 801
San Francisco, Calif.
94108
Tel. (415) 392-5266

Luxembourg
Luxembourg National
Tourist Office
801 - 2nd Ave.
New York, N.Y. 10017
Tel. (212) 370-9850
Fax (212) 697-5529

Malta
Consulate-General of
Malta
249 E. 35th St.
New York, N.Y. 10016
Tel. (212) 725-2345

Monaco
Monaco Government
Tourist and Convention
Bureau
845 Third Ave.
New York, N.Y. 10022
Tel. (212) 759-5227
Fax (212) 754-9320
Telex 424253

Monaco Government
Tourist and Convention
Bureau
407 S. Dearborn St.
Chicago, Illinois 60605
Tel. (312) 939-7836
Fax (312) 939-8727

Netherlands
Netherlands Board of
Tourism
225 N. Michigan Ave.,
Suite 326
Chicago, Illinois 60601
Tel. (312) 819-0300
Fax (312) 819-1740

Netherlands Board of
Tourism
355 Lexington Ave.,
21st Floor
New York, N.Y. 10017
Tel. (212) 370-7367
Fax (212) 370-9507

Netherlands Board of Tourism
90 New Montgomery St. #305
San Francisco, Calif. 94105
Tel. (415) 543-6772 and (213) 678-8802
Fax (415) 495-4925

Northern Ireland
Northern Ireland
Tourist Board
40 W. 57th St., 3rd
Floor
New York, N.Y. 10019
Tel. (212) 765-5144

Norway
(Please see Scandinavia
listing.)

Poland
Polish National Tourist
Office
Information Center
333 N. Michigan Ave.,
Suite 228
Chicago, Illinois 60601
Tel. (312) 236-9013
Fax (312) 236-1125
Telex 282181

Portugal
Portuguese National
Tourist Office
590 Fifth Ave., 4th Floor
New York, N.Y.
10036-4704
Tel. (212) 354-4403
Fax (212) 764-6137
Telex 234140 CTPA

Romania
Romanian National
Tourist Office
573 - 3rd Ave.
New York, N.Y. 10016
Tel. (212) 697-6971

San Marino
Consul General—Attn.
Tourism
1155 - 21st St. N.W.,
Suite 400
Washington, D.C. 20036
Tel. (202) 223-3517
Fax (202) 872-0896
Telex 277566 EXEC UR

Scandinavia
Scandinavian National
Tourist Offices
655 Third Ave.
New York, N.Y. 10017
Tel. (212) 949-2333
(Note: Information is
available for all
Scandinavian countries
at this one office.)

Scandinavian Tourist
Board
8929 Wilshire Blvd.
Beverly Hills, Calif.
90211
Tel. (213) 854-1549
(Note: Information is
available for Denmark
and Sweden.)

Soviet Union, U.S.S.R.
Intourist
630 Fifth Ave., Suite 868
New York, N.Y. 10111
Tel. (212) 757-3884 and -5

Spain
National Tourist Office
of Spain
8383 Wilshire Blvd.
#960 Beverly Hills,
Calif. 90211
Tel. (213) 658-7188
Fax (213) 658-1067

National Tourist Office
of Spain
Water Tower Pl. #915E
845 N. Michigan Ave.
Chicago, Illinois 60611
Tel. (312) 944-0215

National Tourist Office
of Spain
1221 Brickell Dr. #1850
Miami, Fla. 33131
Tel. (305) 358- 1992

National Tourist Office
of Spain
665 Fifth Ave.
New York, N.Y. 10022
Tel. (212) 759-8822

Sweden
Swedish Scandinavian
Tourist Board
150 N. Michigan Ave.
Chicago, Illinois 60601
Tel. (312) 726-1120

Swedish Tourist Board
655 Third Ave.
New York, N.Y. 10017
Tel. (212) 949-2333
(Please also see
Scandinavia listing.)

Switzerland
Swiss National Tourist
Office
150 N. Michigan Ave.
Suite 2930
Chicago, Illinois 60601
Tel. (312) 630-5840
Fax (312) 630-5845

Swiss National Tourist
Office
222 N. Sepulveda Blvd.,
Suite 1570
El Segundo, Calif. 90425
Tel. (213) 335-5980
Fax (213) 335-5982

Swiss National Tourist
Office
608 Fifth Ave.
New York, N.Y. 10020
Tel. (212) 757-5944
Fax (212) 262-6116

Swiss National Tourist
Office
250 Stockton St.
San Francisco, Calif.
94108
Tel. (415) 362-2260
Fax (415) 391-1508

Turkey
Turkish Tourism
Information Office
821 United Nations
Plaza
New York, N.Y. 10017
Tel. (212) 687-2194

Yugoslavia
Yugoslav National
Tourist Office
630 Fifth Ave.
New York, N.Y. 10111
Tel. (212) 757-2801
Fax (212) 459-0130
Telex 825492

European Government Tourist Offices in Canada

Many European nations maintain tourist offices
in Canada, if there is no tourist office of the
countries you wish to visit in Canada, you can
obtain information from the nearest office in the

United States. Postage rates to the United States are slightly higher than within Canada.

Austria

Austrian National Tourist Office
1010 Sherbrooke St. West, Suite 1410
Montréal, P.Q. H3A 2R7
Tel. (514) 849- 3709
Fax (514) 849-9577
Telex 05-267391

Austrian National Tourist Office
2 Bloor St. East, Suite 3330
Toronto, Ont. M4W 1A8
Tel. (416) 967-3381
Fax (416) 967-4101
Telex 06-23196

Austrian National Tourist Office
Suite 1220-1223, Vancouver Block
736 Granville St.
Vancouver, B.C. V6Z 1J2
Tel. (604) 683-5808, Fax (604) 662-8528
Telex 04-51255

Belgium

Belgian National Tourist Office/Office National Belge
    de Tourisme
P.O. Box 760 Succursale N.D.G.
Montréal, P.Q. H4A 3S2
Tel. (514) 487-3387   Fax (514) 489-8965

Bulgaria

Bulgarian Trade Commission
100 Adelaide St. West
#1405   Toronto, Ont. M5H 1S3
Tel. (416) 368- 1034
Fax (416) 368-3505,
Telex 06-23535

Denmark

Danish Tourist Board
P.O. Box 115, Station N
Toronto, Ont. M8V 3S4
Tel. (416) 823-9620
Fax (416) 823-8860

France

French Government Tourist Office
1981 McGill College Ave., Suite 490
Montréal, PQ. H3A 2W9
Tel. (514) 288-4264
Fax (514) 845-4868
Telex 05-267335

French Government Tourist Office
1 Dundas St. West, Suite 2405, Box 8
Toronto, Ont. M5G 1Z3
Tel. (416) 593-4717
Fax (416) 979-7587
Telex 06-23889

Germany, West (FRG)
German National
Tourist Office
2175 Bloor St. East,
Suite 604
Toronto, Ont. M4W 3R8
Tel. (416) 968-1570

Great Britain
British Tourist
Authority
94 Cumberland St.,
Suite 600
Toronto, Ont. M5R 3N3
Tel. (416) 925-6326
Fax (416) 961-2175

Greece
Greek National Tourist
Organization
1233 De La Montagne
Montréal, P.Q. H3G 1Z2
Tel. (514) 871-1535

Greek National Tourist
Organization
68 Scollard St., Lower
Level, Unit E
Toronto, Ont. M5R 1G2
Tel. (416) 968-2220

Ireland
Irish Tourist Board
10 King St. East
Toronto, Ont. M5C 1C3
Tel. (416) 364-1301

Italy
Italian Government
Travel Office
(E.N.I.T.)/Office
National Italien de
Tourisme (E.N.I.T.)
1 Place Ville Marie,
Suite 1914
Montréal, P.Q. H3B 3M9
Tel. (514) 866-7667
Fax (514) 392-1429
Telex 05-25607

Netherlands
Netherlands Board of
Tourism
25 Adelaide St. East,
Suite 710
Toronto, Ont. M5C 1Y2
Tel. (416) 363-1577
Fax (416) 363-1470

Portugal
Portuguese National
Tourist Office
500 Sherbrooke West,
Suite 930
Montréal, P.W. H3A 3C6
Tel. (514) 843-4623

Portuguese National
Tourist Office
2180 Yonge St,
Concourse Level
Toronto, Ont. M4S 2B9
Tel. (416) 487-3300

Soviet Union, U.S.S.R.
Intourist
1801 McGill College
Ave. #630
Montréal, P.Q. H3A 2N4
Tel. (514) 849-6394
Fax (514) 849-6243
Telex 055-62018

Spain
National Tourist Office
of Spain
102 Bloor St. West,
Suite 1400
Toronto, Ont. M5S 1M8
Tel. (416) 961-3131
Fax (416) 961-1992
Telex 06-218206

Switzerland
Swiss National Tourist Office
154 University Ave., 6th Floor
Toronto, Ont. M5H 3Z4
Tel. (416) 868-0584

Travel Agents

Travel agents offer useful and valuable information about where and how to travel. A good agent
can conveniently provide important services at
no direct cost to you, including package tours,
fly-drive combinations, car rentals, tickets, railpasses, and visa information. Most of their income comes from commissions from airlines,
hotels, and other service sellers. Travel agents
may have biases in favor of scheduled airlines,
major tour operators, and large hotel chains.
Some are less likely to want to deal with bucket
shop and charter flight operators, budget-range
small hotels, etc., because those organizations
and establishments offer small (or no) commissions. Some travel agents will bill you directly if
they receive no commission, or what they consider a substandard one.
Select travel agents on the basis of referrals,
their knowledge and trustworthiness. You may
wind up dealing with a single agent, or,
particularly if you use deeply discounted flights,
one for the flights and another for other
purposes.

Sunday Travel Sections

Partly as a service and partly as an advertising
vehicle, many Sunday newspapers have exten-

sive travel sections. These are somewhat scattered in coverage, depending on which writers have been where and which advertisers are aiming for business.

They provide you with the most current information about where to go, what you'll find when you get there, and sometimes how much it will cost. You'll also read articles enticing you to places you hadn't thought about visiting. Some of them you may want to visit—or revisit. The positive is stressed: except for the rare article and letter to the editor, you'll sometimes need to read between the lines to get a balanced view.

Some large city newspapers have developed superior, informative travel sections in their Sunday editions. First among equals is The New York Times. Also excellent are the travel sections of the Los Angeles Times, Boston Globe, and San Francisco Chronicle & Examiner.

The nearest major metropolitan paper—whether named above or not—will be your best source of information about bucket shop, charter, and other cheap flights.

Remember

Above all, you're in control. You can decide intelligently where you want to go, what you want to see, and how to get there.

Passports

Your passport verifies your citizenship. United States and Canadian citizens traveling to Europe are required to have passports, and every airline flying to Europe requires a travel document (usually a passport) before issuing a boarding pass. This is because if you arrive in Europe without such a document, the European immigration officers won't let you in, and the airline will have to fly you back, possibly at its expense.

You need your passport to cross most borders, cash travelers checks, and often to change money. It serves as identification when you register at hotels or rent cars, bicycles, etc. In short, a passport is essential. You should make at least one photo copy of the inside front pages of your passport, and put it in your luggage (but not in your passport case). It will be invaluable if you need to replace your passport.

Since requirements and procedures differ between the United States and Canada, each country is treated separately. Resident non-citizens of the United States should see the end of the United States section.

United States Residents

Passports are readily available to most American citizens. When you apply for the first time, you must complete an application (Form DSP-11). You must apply in person at a Department of

State Passport Agency, major post office, or some courthouses.

To get a passport you need to prove you are a citizen in one of the following ways:

- A certified birth certificate if you were born in the United States. Note that the hospital certificate issued when you were born will not work. If you don't have a birth certificate at hand, order one from the state or county vital statistics department in the state where you were born. A certificate will cost $2 to $15, depending on the state.
- Certificate of Naturalization, Certificate of Citizenship, or Consular Report of Birth if you are a United States citizen born abroad.
- An expired United States Passport. An old passport is always acceptable as proof of citizenship even if you can't renew by mail. (See Passport Renewal.)

If you don't have any of these, contact the nearest passport agency and ask about alternative methods of proving citizenship.

In addition to the above, you will also need identification. It must have your signature and either a physical description or a photograph. A driver license or other government issued identification card is the most acceptable.

The Internal Revenue Service requires a Social Security number (space is provided on the passport application). While you can obtain a passport without including your Social Security number, the Internal Revenue Service could take action against you if you omit it.

Passport Photos

You will need two passport photographs. Black and white is more convenient, though color is acceptable. Instant photos from coin-operated photo booths are not acceptable because they melt during mounting. While most professional photography studios know the standards, here they are:

- Both photographs must be identical. Get two prints from the same negative.

- The photos must be full face forward with your head between 1 and 1⅜ inches in diameter.
- Photos must be taken against a white or light background.
- Overall photo size must be 2 by 2 inches.

Some additional recommendations can ensure that you have the photos you may need in addition to the two for your passport:

- Get at least eight extra prints. They will be useful in obtaining visas, international driving permit, public transit passes, and other secondary identification. You may even give some away to the friends you make.
- Buy or keep the negative and keep it with your passport. This way, if you need additional prints, they will be easy to get and will match your passport picture. This can be important at sensitive borders.
- If your passport picture is black and white, it's easier to get prints quickly from your negative if for some reason you need them fast.

Extra Pages

Most United States passports have 24 pages. You can request 48-page passports when you apply if you think you'll need them for visas. (Most visas take up an entire page and are required for Eastern Europe, as well as many non-European parts of the world.)

If you later find you need added pages, you can get additional pages attached at the nearest passport office (see below) in the United States or the nearest consulate or embassy consular office overseas (see Embassy chapter). There is no charge for additional pages, either when you apply or if you need them added later.

Passport Cost

If you're over 18 years of age, the basic cost is $35. In addition, if you're not renewing an old passport by mail (see below), you'll have to pay an "execution fee" of $7, for a total of $42. Your passport will be valid for 10 years from the date of issue. If you're under 18, the basic cost is $20 plus the $7 execution fee. Your passport will be valid for five years.

Passport Renewal

If you have a passport issued less than 12 years ago (whether current or expired) and you were over 16 when it was issued, you can apply for a new one either in person or by mail. If the passport was issued more than 12 years before the date you reapply, it is valid proof of citizenship (instead of a birth certificate or equivalent), but you cannot renew by mail.

   If you apply for a renewal, follow the procedure above and pay $35. If you renew by mail, get an application (Form DPS-82) at major post offices or from the nearest passport agency (office). Complete the application, get new passport photos, and send them with your old passport to the nearest passport agency with a $35 check or money order. (You save $7 by mailing the application in or going to the passport agency in person.) Both old and new passports will be mailed back to you.

How Long Will It Take?

Your passport will be mailed to you if you apply by mail. If you apply in person, it will be mailed to you unless you specify otherwise. The time can range from as little as a week during the winter to two months during the spring and early summer. Allow extra time, just in case.

Emergency: Need a passport pronto?

In a genuine emergency, you can probably get a passport in as little as a day, but there are conditions. First, you must go in person with your proof of citizenship and identification to the nearest passport agency. And, you will usually have to go in person to pick it up. Bring any documentation of the emergency that you have—it can be a telegram, letter, plane reservation or

ticket (with your explanation). If you don't have
acceptable proof of citizenship, call the nearest
Passport office to determine what you must do
before you go down to the office.

If you cannot contact a Passport Agency
(office), you can also call the State Department at
(202) 634-3600 and ask for the "Passport Duty
Officer."

Passport Agencies (Offices)

Government offices that issue passports are
called "agencies." Applications for passports can
be made in person or by mail to these offices.
These offices' telephone services include both a
24-hour recording with general information, and
an information officer during business hours for
more specialized questions.

Boston
Passport Agency
Thomas P. O'Neill, Jr.
Federal Building,
Room 247
10 Causeway St.
Boston, Mass. 02222
Tel. Recording:
(617) 565-6998
Questions:
(617) 565-6990

Chicago
Passport Agency
Suite 380,   Kluczynski
Federal Building
230 S. Dearborn St.
Chicago, Illinois 60604
Tel. Recording:
(312) 353-5426
Questions:
(312) 353-7155 amd
-7163

Honolulu
Passport Agency
Room C-106,
New Federal Building
300 Ala Moana Blvd.
P.O. Box 50185
Honolulu, Hawaii 96850
Tel. Recording:
(808) 541-1919
Questions:
(808) 541-1918

Houston
Passport Agency
Suite 1100, Concord
Tower
1919 Smith St.
Houston, Texas 77002
Tel. Recording:
(713) 653-3159
Questions:
(713) 653-3153

Los Angeles
Passport Agency
Room 13100
Federal Building
11000 Wilshire Blvd.
Los Angeles, Calif.
90024-3615
Tel. Recording:
(213) 209-7070
Questions:
(213) 209-7075

Miami
Passport Agency
16th Floor,
Federal Office Building
51 S.W. First Ave.
Miami, Florida
33130-1680
Tel. Recording:
(305) 536-5395
Questions:
(305) 536-4681 to -3

New Orleans Passport Agency
Postal Service Bldg. Room T-12005
701 Loyola Ave.
New Orleans, La. 70130
Tel. Recording: (504) 589-6728
Questions: (504) 589-6161 to -3

New York
Passport Agency
Rockefeller Center,
Room 270
630 Fifth Ave.
New York, N.Y. 10111
Tel. Recording:
(212) 541-7700
Questions:
(212) 541-7710
(walk-in applications
only)

Northeast Passport
Processing Center
Federal Building 21108
201 Varick St., New
York, N.Y. 10014-4891
(Mail applications only)

Philadelphia
Passport Agency
Room 4426
Federal Building
600 Arch St.
Philadelphia, Penn.
19106
Tel. Recording:
(215) 597-7482
Questions:
(215) 597-7480 and -1

San Francisco
Passport Agency
525 Market St., Suite
200 San Francisco, Calif.
94105-2773
Tel. Recording:
(415) 974-7972
Questions:
(415) 974-9941 to -5

Seattle
Passport Agency
Room 992
Henry M. Jackson
Federal Building
915 Second Ave.
Seattle, Wash.
98174-1091
Tel. Recording:
(206) 442-7941
Questions:
(206) 442-7945 to -7

Stamford
Passport Agency
One Landmark Square,
Street Level
Broad and Atlantic Sts.
Stamford, Conn. 06901
Tel. Recording:
(203) 325-4401
Questions:
(203) 325-3530, -38, and
-39

Washington Passport Agency
1425 K St., N.W., Room G62
Washington, D.C. 20524
Tel. Recording: (202) 783-8200
Questions: (202) 647-0518

United States Passports Overseas

United States citizens who reside overseas (or
are on a long journey), or whose passports are
lost or stolen can obtain new (or replacement)
passports under the same conditions and costs as
those who live in the United States from the
nearest consulate or the consular section of the
nearest embassy.

Resident Noncitizens

Noncitizen residents of the United States must
take care of a few formalities before leaving for
Europe to ensure admission when returning.
(This includes holders of "Green Cards.")

Contact the nearest Internal Revenue Service
(IRS) office and request a Treasury Sailing
Permit (Form 1040C). Though this document
ensures merely that all your taxes have been
paid before you leave, you must provide a
number of documents to receive it. When you go
to the Internal Revenue Service office, take your
Alien Registration Form (I-151 or Green Card),
valid passport of your own nationality, most
recent federal income tax return and W-2, and a
pay stub or proof of employment. Contact the

IRS before you go to make sure you have everything you need.

If you plan to be out of the United States for more than one year, you must also contact the Immigration and Naturalization Service for a re-entry permit. Allow at least one month to obtain this permit.

Passports for Canadian Citizens

Canadians must obtain passports before traveling to Europe. Passports cost $25 (Canadian) and are valid for five years. At the end of five years, you must apply for a new passport. All applicants must submit documentary evidence of Canadian citizenship: if born in Canada—birth certificate or certificate of Canadian citizenship. Only original documents are accepted. If born in Québec, you can present either an original baptismal certificate, or a municipal or provincial birth certificate, showing the date and place of birth. If you were born outside of Canada, you will need either a Certificate of Citizenship, Certificate of Naturalization, Certificate of Registration of Birth Abroad, or Certificate of Retention of Citizenship. You will need to provide originals, which will be returned to you.

You can apply for your passport in person at the nearest Passport Office. (See list below.) If you apply by mail in Canada, you must send your application to Ottawa. Do not apply by mail to regional offices. The Passport Application Form A can be obtained from any passport office or post office and from some travel agents.

Children under 16 years of age can be included in one of their parent's passports. They can also obtain a separate passport (use Application Form B). Original documentary evidence of citizenship is required in all cases. As well, any court orders relating to the custody of, access to, or mobility of the child(ren), in cases of divorce or separation, are required.

Completing the Application

Complete sections 1 through 7 (sections 1 through 8 on old forms, which are not obsolete). Then you need to have Section 8 (Section 9 on old forms) completed and signed by a "Guarantor," who must have known you for at least two years. He or she must certify that the information you have completed is true and sign the passport form. Guarantors can be chosen *only* from a limited number of categories of persons as listed on the form, including attorneys, notaries public, bank officers, doctors, dentists, and judges.

If you don't have a guarantor who knows you well enough to sign, you can still get your passport by completing one copy of the Declaration in Lieu of Guarantor (Form PPT 132) (two copies outside Canada) and signing it (them) in the presence of an authorized official. The categories of qualified officials are listed on the form.

You must take the application and supporting documents (including original birth certificate or equivalent) in person to the nearest passport office along with the required fee (currently $25). Passports will normally be issued within three to five working days. You can also apply by mail: in this case you must send the same information and fee to Ottawa. You should receive your passport and proof of citizenship by mail within two weeks of their receiving the application.

A passport issued in Canada will not be mailed to an address outside Canada.

Passport Photos

You must submit two passport photographs with your application. The photos must be taken within 12 months of your application and be no larger than 2 x 2¾ inches (50 x 70 mm), with the bottom half inch (13 mm) a blank space. Put your signature in that half inch. The photo must be taken against a plain light background, and the face length from chin to crown of head must be between 1 inch (25mm) and 1⅜ inches (35mm). The photos must be dated and the name and address of the photographer must be on the back of one of the photos. Your guarantor must also sign on the back of one picture. In addition, retouched photos, photos which peel, photos sensitive to heat, or group photographs are not acceptable.

Some additional recommendations can ensure that you have the photos you may need in addition to the two for your passport:

- Get black and white prints. They're easier to reprint quickly.
- Get at least eight extra prints. They will be useful in obtaining visas, international driving permit, public transit passes, and other secondary identification. You may even give some away to the friends you make.
- Buy or keep the negative and keep it with your passport. This way if you need additional prints, they will be easy to get and will match your passport picture. This can be important at sensitive borders.

Emergency: Need a Passport Quickly?

Canadians who need passports quickly should apply in person at the nearest passport office. In most cases, a passport can be issued within three working days. You must have all of the required documentation and photos. Should you require a passport issued in under three days, a plane ticket or other documentation outlining the reason is required.

Canadian Passport Offices

The Ottawa office has nationwide toll-free information numbers: (800) 567-6844 in eastern Canada and (800) 567-6868 in western Canada. Other "800" numbers are limited to the provinces and territories noted. Regional offices, with addresses and phone numbers, follow.

Calgary
Passport Office
220 - 4th Ave. S.E.,
Suite 480
Government of Canada
Building
Calgary, Alta. T2G 4X3
Tel. (403) 292-5171

Edmonton
Passport Office
Suite 1630,
Canada Place Building
9700 Jasper Ave.
Edmonton, Alta. P5J
4C3
Tel. (403) 420-2622 and
(800) 232-9475 (Alberta
& N.W. Territory)

Fredericton
Passport Office
Kings Place, Suite 601
440 King St.
Fredericton, New
Brunswick E3B 5H8
Tel. (506) 452-3900

Halifax
Passport Office
Suite 608
Duke Tower, Scotia
Square
5251 Duke St.
Halifax, N.S. B3J 1P4
Tel. (902) 426-2770 and
(800) 565-7762 (New
Brunswick, Nova Scotia,
P.E.I., & Newfoundland)

Hamilton
Passport Office
Standard Life Building,
Suite 330
120 King St. West
Hamilton, Ont.L8P 4V2
Tel. (416) 572-2217

Jonquière
Passport Office
Suite 208, place St.
Michel
3885 Harvey Blvd.
Jonquière, P.Q. G7X 9B1
Tel. (418) 542-0877

London
Passport Office
Government of Canada
Building, 8th Floor
451 Talbot St.
London, Ont. N6A 5C9
Tel. (519) 679-4366

Montréal
Passport Office
Suite 215, West Tower
Guy Favreau Complex
200 Réné Levesque
Blvd. W.
Montréal, P.Q. H2Z 1X4
Tel. (514) 283-2152
(800) 361-7699 (Quebec)

St-Laurent
Passport Office
3300 Côte Vertu
Main Floor, Suite 112
St-Laurent, P.Q. H4R 2B7
Tel. (514) 496-1343

Ottawa
Passport Office
240 Sparks St. West
Tower First Floor
Ottawa, Ont. K1P 6C9
Tel. (613) 995-8826

Hull
Passport Office
200 Promenade du
Portage
Place du Centre,
6th Floor
Hull, P.Q.
Tel. (613) 994-3500
Nationwide toll-free:
(800) 567-6844/6868

Quèbec
Passport Office
Place Bellecour,
Suite 1000
2590 Laurier Blvd.
Ste-Foy, Québec, Québec
G1V 4M6
Tel. (418) 648-4990

Scarborough
Passport Office,
Suite 828
200 Town Centre Court
Scarborough Town
Centre
Scarborough, Ont., M1P
4X6
Tel. (416) 973-3251

Regina
Passport Office
Suite 502, Canadian
Imperial Bank of
Commerce Building
1867 Hamilton St.
Regina, Sask. S4P 2C2
Tel. (306) 780-7520

St. John's
Passport Office
General Post Office
Building, 4th Floor
354 Water St.
St. John's,
Newfoundland A1C 6C6
Tel. (709) 772-4616

Saskatoon
Passport Office
6th Floor, Room 605
101 - 22nd St. East
Federal Building
Saskatoon,
Saskatchewan S7K 0E1
Tel. (306) 975-5106
and (800) 667-9792
(Saskatchewan)

Toronto
Passport Office
Suite 1031, 10th Floor
Atrium on Bay
20 Dundas St. West
Toronto, Ont. M5G 2C2
Tel. (416) 973-3251 and
(800) 387-3000 (Ontario)
North York
Government of Canada
Building, 2nd Floor
4900 Yonge St.
Willowdale M2N 6A6
Tel. (416) 224-4411

Thunder Bay
Passport Office
Suite 406
Royal Insurance Bldg.
28 Cumberland St. N.
Thunder Bay, Ont.
Tel. (800) 343-5591
(Ontario only)

West Vancouver
Passport Office
Sinclair Centre, Rm. 240
757 Hastings St. West
Vancouver, B.C. V6C
1A1
Tel. (604) 666-0221 and
(800) 663-1656 (British
Columbia and Yukon)

Victoria
Passport Office
Suite 228, Customs
House
816 Government St.
West Victoria, B.C. V8W
1W8   Tel. (604)
388-0213

Windsor
Passport Office
Rm 504 Bank of
Commerce Building
100 Ouellette Ave.
Windsor, Ont. N9A 6T3
Tel. (519) 253-3507

Winnipeg
Passport Office
Suite 308, Revenue Building
391 York Ave.
Winnipeg, Manitoba R3C 0P6
Tel. (204) 983-2190
and (800) 542-3407 (Manitoba)

If you are a Canadian citizen living outside of Canada and need a passport, contact the nearest Canadian embassy consular section or Consulate General. It will provide you with an application form that Canadians requesting a passport abroad must complete. In the absence of a guarantor, you will have to complete two Declaration in Lieu of Guarantor Forms. You will need to provide three photographs rather than the two required of applicants inside Canada.

Visas

A visa is a formal permit to cross a country's border. A government is not required to give you a visa or provide a reason for denying one. American and Canadian travelers don't need visas to visit any Western European countries. Separate visas are required for entry into each Eastern European country, and getting them can be a minor hassle. You can get them either in North America or in Europe. When your visa is issued, your passport is usually stamped, and frequently you are given forms you must keep with you while in that country.

If you were born in or could be claimed as a citizen of an East European country, you should without fail obtain your visa in advance of arrival at the border. Otherwise you could be claimed as a citizen of that country and kept there. Details are available from the United States Department of State and the Canadian Department of External Affairs.

How to get European Visas in the United States and Canada

There are basically two ways to get visas in North America: either directly by yourself or through a visa service. Visa services are easier to deal with but charge for their services.

1. *Do it yourself.* You can apply either in person (preferred) or by mail. Have patience; visas issued by mail in the United States or Canada can take weeks. To obtain a visa issued by mail, you'll have to call or write for a visa application. Send it, your passport, any fee, and any required photographs to the embassy or consulate. A key to French and Eastern European embassies and consulates in the United States and Canada is below.

2. *Use visa services.* You can avoid much of the frustration of getting the visa yourself by using a visa service. These are found in most towns and cities of any size, or can be dealt with through travel agencies. The visa requirements remain the same, but the service's familiarity with the system and its arcane processes ensures more rapid issuance. Generally they offer expedited service to obtain visas quickly. These agencies charge the visa cost plus a service fee. Your passport must accompany your visa application and will be returned.

Key to European Embassies and Consulates in the United States

Albania: United States citizens aren't generally admitted to Albania, and there are no Albanian embassies or consulates in either the United States or Canada. Canadians are admitted on tours only. For further information, contact Albanian embassies in France (131 rue de la Pompe, 75016 Paris, telephone (1) 45.53.51.32) or in Italy (Via Asmara 9, Rome, telephone 8380725), or any Eastern European capital.

Bulgaria:
Embassy of Bulgaria
1621 - 22nd St. N.W.
Washington, D.C. 20008
Tel. (202) 387-7969

Czechoslovakia:
Embassy of
Czechoslovakia
3900 Linnean Ave. N.W.
Washington, D.C. 20008
Tel. (202) 363-6308

Germany, East (DDR):
Embassy of the German Democratic Republic
1717 Massachusetts Ave. N.W.
Washington, D.C. 20036
Tel. (202) 232-3134

Hungary:
Consulate General of
Hungary
8 E. 75th St.
New York, N.Y. 10021
Tel. (212) 879-4127
Fax (212) 734- 6036

Embassy of the
Hungarian Republic
Consular Section
3910 Shoemaker St.
N.W.
Washington, D.C. 20008
Tel. (202) 362-6730

Poland:
Polish Consulate
General
1530 Lake Shore Dr.
Chicago, Illinois 60610
Tel. (312) 337-8166
Fax (312) 337-7841

Polish Consulate
General
233 Madison Ave.
New York, N.Y. 10016
Tel. (212) 889-8360
Fax (212) 779-3062

Embassy of the Republic
of Poland Consular
Division
2224 Wyoming Ave. N.W.
Washington, D.C. 20008
Tel. (202) 234- 2501
Fax (202) 328-6271

Romania:
Embassy of Romania
1607 - 23rd St. N.W.
Washington, D.C. 20008
Tel. (202) 232-4748

Soviet Union, U.S.S.R:
Consulate General of the
U.S.S.R.
2790 Green St.
San Francisco, Calif.
94123-4699
Tel. (415) 922-6642

Embassy of the U.S.S.R
Consular Division
1825 Phelps Place N.W.
Washington, D.C. 20036
Tel. (202) 332-1513

Yugoslavia:
Consulate General of
Yugoslavia
307 N. Michigan Ave.,
Suite 1600
Chicago, Illinois 60601
Tel. (312) 332-0169

Consulate of Yugoslavia
Park Center
1700 E. 13th St.,
Suite 4R
Cleveland, Ohio 44114
Tel. (216) 621-2093

Consulate of Yugoslavia
767 Third Ave.,
17th Floor
New York, N.Y. 10017
Tel. (212) 838-2300

Consulate of Yugoslavia
625 Stanwix St., Suite
1605
Pittsburgh, Penn. 15222
Tel. (412) 471-6191

Consulate of Yugoslavia
1375 Sutter St., Suite
406
San Francisco, Calif.
94109
Tel. (415) 776-4941

Embassy of Yugoslavia
2410 California Ave.
N.W.
Washington, D.C. 20008
Tel. (202) 462-6566

Key to European Embassies and Consulates in Canada

Bulgaria:
Embassy of Bulgaria
325 Stewart Street
Ottawa, Ont. K1N 6K5
Tel. (613) 232-3215

Consulate General of
Bulgaria
100 Adelaide Suite
1410 West Toronto, Ont.
M5H 1S3
Tel. (416) 363-7307

Czechoslovakia:
Consulate-General of
Czechoslovakia
1305 Pine Ave. West
Montréal, P.Q. H3G 1B2
Tel. (514) 849-4495

Embassy of
Czechoslovakia
50 Rideau Terrace
Ottawa, Ont. K1M 2A1
Tel. (613) 749-4442

Hungary:
Embassy of the Hungarian Republic
7 Delaware Ave.,
Ottawa, Ont. K2P 0Z2
Tel. (Visa information) (613) 234-8316
Fax (613) 232-5620

Poland:
Consulate General of
Poland
1500 Pine Ave.
Montréal, P.Q. H3G 1B4
Tel. (514) 937-9481

Embassy of the Republic
of Poland
443 Daly St.
Ottawa, Ont. K1N 6H3
Tel. (613) 236-0468

Consulate General of
Poland
2603 Lakeshore Blvd.
West
Toronto, Ont. M8V 1G5
Tel. (416) 252-5471

Romania:
Embassy of Romania
655 Rideau St.
Ottawa, Ont. K1N 6A3
Tel. (613) 232-5345
Telex 05-33101

Soviet Union, U.S.S.R.:
Consulate General of the
U.S.S.R.
3655 ave. du Musée
Montréal, P.Q. H3G 2E1
Tel. (514) 843-5901
Fax (514) 842-2012
Telex 055-60071

Embassy of the U.S.S.R.
Consular Division
52 Range Rd.
Ottawa, Ont. K1N 8G5
Tel. (613) 236-7220

Yugoslavia:
Embassy of Yugoslavia
17 Blackburn Ave.
Ottawa, Ont. K1N 8A2
Tel. (613) 233-6289

Consulate of Yugoslavia
377 Spadina Rd.
Toronto, Ont. M5P 2V7
Tel. (416) 481-7279

Consulate of Yugoslavia
1237 Burrard St.
P.O. Box 48359
Vancouver, B.C. V7X 1A1
Tel. (604) 685-8391

Getting Visas in Europe

Eastern European visas are more easily obtained
in Western European cities than in the United
States or Canada. Make your application in person. Capital cities are sure to have embassies.
Check the yellow or classified pages of phone
books for a variant of "Embassy,", but look under
"Ambassades et Réprésentations Diplomatiques"
in French and "Botschaft" in German or contact
tourist information offices for addresses. Other
major cities often have visa-issuing consulates.
Look in the phone book for "Consulate" or "Konsulate" in German.
    Western European capitals such as Vienna,
London, Paris, and Brussels are excellent places
to apply, since they have both embassies and
offices of the official travel agencies of the
Eastern nations. Because of long lines, visa

issuance may take a couple of hours. It takes longer to obtain visas to East Germany and the Soviet Union because all travel must be arranged before visas will be issued (see below).

Once you're in Eastern Europe, visas are most easily obtained in other Eastern European capitals, because there are few if any lines, and a visa can be issued in as little as 15 minutes.

Embassies and consulates are often open for visa issuance only from 9 a.m. to noon or 1 p.m. (not always open every day of the week or on national holidays). You will need passport photographs and cash (either dollars or other Western currency). Bring your own pen to complete the application, which will include instructions in the native language, plus English, French, and German. You can answer the questions on any form in English. Most ask your occupation. The consular staff will stamp your passport (except for the Soviet Union) and endorse your visa form. Take good care of the form, since you will have to produce it wherever you stay, whenever you change money, and when you leave the country.

Visa Requirements Key

You must have a current passport before beginning to apply for visas. Many countries require the passport to remain valid for at least six months after the visa is issued. Visas come in several forms: transit visas, issued merely for quick passage across a country; tourist visas, used for tourist travel; and other types for business travel, visits to relatives, or permanent residence. Tourist and transit visas may be issued for a single entry, or for a double or multiple entry without applying again. For visa information for long-term stays and permanent residence, contact the nearest embassy or consulate of the country concerned. Visa costs are given in United States dollars and Canadian dollars for most countries, except for Albania. Visas requirements and costs for Canadians may be different than for United States citizens. Costs elsewhere are roughly equivalent.

Most countries require payment by certified or cashier's check, money order, or cash, made out in the exact amount. They will not accept personal checks or credit cards.

Conditions and costs are subject to change, especially in light of the changes occurring in Eastern Europe in late 1989. Confirm these costs and conditions before you send applications and money.

Albania. Albania will not usually admit United States citizens or journalists. Canadians are admitted only on tours. The £11 visa fee is not included in the tour price. Tours are organized by Regent Holidays, 13 Small St., Bristol BS1 1DE, Great Britain, tel. (0272) 211711, telex 444606. If you want further information, you must contact Albanian embassies in Paris, Rome (see addresses above), or Eastern European capitals.

Bulgaria. You need an application and one photo. Cost is U.S.$16/Can.$15 for transit visa (U.S.$22/Can.$31 for double entry transit visas). Transit visas are also sometimes issued at the border and are valid for 30 hours; a visa into the next country is required. Tourist visas are issued at consulates, embassies, and are valid for 30 days. Cost is U.S.$23/Can.$31, requires one photo.

Czechoslovakia. You need an application and two photos. Visas are issued at Czechoslovak embassies and consulates, and at highway border crossings from Austria, but not at other border crossings. Fill out all of the application, which has no carbon interleaves. Transit and tourist visas cost U.S.$25/Can.$15 for single entry; double entry U.S.$50/Can$30. Visas must be used within five months of issuance. You must prepay your journey or exchange a minimum amount of money when you arrive at the border for each day you'll be in the country.

East Germany (German Democratic Republic or GDR or DDR). Tourist visas are only issued after you have prepaid your accommodations to the Reisebüro der DDR, the official state travel agency. Visas are $9 (15 Marks) for a single-entry visa and $24 (35 Marks) for a nor-

mal visa. This agency, either directly or through
its authorized representatives in other countries,
will provide you with hotel vouchers and a visa
entitlement certificate (Visumberech-
tigungschein). Only then will a visa be issued at
GDR embassies, consulates, and border crossings. All costs must be paid in Western currency.
The West German Deutsche Mark (DM) is the
standard. One DM is officially valued at one
GDR Mark (M). The visa fee is the hard-currency
equivalent of 15 GDR Marks.

The GDR has not been very accommodating to
spur-of-the-moment travelers. Travelers can try
to obtain lodging at the Reisebüro der DDR
offices at most frontier crossings, but hotel space
is scarce and if hotels are full, you may not be
able to enter the country. Unless applying for a
transit visa (see below), you should allow eight
weeks to obtain the hotel voucher and visa. In an
emergency, you will still need at least ten days to
two weeks, and pay all telex charges (50 Marks
per telex).

If you are visiting friends or relatives, you
must follow similar procedures but allow 10 to 12
weeks. You are not required to pay for
accommodations but must exchange the
equivalent of 25 Marks per person per day (7.50
Marks for children 6 to 15 years old).

Some representatives of the Reisebüro der
DDR in the United States and Canada are:

Koch Overseas Co., Inc.   Koch Overseas, Inc.
159-161 E. 86th St.   2015 Peel St.
New York, N.Y. 10028   Montréal, P.Q. H3A 1T8
Tel. (212) 369-3800   Tel. (514) 288-6203
Fax (212) 860-2983
Telex 62187

Berolina Travel, Ltd.
22 Conduit St.
London W1R 9TB England
Tel. 071-629 1664 Telex 263944

You can also contact the Reisebüro directly at:
Reisebüro der DDR
Alexanderplatz 5, Postschliessfach 77
DDR 1026 Berlin
German Democratic Republic
Tel. 21 50 (main desk)
Telex 114648, 114651, and 114652

Transit visas (except to West Berlin) and tourist visas require a visa entitlement certificate or hotel voucher, and completed application.

Transit visas, valid for no more than three days cost DM5 (West German Deutsche Marks) and are issued at consulates, embassies, or road border crossings. If you are going through East Germany to either Poland or Czechoslovakia, you must have your Polish or Czech visa before arrival at the East German border. You will have to make reservations and pay for lodging at the border Reisebüro der DDR office.

Visas for car travel between West Germany and West Berlin are available instantly at road crossings. No photos are required, but you must pay DM5 for one-way and DM10 for two-way passage. Transit visas on trains and busses are free, no photos required. No visa is required to fly from West Germany to West Berlin's Tegel airport.

One-day visas to East Berlin cost 5 Deutsche Marks. In addition, you must exchange at least 25 West German Deutsche Marks for East German Marks, which you have to spend before the end of the day, since they can't be reconverted and can't be taken out. You must return to West Berlin by midnight. These visas are issued while you wait at border crossings between East and West Berlin.

Note: No border crossings into East Germany by bicycle or moped are permitted.

Hungary. You need an application. A 48-hour transit visa costs U.S.$15/Can.$20 and requires two photos. A tourist visa valid 30 days also costs U.S.$15/Can.$20 and also requires two photos. A two-entry visa costs U.S.$30/Can.$37 and requires four photos. Visas are available at consulates, embassies, road border crossings, and Budapest airport and Danube boat landing. No visas are available on trains or Danube boats. There is no minimum currency exchange requirement.

Poland. You need an application and two photos. A tourist visa is required in advance. A 48-hour transit visa costs $14 for a single entry, $20 for a

double entry. A regular (tourist) visa valid for 90
days and for which the first entry must be made
within six months costs $20 single-entry, $33
multiple entry (up to four). There is no longer a
mandatory currency exchange requirement as of
the start of 1990. (Charges are about 30% higher
when paid in Canadian dollars.)

Romania. You need no application and no
photos. A 72-hour transit visa for a single entry
costs U.S. $16 or Canadian $32, for two entries
$20 or Canadian $36. A tourist visa valid six
months from the date of issue costs $16 or
Canadian $32. The required currency exchange
is U.S. $10 per day per person. Visas are avail-
able at highway border crossings, but not at railroad border crossings.

Soviet Union, U.S.S.R. Tourist visas are only
issued after you have paid for your expenses to
Intourist, the official Soviet travel agency (which
can be done through a travel agency at home).

You need a completed visa application, which
you will receive as part of your travel
arrangements confirmation, or upon request
from the consulate. Travel agents usually handle
obtaining the visa if you take a tour. There is no
charge for a tourist visa; business visas are $50,
however the consulate requires U.S. $15 and
Canadian $20 for telex and postage.

The U.S.S.R. is not very accommodating or
flexible for the individual traveler. If you take a
tour and arrange for the visa yourself, you will
need the Intourist Reference Number and the
Voucher Registration Number before a visa will
be issued. If you are not on a tour, you must still
reserve and pay for all accommodations in
advance through an authorized agent of
Intourist; you will also receive an Intourist
Reference Number. You should allow several
weeks to obtain a Soviet visa in the United
States or Canada, or at least six working days in
Europe.

Information is available from:

Intourist
630 Fifth Ave.,
Suite 868
New York, N.Y. 10111
Tel. (212) 757-3884

Intourist
1801 McGill College
Ave. #630
Montréal, P.Q. H3A 2N4
Tel. (514) 849-6394

Yugoslavia. There is no application form or fee, and no photos are required. For United States citizens, one-year visas are issued at embassies, consulates, and border crossings. For Canadian citizens, six-month visas are issued at embassies, consulates, and border crossings. There is no minimum currency exchange.

Getting to Europe

You can get to Europe on jets, ocean liners, freighters, and even yachts. Each choice has its special pleasures and its drawbacks.

How to Pay for Your Transportation

Generally, pay for transatlantic transportation with credit cards or charge cards whenever possible. In these circumstances, you have more leverage with the transportation seller than if you pay with cash or check. Many credit and charge cards provide free flight insurance, and also can be powerful intermediaries if the flight isn't delivered as promised. (After all, you can dispute the bill, which will ultimately result in the transportation company not being paid. Check with the card issuer for specific rights, which can vary from state to state and province to province.)

Flying

Direct and nonstop flights to Europe leave from every major North American airport every day. If you are willing to adjust your plans and your comfort level while in flight, you can save hundreds of dollars. The main choices are between scheduled full fare, APEX fare, or "bulk" fare on scheduled airlines, "bucket shop" flights on scheduled but sometimes obscure airlines, scheduled flights on low-fare airlines, and charter flights on nonscheduled (supplemental) airlines.

Regardless of your choice, every airplane and each airline must meet the same safety requirements. International air fares for the scheduled airlines are in large part set by IATA (International Air Transport Association), an international airline cartel-like organization. Most highly publicized airlines belong to IATA, though some have been known to offer deeply discounts through "bucket shops."

Fares on supplemental airlines are partly set by competition and partly by government regulation in each country. Therefore, changing your European destination by a couple of hundred miles (and across a border or two) can save you substantial amounts of money.

London is usually the cheapest destination, costing approximately $100 less than elsewhere. Other low-fare landing places are Amsterdam and Frankfurt. In general, Austria, Italy, Switzerland, Scandinavia, and most of Eastern Europe are more costly, though there are limited numbers of cheaper fares there, too. You'll just have to look harder for them, and they are likely to be seasonal (for example, winter packages to Scandinavia).

Full Fare on the Scheduled Airlines

Full-fare flights have the most flexibility. You can buy a ticket without advance purchase requirements. Your ticket will be redeemable without penalty if you change your plans. If you do change your plans, however, you may have to repurchase the new ticket at the current (and possibly higher) price. If you lose your ticket and know the name of the issuing agent, your ticket can be replaced, usually at a cost of about $20.

The quickest and by far the most expensive flight from the east coast is via the supersonic Concorde, which flies from Miami, Washington, D.C., and New York to London and Paris. Flight time is approximately four hours. The only carriers are Air France and British Airways.

Regular jumbo jet full-fare flights leave from all over the United States and Canada. Planes include expensive and luxurious first class, business class, and economy (coach).

APEX Fare on Scheduled Airlines

The APEX (Advance Purchase Excursion) fare is the scheduled airlines' answer to the charter flight. While on the plane, you receive the same treatment as the full-fare passengers. However, there are restrictions: in general, the number of seats is limited, you must reserve and pay weeks and occasionally months in advance, and you may have to fly on less popular travel days, such as Tuesday or Wednesday. There is usually a minimum (over a weekend) and maximum (45 to 90 day) length of stay as well. Time limits vary by airline and also by the country you land in. When you make your reservation, you'll have to specify your departure and return dates; changes after you make your initial reservation and certainly after payment have costly penalties. If you want to change your date of return after you arrive in Europe, you may have to pay the difference between the APEX fare and the full- fare flight.

You'll probably find that most travel agents will want to sell you either a regular scheduled flight or an APEX flight. It is far easier for them, and the commission is higher than on charter, bulk fares, or "low-fare" flights.

"Low-Fare" Airlines

In addition to full-service airlines, there are "low-fare" airlines, sometimes also called "supplemental" airlines. These carriers fly a regular but not usually daily schedule, generally only from some major international airports to their home bases in Europe: Virgin Atlantic to Britain, Martinair to Amsterdam, LTU and Condor to Germany, Balair to Switzerland, Minerve to France, and Icelandic to Iceland and continuing to Luxembourg.

The price is hard to beat. You'll often have smaller seats and only a bit less personal attention. These prices are popular with the budget traveler, so make a reservation well in advance.

Bulk Fares and "Bucket Shops"

Bulk fares are blocks of seats that are sold either on supplemental airlines (such as Martinair, Condor, LTU, or Minerve) or extra seats on regularly scheduled airlines (among them Pan Am or even Air France). They are brokered through wholesalers called "consolidators", and sold to the public through travel agents or unlicensed agents known as "bucket shops." (The term "bucket shop" was known as long ago as the 19th century, when they were used for various small-scale stock manipulations in New York.) Bulk fares are lower rates for unsold seats on scheduled flights. Brokers buy them cheaply and sell them for what they can get through ads in Sunday travel sections and from travel agents. The benefit to the airline is to have guaranteed extra revenue; the benefit to the traveler is lower cost.

You can find bucket shop ads in the major city Sunday travel sections, and sometimes in the classified ads under "Transportation—Air." The ads will be simple: a list of cities and prices with a phone number at the end. Call to find out the specifics of the flight: often you'll find the airline, flight number, and departure date.

You can either be ticketed directly or make your reservation and be ticketed through your favorite travel agent. Sometimes, you'll receive the actual ticket, but at other times, you'll receive a voucher good for a ticket, and the ticket itself is held for you at the airport. Often a firm's representative will be at the ticket counter waiting for you; at other times, you call ahead to confirm your place and present your voucher to the airline ticketing staff. Once you have the ticket, you're treated like any other passenger.

It's advisable to charge consolidator tickets on a credit card (especially if you're not receiving the actual ticket), so that you have recourse through the card issuer if the ticket isn't delivered as promised.

Charter Flights

Charter flights are group flights put together by a "Charter Operator," who buys blocks of seats on particular flights. The group consists merely of persons who buy tickets from the operator to travel on those flights.

Widely advertised in Sunday travel sections of major metropolitan newspapers, the ads are indistinguishable from bucket shop ads. The same agencies often handle both. For a complete listing, get a copy of the monthly magazines, "Jax Fax" Travel Marketing Magazine or "Travel World News," which list almost every charter (and bulk fare) flight. Most travel agents have them in their offices, (but not all will let you see it), or order your own directly from:

Jax Fax	Travel World News
397 Post Road	One Morgan Ave.
Darien, Conn. 06820	Norwalk, Conn.
Tel. (203) 655-8746	Tel. (203) 853-4955
$12 per year	Fax (203) 866-1153
	Telex 910 250 9333
	Free to travel agents

Generally, charter flights don't offer the convenience of daily flights. When you call the number in the paper for a charter, ask which airline will be used and the flight time and number. You will find that many charter offerings (at different prices!) are scheduled for the same flight.

Charter flights have some potential drawbacks. For example, the scheduled flight time can be changed by up to 48 hours. If the change is longer, you must be offered a refund. Surcharges of up to 10% of the purchase price may be levied if the flight isn't sufficiently booked. If the price rises by more than 10%, you are entitled to a full refund. If the flight is not completed as promised as a result of some fault of the operator (except for the situations listed just above), you must make all claims to the escrow account holder within 60 days of your scheduled flight.

All charter flights must be bonded before they can be offered to the public. Therefore, your money is actually safer with a charter flight operator than a scheduled airline. Should the charter operator fail, you will not lose your money.

Some travel agents will not be willing to sell you a ticket on a charter flight. Partly, it is a matter of convenience: not all charters are listed on their computers. Partly it is a matter of economics: there is not as much commission in a charter flight.

Buying charter tickets is best accomplished by reserving a seat on the charter by phone. Then send a check payable to the charter flight trust account. This guarantees that your money won't be misapplied. However, all of these warnings are only meant as cautions. Millions of people have successfully taken charter flights with no problems at all.

If you take a lot of baggage or bring home a lot of souvenirs, charters are often less strict about luggage limitations than the scheduled airlines.

Flying as a Courier

One inexpensive way to travel is as a courier. Essentially, you trade your checked baggage allowance for the courier company's part payment (or, more rarely, full payment) of your flight. You can only carry hand luggage. Check in the newspaper classified sections under "Transportation—Air" for courier ads. Depending on the courier company's need, you may or may not be able to negotiate a good deal. But be warned: it may be a rough time and a long wait to get a flight you can afford. Two newsletters, a directory, and a small book specifically give detailed information for couriers:

Travel Secrets
P.O. Box 2325
New York, N.Y. 10108
(Monthly, $30 per year)

Travel Unlimited
P.O. Box 1058
Allston, Mass. 02134
(Monthly, $20 per year)

The Air Courier Directory
Pacific Data Sales Publishing
2554 Lincoln Blvd., Suite 275-F
Marina Del Rey, Calif. 90291
(Quarterly, $5 per issue plus your stamped envelope.)

A Simple Guide to Courier Travel
from The Carriage Group
P.O. Box 2394
Lake Oswego, Oregon 97053
Tel. (800) 344-9375 or (503) 684-3307
($12.45 includes shipping.)

Complaints

If you have a problem with your flight, there are
government agencies that can listen to your complaint.

Safety Violations

If you believe you see a safety violation, you
should contact:

In the United States
Federal Aviation
Administration
Attn.: AOA-20
800 Independence Ave.
S.W.
Washington, D.C. 20591
Tel. (800) 255-1111
Fax (202) 267-5087

In Canada
Transport Canada
Aviation Enforcement
Attn: Chief-AARBC
Ottawa, Ont. K1A 0N8
Tel. (613) 994-1188

All Other Complaints

If you have a complaint about overbooking, flight
cancellations, lost luggage, or other non-safety
issues, contact:

In the United States
Office of
Intergovernmental &
Consumer Affairs
United States
Department of
Transportation
400 - 7th St., S.W.,
Room 10405
Washington, D.C. 20590
Tel. (202) 366-2220

In Canada
Dispute Resolutions
Board   National
Transportation Agency
Ottawa, Ont. K1A 0N9
Tel. (819) 997-6558
Fax (819) 953-8686
Telex 053-3615

Passenger Ships

With the advent of swift, relatively cheap air flights and short and limited vacations, the Europe-to-America passenger ship has become scarce. If you are interested, you should consult a travel agent, who should be aware of what is available and the costs. Cruises aren't cheap and they do take almost a week to cross the Atlantic—a pleasant way to unwind from the daily lives most of us lead. Fly-and-cruise packages (fly one way, cruise the other) are now being offered. Most transatlantic cruises are in the spring or fall, when cruise ships "reposition" from the Mediterranean to the Caribbean.

Most cruise ship lines are members of a cruise line trade association, which can provide a list of all members, including names, addresses, and telephone numbers.

In addition, the Cunard Line's Queen Elizabeth II makes a number of transatlantic passages each year.

Freighters Accepting Passengers

Freighters accepting passengers still exist, and in the past few years, an increasing number of container and other freighters have increased the number of berths. Freighters cost less than cruises but don't offer the social setting or 24-hour food. Additionally they don't always follow an exact schedule and time table. Information about freighters is best found in specialized magazines devoted to this type of travel listed below:

Freighter Travel News, available from:
Freighter Travel Club of America
3524 Harts Lake Road
Roy, Wash. 98580
$18 per year (12 issues)

Ford's Freighter Travel Guide, available from:
Fords Travel Guides
19448 Londelius Street
Northridge, Calif. 91324
Tel. (818) 701-7414
$15 a year (two issues) or $8.95 for one issue.

The following travel agencies specialize in freighter travel and also issue newsletters:
Pearl's Travel Tips
548 East Shore Road
Great Neck, N.Y. 11024
Tel. (516) 487-8351
This agency has a free newsletter.

TravLtips
Cruise & Freighter Travel Association
163-07 Depot Road
Flushing, N.Y. 11358
Tel. (718) 939-2400 or (800) 872-8584
Fax (718) 937-2047
This agency issues a newsletter for $15 per year (6 issues), $25 for two years (12 issues) and also offers a free 8-page pamphlet.

Freighter Space Advisory
Freighter World Cruises, Inc.
180 South Lake #335 S
Pasadena, Calif. 91101
Tel. (818) 449-3106
Fax (818) 449-3106
Telex 675459
This agency issues a newsletter for $27 per year (24 issues).

Yachts

Sometimes it is possible to cross the Atlantic on a yacht, if not as a guest, then as crew. Often, skippers are looking for cooks and cleanup staff as well as sailors. Since yachts aren't on a schedule, working your way across is a matter of luck. You can enhance your luck by being in the main East Coast American yachting centers such as Miami, Newport (Rhode Island), etc. and letting everyone know of your plans and abilities. When returning, try marinas in Britain, the Mediterranean coasts of France, Italy, and Spain, and the yachting centers of Gibraltar and Malta. Don't ignore the bulletin boards at marinas, either. Classified sections of some of the yachting magazines also have help wanted ads.

Traveling Light

The Baggage Squeeze

Decades ago, when ships were the only way to get to Europe, baggage allowances were very generous, with lots of space for huge steamer trunks and boxes. There was little or no extra charge if you went over that nebulous limit. Today's jets don't work the same way: you trade weight and bulk for speed.

If you're a light traveler, there's no problem: everything should fit into a single under-the-seat suitcase, duffle bag, or soft pack. But there are almost always additions most people want to include in their luggage. In general, when flying between North America and Europe, you can check two pieces of luggage each weighing up to 70 pounds (32 kilograms).

Many flights within Europe strictly enforce a 44-pound (20- kilogram or kg) limit for checked luggage on economy and a 66- pound (30-kg) limit on first class, and within Yugoslavia, only a 33-pound (15-kg) limit.

Check with the airline in advance of your flight to determine the rules. In general, the following is the pattern for transatlantic flights:

First Class and Business Class: You may check two pieces of luggage, each with a maximum combined length, width, and height of 62 inches (1m 60cm), each weighing up to 70 pounds (32 kg). In addition, you are permitted a single carry-on with a total combined length, width, and height of 45 inches (1 m 10 cm) and 70 pound (32 kg) weight. Between Europe and North America, excess baggage charges are usually between $20 and $100 per piece. In Europe, excess baggage charges can range up to 1% of the first-class fare per kilogram (2.2 pounds). Check with the airline (in advance if possible—not all counter staff will charge according to the printed tariffs).

Economy Class: You may check two pieces of luggage: one can be up to a maximum combined length, width, and height of 62 inches (1 m 60 cm), and the other with a maximum combined length, width, and height of 55 inches (1 m 40 cm). Each piece can weigh up to 70 pounds (32 kg). You can also have one carry-on, maximum dimensions of 45 inches. Between Europe and North America, excess baggage charges are usually between $20 and $100 per piece. In Europe, excess baggage charges can range up to 1% of the first class fare per kilogram (2.2 pounds). Check with the airline. (in advance if possible—not all counter staff will charge according to the printed tariffs)

Supplemental Carriers and Charter Flights: You may usually check two pieces of luggage, each with a maximum weight of 70 pounds (32 kg), plus one carry-on. Excess luggage charges vary but can range from free to $82 per piece. Some charter flights don't seem to count baggage at all.

Odd Baggage Allowances

Golf Clubs and Skis

Golf clubs must be checked and count as one regular piece of baggage. For the preservation of your complete set, you should arrange to have a cover of some sort for the clubs to prevent them from falling out of the bag. (Golf bags can hold a lot of clothes, too.)

Skis also count as a regular piece of luggage. You should be sure the skis are securely fastened together and each ski clearly labeled with your name and address.

Bicycles

A bicycle usually counts as one piece of checked luggage. While some airlines have bags or boxes available on a limited basis at check-in, you are wiser to pack the bicycle yourself in a bicycle box, obtainable from a bicycle shop. There are several advantages to this. First, bicycles, even more than most luggage, can be fragile if dropped in the wrong way. If you pack and protect it yourself, you have a far better chance of having it arrive in condition to ride away quickly from the airport. The more cushioned the box, the better the chances of its safe arrival. Newspapers wadded up are adequate. Plastic bubble packing is better. Styrofoam peanuts or shells provide excellent cushioning but are a mess upon arrival. Perhaps the best padding consists of other soft items such as sleeping bags, panniers, and clothes. Be sure to bring a number of plastic bags to cover greasy parts such as the chain and derailleurs.

When you pack your bicycle, you will need a few tools to reassemble it on arrival. Your pedals must be removed and taped to the frame. The handlebars must be turned sideways. The wheels should be removed.

If you have a very expensive racing or touring bicycle, be sure to buy excess-value insurance when you check in. To prove the value of your bicycle, have and show to the ticket agent your bill of sale or a recent appraisal from a bicycle shop. Otherwise, the airline (or its insurance company) may refuse to pay a damage claim in full.

Firearms

Warning: Due to various countries' firearms restrictions, and the threat of terrorism, do not carry guns without proper authoriza-

tion! Firearms permits must be obtained from the destination country before boarding. Contact the airline, and pack the firearms in accordance with its instructions. Otherwise, if firearms are found in your luggage, you may be detained and miss your flight, and have your gun confiscated (or worse).

How to Get Extra Baggage on Board

The normal transatlantic allowances should be enough for most travelers. But some travelers using airlines inside Europe with very small baggage allowances, and some shoppers who can't resist heavy and bulky copper cookware, new skis, or antique bronze sculpture, may run over baggage allowances.

Here are a few ways to try to squeeze a little more on the plane . . . most of them free, some requiring a bit of luck, chance, persistence, or fortitude. Some even require a bit of subterfuge at times.

Some possible solutions are:

1. Pay the excess baggage fee (see above, and check with the airline).

2. Arrive at the check-in counter with your allowed luggage after leaving your (heavy) hand luggage at a coin-operated locker. After check in, retrieve the extra piece from the locker and proceed to the boarding area. (Necessary only in flights within Europe, where hand luggage as well as checked baggage is often weighed at check-in.)

3. Plastic shopping bags from duty-free shops or major European department stores aren't usually counted as carry-ons. Fill a bag with light- to medium-weight items. The heavy items should be checked in your baggage, since the bags aren't always very sturdy.

Remember, however, that seats in the front of any cabin just behind the bulkhead have no seats in front of them to store your baggage under. You then have to ask flight attendants to store it somewhere. The somewhere is sometimes inconvenient, especially in crowded planes.

If Your Baggage Doesn't Arrive

If you're baggage doesn't arrive, you can reduce the inconvenience by taking advantage of the airline's lost-luggage system.

Before leaving the luggage-claim area, find the airline's baggage representative (who may be with the airline or the airport baggage service company) and file your claim then and there. You'll need to show your ticket and baggage claim. Fill out forms if needed. You'll be asked the contents and approximate weight of your lost luggage. When claiming, remember that if your luggage is *never* found, your initial declaration of weight will be the basis on which you receive compensation (U.S. $9.07 per pound or $20 per kilogram). If you overestimated . . . well, everyone makes mistakes.

You're entitled to a small "immediate need emergency allowance," which usually amounts to about $100. Before leaving the airport, get authorization for this, and remember to get the name of the authorizing person. Your expenses are reimbursed when you return to the airport *with receipts*.

Most luggage is found within a few days; with the passage of time, the chance of its being found goes down.

Money claims aren't usually paid until at least 30 days after the luggage was lost.

Clothes
Did you really need to take them all?

Comfortable and appropriate clothes can make a large difference in the enjoyment and success of your trip. While there will be seasonal variations in your wardrobe, it is quite reasonable for all your clothes to fit in an under-the-seat carry-on. This small wardrobe can include a few carefully planned accessories. It will serve whether you're going for two weeks or two months, whether hiking your way across the Alps or being chauffeured in a limousine.

Traveling light has obvious benefits: there's less weight to lug around and guard, you have space in your baggage for delectable acquisitions to bring home, and if you don't need to check luggage you'll be first through customs and out of the airport. You also reduce the time spent deciding what to wear each day.

Keep three thoughts in mind as you pack (especially if you are inclined to prepare for everything):

Thought 1: You meet different people every day. They don't know today's outfit is similar to yesterday's.

Thought 2: You can use accessories to transform your clothes.

Thought 3: You can "layer" your clothes, creating varying effects.

More on Thought 1

Most travelers wander from city to city like but-
terflies searching among flowers, alighting for
only a limited time in each. Several of these
cities have millions of people, most of whom you
won't see even once. Those you do see regularly,
such as hotel staff, probably won't even note that
the clothes are familiar. If by off chance they do,
they'll be far too polite to mention it. Travelers
are assumed to have limited wardrobes, anyway.

More on Thought 2

Lightweight, compact accessories such as scarves, belts, ties, stockings, jewelry, and caps can
transform the basic, sturdy, and multipurpose
clothes in your wardrobe. You may want to buy
some along the way. A mathematical figuring of
two outfits and seven or eight accessories will
give you an idea of the variety with which you
can spice your clothes.

More on Thought 3

Europe's climates are varied all year round.
Coastal southern Italy in winter will usually be
pleasant, rather like a cool Alpine summer day.
Northern Europe and mountain areas in winter
will be cold and snowy. Most of the rest of Europe
in winter will be rainy. Southern Spain, Greece,
and Italy in summer will wilt the most energetic
traveler (small children excepted).
    You'll be best prepared for all climates if you
have numerous layers of light clothes. The space
between each layer will trap air, the most
effective insulation and warmth retainer. By the
same token, a thin layer of garments will keep
you cooler in summer. By coordinating the colors
of your layers, you create different looks by using
a basic wardrobe and accessories (see Thought 1
again).
    Special note: The Arctic areas and high Alps in
winter are exceptions, calling for specially
designed wardrobes. Down-filled clothing may be
best as the top layer to combat severe cold.

Care: The Most Important Factor

Permanent-press polyester blends should be the rule for everything except underwear, socks, and dry-clean-only coats. You'll never know exactly how your clothes will be treated by laundries and cleaners, but you should plan on taking care of them yourself (see the chapter about Laundry.)

Men's Clothes

The guiding precepts for men's traveling wardrobes should be simplicity, comfort, and easy care. Above all, take clothes you enjoy wearing, rather than things you think you should wear. Your choices should emphasize quality rather than quantity. You will be able to minimize the quantity by planning your wardrobe around a basic daily "uniform." One or two such uniforms will carry you along for months.

Men's Underwear

Blends with a high cotton content will be by far the most satisfactory; 100% cotton is also good and is the most comfortable but will take longer to dry after washing in humid climates. Colored T-shirts are recommended and can be worn alone on hot days. Some T-shirts can have insignia or lettering on them, and may provoke an interesting conversation. (And you may see shirts proclaiming universities you can't believe exist— and they don't.)

Men's Shirts

Cotton blends are the most durable and resist wrinkles and rigors of travel. Permanent press will stay reasonably crisp even when washed in a hotel sink, submitted to a laundry, or dried in a too-hot laundromat dryer. White or light blue are the most versatile colors for more formal as well as more casual wear.

Men's Trousers

There are two main kinds of trousers that most travelers should have: those that can be used for more formal events as well as street wear, and those that are for more casual wear. Grey cotton/polyester permanent press slacks will serve well for both street and formal wear. You can team them with a blazer or sport coat for dinner, concert, or theatre, or wear them every day without feeling overdressed. Avoid trousers that must be dry cleaned, since rapid dry cleaning is virtually unknown and expensive.

Casual wear can be blue jeans or khakis. Jeans have many pluses: they don't show dirt when worn day after day, they are comfortable, and they are very durable. (In Eastern Europe, you may be asked to sell the very jeans you're wearing, especially if they're original Levi's. The price offered may be high. Sell at your own risk, since the transaction is illegal.)

Khakis, considered more formal than blue jeans, can be worn in many places but show dirt and dust more than jeans.

Shorts aren't widely worn in cities, except by children. Shorts seem to be more acceptable in resort areas, either mountain or beach, and by bicyclists. Solid colors will make you less conspicuous than plaids.

Blazer or Sport Coat

The classic blue blazer is never out of style, doesn't readily show dirt, and with grey slacks lets you go anywhere short of a diplomatic reception. You'll be welcome at the finest restaurants, hotels, and symphony halls. Its fabric composition should be a natural/synthetic blend that is wrinkle-resistant. Otherwise your jacket may resemble a wrinkled prune. It should be the only dry-clean item you have.

A necktie will complete your formal ensemble.

Sweaters

You should have at least one middleweight sweater. Much of Europe is cool, even in summer, especially at night. Your sweater should be of conservative style and color to make it more versatile. This is one item you may wish to buy in Europe, where the quality is high and the prices reasonable. British sweaters are particularly renowned.

Rain Wear

Rain (and snow) are a fact of life in most of Europe, so plan ahead. A lightweight water-shedding windbreaker will serve in most instances. A hood will keep your head dry and avoid the necessity of carrying an umbrella.

Britain sells wonderful raincoats, known for their durability. A plastic raincoat that comes folded in its own pouch is very handy and easy to pack. Heavy rain gear is usually necessary only in winter, since summer rains are usually light and intermittent.

Men's Shoes

Buy your shoes and break them in before you go! Torment and numerous blisters await those who disregard this warning. While you can get by with one pair, an extra pair is almost a necessity. First, if one pair gets wet, you can change them. Simple classic shoes like loafers or oxfords will be formal enough to wear anywhere. The other pair should have shock absorbing soles. Note that some soles can be very slick on smooth, wet surfaces. Running shoes are a good choice if they give enough support. You may wish to take hiking boots, which can be heavy, or cycling shoes if you're cycling.

Men's Swimsuits

You can get a swimsuit at home or in Europe, but be aware that men's swimsuits in Europe are much briefer than you're probably used to in the United States and Canada.

Day Pack or Carry Bag

Packaging in Europe is variable. While you may get some extremely durable plastic bags when shopping, you may also be handed purchases in a twist of paper, in the flimsiest and smallest paper bag you've ever seen, or in nothing at all. Take a tip from the Europeans: have a portable bag along with you. Many European men carry a shoulder bag resembling a purse to cope with the need to easily carry things. More practical is a soft day pack, which can be rolled into virtually nothing. Buy day packs before you leave home. The quality is better and the cost lower in North America. On the other hand, if you want something more like a purse, buy it in Europe. Attaché cases are invaluable for carrying business papers, but awkward for most other purposes because they leave only one hand free.

Men's Clothes Checklist

___ Socks (4 pairs)

___ Undershorts (3)

___ T-Shirts (3)

___ Dress shirts (2)

___ Dress trousers (1)

___ Blue jeans/khakis (1)

___ Blazer or sport coat (1)

___ Necktie (1 or 2)

___ Swimsuit

___ Shoes (dress) (1 pair)

___ Shoes (running, hiking, cycling) (1 pair)

___ Sweater (1)

___ Windbreaker, preferably with hood (1)

___ Rain wear

___ Topcoat (optional)

Women's Clothes

The guiding precepts for women's traveling wardrobes should be simplicity, comfort, and easy care. Above all, take clothes you enjoy wearing, rather than things you think you should wear.

Your choices should emphasize quality rather than quantity. You will be able to minimize the quantity by planning your wardrobe around a basic daily "uniform." One or two such uniforms will carry you along for months. They are most practical when they are medium dark colors such as navy or grey that don't show dirt.

Note: In most churches in Italy, Spain, and Portugal, women are supposed to cover their heads and their arms. A light shawl or large scarf usually suffices.

Lingerie

Your lingerie should above all be comfortable. Generally panties are best when synthetic with a cotton crotch. The bras and slips you wear at home should serve well on the road. Though delicate, you needn't take more than 4 sets, and plan to do laundry fairly frequently.

Dresses

The dress you take should be as all-purpose as possible. It should be durable enough for frequent wear, stylish enough for formal wear with the proper accessories, and comfortable enough for long periods of travel. Avoid colors that show dirt or lint. Material should be a permanent-press synthetic or cotton blend that will wear well. It should not require dry cleaning, since dry cleaning is often slow and always expensive.

Skirts and Blouses

Skirts and blouses should be basic colors that won't show dirt, and be a permanent-press synthetic or synthetic- and-cotton blend. While your outfits should have variety, they should be coordinated to harmonize well in any combination. Generally, two skirts and two blouses should be sufficient.

Women's Slacks

Generally, European women don't wear slacks to the extent that women do in North America. Dresses and skirts are everyday wear for most older European women, although younger women do wear blue jeans as casual wear. In general, fashions are more conservative in southern and Eastern Europe. Nevertheless, pants are so practical that women should include a pair.

Sweaters

You should have at least one middleweight sweater. Much of Europe is cool, even in summer, especially at night. Your sweater should be of conservative style and color to make it more versatile. This is one item you may wish to buy in Europe, where the quality is high and the prices reasonable. British sweaters are particularly renowned.

Rain Wear

Rain in Europe is almost a certainty throughout the year. Lightweight, easy-care rain-shedding shells offer the best protection from the elements. If you don't have an adequate raincoat, you can purchase one in Europe. Britain is particularly noted for excellent rain wear. If your jacket or coat has a hood, you can eliminate taking an umbrella.

Women's Shoes

Women should take two pairs of comfortable shoes. Buy shoes well in advance of departure, and break them in. Torment and blisters await those who disregard this warning.

Each pair of shoes should match the basic color scheme of your wardrobe. Your everyday walking and sightseeing shoes should be low or flats. In part this is because they are better for your feet when walking long distances, and in part because European cities are full of cobblestone or uneven sidewalks and streets. Some women have been very pleased wearing running shoes.

For more formal wear, you should have a pair of medium heels. These should serve in all occasions, and can also be worn during the day to give your other pair of shoes a rest.

While high heels may be "in style," they are poor choices for traveling in Europe. A multitude of holes and cracks await the unwary. In addition, many countries' museums and churches prohibit pointed heels on marble and wood floors.

Women's Swimsuits

If you plan to purchase a swimsuit in Europe, remember that styling is different, swimsuits cover less, and prices are often higher.

Accessories

Accessories are lightweight and compact, and add variety and individuality to your wardrobe. Each accessory, whether belt, hat, pins, or other jewelry, should complement your basic wardrobe. You probably shouldn't take your heirloom jewelry as part of your accessory kit.

Makeup

Most women take a small makeup kit with them.
If you need to add to your kit while in Europe,
makeup is widely available. However, nail
strengthener and other nail supplies are often
unavailable.

Purses and Pocketbooks

If you carry a purse or pocketbook with you every
day, you probably will in Europe, too. However,
traveling provides some special considerations
which may render the ones you now have un-
suitable. Your travel purse should combine
durability and safety with style. Make sure it
will do what you need. Think through very carefully what you'll be taking in your purse, and
where in the purse it will be.

The best travel pocketbook is a hard leather
shoulder bag in a color matching your wardrobe.
Plastic will do, but it's liable to wear at the
corners during the rough use common while
traveling. It should be slightly large, but not a
suitcase.

Security is important. The shoulder strap
should be firmly fastened to the purse. Avoid
flimsy, thin straps and fragile rings holding the
strap onto the purse. A shoulder strap will help
protect your purse because it is harder to pull it
away from you. The main compartment should
be closed by a zipper, as a deterrent to
pickpockets. An additional zippered compartment inside the central compartment is useful
for keeping valuables such as passports and
money. Because you will undoubtedly acquire
small additional items in your travels, your
central purse compartment should expand like
an accordion. Unexpandable purses may burden
you with extra small parcels that are easy to
misplace and lose.

Outside compartments are also invaluable for
items of small value and great utility, such as
paper and pens, and small change (especially for
pay toilets and telephones). You will therefore
avoid exposing the real valuables contained in

the main compartment, and still obtain daily necessities.

Women's Clothing Checklist

___ Stockings (4 pairs)

___ Panties (4 pairs)

___ Bras (3)

___ Dress (1)

___ Skirt (1 or 2)

___ Blouse (1 or 2)

___ Slacks (1 pair)

___ Sweater (1 or 2)

___ Rain wear: water resistant shell raincoat

___ Shoes (2 pair)

___ Swimsuit

___ Accessories: belts, scarves, pins, jewelry, hats.

___ Purse (1)

___ Makeup kit

Camera and Film

A lasting part of your trip will probably be the photos you take. The click of shutters is an everyday sound throughout Europe. From the variety of cameras availabale, a 35mm camera may be your best choice. Single-lens reflex cameras with interchangeable lenses and zoom lenses are the most versatile but are bulkier than the new, more compact autofocus 35mm cameras. A small fixed-focus 110mm camera is also a possibility: it is easier to use, but less flexible than a 35mm, and the prints are of lower quality than from 35mm cameras. These choices are recommended because you can usually find film for them. Instant-image cameras (such as a Polaroid) provide quick prints, but you need to take a lot of film with you (which can be bulkier than film in rolls or cassettes).

More important than the type of camera is the amount of camera gear you take. Keep it to the minimum you know you'll need. Remember: cameras are relatively bulky, valuable, and present great temptation to thieves. Label the camera with your name and a mailing address. Some careful photographers even write the name and telephone number of their hotel on a label on the camera. Many cameras that are lost are not returnable because they carry no identification, according to some authorities.

Take Plenty of Pictures!

Never hesitate to take a picture! Film is relatively cheap, and pictures are easy to take when you're there. When you get home, it will seem as if you took fewer pictures than you thought, and you may think, "If only I'd taken that picture."

Buying Film

You will save money buying film in the United States and Canada. If you do buy film in Europe, not only is it much more expensive, in some out-of-the-way places it may be approaching or even past its expiration date.

Film is readily available in Western Europe, but harder to find in the Eastern Bloc. If you buy film in Eastern Europe, including the Soviet Union, it can be processed only there (which takes a lot of time) or, alternatively, using the Agfa processing system. Other processing systems, including Kodak, will ruin it. Kodak film can occasionally be bought in hard-currency stores in Eastern Europe, but is very expensive.

Film and Security Checks

Your protection from hijackers and terrorists includes inspection of baggage and persons. Film can fog after exposure to X rays of sufficient amounts and strength during security checks. Checked baggage is subjected to X-ray inspection, often at much higher intensity than you and your hand luggage. Therefore, try to avoid putting undeveloped (or developed) film into your checked luggage.

Many people have little trouble with film damage as the result of security inspection. Most X-ray equipment will not harm most undeveloped film for up to about five passes, according to many authorities. After that number, however, fogging may begin to occur, depending on the length and strength of the exposure. In Eastern Europe, however, X rays are reported to be much stronger than elsewhere.

If you use fast film (400 ASA or higher), try harder to prevent exposure to X rays, since it is very liable to fog. Film of less than 400 ASA will not be as severely affected by X rays.

To reduce potential fogging, you can buy lead-lined film bags at photo supply stores. These bags cut down harmful fogging effects. They come in two types: for slow film and a heavier one for fast film.

At security checks, you can always request hand inspection of your film and camera to avoid potential fogging by the X-ray equipment. Allow extra time for inspection if you decide to request hand inspection. However, your request may not be honored, and your film may be exposed to the X rays anyway. If you carry the film with you rather than subjecting it to the conveyor belt X rays, you will reduce the exposure. Hand inspection of film is not allowed in France, Belgium, Denmark, Netherlands, Italy, and Spain. Hand inspection is possible in Switzerland, West Germany, and Scandinavia (except Denmark). These policies are subject to change at any time, and the whim of the inspector.

If you take your film out of the canisters it comes in, you'll make hand inspection easier and quicker. You can also see more readily which film you have used. However, the canisters protect the film and can keep it from excessive battering.

A Modest Note About Photo Composition

Your photos will be more interesting if you include people. They also provide a size scale. If you're not photographing a crowd or a group, ask individuals if you can take their picture. Many will be happy to pose and you'll avoid offending those who don't want their picture taken.

In the Eastern Bloc, do not photograph border crossings, military bases, airports, train stations, or bridges. If you do, it could be considered spying! (As you pass military bases, a circular sign slash bar over a camera will sometimes warn you not to take pictures.)

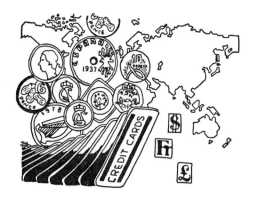

Money
What and How Much to Take?

Travelers checks, cash, and credit cards are the
easiest forms of money to take with you. Less
useful are personal checks and lines of credit.
Money can be wired via telegraph or through a
correspondent bank, but is often difficult to arrange. The more money or convenient credit you
have at hand, the easier it will be to pay your
expenses.

How Much Money to Take?

European travel can be as cheap or expensive as
travel at home. Much depends on the style to
which you are (or become) accustomed. Bear in
mind that large price levels in cities are one-and-
one-half to two times higher than in the
countryside.
   Take more money than you think you'll need.
It will give you peace of mind, and be invaluable
in emergencies. The best advice is to take the
money you expect to spend plus 50% more.
Remember that simple things, such as getting
more money, can become extraordinarily
complicated and difficult when distance and
language differences are involved.

Notification Requirement (United States Only)

It is perfectly legal to cross the United States border with as much money as you wish. However, if you leave or enter with more than $10,000 in cash, travelers checks, or other negotiable items, the government wants to know. You're required to complete Customs Form 4790 when you leave or arrive in the United States. Ask any customs inspector for the form. (When leaving the United States, you may have to go to the customs office for this form.)

Exchange Rates

When changing money, whether travelers checks or cash, you will usually receive 2% to 3% less than the published international New York and London exchange rates because your transaction is considered retail rather than wholesale.

When changing a significant amount of money, you may want to shop around first. Exchange rates between banks often vary widely—as much as 5% to 10% in banks next door to each other. The current rates are often displayed in bank windows facing the street or on boards near the foreign exchange window inside. Over an entire journey, the few minutes spent comparing rates may well pay an extra day of expenses, or at least a fine dinner.

Banks and other money-changing offices at airports and railway stations give lower rates than banks in city centers. In a few countries, including Norway, Denmark, and West Germany, some post offices change money at good rates and without transaction fees.

In some countries, particularly Britain (especially London) but also in France, the Netherlands and Switzerland, exchange booths called "Bureaux de Change" offer long hours, but often add large commissions (often 8% to 11%) to an apparently good rate. Some Bureaux de Change even look like banks, but don't have the word "bank" in their names. Be sure you know the net proceeds of your exchange before handing over your cash or signing a travelers check at these places.

Cash

All people and businesses in Europe will accept cash, if it is the *local* currency. After all, if someone offered you Italian lire or Polish zlotys in change at home, you probably wouldn't accept them either.

In Western Europe, cash-only policies extend to the more modestly priced stores, restaurants, and hotels, and most gas stations. (Gas stations on superhighways will sometimes accept credit cards and traveler's checks.) Surprisingly, some of Europe's most expensive restaurants accept only cash or local checks: they claim they can't afford the credit card commission of 3% to 7%.

The cash-only attitude is particularly pronounced in Eastern Bloc countries, since most individuals and most businesses have no checks or checking accounts, no credit cards, and no extended easy-payment credit plans. Cash substitutes can evoke wonder and incomprehension outside the regular Eastern European tourist hotels, restaurants, and airports. Elsewhere, bystanders will sometimes wonder how you have paid the bill, and whether it will really catch up with you.

Take enough cash to avoid inconvenience; in other words, plan to take between 10% and 25% of your money in cash. It is handy for quick changes of currency—no forms to fill out. Dollars can be very useful if you will be crossing several borders in a short period of time or paying for visas in Eastern Europe. In some places, the anonymity of cash will make certain transactions quicker and sometimes easier. (If you deal in the black market—illegal in Eastern Europe—you must use cash.)

If you're arriving in Europe or crossing a border in the evening or on a Sunday, you may want to buy some currency of the nation where you'll land before you leave the United States or Canada (or any other country).

Major American and Canadian banks will exchange currency, but at a higher commission and a lower exchange rate than you'll receive in Europe. Some major international airports (Los Angeles, Kennedy, O'Hare, etc.) in the United States also have currency exchange booths.

Do not buy money in advance of arrival in the Eastern (Socialist) nations, since the import or export of those currencies is generally forbidden, except that Hungary permits 100 forints and Yugoslavia permits 5,000 dinars (either is worth less than $5).

Travelers Checks

Travelers checks are available from almost every financial institution. Many banks and savings institutions offer them free, rather than the customary one percent charge, even if you're not a customer! The AAA (auto club) also offers travelers checks to members without fee.

Travelers checks are widely available in $20, $50, and $100 denominations (both United States and Canadian dollars). Upon request or at a large bank you can get $500 and $1000 checks, too. These higher denominations are less bulky and easier to carry. American Express will exchange denominations of their travelers checks at no charge (either large to small or small to large).

Travelers checks are also available from many United States and Canadian check issuers in foreign currency. These include British pounds, French or Swiss francs, and West German Deutsche Marks. You will almost always have to pay the 1% commission and will receive a poor exchange rate, too. The Deak International company (offices in most major United States and Canadian cities) offers no-commission travelers checks in all major foreign currencies, but the exchange rate may not be as good as is available in Europe.

Dollar-value fluctuations don't affect the value of your foreign currency travelers checks.

When you get the checks, sign them on the spot. You'll also get receipts which have the serial numbers of the checks printed on them. Make copies of these receipts for your files; leave one at home or with a friend. Keep another one in your luggage—but not with the checks themselves. The receipt is the best proof of ownership in case your checks are lost or stolen. The bank will also keep a copy of this receipt, which is eventually forwarded to the check-issuing company.

Travelers checks are widely used in Europe, so you should have no trouble cashing them at any bank or exchange office. Many Western European hotels and some businesses will accept dollar travelers checks, but will give you 5% to 20% less local currency than a bank.

In Eastern Bloc nations, however, you'll usually get the same rate at hotels, stores, banks, and the official tourist agency. You should get the "tourist" rate in these countries, which is about 50% better than the "official" rate.

Cashing Travelers Checks

Travelers checks receive a slightly better exchange rate than cash in most of Western Europe, but almost always pay a commission not charged on the exchange of cash. According to one European bank manager, there is a rate differential because travelers checks are risk-free to the bank, while cash potentially could be counterfeit. It is harder for banks to care for cash, since it must be counted, tallied, and guarded. Paid and endorsed travelers checks can be easily routed in the bank's paper stream of cancelled checks. On the other hand, many countries charge taxes for handling travelers checks.

Cash is worth more than travelers checks in countries with rapidly depreciating money such as Yugoslavia and Turkey. In those countries, merchants and exchange offices sometimes offer a better rate for cash than banks and a better rate for cash than travelers checks, particularly if you've just made a purchase.

In Yugoslavia, when you exchange money, you can get "Dinarcheck" scrip instead of dinars. This scrip has 10% more value at many government-owned stores or businesses than you otherwise would get. This is an anti-black-market scheme. However, you can't reconvert unused Dinarchecks into Western currency.

To cash a travelers check, you'll have to show your passport as identification. Forms will be filled out, though usually not by you. In many countries, you sign the check, give the signed check and sometimes your passport to the clerk, receive back a numbered slip or copy of the exchange form, and wait at the cashier's window until your name or number is called. You'll get a receipt for the transaction as well. In some places, the whole affair is treated more casually, and everything will be taken care of at one desk or window and you won't have to wait as long.

In some countries such as Norway, there are per-check fees for cashing travelers checks, while in others, such as Belgium, there is a per-transaction fee. In addition, there may be a commission.

Replacing Lost or Stolen Travelers Checks

Each travelers check issuer will give you, upon request, a pamphlet about what to do and where to call if your checks are lost or stolen. Be familiar with the contents: you may even want to take it with you, since specific replacement procedures vary by country.

If lost or stolen, travelers checks can be replaced reasonably promptly if you have copies of the serial-numbered receipts you received with the checks. While there are minor variations in procedures and speed of replacement between companies, you should be able to get them replaced within one or two days by any company.

Replacing travelers checks in the Eastern Europe countries will have to be done in the capital of the country. It will almost always take more time than it would in Western Europe.

Credit Cards

Almost every European country has establishments that welcome credit cards. VISA and the MasterCard European equivalents are the most common. Establishments catering to travelers and affluent locals are likely to take American Express as well. Diners Club and Carte Blanche are not as widely accepted.

When you use a card in Europe, you'll be presented with a familiar-looking charge slip with the money given in local currency, or sometimes just a cash register receipt. Be sure that the total amount has been filled in before you sign. Keep a copy as you would at home, especially since your card statement may be very vague about exactly where and when the transaction took place. For example, gasoline bought at a station in Belgium might be listed as "11-09 posting date, Tecnovo, Malmedy, BE, 10-22 transaction date, converion rate is $0.026111, charge $23.50."

American Express or Diners Club statements will usually include paper copies or photocopies of your charges with the payment coupon. (Certain rental car agencies and airlines will provide a computer-generated substitute without your signature, however, so be sure to keep your original.)

You can also get local currency cash advances at banks in Europe with these cards, although a small fee may be charged for the service.

Credit card companies usually change foreign currency to dollars at the wholesale exchange rate plus a small commission, usually about one per cent. Depending on the rate on the day your charge clears the card's currency exchange department, you could end up paying more or less than you expected.

Charges can take between one week and three months to post.

Credit Limits and "Blocking"

Know the maximum credit limit on each credit card you take. In some European countries, exceeding (or trying to exceed) the maximum is a crime.

In addition, many hotels and car rental agencies "block" your credit card for as much money as you're expected to spend—and sometimes a bit more. Although you haven't actually been charged that amount and the amount won't appear on your statement, you actually don't have credit for the blocked amount.

You're rarely told that your account is being blocked, nor how much the blocked amount is. In particular, when you rent a car, your account may be blocked for the full value of the insurance deductable.

When checking out of a hotel or returning a car undamaged, be sure to ask if the account was blocked, and be sure it is unblocked for you.

It may be worthwhile taking credit cards for more than one account to expand your credit limits.

Charge cards such as American Express and Diner's Club don't have a fixed credit limit, and blocking will not prevent you from using the account.

Personal Checks

Cashing United States and Canadian personal checks in Europe is difficult, but take some with you anyway. They may be useful in a pinch or for large purchases. Surprisingly, some stores will take personal checks for purchases, if you have adequate identification. You don't lose anything by asking.

Before you leave home, ask your bank for the names of its "correspondent banks" in Europe. Even small local banks will have them. These banks have relations with yours and will be slightly more disposed to help. If you do write a personal check in Europe, be sure that it is written in dollars. Otherwise your bank will usually refuse to process and honor it.

Holders of some charge cards, such as the American Express Gold and Platinum cards can cash personal checks at the company's offices.

European Bank Accounts

If you plan an extensive and long journey, you may want to consider opening a checking account at a European bank. This is quite legal and relatively easy to do. With some banks in some countries (such as Switzerland), it can even be accomplished by mail.

While Swiss banks' stability and Swiss secrecy laws are well known, other nations' banks will welcome your money and provide good service, too. A major bank in the nation where you'll spend the most time probably will be more accommodating than small, exclusive merchant banks unless you bring substantial amounts of money with you. A letter of introduction from your local bank will be helpful.

Many European banks will allow checks to be written in various different currencies and will take care of the money exchanging. (Ask at the bank about "Eurocheques," which are special checks backed by a bank guarantee card. Eurocheques can be written in any Western currency; however, the guarantee is limited to a maximum amount for each check in each country, usually running from $60 to $150. Sometimes you may only pay with two or more Eurocheques, each written for less than the maximum guarantee amount. Many establishments, including hotels and restaurants in Western Europe that don't accept credit cards, will accept checks in the local currency with adequate identification.

Special note for United States residents: it is legal to have accounts outside the United States—but the United States government may want to know about them. If you maintain European (or other foreign) bank account(s), with a total value of more than $10,000, you will have to obtain a Report of Foreign Bank and Financial Accounts (Form TDF 90-22.1) each year and file it with the Internal Revenue Service. Instructions are on the form.

Getting Money in a Pinch

If you're out of money, you can call home to get more—collect if needed. Money can be wired to you by telegraph; unless you designate otherwise it will be sent to the local telegraph office and paid to you in local currency. These transfers often take a day or two. Money can also be sent by American Express MoneyGrams to that company's offices; contact American Express in the United States at (800) 543-4080.

Banks will be reluctant to undertake this type of operation unless prearranged. United States and Canadian banks are more likely to suggest picking up the money at their European branches or correspondent banks. Find out from your local bank which European banks are correspondents. This will make it much easier to collect money, cash checks, and undertake other banking transactions.

Avoid sending money into Eastern Europe, since you will most likely be given non-convertible local currency at the "official" and less desirable rate, unless the wire contains clear instructions to pay the amount in the currency in which it is sent or another "convertible" currency.

If you're without money in a major city, and the above methods haven't yielded any, your embassy can make collect calls to try to find you aid. They will not lend you money, but will provide an easy way for money to be sent to you. Be thankful when you get help.

Both United States and Canadian embassies have very small amounts of money to manage as "repatriation loans." Basically, your way could be paid home. Your passport will be restricted to the one-way trip until the loan is repaid. Generally these loans aren't available to the improvident; rather they are used for suddenly destitute, disabled or mentally disturbed individuals. The embassy staff has full discretion in the matter. (See the "Your Embassy" chapter for more details.)

Leftover Foreign Coins and Bills

When you near a border, you should think about the coming change of currency. Try to estimate how much money you'll need in the country you're leaving, since it probably won't be accepted in everyday commerce once you cross the border. Every time you change money, you're charged a commission.

Coins

Coins are of adjoining countries are exchangeable only at some main border crossings in
Western Europe, and only during the hours of
heavy travel. Otherwise, you have bought yourself a pocketful of souvenirs. Change all of your
coins into paper money (see below) or spend them
on inexpensive trinkets or snacks at or near the
border.

The money exchange at Amsterdam's Central
(rail) Station will take coins of most European
nations as well as the United States and Canada.

Paper Money

Paper money from Western European countries
is exchangeable at banks and exchange offices in
any other European country. If you have some
left over, you can save it and change it later when
you need that amount of local currency. If you
bring it home, you can change it for dollars at
airport exchange counters and banks. Commissions at banks are high and the rate of exchange
is much more unfavorable in North America than
in Europe.

You can also keep the money until your next
trip.

Guarding Your Health
Health Care and Insurance

Most people traveling to Europe go in good health and return in good health. While many don't think about health maintenance, emergencies occur.

Many health plans in North America provide "out of area coverage," so you should prepare in advance by contacting your insurance carrier to find out about coverage and claims procedures. Most operate on a reimbursement for charges incurred basis. Ask your insurer for a claim form, and be sure to take it with you.

Special Note to United States residents: Medi-Care benefits (part of Social Security) are not available in Europe.

Medicine and Prescriptions

If you are taking medication, take reasonable amounts of your prescribed drugs with you. You'll also need the prescription form. Be sure to ask your health-care provider to use the generic names of any prescription drugs you use, since brand names of one drug sometimes varies. Be sure that all measurements (for example weight or dose strength) are metric.

If you wear glasses, be sure to take a copy of your current prescription with you. Also, be sure to take a spare pair of glasses.

If you wear contact lenses, take a copy of your current contact lens prescription as well as eyeglass prescription (they're different), a spare pair of contacts, and a pair of glasses as well. Take contact lens supplies: they may be not be available (especially if you react badly to mercury-based thimoserol).

European Emergency Coverage

Each country offers different health-care emergency services at different prices. In general, questions won't usually be asked before emergency service is rendered. This is particularly true after a life-endangering emergency such as a car accident or a heart attack.

In most of Western Europe, you may receive emergency outpatient care at no charge (as in Denmark), but be charged for hospital care and medicines. Countries such as Sweden will charge for all medical services provided, but costs will be much less than in the United States. In Eastern Europe emergency medical care will often be free, including emergency medical, hospitalization, medicine, and dental work.

In general, your health plan or insurance coverage card won't be recognized or accepted by European hospitals as proof of payment or ability to pay. You'll have to arrange for payment and then, if you're properly prepared, submit your claim for reimbursement. (Exception: Some hospitals with names like "The American Hospital," as in Paris, may honor some types of United States and Canadian health coverage.)

When you receive a bill, you will probably have to pay it then and there. Take your own health plan's claim forms with you, and have the physician provide diagnosis and treatment information on the form. Try to have the information written in English. Have the doctor in attendance sign it. Otherwise you may not be reimbursed.

Major Health Plan Procedures

Blue Cross

In general, Blue Cross plans offer foreign coverage to members. You must pay the hospital or other provider and submit a claim form for reimbursement. You may submit it from overseas (if you have the form and supporting documentation), or submit it when you return home.

The forms are relatively simple. Supporting documentation must include your name, the provider's name, date, and the amount charged in local currency. You should retain a copy of everything you send to Blue Cross. The claim should be sent to your Blue Cross plan by registered (or in the United States, certified) mail with return receipt requested.

Because each contract within each plan offer slightly different benefits, check with your local plan office to determine the exact extent of coverage. Get several claim forms and keep at least one with you at all times (with your passport).

Kaiser Foundation Health Plan

Kaiser, a large health maintenance organization, like Blue Cross, is regionalized (mainly on the West Coast, with centers in other parts of the United States). In general, only emergency services are covered when you're out of the "service area"—which includes out of the country.

Your card will not be honored by hospitals, so you will have to pay and be reimbursed.

There are some special limitations: Kaiser *must* be contacted within 48 hours of hospital admission. Get the name of the person contacted at Kaiser if you telephone, or send a telegram.

You will have to have a claim form with you, since the provider will have to furnish a diagnosis, statement of service, and dated signature. Send in the claim form and bills as soon as possible, by registered (or in the United States, certified) mail. Be sure to retain a copy of everything you send.

Travel Health and Emergency Insurance

A number of companies offer travel health insurance coverage and assistance just for
travelers. Most policies (regardless of the amount
of coverage purchased) merely supplement your
regular health insurance at home unless you
have no insurance or your regular policy specifically excludes out-of-area coverage.

Insurance

The actual insurance is only effective over and
above your normal health insurance coverage,
though these companies will usually advance
money for emergency medical care. Some but not
all exclude pre-existing conditions. All of these
coverages include the term "Assignment and
Coordination of Benefits" in the policy's fine
print.

These policies also provide emergency
on-the-spot services to ensure that you receive
the care you need. Some policies also provide
additional non-medical insurance, such as trip
interruption, lost or misplaced baggage, theft,
and legal referrals.

Emergency Assistance Policies

Some companies serve simply as intermediaries
between health care providers anywhere in the
world and your own health insurance, therefore
providing emergency help when you need it.
While they may advance money for care, they
will not pay for care if you don't have health
insurance on your own. Naturally, these intermediaries usually charge less than health travel
insurance. Some also provide non-medical assistance, such as for trip interruption, lost or
misplaced baggage, theft, and legal referrals.

Exact conditions of these policies vary between
companies and even between policies within a
single company. Each company (or its
agents—often including travel agents) will give
you a brochure about the various coverages
offered. Compare the policies carefully—you may

have to wade through long lines of tiny type to
find what each offers.

When comparing various policies, ask these
questions:
- Do I need actual insurance or only inter-
  mediation services?
- How long does the coverage last?
- What are the specific limits to conditions
  covered?
- Are pre-existing conditions included or ex-
  cluded?
- Is the policy renewable?
- How do I contact the service in an emergen-
  cy?
- What deductibles are there, and when must
  they be paid?
- If needed, will air ambulance service be
  provided back home?
- Are incidental expenses of a companion
  covered when an emergency arises? Which
  expenses?
- What non-medical services are provided? Do
  I need them?

Some of the main travel insurance companies
are:
(* if available in the United States, + if
available in Canada)
Access America * +
600 Third Ave.
Box 807
New York, N.Y. 10163
Tel. (800) 284-8300 (United States and Canada)
or (212) 490-5345; Fax (212) 808-5626

Carefree Travel Insurance * +
120 Mineola Blvd.
Mineola, NY 11501
Tel. (516) 294-0220
Tel. (800) 645-2424
Fax (516) 294-0268

Wallach & Company, Inc. * +
243 Church Street N.W.
Vienna, Virginia 22180
Tel. (800) 237-6615 or (703) 281-9500
From Canada, Tel. (800) 446-5116
Fax (703) 281-9504; Telex 292802 IUBUR

In the United States, contact:
Travel Assistance International *
1333 - 13th Street N.W., Suite 400
Washington, D.C. 20005
Tel. (800) 821-2828
or (202) 347-2025
Fax (202) 393-2459

In Canada, contact:
Voyage Assistance Internatinal +
Suite 200
Montréal, P.Q. H2Y 1K9
Tel. (514) 284-3230
Fax (514) 284-3203
Telex 05-24767

Travel Guard International * +
1100 Center Point Drive
Stevens Point, Wis. 54481
Tel. (715) 345-0505 or 800-782-5151

WorldCare Travel Assistance Association, Inc. *
605 Market Street, Suite 1300
San Francisco, Calif. 94105
Tel. (800) 666-4993 or (415) 541-4991
Fax (415) 541-7950

The main intermediary service company is:
International SOS Assistance * +
1 Neshaminy Interplex
Trevose, Penn. 19047
or P.O. Box 11568
Philadelphia, Penn. 19116
Tel. (800) 523-8930 (United States)
or (800) 441-4767 (Canada), or (215) 244-1500
Fax (215) 244-9617; Telex 831598

(* if available in the United States, + if available in Canada)

Credit Card or Charge Card Coverages

Many credit cards (VISA, MasterCard) or charge cards (American Express, Diners Club) offer some emergency coverage to their cardholders. These vary from card to card. Often, emergency insurance through credit and charge cards is offered through the companies listed just above.

Finding a Doctor or Medical Help

The nearest American or Canadian embassy will have a list of qualified English speaking doctors.

Giving you the list is the most they are obligated to do. They will not pay for care.

You can become a member of the nonprofit International Association for Medical Assistance to Travelers (IAMAT). Membership is free, though donations are gratefully accepted. Members receive a membership card and directory of certified English-speaking doctors and other health-care providers. Members receive services according to IAMAT's rate schedule. For membership and information, contact IAMAT six to eight weeks before your departure at:

IAMAT
417 Center St.
Lewiston, N.Y. 14092
Tel. (716) 754-4883

IAMAT
40 Regal Rd.
Guelph, Ont. N1K 1B5
Tel. (519) 836-0102
Fax (519) 836-3412

IAMAT
1287 St. Clair Ave. West
Toronto, Ont. M6E 1B8

In Europe:
IAMAT
57 Voirets
CH-1212 Grand-Lancy-Genève, Switzerland

European Hospitals

European hospitals are, in general, adequate to excellent; in Western Europe, care can be superior to what you would receive at some hospitals at home. In Eastern Europe, buildings may be less modern, and supplies scarce.

Getting Home When You're Ill

If you feel you absolutely must get back home, here are some considerations.

Unless you are totally disabled or contagious, you can come home on a regular flight. Be sure to inform the airline if you need special handling, and explain the nature of your disability.

Air Ambulances

If, after due consideration, you feel you must get home right away, and aren't able to fly on a regular flight, there are air ambulance services, but they are very costly.

Trip Cancellation Insurance

Trip cancellation insurance is available from travel agents as well as most of the emergency medical insurers listed above. It provides payment for air passage home, subject to strict limitations. The limitations are disabling injury or death in the immediate family. The benefit is that you will not need to pay for a separate ticket to get you home in an emergency. On the other hand, the insurance is limited in its coverage and is expensive.

Finding a Drug Store

Drug stores and pharmacies are found in villages as well a cities throughout Europe. All sell prescription medicines, and non-prescription medicine and health aids as well. Usually they don't sell anything but health aids and medicine..

Often, at least one pharmacy in a town must remain open all night; every drug store's door will list the schedule of open druggists.

Drug stores go by many names, usually related to the words "pharmacy" or "apothecary". The terms to look for include "Apotek" in Danish, Norwegian, and Swedish, "Apteekke" in Finnish, "Apotheke" in German, "Apotheek" in Dutch, "Pharmacie" in French, "Farmécia" in Portuguese, "Farmacia" in Italian and Spanish, and "Παρμακειον" (say "Farmakio") in Greek.

In Great Britain and Ireland, look for a "Chemist."

The symbol for a pharmacy in many countries is a green cross, or in Mediterranean countries, sometimes a red cross.

Did You Forget Anything?

Stop just a minute!

In the bustle of getting ready to start your journey, it's easy to leave something essential at home, such as your ticket, your good luck charm, or your prescription medicine.

Knowing each item is in your luggage gives you peace of mind and prevents frustrating experiences. This checklist will eliminate lots of worry and doubt. You may even want to tape a copy of this list to your baggage, and check off items as you pack them in.

Use the list to eliminate excess items—the stuff you'd otherwise lug around, unused.

The Before-You-Leave Checklist

___ Purse or Day Pack

___ Neck pouch

___ Passport

___ Tickets

___ Travelers checks

___ Credit cards (Visa, MasterCard)

___ Charge cards (American Express, Diners Club)

___ Cash

___ Personal checks

___ Reservation slips

___ Prescriptions: medicine and eye

___ Health insurance claim forms

___ International driving permit
___ Pen and paper

___ Small notebook for travel and photo log

___ Flashlight (pocket size)

Carry on luggage (what you'll need as a minimum if the rest of your luggage is lost)

___ Non-electric razor

___ Toothbrush and toothpaste

___ Dental floss

___ Comb

___ Airsickness medicine (if needed)

___ Shampoo

___ Soap

___ Needle and thread

___ Makeup kit

___ Shower cap (for women)

___ Earplugs (if you're easily disturbed while
sleeping)

___ Small towel

___ Washcloth (a very scarce item in Europe!)

___ Medicines: prescription or
non-prescription

___ Spare glasses

___ Spare contact lenses and kit

___ Rubber bands, paper clips, and safety pins

___ Knife (Swiss army or Opinel folding)

___ Roll of fiberglass tape (for emergency
repairs sealing those boxes of purchases
you'll pack along the way)

___ Pocket calculator (to determine prices)

___ Book to read

___ Jewelry

___ One change of clothes

___ Camera(s) (wear around neck)

___ Film

___ Address list or pre-addressed
mailing labels

___ Extra clothes to wear on the plane—
heavy and bulky coats

Checked luggage (suitcase, duffel bag, or
backpack)

___ Clothes not packed elsewhere

___ Clothes washing kit (see chapter on
"Laundry")

___ Guidebooks

___ Presents to friends or relatives overseas

___ Other special items: skis, golf clubs,
bicycle

___ Other items you need:

___ *Did You Remember Your Wallet?*

Crossing the Language Barrier

"Will they understand me?"

Put your fears to rest—if you are polite and can pay your way, most of your worst fears will not come to pass.

English is still the international language. Most students in Western Europe are required to study English in school. In the Eastern Bloc, English is an elective that many students learn. Therefore you're likelier to be understood by a school- aged teenager or college student than an older person. Because you speak what seems to be perfect English, some people will consider you as a teacher or adviser and try their English out on you.

If you speak the language of the country you're in, you obviously have a great advantage. If you can say even a few words, you'll often break through the language barrier and frequently find the person you're talking to is willing to experiment with his or her knowledge of English and gesture.

Many more Europeans are bilingual or multilingual than North Americans. Therefore, if you don't speak the language of the area and they don't speak English, try another language if you know even a few words of it.

In Western Europe, French and to a lesser degree German seems to be the languages most commonly found after English.

In Eastern Europe, German is the more commonly known than French or English, particularly by people over 40. In the Soviet Union, most people speak only Russian.

The short Language Key following will give you at least a few words. Words and phrases are found in other sections, such as the Menu Key in "Food and Drink," the Laundry Key in "Laundry," etc.

In addition, a good phrase book will help greatly. There are many pocket-sized books on the market, so look them over carefully for ease of finding phrases, detail, and pronunciation guides. Also, check the binding for one that will stand up under heavy daily use.

Language Key

English	*French*
Good . . . day	Bon . . . jour
evening	soir
night	nuit
Goodbye	Au revoir
Please	S'il vous plaît
Thank you	Merci
I'm sorry	Je regrette
I don't speak (language).	Je ne parle pas français.
Do you speak English?	Parlez-vous anglais?
Where is . . . a hotel	Où est . . . un hôtel?
a restaurant?	un restaurant?
the train station?	la gare?
the airport?	l'aéroport?
a telephone?	une téléphone?
a bathroom?	une salle de bain?
a toilet?	une toilette (W.C.)?
I would like . . .	Je voudrais . . .
some (drinking) water.	de l'eau (potable).
a room.	une chambre.
with bath (shower).	avec bain (douche).
a table for (number).	une table pour (___).
How much is . . .	Combien est-ce(tte) . . .
this?	Combien est-ce(tte)?
a ticket to (place)?	un billet à (___)?
Open	Ouvert
Closed	Fermé
0	zéro
1	un(e)
2	deux
3	trois
4	quatre
5	cinq
6	six
7	sept
8	huit
9	neuf
10	dix
20	vingt
30	trente
50	cinquante
100	cent
500	cinq cents
1000	mille
I am sick!	Je suis malade!

Language Key

German	*Italian*
Guten Tag	Buon giorno
Guten Abend	Buona sera
Gute Nacht	Buona notte
Auf Wiedersehen	Arrivederci
Bitte	Per favore
Danke	Grazie
Es tut mir leid	Mi dispiace
Ich kann nicht Deutsch.	Non parlo l'italiano.
Können Sie Englisch?	Parla l'inglese?
Wo ist . . . ein Hotel?	Dov'è . . . un albergo?
ein Restaurant?	un ristorante?
der Bahnhof?	la stazione?
den Flughafen?	l'aeroporto?
ein Telefon?	un telefono?
ein Badezimmer?	una stanza da bagno?
die Toilette?	un gabinetto?
Ich Möchte . . .	Vorrei . . .
Trinkwasser.	dell'acqua.
ein Zimmer.	una camera.
mit Bad (Dusche).	con bagno (doccia).
ein Tafel für (___)?	una tavola per (___)?
Wieviel ist . . .	Quanto costa . . .
diese?	questo(a)?
ein Fahrkarte nach (___)?	un biglietto per (___)?
Offen	Aperto
Geschlossen	Chiuso
null	zero
eins	uno(a)
zwei	due
drei	tre
vier	quattro
fünf	cinque
sechs	sei
seiben	sette
acht	otto
neun	nove
zehn	dieci
zwanzig	venti
dreizig	trenta
fünfzig	cinquenta
hundert	cento
fünf hundert	cinquecento
ein tausend	mille
Ich bin Krank!	Sono ammalato!

Transport in Europe

Public transportation is highly developed in most of Europe. Trains, subways, buses, and other public transport will no doubt amaze and usually delight you.

A few trains can whisk you along at 190 miles (300 kilometers) per hour, through tile-roofed villages with steepled churches nestling in forested hills and across carefully tended plains, arriving in stations that are palatial expanses of marble and glass or huge skylighted Victorian crystal palaces.

You take clean to spotless subways that have trains less than two minutes apart during rush hour.

Some intercity buses, with plush velvet recliner seats and thick pile carpeting, have the stereo playing restful Baroque concerti as you glide through the countryside.

Taxis can range from gleaming Mercedes-Benz diesels to battered, pint-size Fiats, Skodas, and Wartburgs.

Not all public transportation in Europe is perfect. City buses can be crowded, and finding your way around can be difficult, even with a good map.

Trains, particularly in southern Europe, can be packed with far more people than seats. Again, mainly in southern Europe but occasionally in Scandinavia, the on-time performance may vary wildly from the precision of the printed schedule. In partial compensation, however, fares in southern Europe run from the low to the ridiculously cheap.

Air Travel

Air fares on scheduled flights within Europe are high: the market is controlled and there is little price competition between airlines, with only a few exceptions. Deregulation of the air is starting to change this, however; a few inexpensive scheduled airlines fly between London and the Netherlands, and some discount fares with restrictions are starting to be offered. There will be additional deregulation by 1992.

European air schedules have less frequent flights between major cities than those in the United States or Canada, in part because trains are competitive in cost and often in time and convenience.

Baggage limitations on many flights are 44 pounds (20 kilograms) for most travelers and 66 pounds (30 kilograms) for first-class travelers. In Yugoslavia, domestic flights limit travelers to 33 pounds of baggage (15 kilograms).

Excess baggage costs are high, often 1% of the full-fare first-class ticket per kilogram.

Exceptions to the high-fare limited service rule are found mainly on the north-south European vacation routes. Britain is the best place to find these flights, though other places—particularly Amsterdam—in northern Europe offer low fare possibilities, too.

Finding Discount Fares Within Europe

Discount fares within Europe are best found after you get there. While this is a little risky if you want to plan every day's travel far in advance, it is not a serious problem if you're flexible.

You can get an idea of the offerings in Britain by looking at a copy of The (London) Sunday Times travel section, available at major North

American libraries (especially at colleges and universities) and some newsstands.

Specific flight offers can often be found by scanning the flight ads in the "Personals" column in the classified sections of The Times, the Telegraph, and other British papers. In London, Time Out and What's On (90 pence each), two weekly entertainment magazines, and a number of free newspapers mainly directed at Australians and New Zealanders, such as TNT and LAM, carry all types of discount flight offers. If you see an ad whose offer meets your needs, don't hesitate to call!

London is by far the best place in Europe to look for discount air fares, though some bargains can also be found in Amsterdam.

Bucket Shops

In Britain, especially London, many flights leave with empty seats to many destinations in Europe, Africa, Asia, and Australia. To try to fill these empties at the last minute, discounted last-minute tickets are offered through legal but un-licensed travel agencies known as "bucket shops."

Bucket shops operate quite openly, advertising not only in the street, but also in the newspapers, and some magazines such as Time Out and What's On. Bucket shop tickets are sold first-come, first- served at whatever price the agents believe someone will pay. Therefore it is wise to find out the full-fare cost from a regular travel agent or airline, and then to call several bucket shops for comparisons.

Often just before (the day before or morning of) the flight, you can negotiate with the bucket shop for a lower price.

Be sure to get your ticket at the time you pay for it. These tickets are usually not refundable, so be sure it's what you want.

Trains in Europe

The European train systems are probably the best in the world, equaled only in Japan. Trains are everyday affairs, whether commuter trains or long-distance intercity expresses. Partly through their excellence and partly through clever promotion, many travelers use trains almost exclusively. Many possibilities exist to take advantage of these trains, including the well known Eurailpass. Trains are one of the best ways to meet people, since the close quarters invite conversation.

Train travel has a few hazards for the unwary traveler. For example, the train may be split during the journey, with some cars going in one direction and the rest in quite another. If you don't watch carefully, you can find yourself hundreds of miles from where you thought you were going. Stops at stations along the route can last only a minute or two, which requires you to be vigilant and prepared.

If traveling in Eastern Europe, you may not be able to cross borders by train unless you have obtained a visa in advance. You'll be unceremoniously left at the border crossing station as the train pulls away.

Schedules

Schedules all over Europe are intricate and often massive. Timetables are usually consistent and stable, but change twice a year (usually in March and September) to reflect winter and summer schedules. In addition, there are special trains to special events and vacation areas on an irregular basis.

Each country publishes an official timetable twice a year, on sale at most large railway stations. In addition, there are sometimes leaflets of mainline train services. In addition, each station has large posters or electronic displays of all trains at that station.

However, if you're going to use trains extensively, it may be worth purchasing a copy of the monthly "Thomas Cook European Timetable" (£4.95 in Britain, higher elsewhere). It includes complete schedules for every country in Europe (except Albania) and is sold at Thomas Cook offices and sometimes other places as well.

Tickets and Reservations

You'll need a ticket unless you have a rail pass. Reservations are required for some (usually first-class) trains. In some areas, a reserved first- or second-class seat can avoid hours of standing in aisles. In Spain, Eurailpass users must obtain a seat reservation 24 hours in advance of all long-distance travel. Otherwise, they may have to stand in the aisles, or, in many cases, be put off the train at the first stop.

For long-distance journeys, both your ticket and reservation are best obtained before you arrive at the station. An authorized travel agent in Europe can sell you a ticket and make you a reservation at the same time and for the same price as if you stood in line at the station. You can recognize these agents by the logo of the national rail company in their windows.

Reservations are required for all EuroCity (long-distance) trains, and for certain special trains in East Germany (Express), France (TGV), and Spain (Talgo), and all long-distance Eurailpass travel in Spain. Reservations can be made up to a year in advance and as little as a two hours before departure (exact conditions vary country by country).

Be sure to specify a smoking or non-smoking seat. In an emergency (such as you're late and didn't buy a ticket, or the ticket sellers are on strike for the day), just get on the train and be prepared to pay cash for the ticket plus a penalty or surcharge. In some countries the penalty can be stiff.

The Rail Station—Highly Organized Chaos

A big city railway station anywhere appears chaotic, with trains arriving only to depart minutes later amid garbled announcements in an unrecognizable language, engine noises, whistles, echoing armies of footsteps. But with a bit of knowledge, finding your railroad car is much easier than you fear—simple, in fact.

Special Note at Smaller Stations: Most small stations have a double track, or a double track that widens to six or seven tracks. To help find your direction, remember that all trains throughout Europe travel on the left.

Departure Information: Finding the Train

When purchasing your ticket, especially from a travel agent, ask which station the train leaves from, since many European cities have more than one.

You'll also need the exact departure time and the platform or track number. Write it down; this information won't always be on your ticket.

As soon as you get to the station, check the poster schedules near the ticket windows. Yellow paper posters are usually departures, white paper posters are usually arrivals. Red print is used for expresses and black print for locals that stop almost everywhere. Or look for the departure board—usually a large scoreboard-like affair in the concourse or shed. It will have the destination (in the local language), departure time (using a 24-hour clock), and track number. Find the right track and go there.

The lobby will also usually have complete 24-hour schedules posted in large displays. Usually departures are shown in red ink and arrivals in black.

Finding Your Rail Car

European trains are often split during a journey. For example, a train from Paris could be split in the north of France, with one part going to meet the ferry at Calais to Britain, the other part to Belgium.

To avoid arriving somewhere you didn't want to be, look for the right car. At the beginning of the platform in the station, look for a signboard marked with the class and destination of each car. Some will have colored plastic cars labeled by class and destination. Others will be little better than words scratched on a chalkboard. This sign may actually not exist at all. In either case, walk along the train. Each car will have a sign (usually white with black lettering) on it near each end of the car, with the starting city, possibly an intermediate stop in smaller letters, and a destination. Example of a car going from Paris to Geneva:

PARIS
Lyon
GENÈVE

The car's destination is almost *never* shown inside the car.

The class of each car (or portion of the car) will be marked at each door: 1 or 2. In addition, first-class compartments' outside window moldings are often edged in yellow or gold. Second-class cars often have a green stripe above the windows.

If you have a reservation, check your car to be sure its destination is also yours. At your seat, you'll usually find either a "Reserved" sign (in the local language, but almost always recognizable) and sometimes also your name inscribed on a paper slipped into a holder at the compartment door or aisle end, or on the seat itself.

If you don't have a reservation, get in the first car of the correct class going your way and look for an unoccupied seat that isn't reserved. Be sure it's smoking or non-smoking to reflect your preference. Sometimes, if you can't find an empty unreserved seat, take a reserved seat until the person who made the reservation comes to take it—often hours later along the route.

When you find your seat, sit down and relax.

Intermediate Stops

If you're getting on or off a train on an intermediate stop (neither the beginning nor end of the route), you'll have to be ready to move quickly when the train gets to the station. Stops can be as short as one, two, or three minutes, and European trains generally adhere to very tight timetables.

Baggage on Trains

All European trains allow you to carry your normal luggage on the train with you at no extra cost. In addition, if you wish, you can check luggage, though sometimes you'll have to pay extra for the service. Sometimes, checked luggage (especially odd-shaped items such as bicycles, golf clubs, and skis, or those checked less than an hour before departure) may not travel on the same train but on a later one, often the next day. Bear this in mind if you plan to leave soon after your arrival at your destination. Otherwise your checked luggage may never catch up with you.

If you have a bicycle with you, you sometimes have to check it as luggage. On some trains, you can take it with you, and hang it on bicycle racks right at the end of some cars. This arrangement is especially common in Belgium, the Netherlands, and Switzerland. In Britain, on many trains you travel with your bicycle safely left in the "guard's van," a carefully monitored baggage car.

Is a Rail Pass Right for You?

Many train travelers wonder if a rail pass of some type is a worthwhile purchase.

Normal rail fares vary by country, and are charged per kilometer. West Germany's charges are almost twice those of Italy. Second-class fares are generally about two thirds of the first-class fare. In general, the northern countries have much higher fares than southern countries such as Greece, Italy, Portugal, and Spain. A national rail pass or other discount fare or possibly individually-bought second-class tickets could have much the same benefits at a much lower cost.

Before running out and buying any pass, think carefully, and ask several questions.

1. Will you make trains your main long-distance travel method? Europe has so many ways to get around, including planes, buses cars, bicycles, balloons, and canal boats.

2. Will you be in the high-fare northern countries or the less expensive southern countries?

3. Will you take a large number of long-distance trips? If you take many long trips or use night trains as hotels, the pass may be a big money saver.

4. How many of you will travel together? For two or more persons, car rental may be more economical.

5. How much do you want to be bound by rail schedules? Not every town and village has frequent service.

Eurailpass and Eurail Youthpass

Most people planning a European trip have considered using a Eurailpass—a pass good for unlimited travel on the national railways of all of Western Europe plus Hungary, except Great Britain. The benefits are obvious—you can hop aboard any train without having to buy a ticket, and your intercity transport costs are fixed in advance.

The Eurailpass is issued for first-class travel (though equally valid in second class) for a period of 15 days to three months. There's also an almost identical Eurail Youthpass, which is good for one or two months of second-class travel. The Youthpass is much cheaper—and limited to persons under 26. Flexible passes allow travel on fixed number of days during the pass's validity at a slightly lower price.

The Eurailpass and Eurail Youthpass are available in the United States and Canada from travel agents and the North American offices of the French National Railways, GermanRail, Italian State Railways, and Swiss Federal Railways (offices in New York, some in Los Angeles, San Francisco, Toronto, and Montreal). If you buy directly from these offices, payment must be made by certified check, cash, or money order. Some accept credit cards as well.

These passes are available in Europe only at 45 main stations' Eurail Aid offices. You must prove you arrived in Europe not more than 6 months before entry (passport entry stamps are required), you must pay a 10% premium over the normal price of the pass, and you must pay in local currency. Sometimes you'll have to press the issue to obtain a pass of your choice.

The Eurail system has also introduced the Eurail-Drive combination, for a minimum of two people from October 1—March 31, and three people from April 1—September 30. If bought in the United States, these passes provide seven days of train travel and three days of a small rental car during two weeks. If bought in Canada, these passes provide nine days of train travel and five days of a small rental car during three weeks. Extra days of car rental can be purchased as well.

The Eurail First Class Saverpass is an off-season pass that provides three persons traveling together (two persons during the winter) with 15 days unlimited rail travel.

Eurail Prices—1990

Eurailpass 1990 (U.S. $ in Roman) *(Canadian $ in Italic)*	Eurail Youthpass 1990 (U.S. $ in Roman) *(Canadian $ in Italic)*
15 days $340/*$408*	15 days (not sold)
21 days $440/*$528*	21 days (not sold)
1 month $550/*$660*	1 month $380/*$456*
2 months $750/*$900*	2 months $500/*$600*
3 months $930/*$1116*	3 months (not sold)

Flexipass (5 days of travel in 15)
198/*$238*   (not sold)

Flexipass (9 days travel in 21)
$340/*$432*   (not sold)

Flexipass (14 days travel in one month)
$458/*$550*

EurailDrive Escape

7 days train plus 3 days car in 21, $309 *$279*
9 days train plus 3 days car in 21, $635 *$529*
(Optional extra days of a car $50 per day.)

There are some reasons why neither the Eurailpass nor Eurail Youthpass may be the best choice for you, even if most of your European travel will be by train. Before rushing out and buying one, ask these questions:

1. Will you be in more than one or two countries? If so, check out the other passes offered by almost every country's rail system. (A Key to these passes is below.)
2. Will you be mainly in the high-fare countries of northern Europe? In the southern low-fare countries, a Eurailpass (or a national railpass) may save you time spent waiting in line for tickets, but probably not money.

If you answered "yes" to all these questions, a Eurailpass is probably a good buy.

Using Your Eurailpass

Your passport number is entered on the pass, either when you buy it or when you first use it in Europe. While in Europe, any conductor may demand to see your passport to make sure it matches the number on the Eurailpass. Eurailpasses aren't transferable under any circumstances.

You don't need to begin using the pass immediately upon arrival in Europe. Validate your pass at the station where you first use it. If you're going to stay at your city of arrival, it's probably a better idea to buy a train ticket into town, and validate it when you take your first long trip; with a Flexipass, validate it when you enter the train station each day you use it.

At the end of the pass period, the pass becomes a worthless souvenir.

Extensions are not obtainable in Europe, but you could buy another one (see above). You could also have someone in North America fill out and send the application and money to a vendor in the United States or Canada, and send you the pass in Europe. Express mail or a courier service such as Federal Express or UPS takes one to three days. Regular air mail takes about a week or sometimes two. Contact the post office for details.

A lost or stolen pass can often be replaced in Europe if you have your purchase receipt and the tear-off stub you get with your pass. Take them to the nearest Eurail Aid office. (They are listed in the information leaflet you get with your pass.) In a dire emergency, far from the offices, contact the station master in major European rail stations.

Other European Railpasses

European passes other than the Eurailpass aren't widely known in North America. Often they can save you money when compared to an equivalent Eurailpass or Eurail Youthpass. Many can be bought on the spot in Europe with little or no formality. If you buy one in Europe, you will often have to present identification such as a passport for name, and, in some cases, proof of age. There are several categories of these passes: Europe-wide, regional, those limited to a single country, and other reduced-fare programs.

Europe-wide Passes

InterRail Junior

InterRail Junior is a one-month, second-class-only card available to persons under 26. Somewhat similar to the Eurail Youthpass, it includes more countries: all the Eurail countries plus Great Britain, Hungary, Romania, Yugoslavia, and Morocco. While it is only supposed to be available to European residents, this seems to be only sporadically enforced, and seemingly infrequently in Belgium and Portugal. It is enforced even less if the pass is bought through travel agents. It costs about 20% less than the one-month Eurail Youthpass. It can be bought at main rail station ticket offices and often through most European travel agents. If you get and use one, you must pay half fare in the "country where you habitually reside"—interpreted to mean the country in which it is purchased. You can ride on other countries' rail systems for free.

InterRail Senior

This is very similar to the InterRail Junior, except that it is available only to men over 65 and women over 60, and sold at the same places. It doesn't include passage in Great Britain, Ireland, or Hungary. The first class Interrail Senior costs about 30% less than a comparable one-month-long Eurailpass. The second-class InterRail Senior costs about half of the month-long, first-class Eurailpass.

Regional Rail Passes

Some nations participate in multi-country regional rail pass offers. The Benelux Tourrail, which includes Belgium, the Netherlands, and Luxembourg, can be bought at railway stations in these countries. The other main regional pass is the Scanrail Pass, which covers all of Scandinavia. Details are provided in the Key below. Both are available for either first- or second-class travel.

National Rail Passes

Many European nations offer single-country rail passes, which are (but not always) sold within the country. They are also usually available from national rail offices in North America. Costs are reasonable, and all of the national passes are available for either first- or second-class travel. See the Key below.

Other Discount Rail Fares

In addition to the rail passes of whatever type, there are dozens of other discount fares. These include the kilometer tickets in a number of countries, family discounts, cheap same-day (almost free return) tickets, and holiday fares. Details of some are given below.

Regional Railpasses

Benelux Tourrail. This pass provides five days unlimited first- or second-class train travel, during any 17-day period anywhere in Belgium, Luxembourg, and the Netherlands, plus bus travel in Luxembourg (First Class 3740 Belgian Francs or Dutch equivalent, Second Class 2490 Belgian Francs, with 35% reductions for ages 12-26 and 47% reductions for ages 6 to 12). Buy it at any rail station in Belgium, Luxembourg, or the Netherlands, or Netherlands Board of Tourism offices in North America.

BritFrance RailPass. This pass provides unlimited travel on both BritRail and the French National Railways systems and one round trip between Britain and France by Hovercraft. Five days' travel in 15 costs U.S.$269/*Can. $329* First Class and $199/*$239* Second Class; 10 days' travel during one month costs $399/*$489* in First Class and $299/*359* in Second Class. Buy it before you leave for Europe from travel agents, or Britrail or FrenchRail offices in North America.

Iberia Tourist Pass. This pass provides unlimited travel on the railways of Portugal and Spain, 15 days' about U.S.$250 First Class and $180 Second Class; and a similar Flexipass providing nine days' travel in 30 days, $255 about first class and $180 second class. Available only in Spain and Portugal, at railway stations and travel agencies.

Scanrail Pass. This pass provides 4 days unlimited travel in 15, U.S.$159/*Can.$189* fist class, $119/*$149* second class; 9 days in 21, $279/*$339* first class, $209/*$249* second class; 14 days in 1 month $419/*$499* first class; $289/*$349* second class; unlimited travel in any Scandinavian country (Denmark, Finland, Norway,

and Sweden), all DSB (Danish) ferries, and some
other ferries, such as those between Stockholm
and Turku (Finland). Buy the pass at any railway station in Scandinavia, or from FrenchRail
offices or through any travel agent in North
America.

National Railpasses and Discount Fares Key

The name of the pass or card is listed in italics in
the foreign language. The English name is either
in the parentheses just after the foreign name or
at the beginning of the description in regular
type. Prices are given in United States dollars in
Roman, Candian dollars *in italics*, and local currency given when available.

Austria

Rabbit Card. This pass offers four days travel in
a 10-day period, and is valid on all national,
state, and private rail lines. Vouchers can be
bought outside of Austria at main railway stations in Western Europe, and the pass is obtained at the first stop in Austria. Or the pass
can be bought in Austria. The price is 1290
Schillings adult first class and 890 Schillings
adult second class (juniors from 6 to 26, about
60% of the adult price in either class).

Bundesnetzkarte (Federal Network Card). This
one-month or one-year first- or second-class pass
provides unlimited passage on all Austrian
trains. Buy at all Austrian railway stations.
(Price example for 1989: one month, 4,650
Schillings first class and 3,000 Schillings second
class.)

Senioren-Ausweis (Senior Citizens' Discount
Card). This card, available to men over 65 and
women over 60, provides half-price passage on
all rail travel, post buses, and lake steamers in
Austria for a calendar year from the date of
issuance. Buy it at any Austrian railway station,
some main post offices, and main railway
stations in Frankfurt, Munich, and Zurich.

Requires one passport photo and proof of age. The price is 200 Schillings.

Belgium

B-Tourrail. This first- or second-class pass provides unlimited passage on five out of a 17-day period on all trains in Belgium. Buy it at any railway station in Belgium. Prices are: 2550 Belgian Francs (BF) first class and 1700 BF second class (juniors from 6 to 26, about 60% of adult price).

Half-Fare Card. A discount card providing a 50% reduction in first- or second-class fares during a one-month period. Buy it at any railway station in Belgium, 500 BF.

Cheap round-trip fares on weekends cost just a small amount more than a one-way ticket. Leave after Friday at 5 p.m., return by Monday morning.

Denmark

Gruppe Billet (Group ticket). This ticket provides discounts for three or more persons traveling together on DSB trains and ferries during off-peak (non-commute) hours. Buy these tickets at all railway stations.

Senioren Billet (Senior citizens ticket). This free card, available only to men and women over 67, provides a 50% discount on round trips taken during off-peak hours. Obtain it at any railway station in Denmark by showing proof of age.

Finland

Finnrailpass. This first- or second-class pass provides unlimited rail passage for 8, 15, or 22 days. Buy it at any railway station in Finland or from:

Holiday Tours of
America
40 E. 49th St.
New York, N.Y. 10017
Tel. (212) 832-9072 or
(800) 223-0567

ScanTours Inc.
1535 Sixth St., Suite
209
Santa Monica, Calif.
90401
Tel. (800) 223-SCAN
(U.S.)
or (800) 233-SCAN
(California only)

Prices for are: 8 days first class 600 Finnish Markka (FIM) or U.S.$135, second class FIM400 or U.S.$90; 15 days first class FIM920 or U.S.$218, second class FIM620 or U.S.$145; 22 days first class FIM1200 or U.S.$272, second class FIM800 or U.S.$181.

Group Rail Tickets. When three or more persons travel together, they can receive a 20% or larger discount, depending on the number of persons. The journey must be at least 75 km (48 miles) in each direction to qualify for this discount.

Senior Citizen Discount. This card, available to any person 65 years of age or more, provides a 50% discount on all journeys of at least 75 km (48 miles) each direction. This card is not valid Friday noon through Saturday noon or Sunday noon through Monday noon. Buy the card at all railway stations in Finland for FIM50.

France

France Rail Pass. This first- or second-class pass provides unlimited passage on the French National Railways (SNCF) for four days in any 15-day period (first class U.S.$149/*Can. $179*, second class $89/*$121*), or nine days in any 30-day period (first class $249/*$299*, second class $175/*$209*). Children 4 to 12 receive a 40% discount. In addition, this card provides free transfers from Paris Charles de Gaulle or Orly airports, a free Paris Metro pass (one or two days), and various discounts on sightseeing. Buy it at French National Railroads offices in North American and Europe, anywhere except France.

France Rail and Drive for at least two persons traveling together. Four days of train travel and three days of car rental, first class $199/$239, second class $149/$179; nine days of train travel and six days of rental car during a 30-day period, first class $329/$399, second class $279/$339 per person.

France Fly, Rail, & Drive Pass. This pass provides a 7-day Rail & Drive Pass plus a one-day Air Inter pass on French domestic air flights, all within a 15-day period. The pass must be bought in North America, first class $449/$339, second class $399/$279; for 9 days rail, six days rental car, and two days flights, $449/$539 first class and $399/$479 second class.

Germany, West

Touristkarte (Tourist Card). This first- or second-class card provides unlimited passage for 4, 9, or 16 days on all German Rail (DB) trains, all Europabus buses including the Romantische Strasse, free passage on KD Line Rhine and Moselle riverboats (mid-April through mid-October only), and passage to West Berlin. Buy it at German Rail offices in North America and Europe, or at any international airport and large railway stations in Germany. A reduced-cost "Junior Touristkarte" is available for 9 and 16 days to travelers less than 26 years of age.

Bundes Netzkarte (National Network Card). This first- or second-class card provides unlimited passage for one month on all DB trains. Buy it at all large railway stations in Germany. Not sold outside of Germany. *Gebiets Netzkarte* (Area Network Card). This first- or second-class card provides unlimited passage for one month on all DB trains in a single region. Buy it at all main railway stations in Germany. Not sold outside of Germany.

GermanRail Flexipass. This first- or second-class pass provides 4, 9, or 16 days' travel within a 21 day period. Second- class passes are U.S. $120/Can. $144 for four days, $180/ $216 for nine days, and $250/$300 for 16 days. First class passes are about 35% more. For travelers under 26, Junior Flexipasses are available for about 55% of the adult fare.

Great Britain

BritRail Pass. This pass provides unlimited train travel for a set period on all BritRail trains. Some also have other material enclosed. Children 5 to 15 pay half-price for the passes. There are senior citizens discounts for first-class but not second-class passes. For passes by students age 16 to 26, there are also discounts of about 20% for students in second class.

BritRail Pass Prices—1990

First Class (U.S. $ in Roman) *(Canadian $ in Italic)*	Second (Economy) Class (U.S. $ in Roman) *(Canadian $ in Italic)*
8 consecutive days $285/*$319*	8 consecutive days $189/*$229*
15 consecutive days $409/*$459*	15 consecutive days $285/*$329*
22 consecutive days $499/*$575*	22 consecutive days $359/*$469*
1 month $589/*$675*	1 month $415/*$469*

These passes are sold at British Rail offices in North America and also in continental Europe (but periods are 7, 14, and 21 days) or through most travel agents. This pass is not sold in Britain. It is not valid for travel in Northern Ireland.

BritRail Flexipass. This pass is similar to the regular BritRail pass, except that it provides unlimited rail travel during half of the pass's validity (either 4 days in 8 or 8 days in 15).

Capital Pack. This pass combines a 4-day BritRail pass with a 3-day Travelcard, providing unlimited use on all London Transport buses and trains plus all British Rail Network Southeast trains.

BritRail Flexipass 1990

First Class (U.S. $ in Roman) *(Canadian $ in Italic)*	Second Class (U.S. $ in Roman) *(Canadian $ in Italic)*
4 days in 8 $229/*$259*	4 days in 8 $159/*$179*
8 days in 15 $329/*$379*	8 days in 15 $229/*$259*
15 days in 30 $479/*$539*	15 days in 30 $329/*$369*

Capital Pack
4 days $99/*$109*
7 days $139/*$169*

Rail Rover. This pass provides unlimited travel for 7 consecutive days (first class £200, second class £120) or 14 consecutive days (first class £300, second class £190) on all British Rail lines. Includes ferries to the Isle of Wight and Firth of Clyde. Sold only in Britain at main railway stations in large towns and cities. Not sold outside of Britain. Not valid in Northern Ireland. Children 5 to 16 travel at half price.

Senior Citizens BritRail Pass. This pass, available to those over 65, provides first-class travel at the second-class fare for one month on all British Rail trains.

BritRail Seapass. This is an add-on to the BritRail Pass, and provides one round-trip ferry or hovercraft trip between Britain and the European continent. Buy it wherever BritRail Passes are sold.

Day Return. This is a regular discount available on all round-trip tickets when you return the same day. The round-trip fare is just a bit more than one-way fares.

Weekend Return. Identical to the day return except you must leave on a Friday, Saturday, or Sunday, and return on a Saturday, Sunday, or Monday.

Emerald Isle Pass. This pass provides unlimited train and bus travel in Northern Ireland and the Republic of Ireland for 7 or 15 days. Buy it at CIE (Irish Transportation Company) offices in main cities in Northern Ireland and the Republic of Ireland.

Rail Runabout. This pass provides unlimited rail passage in Northern Ireland for 7 days. Buy the pass at railway stations in Northern Ireland.

Freedom of Scotland Ticket, 7 days (second class only £38 and 14 days £55) includes all trains in Scotland, plus connections to Carlisle or Berwick-upon-Tweed, and Firth of Clyde boats.

Local Rovers. Available for regional unlimited second-class travel for one or two weeks between Easter and October 1. Sold at all main British Rail stations, but not available outside of Britain.

Note: British Rail offers additional, frequently changing discount tickets and programs available only in Britain. Information is available at main British Rail stations.

Greece

Πασο (Pronounced "Paso") (Touring Card). This pass provides unlimited second-class rail travel for 10, 20, or 30 days, plus travel on the railway system's buses. There are reductions for groups of two or more traveling together. Buy it at main Greek railway stations. This pass is not sold outside of Greece.

Senior Card provides five single trips free and gives a 50% reduction on all other trips during a one-year period. Sold only in Greece.

Ireland

Note: Ireland has only one class on its trains and buses.

Emerald Isle Card. This pass provides unlimited rail and bus service plus city bus service in Irish towns and cities; 8 days' travel in 15 days costs $142; 15 days' travel in 30 days costs $240; just over half price for children. Sold at train and bus station in Ireland and available from CIE Tours, 122 E 42nd St., New York, N.Y. 10168, Tel. (212)

697-3914 or (800) 243-7687 (United States) or (800) 522-5258 (New York State).

Rambler Ticket. This pass provides unlimited passage on all CIE (Irish Transportation Company) buses and trains in the Irish Republic for 8 days out of 15 (U.S. $110) or 15 days out of 30 ($156). You can also buy passes good on only trains *or* buses for the same periods ($78 and $115). Children under 15 pay half of the adult price. Dublin city buses and DART trains are not included in these passes. Sold at all CIE train and bus stations in Ireland and through CIE Tours (address above).

Youth Rambler Pass. This pass is the same as the Rambler Ticket except that it is limited to people 14 to 26 years old, and is sold for the same periods (15% discount if bought before arrival in Ireland). Bicycle passage can be added to this ticket for a $29 supplement.

Italy

Biglietto Turistico di Libera Circolazione (Unlimited Travel Tourist Ticket). This pass provides unlimited first- or second-class train travel in Italy for 8, 15, 21, or 30 days. Reduced price for children under 12. Buy it at Italian State Railways offices in North America and Europe, and through travel agents in North America. It is sold in Italy to foreigners at main rail stations and travel agencies; bring your passport. In Italy, you can pay more to extend the time period of all but the 8-day pass at main railway stations.

Biglietto Chilometrico (Kilometric Ticket). This ticket provides first- or second-class train travel on the State Railways (FS) for up to five people (related or not) for up to 20 trips with a maximum combined distance of 3000 km. Buy it in North America from Italian State Railways offices or at train stations and travel agents throughout Italy. Supplements must be paid for passage on EuroCity and Rapido trains.

Cart ad'Argento (Senior Citizens Silver Card). This card, valid for one year from the day of purchase, provides 30% discount on any rail fare for men over 65 and women over 60. It is not valid Friday through Sunday in July and August or from December 18 to 28. Buy it for 10,000 Lire at any railway station or travel agency in Italy.

Luxembourg

Carte d'Abonnement (Subscription Card). This card provides unlimited second-class train travel and bus travel for one day (217 Francs), five days (658 Francs), or one calendar month (1748 Francs). Buy it at any train station in Luxembourg. Some of these tickets are not valid for trips to a border crossing.

Senior Citizens Discount. Any person over 65 receives a 50% discount by showing proof of age (such as a passport).

Netherlands

All discount cards and fares are available at main railway stations throughout the Netherlands.

Dagkaart (One-Day Network Pass). This pass provides unlimited first-class train travel (80 Gulden) or second-class train travel (53 Gulden) for one day. A pass for local transportation (Stadstreekabonnement) can be purchased for 5.35 Gulden in addition to the Dagkaart.

3-Dagsenetkaart (Three-Day Rover). This pass provides unlimited train travel for three days in first class (U.S. $59) or second class ($40). A pass for local transportation can be added for $4.80. Sold only outside the Netherlands.

Weeknetkaart (Seven-Day Rover). This pass provides unlimited train travel for seven days in first class (159 Gulden) or second class (108 Gulden). Local transportation can be added for 20.15 Gulden. A passport photo or passport number is required.

Maandnetkaarten (Month Network Pass). This pass provides one month's unlimited first-class train travel (616 Gulden) or second-class train travel (419 Gulden).

Dagretour (Same-Day Return). When you buy a first- or second-class round-trip ticket and return the same day after 6 p.m., the return fare is only a few Gulden more than the one-way fare.

NS-Jaarkaart (Annual Rail Card). This card, which can be purchased for 265 Gulden per month (less per person for groups traveling together), provides unlimited use of the Dutch rail network. For further information, and to obtain this card, contact: N.V. Nederlandse Spoorwegen, Klaanten Service, Postbus 2025, 3500 HA Utrecht.

60+ Seniorenkaart (Senior Card). This card provides a 40% discount on all other fares for 75 Gulden, but there are restrictions on weekend travel. It is available from any main railway station in the Netherlands. A passport or other proof of age and a photograph are required.

Note: Some of the above rail passes are sold in the United States and Canada by Netherlands Board of Tourism offices.

Norway

Bargain Rail Pass. This pass is valid for seven days of actual train travel, with unlimited stopovers not counting. For a slightly lesser fare, you can travel 800 kilometers in one direction only. Buy these passes at all Norwegian rail stations. Second class only, 310 Norwegian Kronor. These passes are not sold outside of Norway, and are not valid on Fridays.

Senior citizen rail discount. Persons at least 67 years old (and spouses of any age!) receive a 50% discount on all first- and second-class rail journeys. Show proof of age when buying a ticket.

Poland

PolRailPass. This card is for unlimited first- or second-class travel for 7, 14, 21 days, or 1 month. Buy the card at any Orbis Travel Bureau in Poland and from Orbis' offices outside of Poland.

Portugal

Bilhete Turístico (Tourist Ticket). This card provides unlimited train travel in first- and second-class train travel for seven consecutive days (11,475 Escudos), 14 days (18,300 Escudos), and 21 days (26,140 Escudos). Buy it at rail stations in Portugal.

Bilhete Redução a Velhos (Senior Citizen Rail Discount). Senior citizens over 60 are given 30% to 50% discount on all rail fares. Proof of age (such as a passport) is required.

Bilhete Familiar (Family Ticket). Family groups of at least three persons (including at least one parent) can receive reductions for trips of at least 150 km. One parent pays full fare, other adults pay half fare, and children under 12 pay one quarter of the adult fare. Proof of family relationship (such as passports) are required.

Spain

Tarjeta Turistica (Tourist Card). This card provides unlimited first- or second-class rail travel. Eight days cost 13,000 Pesetas (Pta) first class and 9,000 Pta second class; 15 days cost 21,000 Pta first class and 15,000 Pta second class; 22 days cost 25,000 Pta first class and 19,000 Pta second class. Available at all RENFE (Spanish Railway Network) ticket offices, stations, and travel agencies in Spain, and the RENFE office in Paris, France.

Chequetren (Train Check). This card provides about a 15% reduction on first- and second-class fares on all (RENFE) trains for up to 6 persons traveling together. All the travelers' names must be entered on the Chequetren card at time of purchase. Use for fares, sleeping cars, supplements, or reservation fees. No time or distance limits. Buy this card in Spain at train stations, then spend it like money to buy tickets, sleepers, etc.

Días Azules (Blue Days). You can get a 25% discount for same-day round trip of at least 200 km on 305 days of the year. (The other 60 days are national holidays, etc.) There are larger discounts for groups and families traveling together.

Tarjeta Dorado (Gold Card). This card provides a 50% discount on all train fares on trips of more than 100 km on all Blue Days (see paragraph above) and same-day discounts on trips of less than 100 km each way. Men over 65 and women over 60 can buy the card for 105 pesetas at any RENFE railway station.

Sweden

All second-class fares Monday through Thursday and on Saturday receive a 25% discount from full fare. Full fare is charged only on Friday and Sunday.

Group fares. When two to five persons travel together, if the first pays the full fare, all others receive a 30% discount. This discount is available only in second class, and the discount is calculated from the fare in effect on the day of travel.

Family fares. Parents pay full fare, juniors 16 to 25 pay half fare, and children under 16 are free.

Children's discount. Children under 6 travel free; from 6 to 16 pay half fare.

Senior citizen reduction. Any person over 65 receives a 45% discount on all rail travel in Sweden. Proof of age (such as a passport) is required when you buy tickets.

Switzerland

Swiss Pass. This card provides unlimited first- or second-class post bus and Swiss Federal Railways (CFF- SBB) train travel. Eight days cost U.S.$180/*Can.$220* first class and $125/*$155* second class; 15 days cost $220/*$265* first class and $155/*$185* second class; one month costs $300/*$370* first class and $210/*$260* second class, and includes local streetcar and bus transport in 22 cities and towns. It also provides 50% discounts on most of the private mountain railways. Children under 16 pay half price for the card. Buy the card at Swiss Federal Railways offices and travel agents outside of Switzerland, since the card is not sold in Switzerland.

Environment Ticket (Half-fare Card). Provides 50% discount on all rail, bus, and lake boats in either first or second class. The card costs about $45 for one month and $65 for one year, and can be bought at any Swiss train station.

Swiss Card. Provides a single round-trip ticket from Geneva or Zurich Airport or any border crossing to a single point, plus 50% discount on all other rail travel during one month, first class $80/*$100*, second class $65/*$80*.

Swiss FlexiPass. This card provides 3 days travel in 15 days; first class $149/*$179*, second class $99/*$119*.

Swiss Rail-Drive. This card provides 3 days of rail travel and 2 days of rental cars; $179/*$219* first class, $129/*$159* second class, based on two traveling together. Extra rental car days are $36/*$45* per day.

Long-Distance Buses

Europe has a long-distance bus network, providing both national and international services. The widest network is called "Europabus" on the continent and "Supabus" in Britain. It is affiliated with the national railroads of most (but not all) European nations. Buses not only offer some long- distance services, but also supplement national train services, allowing access to some of the towns and villages inaccessible by trains.

Long-distance buses in a few countries, such as Greece, Spain, Turkey, and Yugoslavia, are often faster and sometimes cheaper than the railroads.

Some regions of Europe, such the Highlands of Scotland or Andorra (wedged between France and Spain), do not have railroads. But these often have adequate bus service.

Austria, Switzerland, and rural parts of Scotland have extensive postal bus networks. These deliver mail as well as passengers at least once a day (except Sundays) to even the most remote villages. Schedules are coordinated with train schedules, so that you can leave the train, and a few minutes later be moving away from the station on the bus.

In Britain, the bus fares between major cities (such as London and Birmingham) are competitive with or even a little cheaper than rail fares.

Bus Stations and Stops

Most large European cities have long-distance bus terminals. Some are adjacent to or near train stations, but most are in other parts of cities or adjacent to access routes.

City maps usually locate bus stations. Tourist information offices can almost always tell you where the terminals are.

Rural bus stops in countries are marked in various ways. When you start a journey, watch for a small sign at the first stop. It may be the symbol of a bus, the word for bus stop, or logo of the bus company.

Public Transit

Subways are the fastest transit method in most major European cities. Buses and trolley cars are usually slower but far more scenic. Some cities also have extensive light rail systems (streetcars on separate rights of way) going to the suburbs, or, in West Germany and Vienna, linking entire regions.

On business days, subways and light rail are the quickest ways to get around: faster than taxis, buses, or foot. Your speed will be about 15 to 30 miles per hour including the walk from your starting point to the subway station, the ride, and the walk from the subway station to your destination. Only bicycle riders can equal the point-to-point speed, and then only by riding in traffic and threading their way through traffic jams.

In general, transit systems are reasonably straightforward, though each city's system has its own aura and eccentricities. Ticket practices vary; some systems charge by distance traveled, others by the ride, and still others by time elapsed. Most, but not all, offer reductions for quantity ticket purchases, or for weekly or monthly or even yearly passes. Still others have special tourist-oriented cards, which often include admission to museums and other attractions, and even shopping discounts. However, the tourist tickets are not usually the most economical.

Many transit systems, particularly in Germany, Italy, the Netherlands, Scandinavia, Switzerland, and the Eastern European nations, use the honor system. No one will check your ticket as you enter or get on the train or bus. However, these systems may include roving ticket inspectors— often plain-clothes—who will impose hefty fines on the spot for unticketed passengers.

Details about mass transit for many major cities in Europe follow. The first listed transit type in each city is roughly an indication of speed, convenience, and coverage. Therefore, subways are frequently listed first.

In the ticket section, the type of ticket is listed first, then the name of the ticket is given in parentheses.

Public Transit Key

Amsterdam

Main types of transit: Streetcar (tram), buses, and subway (Metro).

Operating company name: GVB, or Gemeentevervoerbedrijf (108-114 Prins Henrikkade, Postbos 2131, 1000 CC Amsterdam, tel. 55 14 911, 8:30 a.m.—4:30 p.m., telex 12708. (Note: suburban lines are operated by other companies, though all accept the same tickets.)

Hours of operation: 5 a.m. to 1 a.m., plus night buses on a limited route network and schedule.

Tickets: Fares are charged by distance and time. The same ticket is valid on all forms of transit. Tickets are not collected at the end of the journey. Any journey takes one fare zone to get on plus one additional strip per zone.

How and where to buy tickets:

- Individual tickets *(Uurnetkaart)* are sold only on the bus and Metro, 2.65 Gulden, and 2.50 Gulden at night, valid for unlimited travel during a one-hour period.
- Strip tickets *(Nationale Strippenkaart)* of 10 strips (8.85 Gulden) on buses and trams, and at the GVB office on Prins Henrikkade and post offices, both of which also sell tick-

ets of 15 strips (8.85 Gulden) and 45 strips (25.85 Gulden).

- Rover passes *(Dagkaarten)* for one day (8.65 Gulden) through nine days (8.65 Gulden for the first day plus 2.70 Gulden per extra day) at GVB office in front of Central Station or GVB office on Prins Henrikkade.
- Monthly passes *(Netabonnement)* at GVB offices. Photograph is required and laminated to the card. Cost depends on number of zones purchased. (All of central Amsterdam is in one zone.) Also requires a photo ID card (Stamkaart), available free from GVB offices; bring a photo.

How to find your way around:
Get basic free maps from VVV or GVB offices; complete route map of entire area is 1.50 Gulden. Ask at the VVV office if you need detailed directions.

Special information: Night bus routes are shown in the map at the beginning of the Yellow Pages of the phone directory, or in the GVB pamphlet "Nachtbussen." For transit informa-

Nationale Strippenkaart (reduced)

tion call 27 27 27 (7 a.m.—11 p.m.). Strip tickets
are good on buses, trams, and subways in all
other cities in the Netherlands. Fine for traveling
without a valid ticket: 26 Gulden. All ticket inspectors are uniformed officers.

Exits are marked "Uitgang."

Taxis: Expensive and hard to find. Because of
crowded, narrow, one-way streets, taxis are
sometimes slower than walking, especially in the
central city. Call 77 77 77 for taxis. Tip is included in the fare.

How to get to and from Schiphol airport:
Trains directly between airport (station in front
of the terminal) and Amsterdam Centraal Station every 15 minutes during the day and hourly
between 1 and 6 a.m., costs 4.50 Gulden. Buses
from Schiphol to Royal Sonesta Hotel in the city
center, costs 12.50 Gulden.

Barcelona

Main types of transit: Subway (Metro),
RENFE trains, buses, suburban regional trains,
fenicular, and teleferic lines.

Operating company names: Entitat Metropolitana del Transport, Entitat Metropolitana del
Transport, or TMB (subways, buses, railways)
(Ronda Sant-Pau 43, 08015 Barcelona, telephone
335.08.12, fax 335.86.30, telex 9822 FMTBE),
RENFE (suburban and national rail service),
Estació Sants, information tel. 322.41.42, telex
27632 TERBA, Ferrocarrils de la Generalitat de
Catalunya (suburban rail service), Diputació
237-9, tel. 318.50.24. Information number:
336.00.00, workdays 7:30 a.m.—8:30 p.m., Sundays and holidays 8 a.m.—2 p.m.

Symbols: Metro: Letter M in diamond; RENFE:
initials; Ferrocarils: two intertwined letter "U"s.

Hours of operation: Metro: workdays, 5 a.m. to
1 a.m.; Saturdays from 5 a.m. to 1 a.m.; Sundays
and holidays from 6 a.m. to 1 a.m. Buses run
from around 5 or 6 a.m. to 10 or 11 p.m.

Tickets: Tickets are charged per entry rather
than by distance or time. Each transit organization has its own tickets and passes, which are not
interchangable.

How and where to buy tickets

- Single tickets *(Bitllet senzill)*, workdays (including Saturday) 65 Pta, Sundays and holidays 70 Pta. Allows a single ride on a single line of either Metro or bus. Fenicular, 75 Pta weekdays, 80 Sundays and holidays; teleferic de Monjuïc, 150 Pta.
- Multiple trip tickets *(Targeta Multiviatge)*, allows 10 journeys on Metro, fenicular, and Blue Tramvia, 325 Pta, above plus bus, 380 Pta.
- Combination ticket *(Targeta-bitllet combinat T-3*, 10 Metro trips and 10 Metro rides, 570 Pta.
- Rover passes *(Passo temporal)*, unlimited travel on Metro, fenicular, tramvia, and bus for 1 day (390 Pta), 3 days (800 Pta), or 5 days (1150 Pta).

- Monthly Metro and fenicular pass *(Abonament mensual Metro i Funicular)*, provides unlimited Metro and fenicular travel during a calendar month, 2750 Pta.

Transports Municipals de Barcelona

M

F.C. Metropolita de Barcelona, S. A.
N.º C.I.F. A08 005 795

206715

Tarifa vigent, inclos 6 % IVA
Per presentar a petició de qualsevol
empleat. Conservar fins a la sortida. Sèrie **K**

- RENFE and Ferrocarilles de la Generalitat trains require single tickets, costs depends on distance traveled.

How to find your way around: Transit maps are free, available at information windows at main stations (Sants, Plaça Catalunya, and Plaça Universitat) and the TMB offices at Ronda Sant Pau 43 and Avinguda Borbo 12.

Special information and pitfalls: Microbus service for the disabled is available by calling 352.54.40.

Exits are marked "Sortida," or "Salida" at RENFE stations.

Taxis: Taxis are common and found at taxi stands or by calling 330.03.00, 300.38.11 or any any other number of taxi companies (look under "Taxis" in the Yellow Pages. Charges are metered; if calling, most (but not all) do not charge on their way to pick you up. Tip 10%.

How to get to and from Barcelona airport: RENFE trains from the station at the airport to Sants station, from about 6 a.m. to 10 p.m. daily.

Berlin (West)

Main types of transit: Subway (U-Bahn), light rail streetcars (S-Bahn), and buses.

Operating company name: BVG, or Berliner Verkehrs-Betriebe (Potsdamer Strasse 188, postal district 30, tel. 25 61, fax (030) 216 41 86, telex 302020 BVG).

Symbols: U-Bahn: white U in blue square. S-Bahn: white S in green circle.

Hours of operation: 4:30 a.m. to midnight.

Tickets: Tickets are valid for a trip in any one direction in West Berlin for a maximum of 120 minutes (including round trips), from the minute you time-stamp your ticket. The same kind of ticket is used on all public transit. Transfers (including between bus, U-Bahn, and S-Bahn) are free and no new ticket is needed.

How and where to buy tickets

- Individual tickets *(Einzel-Fahrschein)*, Deutsche Marks (DM) 2.70, at any BVG ticket office, U-Bahn, or S-Bahn station, or buses, provides unlimited use of bus, U-

Bahn, and S- Bahn, including unlimited transfers.

- Individual short-distance tickets *(Kurz-streckentarif)* For less than 6 bus stops or 3 U-Bahn or S-Bahn stations, DM 1.70.
- Five-Ride cards *(Sammelkarte),* for DM 11.50 (a large discount from single-ticket prices). Buy them at BVG offices.
- Rover passes *(Berlin Ticket),* for 24 hours, DM 9 at BVG office at Kleistpark U-Bahn station, at BVG office at the Zoo Station, and most U-Bahn and S-Bahn stations. Unlimited use of the West Berlin transport network, including riverboats.
- Weekday rover ticket *(6-Tage-Karte-Jeder-mann),* DM 26 for entire network except riverboats. Valid Monday through Saturday only. Requires a photograph.
- Group tickets *(Sondernkarte),* for periods at your choice. Buy at BVG offices. Groups must number at least 6, but a member can travel individually on the West Berlin network.
- Monthly pass *(UmweltKarate),* at BVG offices. This pass is transferable and does not require a photograph. Valid for a calendar month, costs DM 65 for entire BVG network.

How to find your way around: Transit maps are sold at all subway ticket windows, DM 2; schedule book DM 2.50.

Special information and pitfalls: West Berlin transit tickets aren't used in East Berlin. Fine for riding without a valid ticket is DM 40.

Exits are marked "Ausgang."

Taxis: Fares are high, with an extra charge for each piece of luggage. Most taxis are immaculate Mercedes-Benz diesels. Taxis are at stands on the street or call for taxis at 69 02, 26 10 26, 21 60 60, or 24 02 02. Tip 10%.

How to get to and from airports:

Tegel (West Berlin) airport: Frequent city buses (Line A9) arrive and depart from Tegel airport. Any regular West Berlin transit ticket can be used.

East Berlin's Schönefeld airport (which is outside East Berlin city limits): buses will take you to East Berlin. You will have to get an East

German transit visa, available at the airport upon arrival (no charge).

Note on transit in East Berlin: You can get a day rover pass for all public transport in East Berlin for 2 Marks (M), or S-bahn for M1 at any S-bahn station or from the tourist office at Alexanderplatz 5. Transit maps are sold (but are rarely in stock). However, you can also buy tickets on buses and S-Bahn stations for M 0.20—0.30. Remember to validate ticket in the stamping machines before you enter (push very hard!).

Brussels

Main types of transit: Subway (Metro), street-cars (called Pre-Metro), trams, and buses.

Operating company name: STIB, or Société des Transports Intercommunaux de Bruxelles (French) and Maatschappij voor het Intercommunaal Vervoer te Brussel (Flemish) (head office at avenue de la Toison d'Or 15, 1060 Bruxelles, tel. for information 515 30 64 Monday through Friday (8:30 a.m.—4:30 p.m.).

Symbol: Metro: stylized white M in blue rectangle.

Hours of operation: 5 a.m. to midnight or 1 a.m., plus limited night bus service.

Tickets: Fares are charged per entry and the same tickets are used on all systems (bus, Pre-Metro, Metro) except suburban (orange) buses. Tickets are valid for a one-hour trip in any direction, plus two transfers in the second hour. Passes can also include suburban trains. Tickets are not collected at the end of the journey.

How and where to buy tickets:

- Individual tickets *(Billet Direct)*, 35 Francs (F) at Metro ticket booths, from bus drivers and on streetcars and trams.
- 5-ride tickets (155 F), sold on buses, streetcars, and Pre-Metro and Metro stations.
- Rover passes *(Carte 24-Heures)*, 140 F for 1 day, at airport tourist information, all subway stations, STIB offices at Rogier and Porte de Namur Pre-Metro stations. (Note: also valid in 25 cities and towns the same day throughout Belgium.)

- Monthly passes *(Abonnement Mensuel)*, 935 F at S.T.I.B. offices; requires a photograph for ID card.
- Annual Passes *(Abonnement Annuel)*, 9350 F at S.T.I.B. offices; requires a photograph for ID card.

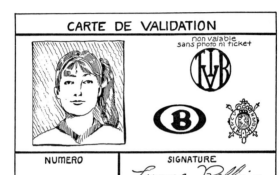

Photo Identification Card and Monthly Coupon (actual size)

How to find your way around: Get free transit maps from all Metro, Pre-Metro, and S.T.I.B. offices in Brussels. Free tourist office map shows some Metro and Pre-Metro routes, but is not as detailed as the S.T.I.B. map.

Special Information: Exits are marked by an arrow pointing out of a box; if in words, "Sortie" (French) and "Uitgang". (Flemish). Fine for attempting to ride without a valid ticket: 1,000 F plus cost of a ticket (first offence) to 10,000 F.

Taxis: Expensive, charging by distance and time. Night taxi fares are double the daytime fare. Hail taxis at taxi stands, train stations, or other busy areas, or call 511 22 44. Tip is included in the fare.

How to get to and from Zaventem (Nationale) airport: Trains between airport basement and Nord and Central (Midi) stations approximately every 20 to 30 minutes from 6 a.m. to 11:30 p.m. Trip takes 20 minutes, costs 75 F.

Copenhagen

Main types of transit: Electric "S" light-rail trains (S-tog) and buses.

Operating company names: HT, or Hovedstadsområdats Trafikselskab (Toftegårds Plads, Gammel Køge Landevej 3, 2500 Valby, tel. 36-44 36 36, fax 36-44 01 19,) and DSB, or Danske Statsbaner.

Hours of operation: 5:30 a.m. (6 a.m. Sundays) to 12:30 a.m., plus a few bus routes until 2:30 a.m.

Tickets: Tickets are valid for one hour within each transit zone. When you go more than one zone, you must have one ticket per zone. Transfers within zone are free. Tickets are valid on both buses and S-tog. Tickets are not collected at the end of the journey.

How and where to buy tickets:

- Individual tickets *(Grundbillet)* 8 Danish kroner (Dkr) for two zones, from bus driver and at S-tog stations.
- 10-ticket books for Dkr 70 at train stations and from bus drivers.

- Rover passes *(1-Day Rover)*, Dkr 80 for 24 hours at railway stations and some large hotels. Two types: Greater Copenhagen includes the city; Metropolitan Area includes suburbs and costs twice as much.
- Area rover passes *(Around the Sound)* Dkr 140 for unlimited travel for 2 days, including travel to Elsinore and Malmö, Sweden.
- Tourist passes *(Copenhagen Card)*, Dkr 80 for 1 day, Dkr 140 for 2 days, Dkr 180, sold for 3 days at airport, railway stations, tourist information offices. Benefits in addition to transport include free admission to almost all museums, Tivoli Gardens, 25% or 50% discount (depending on time) on hydrofoils to Malmö, Sweden.
- Monthly passes *(Maanedsbillet)*, Dkr 240 at Hovedbanegården (main rail station). Good within 3 fare zones nearest to city center; requires one photograph for free ID card.
- All tickets are half price for children from 5 to 11 years old.

How to find your way around: Get free maps from all tourist information offices, or complete transit maps from HT stations, Dkr 5.

Special information and pitfalls: Stamp your ticket at the yellow time-stamp machines on train platforms. Part of the ticket is removed, the remainder is time-stamped. Fine for failure to have a valid ticket is Dkr 150 on buses and Dkr 250 on the S-tog.

Taxis: Plentiful but expensive. Do not tip! Additional night charge of 20% from 6 p.m. to 6 a.m. Call 31-35 35 35 for taxis.

How to get to or from Kastrup airport: SAS (Scandinavian Airlines) buses between airport and bus terminal across street from Vesterport railway station every 15 minutes from 6 a.m. to 10 p.m. Also, HT bus from City Hall Square. Pay the bus driver. Or, take a taxi.

Frankfurt

Main types of transit: Subway (U-Bahn), light rail (S-Bahn), buses, and streetcars.

Operating company name: FVV, or Frankfurter Verkehrs- und-Tarif-Verbund (for all tickets) (Mannheimer Strasse 15-19, Postfach 16349, 6000 Frankfurt 16, tel. (069) 2 69 40, 9 a.m—3:30 p.m.), Stadtwerke Frankfurt am Main (Subway, trams, buses), Deutsche Bundesbahn (DB) for S-bahn, suburban buses.

Symbols: U-Bahn: White U in blue square; S-Bahn: White S in green circle. Bus or tram stop: Green H in yellow circle.

Hours of operation: 5 a.m. to between 10 p.m. and 2 a.m. depending on line.

Tickets: Single tickets are valid for one ride, on any and all forms of transit within a fare zone. (All of central Frankfurt is in the same fare zone.) This system extends as far as Hanau to the east and Wiesbaden and Mainz to the west. Maps at all stations and most streetcar stops show zone boundaries.

How and where to buy tickets:

- Individual short-distance tickets *(Kurz-strecke Fahrschein)* for journeys under 2 km, 2 Deutsche Marks (DM) during peak hours, 1,20 off-peak hours, sold at blue ticket machines at subway stations, and streetcar stops.

- Individual tickets *(Fahrschein)* DM 1.80 at blue ticket machines at subway stations, streetcar stops, and in buses from the driver, provides travel in a single direction within 70 minutes; unlimited transfers permitted. Not sold on U-bahn or S- bahn trains.

- Rover passes *(24-Stunden-Ticket)* for 24 hours day in the city for DM 8 at blue ticket

STADTWERKE FRANKFURT AM MAIN

31 02110   2 7 9 1 4 25 A 0 8.00

Standort   Tag   Uhrzeit   Preis

Nicht übertragbar. Es gelten die Gemeinsamen Beförderungsbedingungen und Tarifbestimmungen. Fahrscheine sind nach Beendigung der Fahrt bis nach Verlassen des Haltestellenbereichs aufzubewahren.

machines at stops and stations, and from bus drivers.

- Seven day passes *(FVV Wochenkarte)* at FVV ticket counters at the Hauptbahnhof (main railway station) and the Hauptwache in the city center. Price varies by number of fare zones purchased.
- Monthly passes *(FVV Monatskarte)* for 30 days at FVV ticket counters at the Hauptbahnhof and the Hauptwache. Price varies with the number of fare zones purchased, maximum DM 165.
- Yearly passes *(Pluskarte)* for 12 months from the first of the month following date of purchase, price varies with number of zones purchased, costs equal 10 monthly passes.

How to find your way around: Get free maps from tourist information offices (or best, the Fairgrounds (Messe) Service- Center). While trams do not have route maps inside them, clear and distinct recorded announcements are made before each stop. Since stops can be short, know the name of your stop to avoid passing it.

Special information and pitfalls: Tickets are sold by zones; while the central city is in one zone, outlying areas and the airport are two to four zones away.

Most tram stops and all subway stations have blue ticket-vending machines, which have signs reading "Fahrscheine." Tickets are time-stamped by the machine or bus driver. You must have a ticket before you enter the subway, trams, or S-Bahn. Fine for failure to have a valid ticket is DM60.

Exits are marked "Ausgang."

Taxis: Expensive, mostly Mercedes-Benz diesels and a few large Japanese cars. Tip 10%. Call 23 00 01 for taxis, or find them at taxi stands. Some take credit cards (and will have appropriate decals).

How to get to or from the Flughafen Frankfurt airport: S-Bahn between basement level of Terminal B to the Frankfurt central station (Hauptbahnhof) every 10 minutes, takes 11 minutes, lines 14 and 15. At the Hauptbahnhof, some trains leave from the underground S-bahn platform, others from the main level, usually at the far left platform.

London

Main types of transit: Subway (Underground or Tube), Docklands light rail, buses (including "Hoppa" minibuses), suburban British Rail trains, and separate river ferry.

Operating company name: London Regional Transport, (55 Broadway, SW1H 0BD, tel. 071-222 5500, fax 071-227 3134). Information offices at Victoria and Euston railway stations, Piccadilly Circus, King's Cross, and Oxford Circus, and both Heathrow Underground stations, or tel. 071-222 1234, 24 hours a day.

Symbol: Circle with horizontal line through it; arrow will point into building or subway.

Hours of operation: Underground, 6 a.m. (Sundays 7:30 a.m.) to midnight. Bus timetables are attached to standards or light poles at bus stops. No transport service on Christmas Day except Airbus A1, and limited service on December 26.

Tickets: Underground and bus tickets are charged by zone, tickets are not interchangeable. No transfers between bus and rail. Underground single-journey tickets are collected at the end of the journey. Bus tickets are not collected after issuance, but should be retained until the end of the journey.

All tickets and a multitude of passes are sold at all Underground station ticket windows.

How and where to buy tickets:

The London region is divided into five fare zones: the Central Zone (1) includes all of the area inside the Circle Line, and a little further in some directions. The Central Zone (Zone 1) includes all of central London; the Inner Zone (Zone 2) includes the rest of London, and the Outer Zones (Zone 3, 4, and 5) include the suburbs to about 15 miles from London.

- Individual tickets: at Underground station ticket booths, and ticket machines at main underground stations, from bus conductors (who may take a minute or two to get to you after you've boarded the bus). Minimum cost is 50p (70p in the Central Zone), up to £2.10 for five zones.
- Daily, weekly, monthly, or annual passes *(Travelcard)*, valid on buses, British Rail,

Docklands light rail, the Underground; sold by zones; valid only in the boundaries of Greater London.

- *One-Day Travelcard*, valid for Zones 1, 2, and 3, costs £2.30, all 5 zones £2.60, sold at every London Transport Travel Information Centre, Underground station, and Bus Garage, cannot be used before 9:30 a.m. No photo required, except by children aged 14 and 15.

- *Weekly Travelcard*, bought any day and valid for seven consecutive days; £7.10 for the Central Zone, up to £19.70 for five zones within the Greater London boundaries. Requires a photograph (photo booth and passport pictures OK), which is placed onto a free identification card.

- *Monthly Travelcard*, bought any day and valid for 30 days; £27.30 for the Central Zone, up to £75.70 for all five zones within the Greater London boundaries. Requires a photograph, which is placed onto free identification card.

- *Annual Travelcard*, bought any day and valid for one year; £284 for the Central Zone, up to £788 for five zones in the

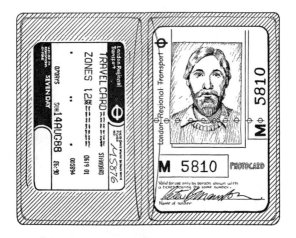

Weekly Travelcard and Identification Card (reduced)

Greater London boundaries. Requires a photograph, which is placed onto a free identification card.

- *Bus Pass*, valid only on buses and sold by zone, but not sold for Central Zone.
- *One-Day Bus Pass*, valid all day (including morning rush hour). Not sold for Central Zone only; ranges from £1 for one zone to £1.90 for five zones. Can be bought ahead of time with scratch-off dates. No photo required.
- *7 Day Bus Pass*, valid for seven consecutive days, sold by zones, for the local area, £2.80, to four zones £7.30, not including Central Zone; including Central Zone, £8.50 to £12.50.
- *Monthly Bus Pass*, valid for one month, sold by zones, £12.30 for the local area, to £28.10 for four zones, not Central Zone; including Central Zone, £32.70 to £48.
- *Annual Bus Pass*, valid for one year, sold by zones, £168 for one zone, to £292 for four zones not including Central Zone; including Central Zone, £340 to £500.

How to find your way around: Get free maps at all London Transport ticket booths. Each underground line has its own color and name, which is consistently used in all maps, signs, and stations.

Special information and pitfalls: Sunday Underground service is infrequent on some lines, and some stations are closed. Underground system is color coded, easy to understand and follow, and the sign design virtually unchanged since developed by calligrapher Edward Johnston in 1907.

If you have a Travelcard or Capitalcard and travel outside your zone, you can use it and pay only an "excess fare" for travel outside the permitted zone.

One-Day passes are not valid on night bus services (line numbers preceded by an N, usually after 11 p.m.). Minimum fare on night buses is £1.

Exits are marked "Way Out."

Taxis: Not cheap but set an unexcelled standard of comfort, roominess, and courtesy. Hail taxis on

the street when "For Hire" sign is lit. Tip 10 to
15%.

How to get to and from airports:

- Heathrow—Underground (Piccadilly line)
  goes directly to Heathrow (all terminals)
  every five to ten minutes; buses from
  Heathrow to the London bus terminal at
  Victoria Coach Station (near Victoria Station) (Bus A1) every 20 minutes from 6:35
  a.m. to 9:40 p.m. Bus A2 goes from Russel
  Square and Euston station every 20 or 30
  minutes. Night bus N97 goes from
  Heathrow to Trafalgar Square and Liverpool
  Street Station, and makes stops upon request. From the southwest, British Rail to
  Woking station (main line), then Railair
  Link Heathrow-Woking bus every 20
  minutes, takes one up to hour (depending on
  terminal), 7 a.m. to 9:15 p.m.
- Gatwick—Gatwick express train every 15
  minutes to and from east end of the air terminal to Victoria Station, journey takes 30
  minutes, £5 second class, £7.50 first class.
  You can't take baggage carts to rail platforms at Gatwick. Green Line 777 buses
  leave every hour from Victoria Coach Station, one block from Victoria Station, takes
  about one hour and a half, and Wandsworth
  Arendale, takes about one hour, £4.50,
  round trip £6. Baggage carts are plentiful at
  Gatwick's bus stop. Greenline information,
  tel. 081-668 7261.
- London City—London Transport bus line
  276 directly to airport (pass by West Ham or
  Stratford Underground stations), or by
  British Rail to London City Airport (Silver-
  town) station, or by riverbus (ferry) from
  Charing Cross Pier at 10 minutes past the
  hour, takes 35 minutes, £5, and from Swan
  Lane at London Bridge at 30 minutes past
  the hour, takes 30 minutes, £4, from 7:20
  a.m. to 6:10 p.m. For ferry information, call
  071-376 3676.
- Stanstead—Train three times per hour be-
  tween Liverpool Street Station and Bishops
  Stortford Station; do not go to Stanstead
  Station. Local bus between Bishops
  Stortford Station and the airport, or take a

taxi (£4). Green Line bus 799 travels from
Stanstead to Redbridge and Stratford Un-
derground stations, and the Victoria Coach
Station, one block from Victoria Station.
• Between Gatwick and Heathrow, buses
every hour, take 90 minutes, £10.

Madrid

Main types of transit: Subway (Metro), and
buses.

Operating company name: ETM, or Empresa
Municipal de Transportes (Alcántara 24, 28006
Madrid, tel. 401-9900).

Hours of operation: Metro: 6 a.m. to 1 a.m.;
bus: 5:30 a.m. to 11 p.m. or to 2 a.m. depending
on line.

Tickets: Fares are charged per ride. Tickets are
not collected at the end of the journey.

How and where to buy tickets:
• Individual tickets *Boleto*, bus, 65 pesetas
(Pta) from bus drivers, Metro: 65 Pta, except
the Colón-Aeropuerto is 200 Pta, from Metro
ticket offices.
• Ticket books 10 bus rides *(Bono-bus)*, 410
Pta, or 10 metro rides *(Taco)*, at EMT kiosks
or EMT headquarters.
• Weekly pass *(Abono Transporte)*, valid on
bus and metro, zone A (all of the central
city), 3000 Pta, to all zones, 4500 Pta.

How to find your way around: Get free maps
from EMT offices (Plaza Cibeles, Plaza Callao,
and Puerta del Sol) and tourist information offices.

Special Information: Microbuses (65 Pta) run
along main routes and are more comfortable and
much faster than regular city buses.

Exits are marked "Salida."

Taxis: Hail taxis on the street (sign "Libre," or
green dome light at night), or from taxi stands
(with sign with large white T on a blue background). Extra charge on Sundays (50 Pta),
holidays (50 Pta), when leaving a bus or rail station (50 Pta), and for each piece of luggage. Night
surcharge after 11 p.m. (50 Pta) Tip 10%. Be sure
meter has been started after you get in.

How to get to and from Barajas airport:
Buses leave every 15 minutes between airport
and City Air Terminal underground at Plaza
Colón, 6 a.m. to 11 p.m., 200 Pta, or take a taxi.

Milan

Main types of transit: Streetcars, subways
(Metro), buses, and trolley-buses.
Symbol: Metro: MM (Metropolitana Milanese),
or ATM in a parallelogram.
Operating company name: ATM, or Azienda
Trasporti Municipali (Foro Buonaparte 61, 20121
Milano, information tel. 8901 0797 and 669 7047,
fax 805 0674, telex 330564 ATMSA).
Hours of operation: 4 a.m. to 2 a.m., depending
on line (some lines have shorter hours).
Tickets: The same tickets are used on all public
transit. Time-stamp your ticket when you first
get on a bus or tram, or enter the Metro station.
Transfers are free, and you need only keep your
original ticket. Tickets are not collected at the
end of the journey.
How and where to buy tickets:
- Individual tickets *(Biglietto Ordinario),* 800
  Lire, at tobacco stands (Tabacchi) with ATM
  logo, all Metro station stands, and ticket
  machines (most take coins and 1000 Lire
  bills). Tickets are valid for one metro ride
  and 75 minutes' unlimited use of the rest of
  the system.
- Carnet *(Carnet di Biglietti Urbani),* a book
  of 13 tickets, 10,000 Lire, at tobacco stands,
  Metro stops, all ATM ticket offices.

Biglietto Ordinario

- Tourist ticket *(Tesserino Turistico Giornaliero)* valid for 1 day, 3,200 Lire, ATM offices at the Piazza Duomo and Centrale railway station Metro stations, and ATM information offices. Proof of non-residence (such as a passport) is required.
- Weekly passes *(Abbonamento Settimanale a Vista)*, valid from Monday to the following Sunday night, 8,400 Lire. Allows unlimited travel on urban Metro, tram, and bus lines. Requires an identification card (5000 Lire and a photograph), and can be obtained at main Metro stations and ATM offices.
- Annual passes *(Abbonamento Annuale di Libera Circolazione)*, valid for a calendar year, 330,000 Lire, requires a photograph. Obtainable only at ATM headquarters at via Ricasoli 2 entrance.

How to find your way around: Get free map at ATM information offices at Metro Duomo and Centrale, and ATM headquarters (even has a street index!); a less-accurate but usable map is free from tourist offices.

Special information and pitfalls: You must stamp your ticket when you enter metro station or bus or tram. The air on Line 1 of Metro is very stuffy most of the year. Large suitcases require their own 800 Lire ticket. Supplemental fares are be charged for suburban travel.

Exits are marked "Uscita."

Fine for failure to have a valid ticket: in city limits 20,000 Lire, outside city limits 10,000 Lire, plus the cost of a single ticket.

Taxis: Numerous, mostly occupied. Tip 5%. Find at taxi stands at train stations and in the central district, or call 8585, 6767, or 5151 for taxis.

How to get to and from the airports:

- Linate: Buses every 20 minutes between airport and city air terminal at Piazza Luigi di Savoia (Metro: Centrale) or take Metro Line 1 to San Babila, then Bus 73 to Linate.
- Malpensa: Buses between airport and city air terminal meet each flight. Malpensa is very far from Milan: take the bus at least 2-1/2 hours before departure. Buses may not serve charter flights. Taxi fares can be up to 50,000 Lire (about $30).

Note: For flight arrival and departure information at both airports, call 74 85 2200.

Munich

Main types of transit: Subway (U-Bahn), light rail (S-Bahn), buses, and trams.

Operating company name: MVV, or Münchener Verkehrs- und Tarif Verbund (Thierschstrasse 2, postal district 22, Postfach 260154, 8000 München 26, fax 2 38 03282. S-Bahn information tel. 128 3660, U-bahn, bus, and tram information 21 91 1).

Symbols: U-Bahn: White U in blue square; S-Bahn: White S in green circle; Tram stop: "Haltestelle" sign on pole.

Hours of operation: 5 a.m. to 1:30 a.m.

Tickets: Munich is divided into fare zones. On transit maps, the inner zone is blue, and outer zones are various shades of green. Single-ride and strip tickets are sold by distance, depending on the number of zone crossed. The same tickets and passes can be used on any public transportation without a separate transfer.

How and where to buy tickets:

- Single tickets *(Einzelkarte)* at ticket-vending machines at U-Bahn and S-Bahn stations, and at tram and bus stops; buy before boarding U-Bahn and S-Bahn. Minimum cost is 2.40 Deutsche Mark (DM), more for extra zones.

- Strip tickets at ticket vending machines at all subway and S-Bahn ticket booths. Tickets of 10 blue strips *(Kleine Streifenkarte)* are blue and cost DM 9.50; tickets of 16 blue strips *(Grosse Streifenkarte)* cost DM 15. For children 4 to 14, tickets are red, cost about half price.

- Rover Passes *(MVV-Day-Ticket)* valid for unlimited travel until 4 a.m. the next morning in the inner (Innenraum) zone costs DM 7.50, and DM 15 for the entire network (Gesamtnetz). Purchase at all ticket vending machines, and subway and S-Bahn ticket booths.

- Monthly Passes *(Monatskarte)* for DM 43—
  DM 178 depending on fare zones included.
  Valid for a calendar month, and requires a
  photograph. Obtain it from MVV offices.

How to find your way around: Free city maps
available from tourist information offices and at
Hauptbahnhof (main railway station). MVV has
a detailed explanation of transit in the multi-lan-
guage publications, "Verbundfahren in München"
and "Rendezvous mit Müchen," available from
tourist information offices or MVV.

Special information and pitfalls: Two blue
strips are required for a journey within the city;
more strips are required on the S-Bahn to suburbs. Time-stamp your ticket in the Entwerter-
automaten machine (blue boxy machine with a
big yellow E) before you get on a bus or tram or
enter the subway or S-Bahn. Fine DM 60 for
failure to have a valid ticket (or enough validated
strips) payable on the spot.

Exits are marked "Ausgang."

Taxis: Expensive; mainly immaculate Mercedes-
Benz diesels and now a few equally immaculate
large Japanese cars. Tip 10%. Find taxis at
stands at railway stations, the city center, or call
21611.

How to get to or from Riem airport: Buses
between airport and Arnulfstrasse on the north
side of the Hauptbahnhof (main railway station)
every 20 minutes from 5:40 a.m. to 8:40 p.m., DM
7.

Paris

Main types of transit: Subway (Metro) and
RER, (Réseau Express Régional) to suburbs, and
buses.

Subway Symbols: Letter M inside circle (infrequently used), or look for word Metro, or sometimes Metropolitain on the 1900's Art Nouveau
entrances. RER—look for letters RER inside
circle.

Operating company name: RATP, or Régie
Autonome des Transports Parisiens (53ter, quai
des Grands Augustins, 75006, 75271 Paris Cedex
06, tel. (1) 43.46.14.14).

Hours of operation: Metro and RER: 5:30 a.m. to 1 a.m. Bus: Full service 5:30 a.m. to 8:30 p.m., reduced service 3:30 p.m. to 1:30 a.m., skeleton night bus schedule hourly from 1:30 to 5:30 a.m. RER: 5 a.m. to 1 a.m.

Tickets: Tickets on subways are valid for one entry. Short bus trips take one ticket, longer trips take two or more. The same type of ticket is used buses and Metro. Tickets are validated when you go through the turnstiles, or when you enter the bus. Use Metro tickets on RER inside Paris, RER tickets when traveling beyond the city (otherwise you will not be able to get out of the suburban RER station). Tickets are not collected at the end of the journey, except on RER lines. In any case, keep your ticket until you pass the "limite de validité de billets" at the exit.

The Paris region is divided into fare zones; all of the city of Paris (inside the Peripherique) is in Zone 1.

How and where to buy tickets:

- Individual tickets *(Ticket à l'Uniteé)* at all Metro stations, on buses, 5 F. Buy RER tickets at all RER stations from coin-operated ticket machines (change given) or from ticket booths.
- Discounted group of 10 tickets *(Carnet)* at all Metro station ticket booths, 31.20 F, little more than half price of ten single tickets.
- Rover pass *(Paris Visite),* good for 3 or 5 days of first-class travel on all Metro, buses, RER, and SNCF suburban trains. Buy at most Metro stations, Paris tourist offices, at SCNF window at Charles de Gaulle 1 airport, and French National Railways offices in other countries. Zones 1, 2, and 3, 3 days

Coupon Orange (Use with Photo Identification Card)

70 F, 5 days 115 F; entire network and airports, 3 days 135 F, 5 days 170 F.

- Daily rover pass *(Formule 1),* provides unlimited second class travel by the day on all
Metro, buses, RER, and SNCF suburban
trains. requires free card plus coupon,
central zones 1 and 2, 21 F; zones 1, 2, and
3, 26 F; zones 1 through 4, 37 F, all four
zones and airport, 63 F. Requires personal
"Carte Formule 1," free at RATP offices and
main stations.

- Weekly passes *(Coupon Jaune)* for bus and
Metro zones 1 and 2, 173 F, and (if desired)
RER zones and SNCF suburban trains.
Valid from Monday through Sunday. Buy it
at all Metro station ticket booths, or RATP
head office. Requires a photograph for the
free identification card *(Carte Orange)*
needed to buy pass.

- Monthly pass *(Coupon Orange)* for Metro
and (if desired) RER, valid for a calendar
month, sold by zones (two zones cover all of
the city, 49 F second class; zones 3, 4, and 5
are in the suburbs, up to 82 F), at Paris
Metro ticket offices, or RATP head office,
and SNCF ticket offices. Photo required for
free identification card *(Carte Orange);* then
buy the pass. This pass is also available as
on annual basis.

How to find your way around: Get free maps
at all Metro ticket booths, Paris tourism offices,
and most French Government Tourist Offices in
other countries.

Coupon Jaune: (Use with identification card)

Special information and pitfalls: Paris subways have first- and second-class cars. First-class cars are in the center of trains, often painted blue and marked with a "1" next to each door. Only first-class ticket holders can use first-class cars between 9 a.m. and 5 p.m.

To find your way in the Metro, you need to know the name of the station at the end of the line in the direction you're going. System is not color-coded, and sometimes signs aren't well located. All Metro signs on every line are either blue on white or white on dark blue.

Exits are marked "Sortie."

Taxis: Expensive and full of hidden but legal charges: luggage (3.50 F per piece); pick-up at train station and air terminals, 4.20 F; evening charges (8 p.m.—7 a.m.). The maximum number

CARTE ORANGE

RATP SNCF APTR

nom
prénom   SMITH JIM

signature

V 777725 ← N° à reporter sur le coupon

rangez ici votre coupon

prenez-en soin

ne le pliez pas et ne l'introduisez pas dans les composteurs des autobus

of passengers in a taxi is usually three, but a fourth can be taken for 5 F extra. Fares more than double from 10 p.m. to 6:30 a.m. Find taxis at the head of taxi stands (Arrêt Taxis, Tête de Station), or by telephone (look in classified under "Taxi"). If you call, you pay for the time and distance the taxi uses until it arrives. Tip 15%. In case of complaints, contact Service des Taxis, 36 rue des Morillons, 75732 Paris Cedex 15, tel. (1) 45.31.14.80.

How to get to and from airports:

- Charles de Gaulle: Frequent buses between airport and Gare du Nord and Gare Montparnasse railway stations. Also, RER line B3 ("Roissy-Rail" goes near the airport, includes free shuttle bus, costs 27.50 F. In addition, Air France buses from Arc de Triomphe and Porte Maillot (Palais de Congrès) every 12 minutes, costs 40 F. RATP bus lines 350 from Gare de l'Est and 351 from Place de la Nation, costs less (varies with destination). Air France bus to Orly every 20 minutes from 6 a.m. to midnight from Gates A3 or B10.

- Orly: Frequent buses between airport and Gare Montparnasse and the air terminal near Les Invalides: trip takes one hour, more during rush hour. Quicker bus service with the "Orlybus" between Orly and Place Denfert-Rochereau Metro station (leaving every 15-20 minutes); trip takes 35 minutes, 18.50 F or 6 yellow Metro tickets or a Coupon Jaune valid for zones 1-4 + Aèroport.

Rome

Main types of transit: Buses, subways (Metro), and trams, plus a few riverboats.

Operating company names: ATAC, or Azienda Tramvie e Autobuse del Comune di Roma for city buses and streetcars (65 via Volturno, 00185 Roma, central tel. 46 951, fax 610091, telex 610091 ATAC), information 46954444; A.CO.TRA.L. (Azienda Consortile Trasporti Laziali) for Metro and suburban buses and streetcars (via Ostiense 131L, 00154 Roma, tel. 57531, fax 57005557) or for information 591 5551.

Hours of operation: Bus: 5:30 a.m. to midnight with skeleton night "Notturno" service on main lines 24 hours. Metro: 5:30 a.m. to 10:30 p.m.

Tickets: One per ride, not collected at the end of the journey, or a pass.

How and where to buy tickets:

- Individual tickets *(Biglietto)*, different kinds for bus and metro, 700 Lire at ATAC offices, ticket machines, tobacco shops, and newsstands. Not available on buses.

- Group of 10 tickets *(Blocchetto da 10 Biglietti di Corsa Semplice)*, provides 10 individual tickets for 6,000 Lire, at ATAC offices, ticket machines, and some tobacco shops and newsstands.

- Half-day rover pass *(Biglietto Orario)*, provides unlimited bus and tram use from either 5 a.m. to 2 p.m. (rose), or from 2 p.m. until midnight (celeste), costs 1000 Lire, at ATAC offices, ticket machines, and some tobacco shops and newsstands. Must be time-stamped when starting the first journey.

- Day rover pass *(Biglietto Integrato Giornaliero or B.I.G.)*, provides unlimited use of the Rome bus, Metro, and urban FS rail system, 2,800 Lire at ATAC offices, ticket machines, and some tobacco shops, and newsstands.

- Tourist rover passes *(Carte Settimanale per Turisti)*, 7 days, 10,000 Lire, at ATAC office in front of Stazione Termini or main ATAC office.

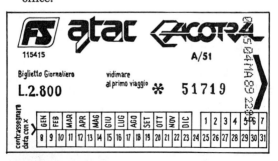

Biglietto Integrato Giornaliero

- Monthly passes *(Tessera di Abbonamento Mensile—Intere Rete Urbana)*, 22,000 Lire at ATAC kiosk in front of Stazione Termini, or main ATAC office. These passes are used on buses and trams but not the Metro. For the same price, a pass can be bought for the Metro and one bus line *(Una Linea ATAC e Linee A e B della Metroplitana.)*
- Passes on A.CO.TRA.L. lines (Abbonamenti) for varying distances and by the week or month are available at all A.CO.TRA.L. offices, require a photocard, L. 5,000.

How to find your way around: Free EPT (tourist office) map shows bus and Metro lines in the city center; the free ATAC "Percorsi di Trianglo" schematically shows the lines to get to particular places. Complete transit maps at ATAC offices, 1000 Lire, or see the "Tuttocittà" section of the phone book has a transit map.

Special information and pitfalls: Metro Line B is dingy and slow south of Termini; Metro Line A is newer, cleaner, much faster. Some stations have long underground corridors. Buses often get stuck in traffic jams.

Most trains leave from Termini station (tel. 4775). Trains to the airport leave from Ostiense station. Commuter trains to the north along via Cassia leave from Giolitti station. Regional trains to Viterbo leave from Piazzale Flaminio.

Taxis: Get taxis at taxi stands or by telephone. Be sure the meter starts after you get in. Extra charges made after 10 p.m., Sundays, holidays, and for each piece of luggage. Tip 10%. Call 3570, 3875, 4994, or 8433. Avoid unlicensed "gypsy" cabs.

Stazione Ostiense at (also called Ferrovie Roma-Lido) at Porta San Paolo (tel. 47 78 90), frequent departures for Lido and Fiumicino airport. There's a 300-meter moving walkway from the Piramide Metro station to Stazione Ostiense.

Regional buses to most areas leave from the vicinity of Termini. Ask at the information stand for exact details.

How to get and from airports:

- Fiumicino (Leonardo da Vinci) airport: Non-stop trains Roma Ostiense Stazione (Metro Piramide) every 10-15 minutes during peak hours; takes 20 minutes for non-stop trains

and 30 minutes for trains with stop. Access
to rail line from Metro line B by moving
walkway, costs L. 5,000.

- Ciampino airport: Metro Line A to Sub-
  augusta station. From there, then
  A.CO.TRA.L bus to the airport. (This airport
  is sometimes used for charter flights.)

Stockholm

Main types of transit: Subways (Tunnelbanan
or T-bana), buses, ferries, and local trains.
Operating company name: SL, or Storstock-
holms Lokaltrafik (Tegnérgatan 2A, Box 6301,
S-113 81 Stockholm, information tel. 23 60 10 (7
a.m.—midnight, head office tel. 786 10 00, telex
19159 SL TRANS S).
Tickets: Tickets for buses, subways and local
trains are interchangeable and are valid for one
hour unlimited travel including unlimited transfers within the city limits. Each zone crossed requires validation of an additional coupon (maximum 8 coupons). Central Stockholm is all in one
zone. Stamp your ticket when you begin to use it.
Tickets are not collected at the end of the journey. (Note: fare increases expected in early 1990.)
How and where to buy tickets:

- Individual tickets *(Biljetter)*, 7 Kronor, at T-
  bana ticket offices, and from bus drivers (actually consists of two 3.50 Kronor coupons).
- 18-strip tickets, *(Rabattkuponger)*, 45
  Kronor, at T-bana ticket offices and
  Pressbyrå shops.
- Tourist tickets, *(Turistkort)*, for 1 day, 22
  Kronor within Stockholm city limits, or entire Stockholm region for 40 Kronor, or 3
  days 76 Kronor, at Pressbyrå shops in subway stations and T-bana ticket offices; full
  use of local transport system and the
  Djurgård ferry; also allows free admission to
  Skansen, Kaknästornet, and Gräna Lund,
  and the Transport Museum.
- Tourist passes *(Stockholmskortet)* for 1, 2, or
  3 days, at tourist information office, in
  Centralstation, and Sweden House. Unlimited transport in Stockholm and suburbs

on subway, bus, and train. Includes free admission to 70 museums, sightseeing tours. Priced from 70 to 240 Kronor.

- Monthly passes *(Månadskort)* for a calendar month for 200 Kronor, at T-bana ticket offices or Pressbyrå shops. Requires photograph for free ID card, plus purchase of monthly ticket.

How to find your way around: Get free maps from tourist information offices, or buy Transport maps *SL Kartor)* at SL offices or Pressbyrå shops.

How to get to and from Arlanda airport: Frequent buses between airport (front of international terminal building), the Vasa Terminal on Vasagatan, with direct access from the T-bana Central station and the Central Railway Station. Buses leave every 5 minutes during peak periods (alternately to international and domestic terminals), and 15 minutes during non-peak periods (all buses serve both terminals). Allow 40 minutes to get to airport check-in from Vasa Terminal, 30 Kronor.

Taxis: Expensive. Call 15 00 00 for taxis. Tip is 10%.

Venice

Main types of transit: Boats (vaporetti, literally little steamers), privately-owned water taxis, and gondolas, and buses in suburban Mestre.

Operating company name: ACTV, or Azienda Consorzio Trasporti Veneziani (Sant' Angelo Corte dell' Albero 3880, Casella Postale 688, 30124 Venezia, tel. (041) 528 780011, fax (041) 5207135, telex 223487 ACTVVE I.

Hours of operation: 24 hours, though vaporetti offer minimal service at night, and none to La Giudecca after about 10 p.m.

Tickets: Valid for one trip (cost depends on distance), not collected at the end of the journey.

How and where to buy tickets:

- Individual tickets *(Biglietto)* at the ticket booth at the landing before you get on the boat. Minimum price 1700 Lire, to 3000 Lire for longer trips.

- Ticket book *(Carnet di Biglietti),* a group of prepaid tickets in various denominations from 100 Lire to 2500 Lire. They can be used as ordinary tickets. Buy them at the ACTV office, or at some tobacco shops. These tickets must be date-stamped before boarding.
- Rover pass *(Biglietto Turistico)* for 24 hours, 9000 Lire at ticket booths at vaporetto stops.
- Discount card *(Carta Venezia),* provides three years of vaporetto service at a two-thirds discount, 10,000 Lire. Buy at ticket booths at vaporetto stops, and ACTV offices. Requires a photograph.
- 3-day discount card *(Biglietto Tre Giorni),* a rover pass for 72 hours from the time of the date stamp at its first use. Includes passage for hand luggage. Excludes lines 2 and 28 and bus lines beyond the Mestre city limits.
- Island Card *(Biglietto Osole),* which provides a one-way journey on a Venice line plus a ride to islands in the lagoon (such as Murano, Burano, Torcello), 3000 Lire.
- Monthly pass *(Abbonamento)* at ACTV offices. The identification card costs 10,000 Lire; requires a photo. After purchasing the card, you can buy a monthly ticket for un-

Carta Venezia (reduced)

limited travel for 29,000 Lire. A monthly pass card can be used as a *Carta Venezia* if the month's coupon has not been bought.

How to find your way around: Get free maps from Venice tourist offices at Piazzale Roma, Santa Lucia railway station, and Piazza San Marco.

Special information and pitfalls: Vaporetti come in three speeds: motoscafi (express), diretto (semi-express), and accellerato (stops at every landing). Also, large pieces of luggage over 50 cm in any dimension cost one ticket per piece.

Gondola prices are unregulated and expensive (50,000 Lire and up). Be sure you agree on length of ride as well as the route before you get in. Singing by the gondolier usually costs extra. Gondola crossings of the Grand Canal cost 300 Lire, and take only a few minutes.

Exits are marked "Uscita."

Smoking is prohibited in vaporetto cabins; fine for smoking inside is 5,000 to 15,000 Lire, payable on the spot.

Water taxis and gondolas: Found at landings or along quays. Agree to a firm price before you get in. Call 32326 or 22303 for water taxis.

How to get to and from Marco Polo airport: Buses (line 5) leave every hour from Piazzale Roma at 10 minutes past the hour, with a stop in Mestre, trip takes 20 minutes. Tickets are sold at the airport in the arrival hall after Customs. Scheduled motorboats also go between the airport and the San Marco vaporetto landing, and meet most flights. Special note: be sure you are on the scheduled boats, since water taxis lie in wait and are exorbitant for this trip.

Vienna

Main types of transit: Subway (Stadtbahn), light rail (Schnellbahn), trams, and buses.

Operating company name: VOR, Verkehrsbund Ost-Region (Postfach 308, Neubaugasse 1, 1010 Wien), telephone 93 95 08-0.

Hours of operation: 5 a.m. to midnight.

Tickets: The system is based on transit zones, using zoned tickets and passes. All of central

Vienna is in the kernel zone (Zone 100). Outlying
areas are in other zones. When using a ticket,
you must stamp it once for each zone boundary
on an uninterrupted journey in a single direction
using subways, trams, and buses. Stamp the
ticket once in the Entwerter machine (insert
ticket in yellow slot) for each zone of your journey
on the bus or at station entrance. Tickets are not
collected at the end of the journey.

How and where to buy tickets:
- Individual tickets *(Fahrschein)* 20 Schillings, at station ticket offices or from bus
  drivers.
- Strip tickets *(Streifenkarte)* with 4 tickets
  (56 Schillings) or 8 tickets (112 Schillings)
  at station ticket offices, tobacco shops
  (tabak). Children 6 to 15 and dogs pay half
  price.

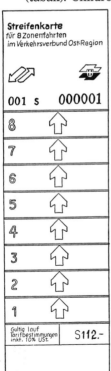

Streifenkarte (reduced)

- One-day rover
  passes *(24-Stun-
  den Wien Netz-
  karte)* for a days'
  travel on all
  public transit in
  the Kernzone,
  sold at Vienna
  tourist informa-
  tion offices and
  VOR station
  ticket offices.
- Weekly Pass
  (Wochenkarte)
  118 Schillings,
  valid for un-
  limited passage
  only in the
  central kernel
  zone one week.
- Monthly passes
  (Monatskarte),
  sold at VOR and
  railway station
  ticket offices,
  tobacco shops
  (tabak). This
  pass is sold by
  zone: costs
  range up to

1,124 Schillings per month. Requires a photo for identification card, available at VOR station ticket offices.

- Yearly passes *(Jahreskarte)*, sold by zone at prices up to 11,240 Schillings, sold at VOR ticket offices. Requires a photo for identification card.

How to find your way around: Get free maps of Vienna from tourist office, or transit map for 35 Schillings from any VOR office.

Special information: Color-coded graphics on subways and Schnellbahn. Signs show the next stop just before leaving the station. Some stations are modern, others date back to the turn of the century.

Dogs and children ride for half of the adult price.

Exits are marked "Ausgang."

Taxis: Many are Mercedes-Benz diesels. Hail a cab from a taxi stand, most often at railway stations and along the Ring, or call 3130, 4369, 6282, or 9101. Taxis charge extra for each piece of baggage. Add 10% tip to the meter charge.

How to get to and from Schwechat airport: Buses every 20 to 30 minutes from 6 a.m. to 7:20 p.m. between the airport and the City Air Terminal at the Hilton Hotel. There are also buses every 30 minutes to the Westbahnhof and Südbahnhof stations every 30 minutes from 7 a.m. to 7 p.m. Buses will wait for planes arriving later in the evening. Also, you can take the train from the airport to City Air Terminal every hour from 7:30 a.m. to 7 p.m. to the Wien Mitte and Wien Nord stations.

Autos and Driving

When you drive, you are unfettered by schedules that may not be convenient. Roads and byways are numerous and pass through almost every village. You can pull over to marvel at a Gothic church or an Alpine peak looming beyond a wildflower-splattered meadow. You can effortlessly cross mountain passes seemingly at the roof of the world, find tranquil picnic spots by the side of the road, and discover cozy, out-of-the-way inns. The charms of the countryside are easy to see at your own pace, since you can stop, even if only to precisely compose a photograph.

You can rent, lease, or purchase cars in Europe, either on the spot or before you leave North America.

If your car has proper registration or a rental contract and insurance (see below), there is no problem crossing borders in a car.

Almost anyone who drives in North America can successfully drive in Europe. To be sure, there are those places—mainly city centers—where driving can be challenging or frustrating, depending on your point of view. Traffic can seem very fast or be agonizingly slow—almost gridlock at times—and a parking place can be almost impossible to find. Fortunately, these same city centers have developed public transport to a fine art: efficient, fast, and cheap.

Driving is somewhat different in Britain and Ireland, where traffic moves on the left side of the road. Your first few minutes there will probably be rather disconcerting. But, after practice, you'll probably do fine, if you watch your right and left turns and the "roundabouts" (traffic circles or rotaries).

Note: If you don't know how to drive a car with manual transmission, your first hours in Europe behind the wheel aren't the best place to learn. Automatic transmission cars may be harder to find and usually cost more. Reserve an automatic in advance or learn to drive a standard transmission before you leave home.

Speed limits and distances everywhere except in Great Britain and older signs in the Irish Republic are in kilometers.

Rules of the Road

1. Speed limits are different from country to country. Freeway and toll road speeds are usually higher than other speed limits in the same country. In West Germany, there is no speed limit at all on the autobahn. In much of Europe, speed limits don't seem to be strictly enforced.

East German autobahns, however, are frequently patrolled and speeds over 100 km per hour, or often poorly-marked lower speed limits, are carefully measured. In some areas with poor maintenance, speed limits are reduced suddenly, and the police lie in wait. Fines are payable on the spot, in Western currency only. A recent fine was approximately $2500!

Some countries have speed traps on main roads that aren't freeways. France is notorious. The fine is imposed and payable on the spot in local currency. No credit cards, travelers checks, or foreign currency are accepted. When you see cars flash their head lights as they come toward you during the day, slow down! Speed trap ahead! They're only trying to save you the cost of a fine.

Usually the speed traps are found on main roads and not autoroutes. Police by the roadside radio ahead and you're pulled over at a more convenient place a couple of miles down the road.

In Finland, fines can be stiff—and, at least for Finns, are based on income (the higher the income, the higher the fine).

2. On a freeway or toll turnpike, flashing high beams from the car behind you mean "move over fast" to a slower outside lane. Most European cars are designed with an easy flash control, which encourages frequent flashing. On the other hand, if you wish to pass another car, the other driver will give way to your flashing headlights.

3. You can't make a right turn (or in Britain or Ireland a left turn) on red signal light! However, you may make turns in the direction shown on green arrows, or, after giving way to pedestrians and cross traffic, on flashing yellow arrows.

4. Road markings are generally like those you're used to. Don't pass on a solid line; don't begin to pass on a short dashed line. All lane lines are white except in construction zones, where they are all yellow, and in Italy, where yellow lines mark lanes reserved for buses and taxis. In Britain, curb markings consist of yellow lines embedded in the street near the curb. One line indicates a loading zone, while a double line means no stopping at any time. There is usually further explanation of parking restrictions on small yellow signs nearby. Don't park at zigzags painted along the roadside in the United Kingdom.

5. Seat belts must be worn in nearly every country. You may have to pay a fine if stopped and you aren't wearing one. In addition, children under six years of age cannot sit in the front seat in most countries even if in seat belts or child seats. In some countries, young children must wear seat belts or be in car seats whether in the front or back seats.

6. Parking restrictions are strictly enforced in some cities, seemingly never in others. But don't park near a sign showing a tow truck taking a car. Tickets are frequently given to offenders. Tickets given in the same country may eventually be charged to you by car rental companies if you don't pay them. Tickets given in one country are almost never passed along to another one. Before disregarding a parking

ticket, search your conscience and check where the car is registered.

7. Parking meters may or may not be similar to those you've cursed at home. There may also be a single meter for an entire block. You park the car, buy a timed ticket, and put it on your dashboard. In some places, there are individual guards, too. Be careful that the guards are official, though. Sometimes they're just neighborhood residents lying in wait for some extra coins.

8. Some countries, including Belgium, France, Germany, and Italy, have "blue zones" where parking is limited in time. The car should come with or you should get a time disk, available in Europe at gas stations, auto parts stores, and curio shops. When you park, place the disk on the dashboard showing your arrival time. The disk will automatically show the time you should leave. If you don't have a disk, put a slip of paper with your arrival time on the dashboard. You probably won't have any problem if you return before your time is up.

9. Roundabouts, the British name for traffic circles or rotaries, are found all across Europe. In Britain and West Germany, do not stop when entering unless there is a dashed line across your lane or a yield sign directed at you. If there is a dashed line across your lane, yield whether entering or already circling. Elsewhere, unless otherwise marked, those entering usually have the right of way.

10. If you are handicapped and have a wheelchair placard, take it with you. In virtually all of Europe, you'll be extended the same courtesies and consideration you would receive at home. The only difference in the placard is that in some European countries the background for the wheelchair symbol is orange, in others it is blue.

11. A few countries have special rules or regulations which drivers should know.

In many countries it is acceptable (and sometimes required) to drive only with parking lights in built-up urban areas with acceptable street lighting.

In Sweden, remember to turn on your headlights night and day. In Finland and Nor-

European Road Sign Key

Remember that there are national variations!

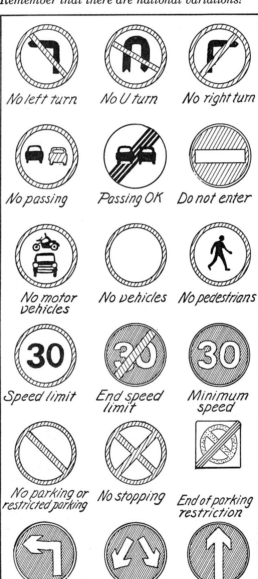

No left turn   No U turn   No right turn

No passing   Passing OK   Do not enter

No motor vehicles   No vehicles   No pedestrians

Speed limit   End speed limit   Minimum speed

No parking or restricted parking   No stopping   End of parking restriction

Left turn only   Pass on either side   Straight ahead only~

European Road Sign Key

Signs can vary from those shown here!

Stop	Yield	Roundabout
Curve	Crossroads	Road work
Danger	Slippery	Pedestrians
Hill	Height limit	Road narrows
Two-way traffic	End divided road	Lane closed ahead
Signals ahead	Rail crossing	Unguarded rail crossing

way, lights must always be on except in cities and towns.

In Switzerland, you have to buy an annual sticker (30 Swiss Francs) to drive on the freeways (defined as any road with green direction signs) and many mountain tunnels. These stickers are sold at every major border crossing by the customs and immigration officers. The fine for driving on an expressway without a sticker is 100 Swiss Francs, plus you have to buy the sticker on the spot. Swiss police are likely to lie in wait at entrances and exits to major tunnels and bridges (particularly St. Gotthard).

12. You are permitted to drive a right- or left-hand drive car anywhere in Europe.

European Road Signs

European road signs are remarkably standard; most are pictograms, similar to the newer signs in the United States and Canada. A key to the common ones is below.

Triangles give warning of hazards. They're white with a red outline and black pictorials.
  Exception: yellow diamonds are used in the Irish Republic.

Circles give orders, prohibitions, or limits. These signs are white with a red outline. Some have the red diagonal slash and some do not.
  Blue circular signs with white arrows give orders, usually permissible turning directions.

Rectangles give information and directions.

Direction and information signs in many countries are color coded. Blue signs with white lettering in most countries point to or are on freeways, expressways, or toll roads.

Exceptions are Italy, Switzerland, and Yugoslavia, where blue is the color of directional signs on ordinary roads. There, green is the expressway color.

In Belgium, green signs with yellow writing direct you to expressways but signs on expressways are blue. In the Netherlands, blue is used for all directional road signs on freeways and surface streets.

Signing shouldn't give you a great deal of difficulty. Signs are particularly well designed and placed in Belgium, Switzerland, and West Germany.

Drunk Driving

Many countries are *very* serious about preventing driving after drinking. Permissible levels of alcohol in the blood are well below those in the United States and Canada. In some nations the limit is 0.0%.

Nations especially strict and severe are Norway, Sweden, Finland, Denmark, and the Soviet Union. In these countries, roadblocks are set up, particularly on Friday and Saturday nights. Everyone driving, whether under suspicion or not, may be stopped and subjected to a breath test. Other countries are hardly lenient. In Italy, breath and blood tests are never given—whether a driver is drunk is strictly up to the discretion of the police.

Driving Paperwork

License

If you drive in Western Europe, your own state or provincial permanent driver license will be accepted (and demanded) when you rent a car or are stopped by traffic police. Some nations (such as Italy) say that you must have a translation of the conditions of your license. This provision is rarely enforced. Many Eastern European nations will accept your license, some subject to a similar condition as Italy.

A few, such as Bulgaria and the Soviet Union, require an International Driving Permit. This permit is available to all licensed drivers at any office of the AAA, CAA, and National Automobile Club for $5. You don't need to be a club member. You will need your driver license and two passport photographs.

Payment must be made in cash if you are not a club member. The permit is issued and signed on the spot. It expires one year from the date it is issued or on the date your regular license expires, whichever comes first.

Get the permit before you leave North America, since you cannot obtain one in Europe with a United States or Canadian license.

Insurance

Insurance is required for all European driving (except in Greece). Your policy at home will probably not cover you. A policy issued in one European country is valid and honored throughout Europe, except in the Soviet Union where you will be required to buy Soviet insurance at the border. If traveling to Spain, be sure that the policy includes a Spanish bail bond endorsement; there is usually no extra charge for this.

Insurance papers are pale green; therefore, they are known as "Green Cards." Further information about insurance is included in the sections on car rental, lease, and purchase sections below.

Your own United States or Canadian insurance is not valid on European rental cars even if it is valid on cars rented in North America. Nor will your own insurance pay the deductible for the Collision Damage Waiver (CDW).

Renting a Car

Car rental agencies are common throughout Europe. While cars can legally be rented to anyone with a valid license, many rental companies require a minimum age as high as 25. Some also have a maximum age—usually 70 or 75. Major companies such as Hertz and Avis are found in Western Europe. Other major American have European affiliates. Still other companies are strictly European.

In some of the Eastern countries, rentals are most easily arranged through the national tourist agencies, though the international companies are opening offices as the opportunities arise.

Rental rates vary widely by company, by country, and by season. Generally, making advance reservations in North America is less costly than a spur-of-the-moment decision to rent a car while in Europe.

If you reserve (and usually pay for) the rental in advance, there are large discounts available, especially if you rent for a week or more. Shop around. In general, car rental is least expensive in Spain, Britain, and West Germany. Prices are usually highest in Eastern Europe and Scandinavia.

Cars rented in West Germany, Switzerland, Belgium, and Scandinavia are usually in the best condition.

Basic liability and collision insurance is included in the rental contract. Deductibles range from about $40 to about $1500, depending on the policy. The deductible amount is quoted in local currency. Rental agencies will press optional no-deductible coverage on you. It is very expensive in proportion to the benefits paid. You can waive it. If you waive, carefully check the car for damage before you accept it. Inspect it for scratches and dents in the body and tears and cigarette burns in the upholstery. Make the agency note the flaws on the contract before you leave. Otherwise you risk having to pay for someone else's damage.

The insurance papers will be in the rental packet or the glove compartment. Be sure you have them before you leave the rental site.

When you rent a car, you get only one set of keys. If you'll be using the car for a week or more, get a spare set made at a locksmith to avoid being stranded. Locksmiths may be hard to find, but a spare key is worth the effort. The rental agencies for some reason rarely want the spare set back to make it easy on the next renter. It is usually easier to have keys made in the country where you obtain the car; otherwise you may have trouble finding the proper blanks (especially for locking gas caps).

Most Western European nations charge Value-Added Tax (VAT) on top of the rental charge. The rental rate you are quoted virtually never includes this tax, which must be paid in local currency or included in credit card bills. When picking up a car in one country and dropping it off in another, the nation where you get the car rental determines the tax rate. When you pick up the car, you must usually leave either a sizable cash deposit or a signed credit card charge slip with the amount left blank. ***blocking credit cards for car rentals Since these rates vary greatly, carefully consider the country where you rent a car. It can make a great difference in the ultimate price of the rental.

Key to Value-Added Tax Rates on Rental Cars

Austria: 21%; if over 21 days, 33.3%
Belgium: 25% (not charged on short-term leases)
Denmark: 22%
Finland: 19.05%
France: 28% (not charged on short-term leases)
Germany (West): 14%

Great Britain: 15%
Greece: 16%
Ireland: 10%
Italy: 19%
Luxembourg: 12%
Netherlands: 20%
Norway: 20%
Portugal: 17%
Spain: 12%
Sweden: 23.46%
Switzerland: 0 (no tax)
Yugoslavia: 15%

Car Rental and Leasing Companies in North America

This list includes only a sampling of the many car rental companies from whom you can rent a car. Absence of a listing for a particular company is no reflection on its services; it is just that it would require a volume the size of a large phone book to include them all. Exact details have to be obtained from each rental agency directly or through your travel agent, since conditions and prices change very frequently.

Auto Europe+
P.O. Box 1097
Sharps Wharf
Camden, Maine 04843
Tel. U.S. (800) 223-5555
or (207) 236-8235
Canada
(800) 458-9503
Telex 760 7562
Fax (207) 236-4724

Avis
900 Old Country Road
Garden City, N.Y. 11530
Tel. U.S. (800) 331-2112
Canada (800) 268-2310
except Toronto 622-0770

Budget
200 N. Michigan Ave.
Chicago, Illinois 60601
Tel. (800) 527-0700

National/Europcar
7700 France Avenue
South Minneapolis,
Minn. 55435
Tel. U.S. and
Canada(800) 227-3876
or (612) 830-2121

Europe by Car, Inc.+*
1 Rockefeller Plaza
New York, N. Y. 10020
Tel. (212) 581-3040
or (800) 223-1516
also at
9000 Sunset Blvd.
Los Angeles, Calif.
90069
Tel. (213) 272-0424
or (800) 252-9401

Europe Auto Travels+*
9367 Wilshire Blvd.
Beverly Hills, Calif.
90210
Tel. (213) 272- 4477 and
273-4477

*Foremost Euro-Car,
Inc..*+*
5430 Van Nuys Blvd.
Van Nuys, Calif. 91401
Tel. U.S. (800) 423-3111
Calif. (800) 272-3299 **or**
(818) 786-1960
Telex 651408

Hertz
Tel. (800) 654-3001
or local offices, check
your phone book.

InterRent
Box 45048
Los Angeles, Calif.
90045-0048
Tel. U.S. (800)421-6878
Canada (800) 421-6868

*Shipside Tax Free
Cars**+
50 6008 Lake St, S.A.
Ramsay, N.J. 07446
Tel. (201) 818-0400

* You can buy new cars to bring home through these companies, too. (See below.)

+ You can lease cars without paying Value-Added Tax from these companies. (See below.)

Some of the smaller companies offer discounts to teachers, students, and certain other professionals. Proof may be requested.

Leasing a Car Tax Free

France and Belgium, with two of the highest Value-Added Tax rates on car rentals, offer an attractive alternative if you plan to use the car for 21 days or more: a short-term lease for three weeks to one year. Spain also has a similar tax-free program. You must be at least 18 years old to lease a car. For slightly more than the lowest priced rental for the identical car and model, you can lease a new, fully insured (zero deductible) car with full factory warranty. In France, your choice is limited to Peugeot, Renault, and Citroen. In Belgium many more makes are offered, including campers and luxury cars. For more information, contact a European manufacturer's North American office, or one of the companies listed in the car rental section above.

In all leases, full payment must be made in advance.

Allow at least two or three weeks to make and confirm arrangements.

Buying a Used Car

If you plan to stay in Europe for at least a couple of months, a used car, van, or camper can save you money. It requires you to be flexible and willing to spend a few days buying and selling your vehicle. You should plan to sell the vehicle in the same country you bought it in to eliminate extra red tape. If you plan to bring the car home, see the end of this section.

You can buy a car at any of the thousands of new and used car dealers in Western Europe. You can also look in classified ads for private parties selling their vehicles. "Exchange & Mart" and "Auto Trader" are weekly classified ad newspapers in London (price 60p). "Paris Hebdo," a classified ad newspaper, issued every week, lists lots of cars for sale. The Paris-based International Herald Tribune newspaper also has a classified column of cars for sale, though they tend to be luxury models.

On weekends in Paris near the Malesherbes Metro station, there is an auto flea market with hundreds of cars for sale; there is also a regular auction at Drouot Véhicules, 17 rue de la Montjoie, 93210 La Plaine St-Denis; payment required by certified check. Near Frankfurt, the drive-in movie (Autokino) also is, on occasion, an auto flea market.

In the Netherlands, there's a car market and auction on Monday at the Olympisch Stadion on Stadionplein in Amsterdam (for information call 71 11 15) and one in Utrecht on Tuesday from 7 a.m. to 5 p.m. at the Terrein Veemarkthallen on Satreweg.

It's impossible for nonresidents to buy a used vehicle in Italy, unless it is for export, which requires immense amounts of patience to deal with the red tape.

Buying a Van or Motorhome

You can also buy a van from a departing traveler. For more than 20 years, travelers have bought and sold cars and vans in London. The weekend Jubilee Road market near Waterloo Underground (subway) Station has been moved. Now it takes place on weekends on Provost Road, just north of the Old Street Underground Station. During the week, it takes place on a reduced scale. This market attracts mostly Australians and New Zealanders selling out after their long holiday or Grand Tour. At some times of the year (especially autumn), there may be dozens of camper vans (mostly Volkswagen), and a few motorcycles for sale. Many cars and vans have left-hand steering wheels suited for driving on the Continent. A camper van is often called a "caravanette" in Britain.

There are weekly used van markets in Amsterdam and Utrecht, Netherlands; information about both is available from the VVV in front of Centraal Station in Amsterdam.

There are a number of specialized dealers handling sales and rental of camper vans in Europe. In the London area, it is easiest to find them listed in free give-away newspapers aimed at Australians and New Zealanders, such as LAM, and TNT, and Australasian Express. In Amsterdam, the VVV at the Central Station has a complete list. While there are many dealers in Germany, there isn't a centralized list of them.

Things to Know When You Buy a Used Car

1. You'll usually have to pay cash. You'll have to pay the registration fee (road tax) and Value-Added Tax (except in Britain, where used cars are exempt).

2. You will have to insure and register the vehicle promptly. While simple to accomplish, you should remember you're dealing with a foreign bureaucracy and a different shade of red tape.

3. It is harder to buy low in June and sell high in September, partly because of tourist demand, and partly because of the arrival of the new model year.

4. If you plan to ship the car home, shipping companies are found at major European ports. Amsterdam, Rotterdam, and Hamburg are usually cheapest. New-car purchase-plan brochures often list the names of shipping companies you can contact directly.

5. Most European countries require regular safety checks. The seller should produce a valid certificate before you buy the car, since it is required for registration and to obtain insurance.

Insuring a Used Car

If you buy a used car from a private party, you must get insurance on your own, since registration may not be issued until proof of coverage is provided. Insurance agencies are common throughout Europe. Auto clubs in many countries can arrange for insurance. A statement of accident-free driving from your insurance company and a copy of your state or provincial driving record in North America can sometimes lead to a lower insurance rate.

In some countries, including Denmark and Austria, nonresidents cannot obtain insurance, and therefore cannot register a car. However, you can often take a vehicle to another country, register it there, and then insure it.

Bringing a Used Car Home

Smog and safety regulations make it impossible or unprofitable to bring home some kinds of used cars. Be sure that the car can be modified to meet emissions and safety standards; otherwise it may be refused entry, or you will have to reexport it at your own expense, or, in the United States, turn it over to Customs for destruction.

All cars imported must meet the United States or Canadian emissions and safety standards in effect during the year of manufacture.

Even if importation and registrations is permitted, you should be a mechanical wizard or be willing to pay several thousand dollars for retrofitting.

United States

All vehicles imported into the United States, except those originally built to meet North American specifications, must be imported by someone holding an "EPA Certificate of Conformity" for the same model and year as the car you propose to import, or, before entry, a signed contract with a certificate holder is submitted with the customs entry. Then, the certificate holder must modify the car within 120 days to meet the required standards. You cannot import this type of vehicle yourself.

You can, however, import cars yourself if they are over 25 years old, or meet certain other very small exceptions.

Certified car modification mechanics can be found scattered around the United States; you must choose from the (free) list of certified mechanics available from the Environmental Protection Agency (address below).

If not a new car originally sold to you, the car must be at least two years old to be registered in California and the New England states, and meet the higher California-New England emissions standards.

In addition to all other fees, cars that do not obtain enough milage per gallon of fuel must pay an additional "Gas Guzzler Tax," which can be as much as $3,850. For information about the Gas Guzzler Tax, contact:

Internal Revenue Service
Public Affairs Office
1111 Constitution Ave. N.W.
Washington, D.C. 20224

For other information about importing a vehicle, contact:

Department of Transportation
National Highway Safety Administration
Vehicle Safety Standards
400 - 7th Street S.W. Room 6115
Washington, D.C. 20590
Tel. (202) 366-2830

U.S. Environmental Protection Agency
Manufacturers Operations Division (EN-340F)
401 M Street, S.W.
Washington, D.C. 20460
Tel. (202) 382-2504

Ask for the information packet "Automotive Imports—Fact Sheet" and "Buying a Car Overseas? Beware!" for additional information and import standards.

Canada

Generally, used or secondhand cars not of the current year model cannot be imported into Canada from Europe, based on the combined regulations of Customs and Excise and Transport Canada.

Transport Canada regulations prohibit import of vehicles modified by anyone other than the original manufacturer without the manufacturer's certification, unless the vehicle is over 15 years old.

Customs and Excise regulations prohibit import of vehicles with the exception of vehicles:

- received as bona-fide gifts
- imported by homecoming returning residents or former residents of Canada
- imported as a replacement for your Canadian vehicle, which was totally destroyed or damaged beyond repair while outside Canada
- over 15 years old.

In Canada, contact:
Road Safety and Motor Vehicle Regulation Directorate
Transport Canada
Ottawa, Ontario K1A 0N5
Tel. (613) 998-2174
Fax (613) 998-4831

Ask for the brochure, "Private Importation of a Motor Vehicle into Canada." Other questions should be directed to the same office.

Also, contact Canada Customs and ask for the brochure, "Importing a Motor Vehicle into Canada," which includes customs requirements and restrictions. This brochure is available from any Customs office or

Revenue Canada
Customs & Excise Travellers Division
Connaught Building, 5th Floor
Ottawa, Ontario K1A 0L5
Tel. (613) 954-6370
Fax (613) 954-1765

Obtaining Information in Europe

In Europe, you should ask the Commercial Officer of the nearest United States or Canadian consulate or embassy for details.

Buying a New Car

Touring Europe in your brand new car can be a dream come true. Not only do you have comfortable transportation during your trip, you can also save money. The purchase price of a European car can be thousands of dollars less when ordered in North America and picked up in Europe than if you take delivery from your dealer at home. If you arrange it right, in many states and provinces you'll avoid paying sales tax on it when it gets home. Also, the car may enter the country as a used car, with a lower rate of customs duty.

The more expensive the car, the larger the potential savings. The maximum savings are found in luxury cars, such as BMW, Mercedes-Benz, Porsche, and Jaguar.

Most European manufacturers who export to the United States and Canada have European pickup plans. Contact the manufacturer's North American offices, a dealer, or one of the sales and rental companies above. Insurance can be arranged through the dealer, sales company, or manufacturer. If you prefer, you can also arrange for insurance on your own after arrival in Europe in most countries (except Austria, Italy, Denmark, and most of Eastern Europe).

If you order a gasoline engine car to drive in Europe, the catalytic converter will already be connected. However, unleaded gas may be unavailable in Eastern Europe, and difficult to find in some parts of Western Europe, since it has only recently been introduced. Leaded gas would ruin the converter, so it may have to be replaced when the car is brought home. Check with the particular dealer before you get to Europe about what to do with the catalytic converter.

Paying for Your Car

You usually have to pay full purchase price to the car sales company before you leave from North America. Unless you deal with the authorized dealer in North America (who will keep part of the potential savings), a new car loan will generally be unavailable.

You can, however, borrow against other assets or draw against an unsecured loan to come up with the money. When you get the car home, it can be used as collateral for a regular auto loan. Often you can arrange the loan before you leave, but it won't take effect until the vehicle is landed on the North American continent and clears customs.

In addition to working with your local dealer, you can contact some independent American-based car sales and rental companies (listed with an * in the Auto Rentals listing). These companies have brochures and catalogues with dollar prices, purchase plans, and shipping arrangements.

Certain cars (Porsches, in particular) should be ordered far in advance. More common makes can be ordered with lead times of one or two months.

Dealers near United States and Canadian military bases in Europe can offer delivery on American- and Canadian-equipped cars.

Planning ahead can avoid the plight of the New Yorker met in Paris cursing the local Mercedes-Benz dealer. When he demanded a Mercedes-Benz blue metallic 300D with American specifications in Paris, the dealer unsympathetically referred him to the Stuttgart factory. Then they escorted him out the front door.

When you buy a car in Europe to bring home, you usually don't have to pay the steep Value-Added Tax and (in some countries, the luxury tax imposed on vehicles) as long as:

1. You aren't a resident of the EEC (Common Market), Sweden, Norway, Finland, or Austria.

2. You ship the car out of the Europe within six months or one year, depending on the country where it is registered. Some manufacturers require a fully refundable bond as part of the

purchase price to ensure export. It is refunded after you prove you have exported the car.

You'll gain a large advantage if you keep the car out of the United States for at least three months after you accept delivery of the vehicle. Your car is likely to enter the United States as a used car, which has a lower customs value and a lesser rate of duty as well.

In some states or provinces, if you pick up the car in person *and* you and the car remain out of your state or province for a set period, you won't have to pay sales tax. Be sure to check the exact requirements with your department of motor vehicles before you place your order.

Fuel

Gas stations are found all over Western Europe. Many brands will be familiar. There may be a few differences, though: Exxon is known as Esso, and Texaco is known as CalTex. Some unfamiliar names are nationalized oil companies: ELF (France) and AGIP (Italy).

Gas is sold by the liter in most of Europe, so don't be fooled by the seemingly low price. Remember that 3.78 liters make a U.S. gallon (Britain uses the Imperial gallon, which is 1⅕ U.S. gallons).

Unleaded gasoline is now common in most of in Western Europe, but because it was recently introduced, may be difficult to find, particularly in the countries of southern Europe that are slower to promote it (Greece, Italy, Spain, and Portugal). It is known as "bleifrei" in German, "loodvrij" in Dutch, "sans plombe" in French, "senza piomba" in Italian, and "sin plomba" in Spanish. Unleaded is most likely to be found at stations on superhighways.

In general, with a car that can use leaded gas, most cars will take "super," a universally known term. Cars such as Volkswagens, Fiats, and Renaults will take regular. This may be known as "essence" in French, "benzin" in German, or a similar term.

In Eastern Europe, almost all gasoline is sold at the infrequent state oil company stations. Unleaded gas is very rare in Eastern Europe, and available only at a few stations for foreign tourists. Usually, there's only regular and super. All cars should be filled with super (or unleaded if your vehicle requires it) in these countries.

Diesel fuel is generally available throughout Europe, though it goes under many names: "diesel" in English, "gazole" in French, "gasoil" in German, and "gazolio" in Italian.

Gasoline prices in Europe are much higher than in North America. Diesel is often from one-third to one-half the price of gasoline.

Oil is available at gas stations, and for less money at many discount stores and supermarkets. Sometimes it is only available in two-liter containers, and is relatively expensive compared to prices at home.

Many service stations throughout Europe are the full-service type, especially in large city centers. Your windows will on occasion be washed, the oil checked, and water added to the radiator. The attendants pump gas, and even smile sometimes.

Self-service stations are a bit cheaper—but not by much. They are most often found on approach roads to major towns and on some main highways and expressways, and at discount grocery stores. Procedures at self-service stations are different. Lift the pump nozzle and the pump is ready. There are no levers to turn or buttons to push. The pump shuts off automatically when you put the nozzle back in its slot. Pay at the cashier's counter, usually inside, after you finish pumping.

Gas stations in Eastern Europe are not as common as in Western Europe, and are found on main routes but there may be only one in a town. There may be long lines. In some countries (Bulgaria East Germany, Poland, U.S.S.R.) you may have to buy gas coupons with Western currency at the border or at the official tourist offices in the country. Having foreign license plates may get you quickly to the front of the line (their orders, not your choice) or, alternatively, into special gas stations reserved only for foreigners.

Discount Gas Coupons

Bulgaria

Gas and oil are only supposed to be bought with coupons sold at the offices of the Shipka Tourist Agencies at the border, and all BalkanTourist hotels, and other large hotels and motels.

Czechoslovakia

Coupons for gasoline and diesel are sold by Cedok at the borders. The coupons entitle you to about a 20% discount on fuel and are accepted at all gas stations in Czechoslovakia.

East Germany

Coupons for oil and gas are sold at all branches of the Reisebüro der DDR and international service stations, only for hard (not local) currency in denominations of M5, M10, and M20. West German Deutsche Marks are accepted at gas stations on West Berlin access routes.

Italy

Italy offers packets of discount coupons for gasoline at border crossings, some Automobile Club d'Italia offices inside Italy, and some Italian tourist offices in Western Europe to all persons not resident driving a car registered outside of Italy. The discount is approximately 20%, and the packets include coupons good for free passage on the autostrade (toll expressways). Almost every gas station in Italy accepts these coupons (and will give change in money for the excess coupon value).

Poland

Motorists can receive an approximately 40% discount on fuel if they buy coupons. They are sold for hard (Western) currency only at border crossings and all Orbis offices inside Poland. Unused coupons can be reconverted to hard currency at the border; you may receive the money in several different foreign currencies. (This coupon system is subject to change in 1990).

Romania

Fuel will only be sold for foreign-registered cars if you have fuel coupons. They are sold—for hard (Western) currency—at border crossings, tourist offices, and service desks of hotels catering to Western travelers.

Soviet Union (U.S.S.R.)

Motorists driving foreign-registered cars in the Soviet Union should buy gasoline coupons from Intourist service desks and offices. They come in 5-, 10-, and 20-liter values, and must be bought in hard (Western) currency.

Yugoslavia

Coupons usable for gasoline or diesel are sold at border crossings. They entitle you to 5% more fuel than you pay for. Coupons must be paid for in hard (Western) currency or travelers checks. These coupons are available in various denominations. Fuel can also be bought with Yugoslav dinars.

Special Note: No Gasoline Credit Cards

Oil company credit cards are not accepted at any European gas station, not even the credit card you use at the same company's stations at home. Sometimes, especially on autobahns and other express highways, Visa or MasterCard charge cards are accepted (some stations may display old "BankAmericard" or "Barclaycard" signs for Visa, and "Access" for MasterCard.

Auto Repairs

If your car needs repairs, garages are plentiful throughout Western Europe. Service is widely available for major European cars. Garages will most likely have parts for cars made in the same country: Fiat in Italy; Peugeot, Renault and Citroen in France; and BMW, Volkswagen, German Ford, and Opel (GM) in Germany. Finding parts for foreign cars will be easiest in major cities.

The Michelin red guides list all factory-authorized service locations in the countries and cities they cover. The listing for each city includes the makes serviced, along with the garage name, address, and telephone number. The garages are pinpointed on the city maps found in the guide. If you don't have a Michelin red guide or are in an area for which no guide is issued, the police will know the local garages.

In the Eastern European countries, service and parts are much more difficult to find. Garages are few and far between. Those that exist are accustomed to working on Eastern European makes such as Skoda (Czech), Lada (Soviet), and Polski Fiat (Polish). Take parts with you if you think you'll need them. Sometimes the only alternative is to make a special quick trip West to buy parts. If you drive into the Soviet Union, you must promise to take your car out with you, even if it becomes a total wreck. Otherwise, *you* may not be permitted to leave either.

Not all garages, whether in Eastern or Western Europe, are full of expensive modern equipment that makes the garage look more like a laboratory. Don't be upset as your car is taken apart and laid out on the plaza. It will most likely run well when the parts are put back together.

When you need a flat tire repaired, do not go to a gas station or garage, except to ask, "Where is the nearest tire repair shop?" Tires are repaired at tire repair shops and tire stores.

Emergency Road Service

Most nations have breakdown and towing services provided by national auto clubs. Many motorways and main highways have emergency phones every kilometer or so. If you have an emergency, use the phones: a repair car or tow truck will be dispatched. In some countries, members of AAA or CAA receive breakdown service on the same terms as members of the local clubs. (The AAA brochure, "Offices to Serve You Abroad," explains all services available to its members in Europe.) Service is sometimes round the clock, though it is more likely to be dawn to dusk. On expressways and certain other main highways, there may be roving patrols to provide service.

If you're not on a highway with emergency phones or auto club patrols, the phone numbers and names of some auto club emergency services are given below.

You can often purchase a membership a European auto club from any office in that country.

Phone Numbers for Emergency Road Service

An asterisk (*) indicates that emergency service to AAA members is on the same basis as its own members. In some countries, this is free, in others, a charge is made.

Austria*: Tel. 95-40 nationwide, but use emergency call boxes on Autobahns. Free breakdown service; charge for towing. (Service provided by ÖAMTC, the Austrian Automobile and Motorcycle Club.)

Belgium: Tel. (Brussels area) (02) 736 59 59 for service by Royal Automobile Club de Belgique (numbers vary in other areas), or (02) 512 78 90 for service by Touring Secours (numbers vary in other areas).

Bulgaria: Tel. 146 in main towns and along main roads. (Service provided by SBA, Union of Bulgarian Motorists.)

Czechoslovakia: No general breakdown number.

Denmark*: Use emergency call boxes on motor-ways, or call FDM at (01) 38 21 12 from 9 a.m.—5 p.m. (Service arranged by FDM, Federation of Danish Motorists, but service provided by con-tracted garages has a fixed price.)

Finland*: Tel. (90) 694 0496 (Finnish Automobile and Touring Club).

France: You must call local garages, except on some main roads and all autoroutes, which have emergency phones every kilometer.

Germany, West (BRD)*: "Strassenwacht" road service patrols on autobahns by ADAC (German Auto Club), or phone number in most areas (city code) + 19 21 1, or by Avd (Auto Club of Ger-many) service patrols.

Great Britain*: AA (Automobile Association) and RAC (Royal Automobile Club) Road Patrols on main roads. Some motorways and main roads have emergency call boxes. Otherwise check phone book for nearest AA Service Centre.

Greece*: ELPA (Automobile Touring Club of Greece) road patrols on motorways provide free service, or tel. 104, 7 a.m.—10 p.m. in main cities and highways, or head office in Athens Tel. (01) 779 1615 or 363 8632.

Hungary: Budapest: 260-668. Service provided by MAK (Hungarian Auto Club).

Ireland*: AA Road patrols on a few main roads. Otherwise check phone book for nearest AA Ser-vice Centre.

Italy*: Call boxes every two kilometers on autostrade, or tel. 116. (Service provided by ACI, Automobile Club d'Italia.) A service fee is charged except to foreign-registered vehicles.

Luxembourg*: Road patrol service on main roads or tel. 45 00 45, 24 hours a day. (Service provided by ACL, the Luxembourg auto club.)

Netherlands*: Road patrols on motorways and main highways. Emergency phones along motor-ways also summon help. If you are not an auto club member, the charge is 75 Guilders. (Service provided by ANWB, the Dutch auto club.) No auto club service in most cities; private garages charge for service.

Norway*: Road patrols on main roads 10 a.m.—8 p.m. provide free assistance from June through August; at other times, it must be paid for. Tel. (02) 42 94 00 for help 24 hours a day for a contract service, with fixed prices. (Services provided by NAF, the Norwegian Automobile Federation.)

Poland: Tel. local offices of PZM (Polski Zwiazek Motorowy), the Polish Auto Club; Warsaw tel. 29 62 52.

Portugal: Tel. (01) 73 61 21 for service from the ACP (Automövil Club de Portugal.

Romania: Call local offices of the ACR (Automobil Clubul Roman) for emergency service. The numbers are on road signs as you cross regional boundaries; record them if you think you'll need them, since there are no phone books.

Switzerland: Tel. 140 or use emergency telephones on motorways to summon help. A reasonable charge is made for each service call.

Turkey: You must call local garages, since there is no central breakdown service.

Yugoslavia: Tel. 987 from 8 a.m.—8 p.m. (Service provided by AMSJ, the Yugoslav Auto Club.)

Where is that Car From?

European license plates come in many sizes, colors, and shapes. Most plates are rectangular or square, though some temporary West German plates are oval. The name of the country on license plates is found only on those from Monaco and Andorra, and on personal cars of United States and Canadian military personnel. Separate white ovals with letters designating the country of registration are found on the backs of cars. Letter codes are listed below.

Exceptions: military vehicles almost never have license plates; rather, the number is painted on near the license plate space. Small national flags may also be painted on near the numbers. In some countries, tractors and farm machinery are unlicensed—but rarely cross national boundaries.

Autos and Driving

Country codes for the ovals you're likely to see are listed in the following Key:

Code	Country	Country in foreign language
A	Austria	Österreich
AL	Albania	Shqiperia
AND	Andorra	Andorra
B	Belgium	Belgique (French), Belgïe (Flemish)
BG	Bulgaria	България
CDN	Canada	Canada
CH	Switzerland	Suisse (French), Schweiz (German), Svizzera (Italian). CH stands for Confoederatio Helvetica (Latin)
CS	Czechoslovakia	Ceskolovenskò
CY	Cyprus	Κνπροζ (Greek)
DDR	Germany, East	Deutsche Demokratische Republik
D	Germany, West	Bundesrepublik Deutschland
DK	Denmark	Danmark
DZ	Algeria	(arabic or Algerie)
E	Spain	España
F	France	France
FL	Liechtenstein	Furstentum Liechtenstein
GB	Great Britain	including Northern Ireland
GR	Greece	Ελλαζ (Ellas)
H	Hungary	Magyarorszag
I	Italy	Italia
IL	Israel	Israel
IRL	Ireland	Éire
L	Luxembourg	Luxembourg
M	Malta	Malta
MA	Morocco	Maroc (French)

MC	Monaco	Monaco
N	Norway	Norge
NL	Netherlands	Nederland
P	Portugal	Portugal
PL	Poland	Polska
R	Romania	Romana
RL	Lebanon	Liban (French)
RSM	San Marino	Repubblica di San Marino
S	Sweden	Sverige
SF	Finland	Suomi/Finland
SU	Soviet Union, U.S.S.R.	CCCP
TN	Tunisia	Tunisie (French)
TR	Turkey	Türkiye
USA	United States	
V	Vatican City	Cittá Vaticano
YU	Yugoslavia	Jugoslavija

In addition, you may also see other ovals, including:

CD	Diplomatic Corps
C	Consular Corps

Mail and Packages

When you're far from home, letters are a pleasure to receive.

You may also bring joy to people by sending letters and postcards, and maybe keep in contact with your business.

Sometimes you'll need or want to send or receive packages.

This chapter gives details on how.

Dealing with post offices and express offices in Europe is something most travelers do: it can be an adventure in many places. Sometimes, especially in southern Europe, you can bypass the post office to buy stamps. For packages, however, the post office or express office often can't be avoided.

Sending Mail to Europe

There are be sure that mail sent to you is received: each one has plusses and minuses. All require a bit of planning on your part so that you and your mail eventually meet. A few instructions apply to your correspondents regardless of whether they write to a post office, American Express office, or hotel, or in care of a business or personal acquaintance.

How Can You Be Sure It Arrives?

If you send a letter, there's no assurance that it will arrive, unless you either send it by "Registered" mail, or use an air express company.

Post offices don't keep track of mail unless it is registered. With registered mail, each clerk and handler must sign for it when receiving it and when handing it to another person. Tracing registered mail is a time-consuming process.

Air express companies automatically track every single item given to them for carriage. Through the wonders of computerization, many air express companies can tell you where in the system it is at any one time (while you wait).

How to Address Mail Sent to Europe

Proper addressing will increase the chances that your mail—all of it—will reach you.

1. All mail addressed to you should have your last name written in capital letters and preferably underlined. Mail is held for pickup in alphabetical order and, if your last name isn't clear, it may be filed under your first name, or even filed under Mr., Mrs., or Ms. (If you expect some mail and don't receive it, you probably should ask the clerk to check under your first name also.) Typed addresses are preferable, since each nation's handwriting characteristics vary widely. If not typed, addresses should be printed.

2. Addresses should be in the local country's style whenever possible, using its order for addresses. For example, many countries put street numbers after the name of the street, and others put the postal code before the name of the city. In the Soviet Union, the country comes first, then the region, then city, then the street address, and at the bottom, the individual's name. When sending mail to Bulgaria, Greece, the Soviet Union, or parts of Yugoslavia that use other alphabets, you can neatly address it only in Latin letters and it will still be translated and delivered.

3. Mail is usually held for 30 days from its receipt. If you're not sure you'll be able to claim it in time, it may be held longer if the envelope requests that the mail be held until a specific date before it's returned as unclaimed.

The request is likelier to be honored if written in the local language. Remember that numerical dates should always be written in DAY/MONTH/YEAR order. Often, the months are written in Roman numerals. For example, if writing to France and you want the mail held until September 20, 1990, write on the envelope, "SVP Tenir jusqu' à 20 IX 1990." Even better is to write out the name of the month rather than using figures, but in this case the month should be written in French: "20 septembre 1990."

4. When sending mail inside Western Europe, you can either put the country name on the address or use the one-, two-, or three-letter country designation in front of the post code or city. The designations are the same ones used on autos: see the last pages of Autos and Driving in this book for all the codes. For example, Switzerland's letters are CH: a letter would be properly addressed and correctly delivered from anywhere in Western Europe when addressed:

Roger SMITH
Post Restante
CH-6900 Lugano

Sending to Post Offices

Mail sent to post offices can be held for pickup if you have no local address. This service, equivalent to general delivery, is called "Poste Restante" in most of Europe: every post office employee will know this French term even if the local language has another word, such as "Postlagernd" in German, "Fermo Posta" in Italian, and "Lista de Correos" in Spanish.

When writing to Poste Restante, in large cities include the address of post office at which you'll be picking it up. (Large cities may have dozens.) If not sure, mail should be sent to the main post office. You can ask at the tourist information office for the location of the main post office.

For example, letters sent to the main post office in Paris, should be addressed:

Susan JONES
Poste Restante
Hôtel des Postes
52 rue du Louvre
75001 Paris
France

It is usually easier to receive Poste Restante mail in small towns and villages than in large cities, because there are fewer people calling for mail (which reduces the chance of missing a letter that's waiting for you), and also because small town post offices are usually much less crowded.

Since small towns and villages usually only have one post office, mail can simply be addressed:

Roger SMITH
Poste Restante
8113 Kochel am See
West Germany

Sending to American Express

American Express offices are located in most major cities of Europe and will hold mail for pick-up. Look for their addresses in an American Express pamphlet available at all their travel agency offices or from banks selling American Express travelers cheques. Send mail in care of "Client Mail Service."

Mail is held 30 days, unless a specific "hold until" date is placed on outside of the envelope. If you use all numbers for dates, remember use the day/month/year sequence.

American Express' Client Mail Service is free to American Express clients (such as a holder of an American Express card or even a single American Express travelers check); to all others, a charge is made for each *search,* whether or not there is any mail.

Sending to Hotels

You can have mail sent to hotels you plan to stay at. Correspondents should note the estimated date of arrival on the outside of the letter, and address care of the hotel. For example:

Susan JONES
(Please hold until 15 October 1990)
c/o The George Hotel
High Street
Salisbury, Wiltshire SP5 5RS
England

The easiest way to send letters to the Soviet Union is to mail them to hotels, since there are only a few hotels open to Western travelers, and they are usually listed in the planned itinerary.

Sending to Businesses or Private Residences

Just write to the individual, care of the business or person whose address you're using, just as if it were a hotel.

Sending Small Packages to Europe

Through the post office, you can send small packages to Europe either by air or by surface (parcel post). You must provide a postal address for pickup, though this can include a Poste Restante address. The post office provides the only ground/sea service to Europe from the United States and Canada.

The post office also offers small parcel service by air, though at higher rates. Air mail parcel service takes about a week to 10 days to most of Western Europe, longer to Eastern Europe. Italy is a special problem, since service is so unreliable: one parcel will take a week, another will take six months.

Sending by Express Mail or Private Air Express Services

Sending letters and small packages by Express Mail or air express delivery services (such as Airborne, DHL, Emery, Federal Express, and United Parcel Service) is easy though relatively costly. Delivery to major cities in Western Europe is usually within two days, though some services can offer overnight delivery to London, Paris, Frankfurt, and Milan from a few major metropolitan areas such as New York, Chicago, Los Angeles, Toronto, and Montréal.

Delivery (where available) takes three to five business days to smaller cities, and to those cities in Eastern Europe that are served. (Note: Eastern Europe isn't served by Federal Express, but most Eastern European capitals are served by Airborne Express, DHL, Emery, and United Parcel Service.)

Most express companies serving Europe will provide a service guide upon request, listing their office addresses and rates (which are sometimes called tariffs). A few don't have service guides, but their 800-number staff will be able to quote delivery times and rates.

Letters weighing less than eight ounces generally are about $20-25 from the United States to Western Europe and about $25-30 from Canada to Western Europe. Three-pound packages are $10 to $20 more. To Eastern European countries, the costs are approximately $110 for letters and $130 for three-pound packages, with delivery in two or three working days for letters and five working days for packages. In Eastern European countries, many deliveries are made by airline companies working under contract with the delivery service.

Private air express companies cannot deliver to post offices (including Poste Restante), but can usually have items held at their offices or delivered to any street addresses.

You must use a special international air bill or express mail form for international shipments. Ask the post office or air express company for the proper form.

Packages require a customs declaration, which will be furnished by any post office or the shipping company. Particularly for air express companies, be sure to ask about special restrictions or documentation that may be required before shipment.

Check to be certain the contents of the package are allowable in the country of destination (some items won't be cleared by European customs).

Airline Air Freight

Most airlines will accept unaccompanied baggage or packages as air freight, and hold it for pickup at the airport terminal in Europe. Call the airlines you're considering for detailed information. The minimum charge, which varies by airline, is based on weight and destination.

Parcel Post

Every post office in the United States and Canada can accept parcels for shipment to Europe. While maximum weight for packages mailed from the United States is 44 pounds (20 kilograms) for most countries (though some vary, such as the maximum to Greece: 11 pounds, or 5 kilograms), in Canada, the maximum weight is often limited to 11 pounds (5 kilograms).

Surface mail may take a month to six weeks to Western Europe, and up to six months to Eastern Europe, and Italy and Greece.

Be sure the packaging is secure, especially for shipments to southern Europe, where post offices can be chaotic behind the counter as well as in front of it.

Receiving Mail in Europe

You can pick up mail at many places: post offices, American Express offices, hotels, and (for Canadians) embassies and consulates.

Identification Required for Pickup

You must prove your identity to receive mail at any place except a private home or business address.

If you're a United States or Canadian citizen, your passport is the acceptable proof.

If you are a citizen of a European country, your national identity card is acceptable.

Other identification (often including driver licenses and credit cards) will not be as readily accepted, and many types may not be accepted at all.

Post Offices

Post offices are usually open Monday through Friday and often on Saturday mornings.

Some post offices in large city centers, main railway stations, and airports have extended hours. In the largest cities such as Paris, Munich, and Vienna, they are open on Sundays; a few are open 24 hours a day year round.

Go to the Poste Restante counter or window, present your passport or identity card, and receive your mail.

Delivery Service Charge

Some countries, including France and Italy, charge for the pickup mail service at Poste Restante windows. The fee is equal to the rate for a first-class letter, regardless of the weight of the letter or whether it has been sent by air or surface mail.

American Express Offices

Mail service at American Express offices is free and to be used by American Express customers. A customer is a holder of an American Express Card or at least one American Express travelers' cheque.

If you're not an American Express customer, some offices will refuse to search and others will charge a stiff fee for looking and giving you any mail they have. (You can always buy some American Express cheques at banks or American Express offices and instantly become a customer.)

American Express offices are usually conveniently located in large city centers in Western Europe, but are not found in some Communist countries. Local telephone books always list their addresses under American Express in the White Pages. You cannot, however, call to find out if you have mail there—you have to go in person.

Mail is usually held a maximum of 30 days, but if the envelope requests holding it a bit longer, it will usually be held.

Some large city American Express offices (mainly in southern Europe but also sometimes including Paris) can be overcrowded and frustrating places to retrieve mail. Others (often in northern Europe) are uncrowded and offer comfortable lounges where you can read the mail you've just received.

Hotels

To ask for mail, go up to the reception desk and ask. If you have a confirmed reservation at a good to luxury hotel, mail will often be automatically put in your box.

Hotels are usually accommodating about holding mail for longer periods than either post offices or American Express offices.

Embassies and Consulates

Canadian embassies and consulates will hold mail for Canadian citizens. Mail it to the embassy; it will be held for about one month or until the date you put on the envelope. For locations and addresses of Canadian embassies and consulates, please see the chapter on Embassies.

In some countries, particularly in southern Europe (where post offices and American Express offices can be chaotic), this can be the most convenient way to receive mail.

You must present your passport to receive mail.

In Eastern Europe, United States embassies and consulates will also hold mail for pickup but do not encourage use of this service.

Receiving Packages

Parcel post or post office Express Mail packages can be received at most locations, including Poste Restante windows at post offices.

Air express packages must be held at the express company or airline offices for pick up or delivered to a street address (including hotels).

Sending Mail to the United States and Canada

Sending mail home can be either easy or complicated, depending on the country you're in and the type of item you're sending. Packages are usually more difficult to send than letters and post cards.

Postcards and Letters

Postcards and letters are handled in the same way, though the costs may be different. They can be sent air mail (usually a week to 10 days delivery time) or surface mail (at least a month, often two months, and sometimes almost three months).

In a few countries, all first-class mail to the United States and Canada (both letters and postcards) are automatically sent air mail at no extra charge if the weight is less than 5 grams—one sheet of paper folded on itself (Denmark) or 15 grams—one thin sheet of paper in an envelope (Finland, Norway, and Sweden).

Postal Services Key *(Continues across)*

English	*French*
Air Mail	Par Avion
Letters	Lettres
Stamps	Timbres
Packages	Colis/Emballages
General Delivery	Poste restante

Where to Send Mail From

Post Offices

Post offices are found in every city, town, and village in every country of Europe. Rate information is available from counter clerks, or occasionally from information provided on posters or reference guides in post office lobbies. A few countries' post offices, including Great Britain, France, Italy, and West Germany, have free brochures available that list rates.

Waiting in lines in the British Isles, Scandinavia, Switzerland, and West Germany is like waiting in the United States and Canada. In France, lines form along the counter, the right side of the window. One line can cross right through another without losing its identity. In Italy, people just crowd up at each open window. Don't be bashful, and eventually you'll get to the front of the mob.

Most post offices have specialized counters for bill paying and postal savings banks: don't go to them for stamps. If you're sending air mail letters and post cards, be sure to ask for free air-mail stickers, and be sure that every envelope or card has at least one.

Sending letters and post cards from Europe will usually strike you as expensive: for example, an air-mail post card from Austria to either the United States or Canada will cost 8 Austrian Schillings, or about 50 U.S. or 60 Canadian cents.

Letters are often more expensive: for example, sending a letter from Norway will cost 4 Kroner (about 80 U.S. or 90 Canadian cents) and a

Postal Services Key *(Continued)*

German	*Italian*
Luftpost	Per via aerea
Brief	Lettere
Briefmarken	Francobolli
Paketen	Pacchi
Postlagernd	Fermo Posta

postcard 3.50 Kroner (about 70 U.S. or 95 Canadian cents). In some countries, such as France, if you write more than 10 words on a post card in addition to the address, it may be charged as if it were a letter.

Buying Stamps—Not at Post Offices

Alternatives to crowded—and often chaotic—post offices are available for buying stamps in many countries, particularly in southern Europe. If you buy stamps at places other than post offices, be sure you already know the postage rates to the United States and Canada, because most vendors may not know them.

Tobacco shops are the best places to buy postage stamps. Where tobacco sales are carefully regulated or a monopoly, such as Spain, Austria, and France, you're likely to be able to buy stamps at cost.

Most hotels will have stamps to sell or send letters at cost, if you're a hotel guest.

Occasionally souvenir and post card vendors will have stamps, but there is occasionally a markup.

Mail Boxes

Mail boxes are always found near post offices, but mail drop slots are often only outside the building. Boxes are also found in main streets and village centers. They come in all sizes and colors, but many countries' boxes have a post horn on them.

In very large city centers, boxes may be scarce, except in front of the post offices or in office building lobbies.

Sending Packages to the United States and Canada.

Packages can be sent from most post offices, but in some countries if packages weighing more than 11 pounds (5 kilograms) can only be sent by ground or air express to the United States.

Canada enforces this 11-pound maximum from most countries, but excludes air shipments and books and certain other shipments from this rule.

You must fill out a customs declaration for each package. Usually it is printed in green, or printed on green paper, and one section is glued or taped to the package. It is always in French and in the language of the country you're in. Only sometimes will it also be in English. In general, the form requires the names and addresses of the sender and recipient, the value (spelled out as well as in figures), a description of contents, and often type of packaging as well.

In Portugal, every package must be properly packaged and sealed (which involves lots of string, wax seals, etc.) before being presented at the post office. In others countries, it must be inspected by Customs before sealing. Near major city post offices, you usually can find packing shops near by.

Unsolicited Gifts

Packages sent to friends and relatives (but not to yourself!) in the United States can enter duty-free if they clearly state "Unsolicited Gift—Value Under $50" on the outside of the package.

Packages sent to friends and relatives in Canada (but not to yourself!) can enter duty-free if they clearly state "Unsolicited Gift—Value Less Than $40 Canadian." In addition, you'll have to complete a small green customs declaration, which describes the contents of the package and its value.

If you're returning items originally brought from the United States or Canada, and you're shipping them back, be sure to state on the contents "Returning goods of (United States) (Canadian) Origin" to avoid the payment of duty.

Sending Express Documents and Packages to the United States and Canada

Express documents and small packages can be sent from many post offices in Europe. The process is described above.

You can also call air express companies such as Airborne, Emery, or Federal Express, or the United Parcel Service, who will come and pick up the documents or small packages. If you have an account, you can even have the packages billed to your business or personal account, or pay for it at pickup.

Large Shipments

Very large shipments are usually sent to the United States or Canada by shipping crate or container. Containers are the cheapest way to move large quantities of goods from Europe to the United States. You may wish to contact shipping companies for details, or see any of the "Manston's Flea Markets" books for detailed information.

Using European Telephones

We take the telephone for granted, always there when we need it, familiar, easy to use. But each European country's telephone system has its unique variations. Unfamiliarity with the system can cause phone frustration.

Obviously, United States and Canadian coins won't work in European coin phones. Less obviously, in some countries local coins won't work either. You may need to buy a special token or phone card. Operators may be difficult to reach, never at "0," and calls to them may not be free. In some countries, operators can speak English, in others many cannot.

Telephones may have either rotary dials or touch keys. Though the touch key phones resemble the touch-tone phones found in North America, they aren't. Except in France, touch the keys as slowly as if you were dialing the call on a rotary phone.

Telephone service in almost every European country is government-run rather than privately owned. Since most countries have organized the phone service as part of the postal system, post offices are usually excellent places to find phones, particularly for making long-distance and international calls. In major cities, some offices are open for extended hours: a few (such as 52 rue du Louvre in Paris and 4 Gurku in Sofia) are open 24 hours.

Some countries, such as Italy, Great Britain, Greece, and Spain, have national phone companies separate from the post office. In those countries, look for the telephone calling offices (see Telephone Keys for names). Many post offices in those countries don't have coin phones.

Most countries in Europe charge telephone calls by "pulses," even for local calls. Each pulse gives you a certain amount of time, depending on distance and often the time of day. A pulse on a long-distance call may last only a few seconds, particularly on an international call, though a local call pulse may last up to eight minutes. The pulse system is used with both pay phones and non-coin phones, for local, long-distance, and international calls placed without the help of an operator.

When your time is almost up at a pay phone, you will usually be warned in some way to put in more money or be cut off.

Local Calls

The minimum rates from pay phones are shown in the Telephone Key for each country. The rates for local calls from pay phones are often different and a bit higher (almost double in Britain) than from non-coin phones. Note that every year, one or two countries raise the price of a local phone call. In countries with rapid inflation or currency of uncertain value (such as Poland, Turkey, and Yugoslavia), changes may come quickly, and prices may change several times within a year.

Long-Distance and International Calls

Long-distance calls can be made from telephone offices (whether at the post office or elsewhere), coin and card phones in many but not all countries, and hotels, as well as private homes and businesses. In addition to the phone number you want to reach, you'll need the access code (which gets you into the long-distance or international network). In some countries, after dialing the access code, you must wait for a second dial tone before continuing to dial the country and city or area code. In Sweden, the second dial tone comes after you dial the country code.

The access code for each country and dialing instructions are included in each Telephone Key. Each Key also includes the complete code for dialing the United States and Canada.

Where to Call From

Telephone Offices

The usual procedure is to tell the clerk in the office where you want to call. You will be directed into a booth, and in most countries you will actually direct dial the call. As soon as your connection is completed, a meter at the cashier's desk begins counting pulses, much like a remote-controlled self-service gas pump. At the end of your call, you pay the cashier or clerk.

In a few countries, calls must be placed through an operator. In this case, you tell the clerk the country and number you want to call. In other respects the procedure is similar. There will usually be a three-minute minimum charge if an operator dials the number.

Pay Phones

Direct-dial long-distance and international calls can be made from pay phones in many countries. Calls made from phone booths and telephone offices offer the lowest available rates.

In many countries, some pay phones accept only prepaid telephone cards. These are for sale at post offices and telephone offices, and often at some tobacco shops or newsstands. Most countries' cards come in various denominations, each one providing a certain number of pulses. In general, you insert the card into the slot on the telephone and then make calls until the pulses on the cards run out.

Cards can only be used in one country's ¹ephones, and you cannot receive pro-rata ⁿds on partially used cards when you leave.

In a few phones in London, you can use most credit and charge cards (such as Visa, MasterCard, and American Express) in special telephones for calls.

Private Homes

All kinds of calls can be made from private home telephones. In most countries you can direct dial from telephones in private homes, including countries in Eastern Europe, even those where you cannot make long-distance calls from pay telephones.

Offer to pay for the calls when you make them: many people have pulse counters right by the telephone, or you can ask them to have the operator call back with the charges.

Hotels: Watch Out!

European hotels have long considered the telephone a prime profit-producing instrument. Most hotels own their own internal systems and run them as a major profit center. The method is simple and unsubtle: the hotel adds a surcharge, whether local, long distance, or international, on calls made from all its phones. Surcharges can be "modest" (up to 40%) but can also be 300% more than the normal cost of the call. This practice isn't limited to luxury palaces or run-down pensions, or to particular countries.

Some establishments have agreed to limit their surcharges; in any case, the first rule is to check *before* using any hotel phone to avoid unpleasant and expensive surprises. In some hotels, there are cards near the telephone listing the amount of surcharge. In most, however, there is none—and the hotel operator may not be willing to tell you in advance the amount or percentage of the surcharge.

Look for dialing instructions near the phone in the room or ask the hotel operator to place your call. In some large hotels, you need to dial the numeral "8" or "0" to get an outside line. This starts the time-and-charges counter. Operators are not reached by dialing "0."

Some hotels even make a charge for collect or telephone calling-card calls. A few have even put on an automatic block to prevent collect or telephone calling-card calls. If you must talk from a hotel house phone, either in the lobby or in your room, arrange to be called, or keep the call short and ask to be called back immediately. No hotel ever charges for calls made to your room.

A number of countries and hotel chains have agreed to somewhat limit their charges for calls to the United States with the Teleplan program. This program is promoted by AT&T, which has a brochure listing them.

Contact AT&T at:
International Calling Information Center
AT&T Communications
(800) 874-4000 (United States only)

If there is a country-wide limit to telephone surcharges, it is shown in the "Hotel Surcharges" section of each Telephone Key. Only Ireland and Portugal currently have a nationwide maximum surcharge.

Businesses and Government Offices

As in North America, many large organizations in Europe, including large businesses and government offices, have internal telephone systems. Often, these systems require you to dial an access number, usually "0" (zero), or sometimes "8" or "9", in order to use an outside telephone line. Then wait for another dial tone and dial the number you want to call. The "0" will not connect you to an operator.

Dialing Your Call

Local Numbers

Local phone numbers in a single city can have from two to eight digits. Phone numbers in Italian cities, for example, can have from four to eight or even nine digits. Sometimes this is because there are different number of digits in the numbers assigned by the telephone company, in other cases it is because of four- or five-digit extension numbers from a telephone central at a business or government office. All can be dialed from any phone.

Long Distance: City or Area Codes

Area codes or city codes, which have from one to six numerals, begin with the numeral "0" in many countries. You must dial the "0" when making long-distance calls within a country, just as in much of North America you must dial "1" before you dial the area code. In most countries using this system, the "0" is written on all phone numbers on letters, cards, and brochures. In Spain and Finland, the numeral "9" is used.

When calling from another country, do not dial the "0." For example, when making a call to central London from elsewhere in Britain, dial 071-XXX XXXX. When calling the same number from another country, dial the access code (which varies), then the country code (44), then the city code (71), and the number (XXX XXXX). Exceptions are Finland and the Soviet Union, where the "0" is a necessary part of some city codes, whether called from inside or outside of the country. If calling Spain or Finland, do not dial the initial "9."

Toll-Free Calls Inside a Country

A number of European countries have set up toll-free numbers similar to the "800" numbers in North America and Canada. Generally, you just dial as any long-distance call. These have various names, such as "0800" in Britain, "Appel Vert" in France. Where such systems exist, they are listed in each country's Telephone Key.

Answering Machines

If a phone customer has an answering machine, in many countries that person's number in the telephone directory will be noted with a reversed

Q symbol (∅) or in Spain, with an asterisk (*). You will be charged for the call when answered.

International Telephone Calling Costs

You can make brief calls home for only a few dollars. Some countries, such as Britain, offer relatively low telephone rates, especially from private residential or business phones (except most hotels). When using a pay phone, you can budget the amount of money you want to spend, since the connection is cut when the money runs out.

Calling the United States and Canada

Generally, calling North America from Europe is more expensive than calling from the United States or Canada to Europe. For example, from Italy to North America, a direct-dialed call is about three times more expensive than from North America to Italy. A direct-dialed call from Italy to North America costs about twice as much as the same call placed collect or charged to a calling card.

Reaching "800" Numbers from Europe

Usually, toll-free "800" numbers in the United States and Canada can't be called with coins, calling cards, or even through a regular operator. However, if you're willing to pay for the call to New York from wherever you are (using local access numbers), you can use the Credit Card Calling System's operator-assisted lines to reach "800" numbers in the United States and Canada. Information on this company's services is listed under the "Telephone Calling Cards" section below.

Telephone Calling Cards

You can use your telephone calling card (sometimes called a credit card) in almost every

European nation. The call is billed at the higher operator-assisted rate with a three-minute minimum charge rather than the direct-dial rate. You should remember that to receive a night or Sunday discount, the call must get to the North American destination during the discount periods in North America.

You can only use your telephone calling card to make calls to your country of residence. You generally cannot, for example, use it to make a call from France to Germany if you live in the United States, Britain, or Canada.

You can make calling-card calls from virtually any pay phone—even most of those from which you usually can make only local calls. In many countries, especially in Eastern Europe, you can use your calling card only through an international operator. Local operators may not even know what a telephone calling card is.

Call Home "Direct"

In a number of Western European countries, you can make a special local or free call, which connects you with an operator of a long-distance company in the United States or Canada. You will be billed to your own calling card or to your telephone number at the operator-assisted rate (higher than the direct-dial rate but lower than a collect call through the foreign operator).

The telephone numbers to call for this service are listed in the "Special Information" section of each country's Telephone Key.

Calls made on any program usually will be billed on your regular telephone statement, even if the company you choose is not your regular long distance company.

"USA Direct"

AT&T introduced this service to call home without the use of foreign operators. Calls can only be made to the continental United States (not to Alaska or Hawaii). For information, call (800) 874-4000. From overseas, call (816) 556-5000 *collect*. (Not available in Canada.)

"MCI Call USA"

MCI introduced this service in late 1988. Calls can be made to any number in the United States. (Not available in Canada.) For information, contact:
MCI Communications Corporation
1133 - 19th St. N.W.
Washington, D.C. 20036

   or your nearest MCI office (various (800) numbers throughout the United States)

"Canada Direct"

Teleglobe Canada, in association with Telecom Canada, a consortium of Canadian telephone companies, introduced this service to call Canada without using a foreign operator. Calls can only be made to Canada. (Not available in the United States.) Further expansion is planned in the near future. This service is now available from Belgium, Finland, Italy (Rome and Milan only), the Netherlands, Norway, and the United Kingdom. For more information, contact:
Canada Direct
Telecom Canada
410 Laurier Ave. West
Box 2410, Station 'D'
Room 950
Ottawa, Ontario K1P 6H5
Tel. (800) 561-8868 or (613) 560-3000
Fax (613) 453-9540
Telex 610-562-1911

Credit Card Calling Systems (CCCS)

This system provides U.S. operator connections, and calls can be billed to any credit card (Visa, MasterCard), charge card (American Express), or to your *local* telephone or long distance company calling card—except *not* to your AT&T card. (If you have the same number from both your local company and AT&T, be sure to give only the name of your local company.) Prices are U.S.$4.80 to set up a station-to-station call plus

$1.35 per minute from Great Britain and $1.55 per minute from the rest of Europe. At times, some calls are made only on a person-to-person basis (at no extra charge) as a fraud prevention measure. This is the only service that will let you reach "800" numbers in the United States—but you must still pay for the call. For more information, contact:

Credit Card Calling Systems, Inc.
67 Wall Street, Suite 2411
New York, N.Y. 10005
Tel. (212) 323-8030 or (800) 950-8810

"UK Direct"

British Telecom introduced this program. Calls can only be made to the U.K. (Not available in the United States or Canada.) For information, contact the nearest British Telecom office.

Receiving Calls at European Pay Phones

The least expensive calls between North America and Europe are made *from* North America to any phone in Europe, including hotels, businesses, and homes, as well as those pay phones where you know the number.

However, only some countries allow you to receive calls at pay phones. Most pay telephones in Britain, France, Switzerland, among other countries have their numbers written on or near the phone. Some phones in West Germany also can receive calls. But in much of Europe, pay phones are one-way communications devices, and cannot usually be called. Countries with this system include Austria, Belgium, Italy, the Netherlands, and Spain.

Calling Europe

If you call Europe from either the United States or Canada, you can in most areas direct dial from your phone at home or office. To do so, dial the access code (011) + country code (see top right of the each country's Telephone Key) + the area or city code + the subscriber's local number.

If you don't live in an area where direct-dialed international calls are possible, call the operator, who will put your station to station call through at the same price as a direct dialed call.

Remember that the time of day in Europe is five or six (Atlantic time) to eight or nine hours (Pacific time) later than it is at your home right now.

International Directory Assistance

Do you need and don't know the telephone number of a hotel, a friend, or the opera house box office? International directory assistance can get it for you at no charge, regardless of where you are. (This no-cost feature is guaranteed by international agreement and is not subject to change.) In the United States and Canada, dial the long-distance operator (either "00" or "0") and give the operator your request. Your operator will be connected with an English-speaking operator in the country you're requesting information from, as you listen in.

Telephone Tones

When you pick up a telephone receiver, you will hear a variety of sounds that may differ greatly from those you're familiar with at home. Standardization of dial tones in Western Europe by the year 2000 is planned, but progress is glacially slow.

The tones found in each country are shown schematically and described in the country Telephone Keys. The diagrams show the type of signal, its sound (with passing time shown in seconds), and a description of the tones. In some countries there may be more than one tone representing the same result.

In your travels you may find some variations that aren't listed in the charts, as the result of differences in equipment and varying national or local standards.

On international calls, any sounds you hear after you dial the country code (such as ringing, busy, or out of order) will be those of the country you're calling, not the country you're calling from.

Using Computers and Modems with European Telephone Systems

Most Western European countries' telephone systems are of adequate quality for data transmission. However, wiring connections to telephone lines vary from country to country. Generally, they are compatible with CCITT data transmission standards. However, you'll either need to rewire your modem, use a modem made for that country, or use an acoustic modem, or (carefully) take apart the telephone mouthpiece.

In Eastern Europe, clarity of transmission is not always adequate for data transmission without a good error-checking feature in your modem. In addition, modems are virtually unknown in those countries.

If you are a United States resident, taking certain types of computers (usually the newest, highest-level machines) with you to Eastern Europe requires a permit from the United States Government Department of Commerce.

Since these standards are changing rapidly, check with local computer users or (with less hope of success) the data transmission bureau of the telephone system of the country you're in.

In some countries such as France (almost always) and Britain, when using public (coin or card) telephones, the end of each pulse is marked by an audible tone that make it almost impossible to transmit files by modem. This doesn't seem to occur when calls are made from private or business non-coin or card phones. It also never occurs when calls are made from North America to Europe, even if the calls are received at pay phones.

Fax Machines

Fax (sometimes called facsimile or telefax) use is
increasing rapidly in Europe. Many businesses
have dedicated fax lines. In addition, travelers
can find public fax machines in some telephone
offices, main post offices, airports, businesses,
hotels, and occasionally other locations. Most
European fax machines are CCITT Group III
compatible, so that transmissions can easily be
made.

Telephone Keys

The next pages are country-by-country Keys to
using the telephone in each country. They include not only how much money to put in a
phone for a local call, they also tell you in what
order and also about special tricks you need to
know to cope successfully with a particular system.

Austria
Country Code: 43. Telephone: TELEFON.

Pay Phones are found at post offices, train and subway stations, street booths, and on some special trains. Card phones are found in similar locations (about 3,500 card phones throughout the country).

Phone Directories contain White and Yellow Pages, often in separate volumes. There is no English summary for either local or long-distance calling. Find directories at post offices, phone booths, and hotels.

Using Pay Phones: Use 1 Austrian schilling coin per minute for local calls. Other coins accepted are 5, 10, and sometimes 20 schillings.

How to make a call:

1. Pick up receiver, wait for dial tone.
2. Put in money.
3. Dial number.
4. With pushbutton pay phones, speak when phone is answered. With older rotary phones, push the button (Zahlkopf) when party answers so you can be heard.
5. Put in more money when you hear buzz signal or you'll be cut off.

Using Telephone Card Phones: Buy telephone cards "Telefon-Wertkarte" (50 pulses, 48 schillings; 100 pulses, 95 schillings) at post offices and Tabak Austria shops.

How to make a call:

1. Pick up receiver.
2. Put card in slot at bottom; see how many units remain on digital display.
3. Wait for dial tone.
4. Dial number.
5. After call, card is disengaged from phone; don't forget to take it with you!

Operator calls for local services cost 1 schilling per minute; international operators are free; most international operators speak English, local ones may not.

Local information and local directory assistance dial 08, international operator 09.

Long distance information and long-distance directory dial 16.

Emergency calls from pay phones are free (no coin required). Police dial 133; Fire dial 122; Ambulance dial 144.

Long-Distance Calls inside Austria, made from post offices and pay phones that take 5-, 10-, and 20-schilling coins. Dial 0 + city code + subscriber number. (If the city code you have starts with 0, don't dial another zero.)

International Calls from Austria, made from post offices and private phones, and all card phones, and pay phones that take 5- and 10-schilling coins. Dial: for Italy 040 + city code + subscriber number.

For most of the rest of Europe dial 00 + country code + city or area code + subscriber number.

For rest of world dial 900 + country code + city or area code + subscriber number.

To call the U.S. and Canada dial 900 + 1 + area code + number. In some provincial areas dial 00 + 1 +area code + number.

"Dial Direct" access codes: AT&T USA Direct dial (022) 903 011 (this is a toll call to or in Vienna).

Hotel Surcharges: No maximum percentage.

Things You Should Know: There is no reduced-rate international calling time from Austria to foreign countries. Telephone credit cards are accepted, but not for calls made from coin phones. If you don't start dialing within 10 seconds, your dial tone becomes a busy signal, and then you can't make a call.

Telephone sounds you may hear:

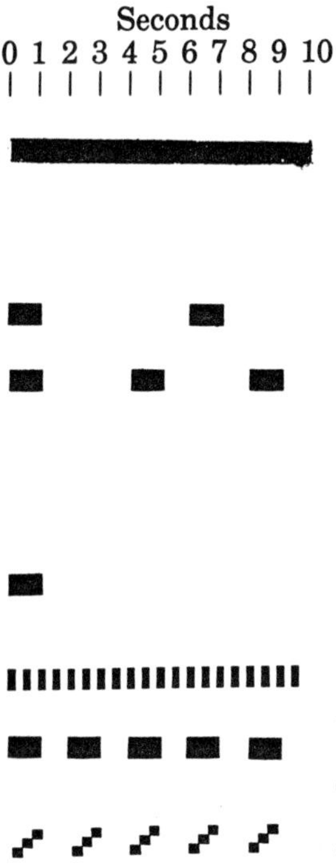
Seconds
0 1 2 3 4 5 6 7 8 9 10

Kind	Description
Dial tone	Steady Tone
Ringing	1 sec. ring and 5 sec. intervals.
or	1 sec. ring and 3 sec. intervals.
Add money	Watch indicator on phone; add when flashing.
or	Buzz 10 sec. before time is up.
Busy	¼ sec. tone and ¼ sec. interval.
or	1 sec. tone and 1 second interval.
Out of Order	3 rising tones in 1 sec. and 1 second interval.
or	Recording.

Belgium
Country Code: 32. Telephone: French area:
TÉLÉPHONE. Flemish area: TELEFOON.

Pay Phones are found at post offices, transit
stations, airports, and on street. Two types of
coin phones: Belgium only and international, and
telephone card phones.

Phone Directories contain White and Yellow
Pages. Yellow pages have an English index of
classifications but no summary about making
either local or international calls. There is also a
fax directory at RTT offices. Find directories at
post offices, hotels, shops, and most phone
booths.

Using Pay Phones: Use two 5-franc (F) coins
per 2 minutes 40 sec. 8 a.m.-6 p.m. (5 min. 20
seconds nights and weekends) for local calls.
Other coins accepted are 5 F and 20 F in international coin phones.

How to make a call:
1. Pick up receiver.
2. Deposit coin and wait for dial tone.
3. Dial number.
4. Coin will be returned if number is busy or
   not answered.

Using Telephone Card Phones: Buy
"Telecards" (20 units, 200 F; 105 units, 1,000 F)
at post offices and telephone calling offices
(found in transportation centers).

How to make a call:
1. Pick up receiver.
2. Insert card into slot near bottom of phone
   and wait for dial tone.
3. When you see number of units left in digital
   display (may be faint), dial number.
4. Card will be disengaged when you hang up.
5. If you run out of units and have another
   card, remove old card and insert another
   card as it uses the last unit.

Operator calls cost 10 F; most local and all international operators speak English, especially
at the Flemish-language numbers.

Local information and directory assistance dial
1207 (Flemish); 1307 (French).

Local operator for assistance dial 1280 (Flemish); 1380 (French).

Long-distance information in Belgium dial 1208 (Flemish); 1308 (French).

Long-distance operator for assistance dial 1229 (Flemish); 1329 (French).

International information in Europe, North Africa, and Greenland dial 1204 (Flemish); 1304 (French).

International-telephone country and city codes dial 1224 (Flemish); 1324 (French).

International operator to make calls in Europe, North Africa, and Greenland dial 1224 (Flemish); 1324 (French).

International information outside Europe, North Africa, and Greenland dial 1222 (Flemish); 1322 (French).

International operator to place calls outside Europe dial 1222 (Flemish); 1322 (French).

Emergency calls are free. Police dial 101; Fire dial 100; Ambulance dial 100.

Tourist information dial 513 30 30 (Brussels Tourist Office).

Long-Distance Calls inside Belgium, made from post offices and all coin phones. Dial 0 + area code + subscriber number.

International Calls from Belgium, made from post offices and phone booths with European flags, and telephones accepting 20 F coins, and all telephone card phones. Dial 00 + wait for second dial tone (in some

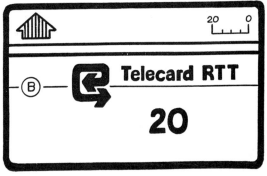

but not all exchanges) + country code + city or area code + subscriber number.

To call the U.S. and Canada dial 00 + second dial tone + 1 + area code + number.

"Dial Direct" access codes: AT&T USA Direct dial 110010; CCCS dial 115454; Canada Direct dial 110011; MCI Call USA dial 110012.

Hotel surcharges: No maximum percentage.

Things You Should Know: 1. Reduced-rate direct-dialed international calls 6:30 p.m.—8 a.m. and all day Sunday.

2. Information numbers are Flemish (start with 12) and French (start with 13). Flemish operators are likelier to speak English.

3. Some Telecards have pictures below the band.

4. Long-distance free (similar to "800") or local-rate (similar to "900") numbers are called "Numéros Verts/Groene Nummers." Free calls start with "11," and local-rate calls start with "15." These numbers are listed in the directory just before the alphabetical listings.

Telephone sounds you may hear:

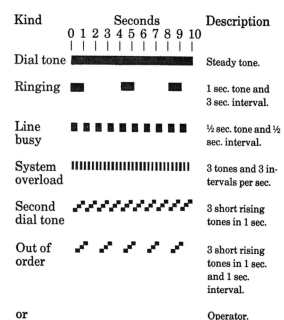

Kind	Seconds	Description
	0 1 2 3 4 5 6 7 8 9 10	
Dial tone		Steady tone.
Ringing		1 sec. tone and 3 sec. interval.
Line busy		½ sec. tone and ½ sec. interval.
System overload		3 tones and 3 intervals per sec.
Second dial tone		3 short rising tones in 1 sec.
Out of order		3 short rising tones in 1 sec. and 1 sec. interval.
or		Operator.

Bulgaria
Country Code: 359. Telephone: ТЕЛЕФОН.

Pay Phones are found at post offices, restaurants, hotels, and phone booths on the street.
Phone Directories have "private" and "public" pages. There are no English summaries or instructions. Find directories at some post offices and some hotels.
Using Pay Phones: Use 5-stotinki coin or token (costs 5 stotinki) for untimed local calls. Some special long-distance phones accept 5- and 50-stotinki coins.

How to make a call:

1. Pick up receiver.
2. Place coin in slot at top of phone.
3. Wait for dial tone.
4. Dial number.
5. On some pay phones you must push a button to be heard.

Operator calls cost 5 stotinki or 1 token; some international operators speak English, local ones almost never do.
Local information dial 145.
Local directory assistance dial 144.
Long-distance information and international operator dial 0123.
Emergency calls cost 5 stotinki. Police dial 166; Fire dial 160; Ambulance dial 150.
Tourist Information from Balkan tourist offices—various numbers in different cities (Sofia: 84-131).
Long-Distance Calls inside Bulgaria, made from post offices, hotels, long-distance pay phones (50 stotinki per 2 minutes). Dial city code + subscriber number.
International Calls from Bulgaria, made from post offices, hotels (but not from coin phones). International direct dialing from coin phones is not possible.
To call the U.S. and Canada dial Operator at 0123.
Hotel surcharges: Maximum surcharge unknown.
Things You Should Know: 1. International calls take up to one hour to be connected.

2. Sometimes lines are crossed during a conversation.

3. Main Post Office telephone office (4 Gurku St., Sofia 1000) is open 24 hours a day, includes calling booth for direct-dial international calls to Western Europe and North America.

Telephone sounds you may hear:

Kind	Seconds	Description
	0 1 2 3 4 5 6 7 8 9 10	
Dial tone	▮■ ▮■ ▮■ ▮■ ▮■	Short tone and interval, then long tone and interval.
Ringing	■■	1 second tone and 9 second interval.
Busy	■ ■ ■ ■ ■ ■ ■ ■ ■	½ second tone and ½ second interval.
Out of order		Busy signal or silence.

Czechoslovakia
Country Code: 42. Telephone: TELEFON.

Pay Phones are found on the street (orange or green booths), in hotels and restaurants, and at post offices.

Phone Directories contain White Pages. There is sometimes a short English summary, including international instructions. Find directories at all post offices, most hotels, and some phone booths.

Using Pay Phones: Use 1 koruna (Kcs) per untimed local call. No other coins are accepted, except at new long-distance and international booths accepting 1-, 2-, and 5-Kcs coins.

How to make a call:
1. Pick up receiver.
2. Wait for dial tone.
3. Dial number.
4. When answered, insert coin.
5. Do not put in money until you hear the right person.
6. If you already put coin in, it is returned if you hang up with no answer.

Operator calls cost 1 koruna; few operators speak English.

Local information and local directory assistance dial 120.

International directory assistance dial 0149.

International operator dial 102 or 108.

Emergency calls cost 1 koruna (free from some phones). Police dial 158; Fire dial 150; Ambulance dial 155.

Long-Distance Calls inside Czechoslovakia, made from pay phones, post offices, and hotels. Dial 0 + city code + subscriber number.

International Calls from Czechoslovakia, made from post offices, hotels, private phones, and pay phones accepting 2- and 5-Kcs coins. Dial 00 + country code + area or city code + subscriber number.

To call the U.S. and Canada dial 00 + 1 + area code + number.

Hotel surcharges: No maximum percentage.

Things You Should Know: 1. U.S. and Canadian telephone calling cards are accepted only on calls made from post offices.

2. Some old pay phones have no coin return.

Telephone sounds you may hear:

Kind	Seconds 0 1 2 3 4 5 6 7 8 9 10	Description
Dial tone	▮▮ ▮▮ ▮▮ ▮▮ ▮▮	Short tone and short interval; then long tone and long interval.
Ringing	▮▮ ▮▮	1 second tone and 4 second interval.
Busy	▮▮▮▮▮▮▮▮▮▮▮▮▮▮▮▮	5 tones and 5 intervals per 3 seconds.
Out of order		No sound.

Denmark
Country Code 45. Telephone: TELEFON.

Pay Phones are found at telephone offices, post offices, transport stations, airports, cafes, and a few booths in the street.
Phone Directories contain White alphabetical and Classified pages, often in separate volumes. There is an English summary, including international calling information. Find directories in telephone offices, phone booths, hotels, and shops.
Using Pay Phones: Use 2—25-øre coins per 3 minutes local call (per 6 minutes 10 p.m.—8 a.m.). Other coins accepted are 1 krone, 5 kroner, 10 kroner.
How to make a call:
1. Pick up receiver.
2. Put in money.
3. Dial number.
4. If no answer, try another call (there is no coin return).
5. Add money when you hear rising tones.

Operator calls cost 50 øre (2 x 25 øre); most operators speak English.
Information dial 0030, local directory assistance dial 0034.
Long-distance operator and directory assistance dial 0038.
International operator dial 0039.
Emergency calls are free and no coin is needed. Police, Fire, and Ambulance dial 000.
Long-Distance Calls inside Denmark, made from telephone offices, all coin phones. Dial 0 + two digit area code + subscriber number.
International Calls from Denmark, made from telephone offices, all pay phones (from pay phones you'll need a lot of coins). Dial 009 + country code + city or area code + subscriber number.
To call the U.S. and Canada dial 009 + 1 + area code + number.
"Dial Direct" access codes: AT&T USA Direct dial 8001-0010; Canada Direct (begins June 1990, code not available at press time); CCCS dial 8001-0800; MCI Call USA dial 8001-0022.

Hotel Surcharges: No maximum percentage.
Things You Should Know: 1. Pay phones have no coin return—if no answer, try calling another number. Otherwise, you'll lose your money.
2. Some phones have a squeeze button on receiver: if you don't squeeze during the conversation, the other party can't hear you.
3. These letters are at the end of the Danish alphabet: å/aa, ä, æ, ö/ø, and ü.
4. Phonecards will be introduced in the near future.

Telephone sounds you may hear:

Kind	Seconds	Description
	0 1 2 3 4 5 6 7 8 9 10	
Dial tone	▬▬▬▬	Steady hum.
Ringing	▪ ▪	1 sec. ring and 7 sec. interval.
Add more money	♪ ♪ ♪ ♪ ♪	3 rising tones in 1 second and 1 sec. interval.
Busy	▌▌▌▌▌▌▌▌▌▌▌▌▌▌	Rapid buzz and interval (3 per 2 seconds).
Out of order	♪ ♪ ♪ ♪ ♪	3 rising tones in 1 second and 1 sec. interval.
or		Operator.
Phone off hook	▌▌▌▌▌▌▌▌▌▌▌▌▌▌▌▌	Short rapid tones and intervals.

Finland
Country Code 358. Telephone: PUHELIN.

Pay Phones are found on the street, in official buildings, Teleservice calling offices, and transit stations.

Phone Directories contain White Business and Residence Pages and Business Yellow Pages. White Pages have English summary, including international calling information. Find directories at post offices, telephone offices, phone booths, hotels, and shops.

Using Pay Phones: Use 1-markka coin for timed local calls. The other coin accepted is 5 markka. At major airports, ferry terminals, and train stations, some pay phones accept major credit and charge cards.

How to make a call:

1. Pick up receiver, wait for dial tone.
2. Put in coin.
3. Dial number.

Operator calls cost at least 2 markka; most operators speak English. For information dial 09, for local directory assistance dial 012.

Long-distance operator and long-distance directory assistance dial 020.

International operator (no charge) dial 92022.

International calling cost dial information, 92020.

Emergency calls are free; Police, Fire, and Ambulance dial 000.

Tourist Information English recording: Helsinki dial 058 (50 pennis per minute), or Helsinki Tourist Office dial 169-3757 (local call). Daily news in English dial 040 (129 pennis per minute).

Long-Distance Calls inside Finland, made from coin phones, post offices, teleservice offices. Dial area code + subscriber number.

International Calls from Finland, made from coin phones, post offices, teleservice offices. Dial 990 + country code + area or city code + subscriber number.

To call the U.S. and Canada dial 990 + 1 + area code + number.

"Dial-Direct" access codes: AT&T USA Direct dial 9800-10010; CCCS dial 9800-10110.

Hotel Surcharges: No maximum percentage.

Things You Should Know: 1. Å, Ä, Ö, are listed after Z in the alphabet.

2. Reduced-rate international calls (direct-dialed calls only) 10 p.m.—8 a.m. weekdays and all day Sunday.

Telephone sounds you may hear:

Kind	Description 0 1 2 3 4 5 6 7 8 9 10	Description
Dial tone	▬▬▬▬▬▬▬▬▬	Steady hum.
Ringing	▪ ▪	1 second tone and 4 second interval, or
or	▪	1 sec. tone and 9 second interval.
Busy	▪▪▪▪▪▪▪▪▪▪▪▪▪▪▪	5 tones and 5 intervals per 3 seconds.
Out of order		Busy, silence, or ringing.

France

includes Andorra & Monaco, Country Code 33.
Telephone: TÉLÉPHONE.

Pay Phones are found in street booths, post offices, train stations, airports, and most bars and cafés.

Phone Directories contain White and Yellow Pages, separate volumes in large cities (Paris has five volumes). Instructions are at the beginning of the Yellow Pages. There are only short or no English summaries or instructions. Find directories at post offices (all of France!), hotel reception desks, bars and cafes, and a few phone booths (usually binders are there but books are missing).

Also, every post office and many residences and businesses in France have terminals for the national Minitel system, which includes a complete national directory. To use Minitel's directory, dial 11, then press "connection" key, then enter name ("nom)," business classification ("rubrique") and town ("localité)", then press send key ("envoi"), and wait for answer.

Using Coin Phones: Use 1-franc coin for local calls of 6 minutes during the day, 12 minutes during the evening, and 20 minutes from 10 p.m. to 7 a.m. Other coins accepted are ½ F, 1 F, 5 F, and occasionally 2 F.

How to make a call:

1. Pick up receiver.
2. Put in coin(s).
3. Wait for dial tone.
4. Dial number.
5. Coins are taken smallest first to larger later.
6. When finished, hang up.
7. Unused coins are returned.

Using Telephone Card Phones (found in most major cities and almost exclusively in Paris): Buy a "Telecarte" (40, 50, or 120 units, each unit about 0.76 F) at any post office and some tobacco shops.

How to make a call:

1. Pick up receiver.
2. Put card in slot.

3. Close door over the card.
4. Dial when you see "Numerotez" on digital readout.
5. When completed, hang up and door will open.
6. Remove card (don't forget it).

Operator calls are free from card and some coin phones; at others, pay 3.50 F. Some local and most international operators speak English.
Information and directory assistance dial 12.
Electronic directory dial 11 (first 3 minutes free).
International operator dial 19 + dial tone + 3333.
International information dial 19 + dial tone + 3312 + country code (U.S. and Canada = 11).

Emergency calls are free—deposit coin, which is returned. Police dial 17; Fire dial 18; Ambulance dial 18; 24-hour English SOS dial (Paris) 47.23.80.80.

Long-Distance Calls inside France, made from post offices and all pay phones:
1. Within Paris region: dial 8-digit number.
2. From Paris region to provinces: dial 16, wait for second dial tone, dial 8-digit number.
3. Provinces to Paris: dial 16, wait for second dial tone, dial 1 then 8-digit number.
4. Provinces to provinces: dial 8-digit number.

International Calls from France, made from post offices, all coin phones. Dial 19 + wait for

second dial tone + country code + city or area code + subscriber number.

To call the U.S. and Canada dial 19 + wait for second dial tone + 1 + area code + number.

"Dial Direct" access codes: AT&T USA Direct dial 19, wait for second dial tone, then 0011; Canada Direct dial 19, wait for second dial tone, then 0016; CCCS dial 19, wait for second dial tone, then 05902747; MCI Call USA dial 19, wait for second dial tone, then 0019; UK Direct dial 19, wait for second dial tone, then 0044.

Hotel Surcharges: No maximum percentage.

Things You Should Know: 1. To extend long-distance calls made from pay phones, watch for flashing red light at top left of phone about 10 seconds before money runs out.

2. Operators may take several minutes to come on the line—let it ring.

3. Reduced-rate international direct-dial calls (including from pay phones) 10 p.m.—10 a.m. and all day Sunday.

4. Toll-free calls (similar to "800" calls) are called "numéro vert," always begin with "05." For national information dial 05-00 00 01; for international information dial 05-19 3333.

5. You can receive calls at telephones with a blue sign of a bell and the booth telephone number (see similar illustration in Germany (West) Telephone Key).

6. Privately owned phones in hotels, bars, cafes, etc. marked "Point-Phone" can charge higher than standard prices (usually at least double).

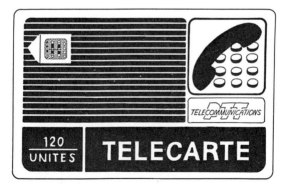

Telephone sounds you may hear:

Kind	Seconds 0 1 2 3 4 5 6 7 8 9 10	Description
Dial tone	▬▬▬▬▬▬▬▬▬▬▬	Steady tone.
Ringing	▬ ▬	1½ second tone and 3½ second interval.
Add more money	▬	High rapid tone and/or flashing light at top left of box.
Busy	■ ■ ■ ■ ■ ■ ■ ■ ■	½ sec. tone and ½ sec. interval.
Routing tone (call going through)	‖‖‖‖‖‖‖‖‖‖‖‖‖‖‖‖‖‖‖‖‖	10 short tones and intervals per sec. (May last 40 seconds)
Out of order	♪ ♪ ♪ ♪ ♪	3 rising tones in 1 sec. and 1 sec. interval, then recording.

Germany (East)
Country Code 37. Telephone: TELEFON.

Pay Phones are found at post offices, train stations, subway and public transit stations, and on the street.

Phone Directories are found in post offices, hotels, and shops (but infrequently).

Books have only White Pages with some classifications listed in the book. There is no English summary for either local or international calling.

Using Pay Phones: Use 20 pfennig per 3 minutes for local calls. Some phones also accept 20-, 50-pfennig and 1-mark coins.

How to make a local call:

1. Pick up receiver.
2. Deposit coin, wait for dial tone.
3. On phones taking 20-, 50-pfennig and 1-mark coins, dial while light at coin slot is red (about 10 seconds).

Operator calls are free; local operators rarely speak English, but international operators often do. Local directory assistance dial 180.

Long-distance operator dial 181 (deposit money, returned).

International operator to U.S. and Canada dial 01-12. For operator to call other countries see page 1 of phone book (numbers vary). For international information and directory assistance dial 183.

Emergency calls are free, no coin needed. Police dial 110; Fire dial 112; Ambulance dial 115,.

Tourist Information dial 2150 (Berlin, Reisebüro der DDR).

Long-Distance Calls inside the GDR, made from post offices, hotels, phones accepting 20-, 50-pfennig, and 1-mark coins. Dial city code + subscriber number.

International Calls from the GDR, made from post offices, hotels, private phones, pay phones accepting 1M coins. No direct-dial international calls from pay phones, except to West Berlin and the rest of Europe from East Berlin on phones accepting 1-mark coins. (Calls not possible to the United States or Canada.) Dial 06 + country code + city or area code + subscriber number (in some areas outside of East Berlin, access code is 000 or 012).

To call the U.S. and Canada dial 06 + 1 + area code + number. In many areas, can call only through international operator.

Hotel Surcharges: No maximum percentage.

Things You Should Know: Allow 30 seconds for international direct-dial calls to be connected. Keep trying to call, because there aren't enough international lines to provide instant access.

Telephone sounds you may hear:

Kind	Seconds	Description
	0 1 2 3 4 5 6 7 8 9 10	
Dial tone	■ ■■ ■■ ■■ ■■ ■	¾ sec. tone, ¾ sec. interval, ¼ sec. tone and interval.
Ringing	■■ ■■	1 sec. tone and 4 sec. interval,
or	■ ■■	1 sec. tone and 5 sec. interval,
or	■■	1 sec. tone and 9 sec. interval.
Busy	‖‖‖‖‖‖‖‖‖‖‖	0.1 sec. tone and ½ sec. intervals.

Germany (West)
Country Code 49. Telephone: TELEFON.

Pay Phones are found in booths on the street, transit stations, airports, autobahn rest stops, and at all post offices.

Phone Directories contain White and Yellow Pages, often in separate volumes. Directories do not have English summary or international calling information. Find directories in phone booths (sometimes, in large cities), at post offices (for entire country), hotels, and shops.

Using Pay Phones: Use 3—10l-pfennig coins (30 pfennig) per 8 minutes 8 a.m.—6 p.m. weekdays (12 minutes all other times) for local calls. Two types of pay phones:

Rotary-dial phones for calls within Germany only; accept 10-, 50-pfennig, and DM 1 coins. Pushbutton pay phones (with "Ausland" or "International" sign) can make calls within Germany and direct-dial international calls also; accept 10 Pf, DM 1 and DM 5 coins. Some pushbutton phones also accept 50 Pf, and DM 2 coins.

How to make a call:
1 Pick up receiver.
2. Deposit coin(s).
3. Dial number.
4. Add money when "Bitte Zahlen" or arrow at coin slot lights up.
5. If calling long distance, add several coins in advance.
6. Unused coins will be returned. You can add small coins to obtain refund of partially-used high-value coins *before* you replace the receiver.

Using Telephone Card Phones: Buy telephone cards, ("Telefon-Karte") at main post offices; 45 units cost DM 12, and 200 units cost DM 50. These phones are new, set on a round base, and are found only in a few city centers and airports.

How to make a call:
1. Pick up receiver.
2. Insert card into slot near bottom of phone.
3. When you see number of units left in digital display (may be faint), dial number.
4. If you run out of units and have another

card, you can insert another card as it uses the last unit.

5. Card will be disengaged when you hang up.
6. Remove your card—don't forget it!

Operator calls cost 30 Pf; some local and most international operators speak English.

Local information and directory assistance dial 1188 or 0188.

Long-distance operator dial 010.

International operator dial 0010.

International information dial 00118.

Emergency calls are free; deposit 30 pf, coins returned. Police dial 110; Fire dial 112; Ambulance dial 112. Some booths marked "SOS" have a direct no-coin box with SOS knob for police and fire. Just push the SOS knob to the left (green) for police, to the right (red) for fire. Emergency Numbers vary in some rural areas: check front of phone book for "Notruf."

Long-Distance Calls inside West Germany from all coin phones, at post offices, hotels. Dial city code + subscriber number.

International Calls from West Germany, made from post offices, "Ausland" coin phones, hotels. Dial 00 + country code + subscriber number.

To call the U.S. and Canada dial 00 + 1 + area code + number.

Telefonkarte

Gebühr
12 DM
40 Einheiten

Deutsche
Bundespost

"Dial Direct" access code: AT&T USA Direct dial (0130) 0101; CCCS dial (0130) 2928.

Hotel Surcharges: No maximum percentage—could be 300%!

Things You Should Know: 1. You can't use U.S. and Canadian telephone calling cards in West Germany.

2. Don't use "0" as part of city code except when calling another West German city.

3. You can be called at any booth with a red sign and white bell with the phone number written in under the bell (see illustration).

Anrufbares Telefon
You can receive calls here, too
Cette cabine peut être appelée

Telephone sounds you may hear:

Kind	Seconds 0 1 2 3 4 5 6 7 8 9 10	Description
Dial tone	▬▬▬▬▬▬▬▬▬	Steady tone.
Ringing	▪ ▪	1 second tone and 4 sec. interval.
Add more money		No tone, but watch for flash at coin slot.
Busy	▪ ▪ ▪ ▪ ▪ ▪ ▪ ▪ ▪	½ sec. tones and intervals.
Out of order	⌁ ⌁ ⌁ ⌁ ⌁	3 rising tones in 1 sec. and 1 sec. interval or
or		Recording

Great Britain
Country Code 44. Telephone: TELEPHONE.

Pay Phones are found in old-fashioned red phone booths (call boxes) or newer yellow (for coins) and green (for "Phonecards") half-booths on streets, in transit stations, airports, large department stores, pubs, and British Telecom calling offices.

Phone Directories contain White and Yellow Pages, with separate volumes in most areas. Instructions and international calling information are in English. Find directories at phone booths in transit terminals and rural areas, sometimes in city phone booths, and in hotels, shops, and Telecom offices. Business-to-business Yellow Pages are published for London and a few other large cities, but are never found at phone booths.

Using Pay Phones: Use 10-pence coin per 5 minutes (varies with distance and time of day). Different types of phones take different coins.

How to make a call:

"Pay and Answer" rotary-dial phones take only 10-pence, rarely 50-pence, coins; found in many hotels, shops, pubs, and rural areas.

1. Have money ready.
2. Pick up receiver for dial tone.
3. Dial number.
4. When answered, you will hear high pips—push coin(s) in immediately. When money is accepted, pips will stop and you can begin talking.
5. If you hear more pips, add more money or you will be cut off.

Note: International calls can be made from this type, but are not recommended, since you can't push money in fast enough.

"Blue Payphone" pushbutton phones take 2-, 10-, 50-pence coins in separate slots; if a single slot, takes 5-, 10-, 20-, 50-pence and £1 coins.

1. Pick up receiver.
2. Put in coins.
3. Watch value of money on digital display (sometimes, credit doesn't register and you have to redeposit money).
4. Dial number.

5. During conversation, digital display shows how much credit is left and flashes when you need to add more money.
6. Unused coins are refunded.
7. These phones are rare—only in airports, train and subway stations, a few city-center phone booths.

Using Telephone Card Phones: Buy "Phonecards" (10 units £1, 20 units £2, 40 units £4, 100 units £10, 200 units £20) at main post offices and newsstands, kiosks, and railway station buffets where the green Phonecard decal is found.

How to use a Cardphone:
1. Pick up receiver.
2. Push card into slot in phone.
3. When digital display shows remaining credit, continue as for "Blue Payphone."
4. When you hang up, card will be pushed out of slot.
5. Only some operator services are available from these phones.

Operator calls are free; all operators speak English.
Local information dial 100. Local directory assistance dial 142 (for London numbers), or

192 (for numbers elsewhere).

Long-distance operator and directory assistance dial 191.

International operator for Europe dial 104 or 105. For directory assistance for Europe dial 102 or 103.

International operator and directory assistance for the U.S. and Canada dial 155.

International operator and directory assistance for the rest of the world dial 108.

Emergency calls are free and require no coins. Police, Fire, and Ambulance dial 999.

Tourist Information call London 246-8041 (recording), Edinburgh: 246-8041 (summer only).

Long-Distance Calls inside Britain, made from any coin phone, Telecom offices, hotels. Dial 0 + city code + subscriber number. City codes are listed in the front of the White Pages.

International Calls from Britain, made from coin phones, telephone offices, some post offices. Dial 010 + country code + area code + subscriber number.

To call the U.S. and Canada dial 010 + 1 + area code + number.

"Dial Direct" access codes: AT&T USA Direct dial 0800-89-0011; Canada Direct dial 0800-89-0016; CCCS dial 0800-89-1800; MCI Call USA dial 0800-89-0222.

Hotel Surcharges: No maximum percentage.

Things You Should Know: 1. City codes have two to five digits, beginning with "0" (zero); numbers have 3 to 7 digits.

2. You may have to wait a long time to be connected to operator. Be patient; let it ring.

3. You'll find some coin phones out of order.

4. Toll-free numbers (similar to"800") are called "Freefone," or have 0800 as the city code.

5. Reduced-rate direct-dialed international calls from pay phones and private phones 8 p.m.—8 a.m. weekdays and all day Saturday and Sunday.

6. When coin boxes are full, you can dial only emergency (999).

Telephone sounds you may hear:

Kind	Seconds 0 1 2 3 4 5 6 7 8 9 10	Description
Dial tone	▬▬▬▬▬▬▬▬	Low hum.
Ringing	▪▪ ▪▪ ▪▪ ▪▪	2—0.4 sec. tones separated by 0.2 sec. interval, then 2 second interval.
Add more money	‖‖‖‖‖‖‖‖‖‖‖‖‖‖‖‖‖‖‖‖	4 rapid pips and 4 intervals per second.
Busy	▪ ▪ ▪ ▪ ▪ ▪ ▪ ▪ ▪ ▪ ▪	⅜ sec. tone and ⅜ sec. interval.
Out of order	▬▬▬▬▬▬▬▬	Steady high tone, or
or		Silence, or
or	▱ ▱ ▱ ▱ ▱	3 rising tones in 1 sec. and recording.

Greece
Country Code 30. Telephone: Τηλεφωνο.

Pay Phones are found at newsstand kiosks, OTE (Greek telephone company) offices, bus depots, railway stations, airports, and booths.

Phone Directories have White and Yellow Pages, with short Latin-alphabet listings at end of White Pages and short classified listing of the Yellow Pages. There are no English instructions or international calling information in these. There is also an English-language Blue Pages Classified directory, which includes international calling information. Find directories at OTE telephone offices, hotels, and shops.

Using Pay Phones: Use 7 drachma (5-drachma coin plus 2-drachma coin) per 5 minutes for local calls. No other coins are accepted.

How to make a call:
1. Pick up receiver.
2. Deposit coins for dial tone.
3. Dial number.

(If phone doesn't have coin slot, you'll have to pay the kiosk attendant; price may be higher.)

Operator calls are free. A few local operators and most international operators speak English. Local information dial 134.

Local directory assistance dial 131 (Athens and Attica).

Long distance operator dial 151.

Long-distance directory assistance dial 132.

International operator dial 161.

Emergency calls are free. Police dial 100; Fire dial 199; Ambulance dial 150 or 166. In Athens, dial the English- speaking Tourist Police at 171.

Long Distance Calls inside Greece, made from OTE telephone offices, public phones at kiosks with pulse meters. Dial 0 + city code + subscriber number.

International Calls from Greece, made from OTE telephone offices, public phones at kiosks with pulse meters. Dial 00 + country code + city or area code + subscriber number.

To call the U.S. and Canada dial 00 + 1 + area code + number.

"Dial Direct" access codes: (not available from red pay phones) AT&T USA Direct dial 00-800-1311; MCI Call USA dial 00-800-1211.

Hotel Surcharges: No maximum percentage.

Things You Should Know: 1. If making a long-distance call from a kiosk without a pulse meter, price could be exorbitant.

2. It is much harder get a long-distance connection from the provinces than from Athens (the calls originating in Athens seem to get priority).

Telephone sounds you may hear:

Kind	Seconds	Description
	0 1 2 3 4 5 6 7 8 9 10	
Dial tone	▮▮ ▮▮ ▮▮ ▮▮ ▮▮	2 short tones in 1 sec. then 1 sec. interval.
Ringing	▬ ▬	1 sec. tone and 6 sec. interval.
or	▬ ▬	1 sec. tone and 4 sec. interval.
Busy	▮▮▮▮▮▮▮▮▮▮▮▮▮▮▮▮	0.3 second tone and 0.3 second interval.
Out of order	▮ ▮ ▮ ▮ ▮ ▮ ▮ ▮ ▮	½ sec. tone and ½ sec. interval.
or		Silence.

Hungary
Country Code 36. Telephone: TELEFON.

Pay Phones are found at post offices, street booths, bars, railway stations, and most pastry shops.

Phone Directories have White Pages and Yellow Pages in separate volumes. There is an English-language summary in the Yellow Pages. Find directories in post offices, hotels, shops, and many phone booths.

Using Pay Phones: Use 2-forint coin per 3 minutes 7 a.m.—6 p.m. (6 minutes 6 p.m.—7 a.m.) for local calls. No other coins accepted, except red pay phones with pushbutton dialing also take 10- and 20-forint coins.

How to make a call:
1. Pick up receiver, wait for dial tone.
2. Insert coin(s).
3. Dial number.
4. Add money before time is up to extend call— sometimes no warning signal before connection is cut off.

Operator calls cost 2 forints; only a few local and some international operators speak English. Local information dial 01, local directory assistance English in Budapest dial 117-2200 (weekdays 7 a.m.—8 p.m.

Long-distance operator and long-distance directory assistance dial 01.

International operator dial 09 (no charge).

Emergency calls are free—deposit coin, which is returned. Police dial 07; Fire dial 05; Ambulance dial 04.

Tourist Information (English) dial 117-2800 in Budapest.

Long-Distance Calls inside Hungary, made from post offices, red and yellow coin phones that take 2-, 10-, 20-forint coins. Dial 06 + and wait for second dial tone + area code + subscriber number.

International Calls from Hungary, from post offices, red pay phones accepting 2-, 10-, and 20-forint coins. Dial 00 + wait for second dial tone + country code + subscriber number.

To call the U.S. and Canada dial 00 + wait for second dial tone + 1 + area code + number.

"Dial Direct" access code: AT&T USA Direct dial 00 + wait for second dial tone + 36-0111.

Hotel Surcharges: Maximum 50%.

Things You Should Know: 1. Sometimes (maybe 5%) you'll get a wrong number even though you dialed correctly. Hang up and try again.

2. When making a long-distance or international call from a red pay phone, you must put in at least 40 forints. Also, second dial tone is high-pitched. After you finish dialing, you will hear a single routing tone; wait while your call is connected.

3. Dial slowly, or you will hear a busy signal.

Telephone sounds you may hear:

Kind	Seconds	Description
	0 1 2 3 4 5 6 7 8 9 10	
Dial tone	▬▬▬▬▬▬▬▬▬	Steady hum.
Ringing	■　　　　　■	1 sec. tone and 6 sec. interval.
Add money		No warning tone or signal.
Busy	❚❚❚❚❚❚❚❚❚❚❚❚❚	0.3 second tone and 0.3 second interval.
Out of order	✔ ✔ ✔ ✔ ✔	3 rising tones in 1 sec. and 1 sec. intervals.
or		Operator.

Ireland
Country Code 353. Telephone: TELEFÓN.

Pay Phones are found at post offices, hotels, restaurants, pubs, and blue and white concrete boxes, and silver, orange, black and gold aluminum boxes.

Phone Directories contain White and Yellow Pages (entire country: 7 volumes White and Yellow Pages). Instructions and international calling information are in English. Find directories at post offices, hotels, shops, and phone booths (sometimes missing or vandalized).

Using Pay Phones: Use 2 10-pence coins per 4 minutes 45 seconds for local calls. There are several different types of pay phones. Other coins accepted are 5 P on all types and 50 P on new STD (Subscriber Trunk Dialing) phones only.

How to make a call:

Type 1—STD Type:
1. Line up coin(s) on ramp at top of phone (at least 20 P local, 50 P long-distance, £1 international).
2. Pick up receiver.
3. Listen for dial tone: may take 20 seconds.
4. Dial number.
5. When answered, the first coin(s) will be taken automatically. Additional coins will fall in as needed.
6. 10 seconds before time is up, you will hear a beep. Add money quickly to continue call.
7. No coin return on this kind of phone; but you can make another call to use up credit if you dial within 30 seconds.

Type 2—A and B Button Phones:
1. Pick up receiver, listen for dial tone.
2. Insert money.
3. Dial number (for long distance, dial operator).
4. When call answered, press "A" button usually on right side of phone box.
5. If call not answered, press "B" button to return coin.

Operator calls are free; except extra 20-P charge to make a connection. All operators speak English.

Local information and directory assistance in entire Republic of Ireland dial 190.

Long-distance operator and directory assistance dial 10.

International directory assistance dial: for UK International dial 114.

For international operator-assisted calls dial 10, except in Dublin calling area dial 10 for the U.K. and 114 for the rest of the world.

Emergency calls are free; Police, Fire, and Ambulance dial 999.

Long-Distance Calls inside Ireland, made from post offices, Telecom Eireann calling offices, all coin phones. Dial 0 + city code + subscriber number. (Most written phone numbers include the 0.)

International Calls from Ireland, made from post offices, Telecom Eireann calling offices, and STD pay phones. For Great Britain dial 03 + city code + number; for all other countries dial 16 + country code + city or area code + number.

To call the U.S. and Canada dial 16 + 1 + area code + number.

Hotel Surcharges: A 25% service charge or $10 per call, whichever is less; $1 service charge for collect or telephone credit-card calls. (Ireland is a Teleplan country.)

Things You Should Know: 1. Wait up to 20 seconds after dialing to hear any further sounds for calls inside Ireland; 30 seconds on international calls.

2. In some phones, call can't be extended by adding more money. When cut off, call again.

3. When all long-distance lines are busy, priority service is available from operator at double the normal cost.

4. Only telephone credit-card and collect calls outside of Europe can be made from Type 2 pay phones.

5. Reduced-rate international calls weekdays 10 p.m.—10 a.m. and all day Sunday.

Telephone sounds you may hear:

Kind	Seconds 0 1 2 3 4 5 6 7 8 9 10	Description
Dial tone	▬▬▬▬▬▬	Low hum.
Ringing	■■ ■■ ■■ ■■	2—short tones in 1 sec. and 2 sec. interval.
Add more money	▬	Single tone 10 sec. before time is up.
Busy	■■■■■■■■■■■■	0.4 sec. tone and 0.4 second interval.
or	♪ ♪ ♪ ♪ ♪	3 rising tones in 1 sec. and 1 sec. interval.
Out of order	♪ ♪ ♪ ♪ ♪	3 rising tones in 1 sec. and 1 sec. interval.

Italy
includes San Marino and Vatican City,
Country Code 39. Telephone: TELEFONO.

Pay Phones are found at transit stations, airports, telephone offices 169posti telefonici", bars
and cafes with a yellow telephone dial sign.

Phone Directories contain White and Yellow
Pages. There is no English summary or international calling information. Find directories at
SIP (telephone company) offices, hotels, shops,
and about half of the phone booths.

Using Pay Phones: Use 1 gettone (telephone
token, costs 200 lire) or 200-lire coin, or per pulse
on a telephone card (Scheda Telefonica) per 6
minutes for local calls (in some areas, calls are
not timed). Buy tokens and telephone cards (for
5,000, 10,000, 20,000 lire) at SIP offices, tobacco
stores, bars, and cafes. Some phones have token-
vending machines. Only some phones will take
100-lire and 200-lire coins as well as tokens.

How to make a call:

Coin and gettone telephones:
1. Buy token(s) if needed.
2. Put in gettoni or coins (at least 1 for local
   call, 6 for long distance).
3. Pick up receiver.
4. Dial number.
5. If busy, hang up and try again immediately.
6. Add more tokens to extend call.
7. Unused coins or tokens will be returned
   when you push the red button halfway down
   the telephone box.

Card phones (found at airports, main train stations, city centers, SIP and ASST offices, and rest
stops on the autostrade):
1. Pick up receiver.
2. Insert card into blue box at the right of the
   telephone. (Tear off the corner tab from the
   card before first use.)
3. Dial number.
4. When call completed, hang up; card will
   be returned.
5. When you see the flashing light as you run
   out of units, you must replace the card with
   an unused one to continue the call.

Operator calls: some cost 1 gettone or unit, others are free; a few local operators and most international operators speak English.

Local information and directory assistance dial 12.

Long-distance information (no charge) dial 184.

Long-distance directory and long-distance operator dial 184.

International operator (no charge) for Europe and North Africa dial 194; rest of the world dial 170.

Emergency calls are free. Police dial 112; Fire dial 115; Ambulance dial 113.

Long-Distance Calls inside Italy, made from SIP offices, most coin phones with "Interurbano" or "Teleselezione" signs, and all card phones. Dial 0 + city code + subscriber number.

International Calls, made from SIP offices, "Teleselezione" or "Interurbano" pay phones. Dial 00 + country code + city or area code + number.

To call the U.S. and Canada dial 00 + 1 + area code + number.

"Dial Direct" access codes: AT&T USA Direct dial 172-1011 (major cities only); Canada Direct dial 172-1001 (Milan and Rome only); CCCS dial 1678-79074 (charged as a local call, excess coins are refunded); MCI Call USA dial 172-1022 (Milan and Rome only).

Hotel Surcharges: No maximum percentage.

LIRE 3,000

← **CARTA TELEFONICA**
Validità 30.06.90

A 016179508088   **SIP**

Things You Should Know: 1. Sometimes at the end of a timed local call, you'll be cut off. Adding coins or gettoni won't prevent cutoff.
2. You can get a busy signal at any time: before you dial, during dialing, and at the end of dialing. It means system overload—try again immediately.
3. You'll need a lot of gettoni for all but a short local call.
4. Phone numbers in a single city can have varying number of digits: for example numbers in Rome range from 4 to 8 digits.
5. Reduced-rate long-distance and international calls 8 p.m.—8 a.m. and all day Sunday.
6. Italians answer the telephone with "Pronto."
7. Almost-toll-free calls are called "numero verde," start with prefix 1678, you are charged a single pulse regardless of the length of the call or its destination.

Telephone sounds you may hear:

Kind	Seconds	Description
	0 1 2 3 4 5 6 7 8 9 10	
Dial tone	■ ■■ ■■ ■■ ■■ ■	0.6 sec. tone, 1 sec. interval, 0.2 sec. tone and 0.2 second interval.
Ringing	■■ ■■	1 sec. tone and 4 sec. interval.
Busy	‖‖‖‖‖‖‖‖‖‖‖‖‖‖‖‖‖	0.2 sec. tones and intervals.
Out of order		Busy or ringing tone.

Luxembourg
Country Code 352. Telephone: TÉLÉPHONE.

Pay Phones are found in front of or in post offices, at train stations, the airport, and on the street.

Phone Directories contain White Pages only, but some classified listings are included. Directories do not have an English summary or instructions for international calling. Entire country is in two volumes. Find directories at post offices, most pay phones. Private Yellow Pages directory "La Ligne Bleu" is found at shops, hotels, and homes.

Using Pay Phones: Use 5-franc (F) coins from Luxembourg or Belgium for untimed local calls. Two types of telephones: one takes only 5-F coins, for national calls only. Other type takes 1-, 5-, 20-coins, has worldwide automatic direct dialing.

How to make a call:
1. Pick up receiver.
2. Insert coin(s) (5 F minimum), wait for dial tone.
3. Dial number.

Operator calls are free; many operators speak English.

Local information and directory assistance dial 017.

Long-distance operator dial 0010; for international directory dial 016.

International operator dial 0010.

Emergency calls cost 5 F. Police, Fire, and Ambulance dial 012.

Long-Distance Calls inside Luxembourg, made from post offices, all coin phones. Dial the number (there are no area or city codes).

International Calls, made from post offices (metered), hotels, some phone booths. Dial 00 + country code + city or area code + subscriber number.

To call the U.S. and Canada dial 00 + 1 + area code + number.

Hotel Surcharges: No maximum percentage.

Things You Should Know: 1. In long-distance calls, you will hear a single short tone 20 seconds before money runs out. Add money or you will be cut off.

2. Reduced-rate international calls (33% discount) to U.S. and Canada 10 p.m.—10 a.m. every day.

Telephone sounds you may hear:

Kind	Seconds	Description
	0 1 2 3 4 5 6 7 8 9 10	
Dial tone	▬▬▬▬▬▬▬▬	Steady tone.
Ringing	▪ ▪	1 sec. tone and 4 sec. interval,
or	▪	1 sec. tone and 9 sec. interval.
Add more money	▬	Short single tone 20 seconds before cut-off.
Line busy	▪ ▪ ▪ ▪ ▪ ▪ ▪ ▪ ▪	½ sec. tone and ½ sec. interval.
System overload	▮▮▮▮▮▮▮▮▮▮▮▮▮▮▮	¼ sec. tone and ¼ sec. interval.
Out of order		Recording

Netherlands
Country Code 31. Telephone: TELEFOON.

Pay Phones are found in transit stations, airports, PTT telephone offices, department stores, and on the street.

Phone Directories contain separate White Pages and Yellow Pages volumes. White Pages include classified listings, but no advertising. There is no English summary or international calling information. Yellow Pages have an English classified index inside the back cover and indexed city map at the front. Find directories at telephone offices, shops, and hotels (White Pages only when not missing).

Using Pay Phones: Use 25-cent coin per untimed local call. Other coins accepted are 1 guilder and 2½ guilders. For card phones, buy "Telefoonkaart" at post offices, telephone offices, railway stations, and some other shops; 20 units 5 guilders, 45 units 10 guilders, and 115 units 25 guilders.

How to make a call:

Coin phones:

1. Pick up receiver, wait for dial tone.
2. Deposit money.
3. Dial number.
4. Unused coins will be returned.

Card phones: (rare, found in city centers, airports, and main transit stations).

1. Remove receiver.
2. Insert card into slot, wait for dial tone.
3. Dial number.
4. After the call, replace receiver.
5. Take card out (don't forget).
6. If card runs out while talking, press black button above touch pad, take out old card, and insert new card.

Operator calls cost 25 cents; almost all operators speak English.

Local information dial 004 (free), 8:30 a.m.—4:30 p.m., Monday—Saturday.

Local directory assistance dial 008.

Long-distance operator and directory assistance dial 0016.

International operator to make a call dial 0010.

International information dial 0018.

Emergency calls cost 25 cents. Police dial 22-22-22; Fire dial 21-21-21; Ambulance dial 555-5555. (Numbers may vary in rural areas.)

Tourist Information: Look under VVV in phone directory.

Long-Distance Calls inside the Netherlands, made from post offices, almost all coin and card phones. Dial area code (starting with "0") + subscriber number.

International Calls from the Netherlands, made from coin phones accepting 1, 2½-guilder coins, post offices. Dial 09 + dial tone + country code + city code + subscriber number.

To call the U.S. and Canada dial 09 + dial tone + 1 + area code + number.

"Dial Direct" access codes: AT&T USA Direct dial 06 + second dial tone + 022-9111, costs 25 cents; Canada Direct dial 06 + second dial tone + 022-9116; CCCS dial 06 + second dial tone + 022-6202; MCI Call USA dial 06 + second dial tone + 022-9122.

Hotel Surcharges: No maximum percentage; check before placing call.

Things You Should Know 1. Many White Pages have **no** instructions or information in them.

2. Reduced rate and international calling Mon.—Sat., 10 p.m.—10 a.m., and all day Sunday.

3. Pay phones in restaurants, hotels, and other private places charge double or even triple for all calls.

In Amsterdam, 24-hour telephone office is open at "Telehouse," 46-50 Raadhuisstraat. (Fax and telex available, too.)

Telephone sounds you may hear:

Kind	Seconds	Description
	0 1 2 3 4 5 6 7 8 9 10	
Dial tone	▬▬▬▬▬▬▬▬	Steady tone.
Ringing	■　　　　■	1 sec. tone and 4 sec. interval.
Add more money	■	1.6 sec. tone 15 seconds before line is cut off.
Busy	‖‖‖‖‖‖‖‖‖‖‖	¼ sec. tones and ¼ sec. intervals.
Out of order	✎ ✎ ✎ ✎ ✎	3 rising tones in 1 sec. and 1 sec. interval.
or	▪▫▪▫▪▫▪▫▪▫▪	2 alternating ½ sec. tones.

Norway
Country Code 47. Telephone: TELEFON.

Pay Phones are found on streets and at transit stations and Televerket (telephone calling) offices.

Phone Directories contain White and Classified White Pages. There is an English summary with international calling information near the front of the White Pages. Find directories at Televerket offices, hotels, shops, and in phone booths.

Using Pay Phones: Use 2 kroner per 3 minutes 8 a.m.—5 p.m., weekdays (untimed at other times).

How to make a call:
   1. Pick up receiver, wait for dial tone.
   2. Deposit coins and dial.
   3. Unused coins will be refunded (if you're lucky).

Operator calls are free; many operators speak English.

Guaranteed English-language operator dial 0115.

Local directory assistance dial 0180. For long-distance operator dial 0111 and 0115.

Long distance directory dial 018.

International operator for Scandinavia dial 090. Outside Scandinavia dial 093.

Emergency calls cost 2 kroner; numbers vary city by city, but 000 emergency number has been introduced in most cities. Oslo numbers: Rescue Police dial 66 90 50; Fire dial 144 55; Ambulance dial 20 10 90.

Long-Distance Calls inside Norway, made from Televerket offices, coin phones. Dial 0 + area code + subscriber number.

International Calls from Norway, made from Televerket calling offices, coin phones. Dial 095 + country code + city or area code + subscriber number.

To call the U.S. and Canada dial 095 + 1 + area code + number.

"Dial Direct" access codes: AT&T USA Direct dial 050-12-011; Canada Direct dial 050-12-111; CCCS 050-12-050.

Hotel Surcharges: No maximum percentage.
Things You Should Know: 1. Extra charge for
operator if long-distance call can be dialed direct.
2. Reduced international rates 10 p.m.—10 a.m.
and Sundays.
3. Accented vowel letters are listed after Z in
telephone books.

Telephone sounds you may hear:

Kind	Seconds	Description
	0 1 2 3 4 5 6 7 8 9 10	
Dial tone	▬▬▬▬▬▬▬	Steady tone.
Ringing	▪ ▪ ▪	1 sec. tone and 3 sec. interval.
or	▪ ▪	1 sec. tone and 4 sec. interval.
Add more money	▪	Single buzz 20 seconds before time runs out.
Busy line	▪ ▪ ▪ ▪ ▪ ▪ ▪ ▪ ▪	½ sec. tone and ½ sec. interval.
System overload	▪▪▪▪▪▪▪▪▪▪▪▪▪▪▪▪▪	¼ sec. tone and ¼ sec. interval.
Out of order	▨▨▨▨▨▨▨▨▨	3 rising tones in 1 sec.
or		Recording.

Poland
Country Code 48. Telephone: TELEFON.

Pay Phones are found at post offices, transit stations, some hotel lobbies, outside walls of some buildings, and phone booths.

Phone Directories contain White and Yellow Pages (separate volumes in Warsaw). Books are issued every five years or so. There is no English summary or international calling information. Find directories at post offices, hotels, shops.

Using Pay Phones: Use 2—5-zloty coins per un-timed local call, for local calls only. Other coins phones accept 10- and 20-zloty coins, can be used for long-distance calls. (Note: due to high inflation, prices will be substantially raised during 1990.)

How to make a call:
1. Pick up receiver, or, with some phones, insert coin first.
2. Wait for dial tone.
3. Dial number.

Operator calls cost 20 zloty; few local and some international operators speak English.

Local information dial 911.

Local directory assistance dial 912.

Long-distance operator dial 900.

Long-distance directory assistance dial 912.

International operator dial 901.

Emergency calls are free. Police dial 997; Fire dial 998; Ambulance dial 999.

Tourist Information dial tourist information (Warsaw 21-36-73 or 27-81-31).

Long-Distance Calls inside Poland, made from post offices, from special long-distance phones. For major cities dial 0 + city code + subscriber number. For smaller cities dial 8 + city code + subscriber number. (You will hear routing tone while connection is being made.)

International Calls, made from post offices, hotels, private phones, but no pay phones. Dial 00 (for Austria, East Germany, Hungary, Great Britain, Soviet Union, Switzerland), or 80 (for Bulgaria, France, Italy, Spain, Sweden, Yugoslavia) + country code + city or area code + subscriber number. (You will hear routing tone while connection is being made.)

To call the U.S. and Canada dial 901 for operator (no direct-dial calls are possible.)

Hotel Surcharges: 10% and up.

Things You Need to Know: 1. System is overloaded and many calls are either not connected or are connected to a number other than that which you dialed.

2. Sound quality is often poor.

Telephone sounds you may hear:

Kind	Seconds	Description
	0 1 2 3 4 5 6 7 8 9 10	
Dial tone	▬▬▬▬▬▬▬▬	Steady tone.
Ringing	▪ ▪	1 sec. tone and 4 sec. interval.
Busy	▪ ▪ ▪ ▪ ▪ ▪ ▪ ▪ ▪	½ sec. tone and ½ sec. interval.
Routing tone	‖‖‖‖‖‖‖‖‖‖‖‖	¼ sec. tone and ¼ sec. interval.
Out of order	✦ ✦ ✦ ✦ ✦	3 rising tones in 1 sec. and 1 sec. interval.
or		Recording.
or		Silence.

Portugal
Country Code 351. Telephone: TELEFONE.

Pay Phones are found at post offices, bars, cafes, transit stations, and a few booths in streets and squares.

Phone Directories contain White and Yellow Pages, separate volumes in Lisbon. There is no English summary or international calling information. Find directories in post offices, phone booths, hotels, and shops.

Using Pay Phones: Use 5 escudos ($) per 3 minutes for local calls, or phone card (Credifone). Other coins accepted are 10 $, 20 $. New phones take only 10 $-, 20 $-, and 50 $-coins.

How to make a call:
1. Pick up receiver.
2. Put in coin on ramp on top of phone and wait for dial tone (may take 15 seconds).
3. Dial number. Wait up to 10 seconds for ring.
4. If busy, hang up and try later (coin returned).

Using Card Phones, found in cities and transportation centers. Buy Credifone cards at post offices, some other locations (often the nearest is shown inside the phone booth).

How to make a call:
1. Pick up receiver.
2. Insert card in telephone, listen for dial tone.
3. Dial number.
4. After call, remember to retrieve card.

Operator calls cost 10 $; a few local and many international operators speak English.

Information and local directory assistance dial 12. (Free if number is not listed in phone book—coin returned.)

Long-distance operator and directory assistance dial 090.

International operator dial 099 for Europe; dial 098 for elsewhere.

Emergency calls are free; Police and Ambulance dial 115; Fire calls are 5 escudos, number varies by town, Lisbon dial 32-22-22. Lisbon poison center dial 76-11-81, cost 10 escudos.

Tourist Information: Lisbon dial 57-50-86 or 36-33-14.

Long-Distance Calls inside Portugal, made from post offices, coin phones. Dial 0 + city code (which may include another 0) + subscriber number.

International Calls from Portugal, made from post offices, hotels, private phones.

For Europe dial 00 + country code + city or area code + subscriber number.

For elsewhere dial 097 + country code + city or area code + subscriber number.

To call the U.S. and Canada dial 097 + 1 + area code + number.

"Dial Direct" access code: Canada Direct (service to start June 1; number not available at press time).

Hotel Surcharges: A 20% surcharge or two dollars (U.S.) maximum. per call. (Portugal is a Teleplan country.)

Things You Should Know: 1. Operators answer calls in order received—be patient and wait.

2. To make collect calls, call 099 (for calls in Europe) and 098 (rest of the world) and ask for "Communicações pagaveis no destino."

3. You cannot use telephone credit cards in Portugal.

4. Mass telephone prefix changes for the year are listed at the beginning of White Pages.

5. Reduced costs for and international calls weekdays midnight—8 a.m. and all day Sunday.

Telephone sounds you may hear:

Kind	Seconds 0 1 2 3 4 5 6 7 8 9 10	Description
Dial tone	▬▬▬▬▬▬▬▬	Steady tone.
Ringing	■ ■	1 sec. tone and 5 sec. interval.
Busy	■ ■ ■ ■ ■ ■ ■ ■ ■	½ sec. tone and ½ sec. interval.
Out of order	‖‖‖‖‖‖‖‖‖‖‖‖‖‖	0.2 sec. tones and intervals.
or		Busy tone.

Romania
Country Code 40. Telephone: TELEFON.

Pay Phones are found in post offices, street booths, restaurants, hotels.

Phone Directories contain only White Pages. There is no English summary or international calling information. Directories are scarce, but can sometimes be found in post offices, hotels, and shops.

Using Pay Phones: Use 1 leu coin per 3 minutes local call.

How to make a call:
1. Pick up receiver.
2. Deposit coin in slot.
3. Wait for dial tone.
4. Dial number.

Operator calls are free; no local and some international operators speak English.

Information dial 051.

Local directory assistance: public numbers dial 030, private numbers A-L dial 031, private numbers M-Z dial 032.

Long-distance operator dial 091.

Long-distance directory dial 031.

International operator dial 071.

Emergency calls; Police dial 055, Fire dial 081; Ambulance dial 061.

Tourist Information dial 14 51 60 (Bucharest); other cities vary.

Long-distance calls inside Romania, made from post offices, hotels, private phones. Dial city code + subscriber number.

International Calls from Romania, made from post offices, hotels, private phones, dial access code + country code + city or area code + subscriber number. Special note: calls made from Romania are exorbitant, and cost per minute *rises* with length of call. First 3 minutes, 240 lei; 4th to 6th minute, 120 lei per minute; 7th to 10th minute, 160 lei per minute; 11th to 21st minute 240 lei per minute; above 20 minutes, 320 lei per minute.

To call the U.S. and Canada dial operator at 071.

Hotel Surcharges: Maximum percentage unknown.

Telephone sounds you may hear:

Kind	Seconds 0 1 2 3 4 5 6 7 8 9 10	Description
Dial tone	████████████████	Steady tone.
Ringing	██ ██	2 sec. tone and 4 sec. interval.
Busy	‖‖‖‖‖‖‖‖‖‖‖‖‖‖‖‖	3 tones and intervals per sec.
Out of order	‖‖‖‖‖‖‖‖‖‖‖‖‖‖‖‖	0.4 sec. tone and 6 - 0.1 sec. tones and 7 0.1 intervals. (1.7 sec. cycle.)
or	‖‖‖‖‖‖‖‖‖‖‖‖‖‖‖‖‖‖‖	⅛ sec. tone and 3 – 0.075 sec. pips and 4 – 0.075 sec. intervals. (⅔ sec. cycle).

Soviet Union
U.S.S.R.
Country Code 7. Telephone: **ТЕЛЕФOН**.

Pay Phones are found on the street (especially near subway stations) and at telephone calling offices.

Phone Directories do not exist in much of the Soviet Union. In Moscow, a small edition was printed in 1986; almost impossible to find. "Information Moscow," published in English every 6 months, is alternative to Moscow phone book (find it at hotel service desks, embassies, shops reserved for foreigners).

Using Pay Phones: Use 2-kopeck coin per untimed local call. Some phones accept 1- and 10-kopeck coins.

How to make a call:
1. Put coin(s) in slot before lifting receiver.
2. Wait for dial tone.
3. Dial number. (If there is a button marked "OTBET" (means answer), push it when you're answered to complete the connection.)
4. Coin returned if number is busy or no answer.

Operator calls cost 2 kopecks; most operators speak only Russian; many long-distance operators speak English.

Information and local directory assistance dial 09.

Long-distance directory dial 07.

Long-distance operator dial 8-196 (free).

International operator dial 8-194; in Leningrad dial 312-7383.

Emergency calls are free; Police dial 02; Fire dial 01; Ambulance dial 03.

Tourist Information Intourist (Moscow) dial 203-6962. Intourist numbers in other cities are found in the brochure, "Visiting the U.S.S.R.," available from Intourist.

Long-Distance Calls inside the U.S.S.R., made from long-distance telephone offices (Peregovorny Punkt), hotels, private phones. Dial code varies depending on the city. Call 07 for information.

International Calls from the U.S.S.R, made from long-distance telephone offices (Peregovorny Punkt), hotels, private phones. No international or long-distance calls from pay phones.
To call the U.S. and Canada dial operator at 333-4101. (U.S. or Canada cannot be dialed direct.)
Hotel Surcharges: Maximum percentage unknown.
Things You Should Know: 1. If no dial tone or line is busy when you lift receiver, hang up and try again immediately.
2. From hotel rooms, local calls are often free.
3. If at a public phone and someone else is waiting to use it, limit your calls to 3 minutes.
4. It may take hours to place an international call.
5. If direct dialing a number in the Soviet Union from abroad, you must dial the "0" in the city code (example: Moscow 096).
6. If making a long-distance call from a telephone office, you must prepay the call.
7. When making an international call, if you are connected to a wrong number, you will still be charged.

Telephone sounds you may hear:

Kind	Seconds	Description
	0 1 2 3 4 5 6 7 8 9 10	
Dial tone	▬▬▬▬▬▬▬	Steady tone.
Ringing	▮ ▮ ▮	1 sec. tone and 3 sec. interval.
Busy	▪▪▪▪▪▪▪▪▪▪▪▪	0.4 sec. tone and 0.4 sec. interval.
Out of order		Silence.

Spain
Country Code 34. Telephone: TELEFONO.

Pay Phones are found at the telephone company calling office (Telefonica) in each town, major department stores, bars, cafes, and booths on street.

Phone Directories contain White and Yellow Pages, separate volumes in large cities. Find directories at telephone company offices, hotels, and shops.

Using Pay Phones: Use 5-peseta (Pta) coin per 3 minutes local call. Other coins accepted 25, 50, and 100 Pta at long-distance phones. (The first card phones were installed in 1987.)

How to make a call:
1. Pick up receiver.
2. Wait for dial tone.
3. Dial number.
4. Deposit money at short tone.
5. During call, add more money quickly at short tone or you will be cut off.

Operator calls: few local operators will speak English, long-distance operators often can. Information dial 098, costs 25 Pta.

Local directory assistance dial 003.

Long-distance operator dial 025-041 + regional code (see front pages of White Pages for map with regional codes).

Long-distance directory assistance dial 003, free. International operator, free, dial:

- For Europe dial 008 (will usually answer in French, but will pass you to an English-speaking operator)l
- For elsewhere dial 005 (operator will usually answer in Spanish, switch to English).

Emergency calls cost 5 Pta; National Police dial 091; Municipal Police dial 092; Fire varies by city, see beginning of White Pages, look for "Bomberos" (Madrid and Barcelona dial 080); Ambulance varies by city, see beginning of White Pages.

Long-Distance Calls inside Spain, made from telephone company offices, coin phones marked "telefono interurbano" or "larga distancia" (these phones will accept 25-, 50-, and 100-Pta coins).

Dial 9 + area code (indicativo interurbano) + sub-scriber number.

International Calls from Spain, made from telephone company offices and coin phones marked "telefono interurbano." Dial 07 + high pitched dial tone + country code + city or area code + subscriber number.

To call the U.S. and Canada dial 07 + high pitched dial tone + 1 + area code + number.

"Dial Direct" access code: AT&T USA Direct dial 900- 990011.

Hotel Surcharges: Maximum 25%, with a min-imum of 15 Pta per call. You will be charged whether the call is completed or not.

Things You Should Know: 1. Long-distance calls may take 30 seconds after dialing to make connection.

2. Reduced international rates 10 p.m.—10 a.m. every day.

Telephone sounds you may hear:

Kind	Seconds	Description
	0 1 2 3 4 5 6 7 8 9 10	
Dial tone	▇▇▇▇▇▇▇▇▇▇	Steady tone.
Ringing	▇▇ ▇▇ ▇	1½ sec. tone and 3 second interval.
Add more money	▇	Short tone 5 seconds before time is up.
Busy	‖‖‖‖‖‖‖‖‖‖	0.2 sec. tone and 0.2 sec. interval.
Out of order	▞ ▞ ▞ ▞ ▞	3 rising tones in 1 sec. and 1 sec. interval.

Sweden
Country Code 46. Telephone: TELEFON.

Pay Phones are found at transit stations, shopping centers, restaurants, and some on streets.

Phone Directories have White and Yellow Pages—but sometimes Yellow Pages are printed on white paper (separate volumes for Stockholm). There is an English-language summary with international calling information at end of introduction in White Pages. Find directories in phone booths, hotels, and shops.

Using Pay Phones: Use two 1-krona coins per 12 minutes local call.

How to make a call:
1. Pick up receiver.
2. Insert coins, wait for dial tone.
3. Dial number.

Operator calls cost 1 krona; all operators speak English.

Local information and local directory assistance dial 90-140.

Long-distance operator and directory assistance dial 90-140.

International operator for Scandinavia dial 0013; elsewhere dial 0019.

Emergency calls are free; Police, Fire, and Ambulance dial 90000, or at pay pnones push red button below for instant connection to SOS operator (no coin required).

Tourist Information dial 221 840 (Stockholm).

Long Distance Calls inside Sweden, made from all pay phones, telephone calling offices, hotels. Dial area code + subscriber number. (Area codes are in front pages of directory.)

International Calls from Sweden, made all phones, telephone calling offices, hotels. Dial 009 + country code + dial tone + city or area code + subscriber number.

To call the U.S. and Canada dial 009 + 1 + dial tone + area code + number.

"Dial Direct" access codes: AT&T USA Direct dial 020-795-611; CCCS dial 020-795-679; MCI Call USA dial 020-795-922.

Hotel Surcharges: No maximum percentage.

Things You Should Know: 1."0" is before 1 on dial telephones—not after 9.
2. Stockholm directory has good city maps in after the Yellow Pages in Part 2.
3. Phone book listings A-Z, then å, ä, ö.
4. Reduced long-distance and international rates Mon. through Fri. 10 p.m.—8 a.m. and all day Saturday, Sunday, and holidays.

Telephone sounds you may hear:

Kind	Seconds	Description
	0 1 2 3 4 5 6 7 8 9 10	
Dial tone	▬▬▬▬▬▬▬▬▬▬	Steady tone.
Ringing	▪ ▪	1 sec. tone and 5 sec. interval,
or	▪	1 sec. tone and 9 sec. interval.
Busy	▮▮▮▮▮▮▮▮▮▮▮▮▮	¼ sec. tone and ¼ sec. interval.
Out of order	⌁ ⌁ ⌁ ⌁ ⌁	3 rising tones in 1 sec. and 1 sec. interval.
01		Operator.

Switzerland

includes Liechtenstein, Country Code 41.
Telephone: TELEFON (German),
TÉLÉPHONE (French), TELEFONO (Italian).

Pay Phones are found at train stations, airports, all post offices, most restaurants, and on streets.

Phone Directories contain White Pages, which include alphabetical classified headings, and, in a few cities, Yellow Pages. There is an English-language summary, and international calling information, near the front of the book. Find directories at post offices, hotels, shops, and phone booths. Directories for all of Switzerland are found in all of these places.

Using Pay Phones: Use 2—20-centime (French) or 20-rappen (German) coins (same coin) per 4 minutes 6 a.m.—9 p.m., Mon. through Fri. (12 minutes all other times) per local call. Other coins accepted are 10, 20 centimes, ½, 1, and 5 franc. (Some coin phones only take 20-c coins.)

How to make a call:

1. Pick up receiver, wait for dial tone.
2. Put in coins.
3. Dial number.
4. Watch display for money left on your call: add more if needed.
5. Unused coins are returned.

Operator calls cost 40 centimes/rappen; almost every operator speaks English.

Local information and local directory assistance dial 111.

Long-distance directory dial 111.

Long-distance operator dial 114.

International operator dial 191 (no charge to place a call—coins returned).

International telephone rates dial 115.

Emergency calls cost 40 centimes/rappen; Police dial 117; Fire dial 118; Ambulance dial 144.

Tourist Information dial 120 (English recording); cost 40 centimes/rappen.

Long-Distance Calls inside Switzerland, made from all coin phones, post offices, and hotels. Dial 0 + city code (1 or 2 digits) + subscriber number.

International Calls from Switzerland, made from post offices, pay phones. Dial 00 + country code + city or area code + subscriber number.

To call the U.S. and Canada dial 00 + 1 + area code + number.

"Dial Direct" access codes (charged as a local call): AT&T USA Direct dial 046-05-0011; CCCS dial 046-05-2928; MCI Call USA dial 046-05-0222.

Hotel Surcharges: No maximum percentage.

Things You Should Know: 1. No operator-assisted calls to another Swiss number are possible.

2. Operator-assisted international calls cost much more than direct-dialed.

3. Phone numbers printed on cards, letterheads, advertisements, etc. include the access code "0" as part of the area code.

4. Swiss area codes are in front of every phone book in the Red Pages in front of White Pages directory.

5. Most pay phones can be called; the number is written on or near the telephone.

Telephone sounds you may hear:

Kind	Seconds	Description

0 1 2 3 4 5 6 7 8 9 10

Kind		Description
Dial tone	▬▬▬▬▬▬▬▬▬	Steady hum.
Ringing	■ ■	1 sec. tone and 4 sec. interval.
Add more money		None—watch the display showing amount left.
Busy (line)	■ ■ ■ ■ ■ ■ ■ ■	½ sec. tones and ½ sec. intervals.
System overload	▮▮▮▮▮▮▮▮▮▮▮▮▮▮	¼ sec. tones and ¼ sec. intervals.
Out of order	♪ ♪ ♪ ♪ ♪	3 rising tones in 1 sec. and 1 sec. interval.
or		Recording.

Turkey
Country Code 90. Telephone: TELEFON.

Pay Phones are found at post offices, hotels, large stores, and on the street.

Phone Directories contain White and Yellow Pages, separate volumes in large cities. There is no English-language summary or international calling information. Find directories at post offices, hotels, and shops.

Using Pay Phones: Use small telephone token (jeton), cost 150 lira, per 3 minutes local call. Use 750-lira tokens (normal jeton) for local and long-distance calls, and 2250-lira tokens (büyük jeton) for long-distance and international calls. No other coins or tokens accepted, except some phones accept "Telecards", bought at post offices (20 units, 2,850 lira; 30 units, 4,300 lira; 60 unites, 8,600 lira and 120 units, 17,100 lira.) Due to inflation, prices are liable to rise during the year.

How to make a call:

Buy jetons or Telekarti at post offices and tobacco shops.

Automatic telephones (yellow, pushbutton dial, has slots for all three types of jetons or one slot for telecard.)

1. Check for red out-of-order light below pushbuttons: if lit, the phone is broken.
2. Pick up receiver, insert jeton or telecard gently.
3. Wait for dial tone.
4. Dial number if a local call.
5. For long-distance calls, look for light at right of instructions. When it goes out, dial 9.
6. Wait for second dial tone, then dial.
7. For international calls, when light goes out, dial 99 + country code and number.
8. If light goes on and you hear tone, add more jetons.

Operator calls are free; local operators speak only Turkish, many international operators speak English.

Local information and directory assistance dial 011.

Long-distance operator and directory assistance dial 031.

Extra-quick service at extra cost dial 091.

International operator dial 032.

Emergency calls cost 1 jeton; Police dial 055; Fire dial 000; Ambulance dial 077. Check front page of White Pages.

Long-Distance Calls inside Turkey, made from post offices, coin phones accepting large jetons (have lots of jetons) or telekarti. Dial 9 + city code + subscriber number.

International Calls from Turkey, made from post offices, hotels, private phones, pay phones accepting 750 L and 2250 L jetons. Dial 9 + dial tone + 9 + country code + city or area code + subscriber number.

To call the U.S. and Canada dial 9 + dial tone + 9 + 1 + area code and number.

Hotel Surcharges: No maximum percentage.

Things You Should Know: 1. Long-distance calls may require a long time to go through, especially if placed through an operator.

2. Reduced long-distance rates inside Turkey every day 6 p.m.—8 a.m., plus Saturdays, Sundays, and holidays. Reduced rates for international calls everyday 10 p.m.—a.m. and Sundays.

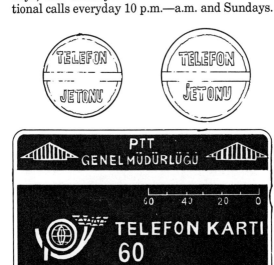

Telephone sounds you may hear:

Kind	Seconds	Description
	0 1 2 3 4 5 6 7 8 9 10	
Dial tone	▬▬▬▬▬▬▬▬	Steady tone.
Ringing	■ ■ ■	1 sec. tone and 3 sec. interval.
or	▬ ▬	2 sec. tone and 4 sec. interval.
Busy line	■ ■ ■ ■ ■ ■ ■ ■	½ sec. tone and ½ sec. interval.
System overload	■‖‖■‖‖■‖‖■‖‖	0.6 sec. tone, 4 tones and intervals of 0.2 sec.
Out of order		Ring, busy, or silence.

Yugoslavia
Country Code 38. Telephone: TELEFON.

Pay Phones are found in public places, transit stations, and on the street.

Phone Directories contain White Pages only. Some directories have English-language summary and international calling section. Find directories in post offices, hotels, shops, and some phone booths.

Using Pay Phones: Use 2800-dinar (A) token per 3 minutes local call. Some phones also accept 5,000 dinar (B) and 10,000 dinar (C) tokens. There are also phone cards (telekarta). Tokens and phone cards are sold at post offices. Due to rapid inflation, prices are liable to change during the year.

How to make a call:
1. Pick up receiver.
2. Deposit token(s) or insert phone card, wait for dial tone.
3. Dial number.

Operator calls usually free (token returned); few local and many international operators speak English.

Local directory assistance dial 988.

Long-distance operator dial 989.

For calls that can't be direct-dialed call 901.

Emergency calls (free, no token required): Police dial 92; Fire dial 93; Ambulance dial 94.

Long-Distance Calls inside Yugoslavia, made from post offices, hotels, and private homes. Dial access code + city code + subscriber number.

International Calls from Yugoslavia, made from post offices, hotels, and private phones. Dial 99 + country code + city or area code + subscriber number.

To call the U.S. and Canada dial 99 + 1 + area code + number (but not possible from coin phones).

Hotel Surcharges: No maximum percentage known.

Things You Should Know: 1. Reduced long-distance and international rates all day Sunday.
2. There is no operator service from some telephones accepting B and C tokens.

3. Area code map for Yugoslavia is near beginning of the phone book.

Telephone sounds you may hear:

Kind	Seconds 0 1 2 3 4 5 6 7 8 9 10	Description
Dial tone	■ I■ I■ I■ I■ I	0.7 tone, 0.8 sec. interval, then 0.2 sec. tone, 0.3 sec. interval.
Ringing	■ ■	1 second tone, 4 second interval.
or	■	1 second tone, 9 second interval.
Busy	■ ■ ■ ■ ■ ■ ■ ■	½ sec. tone and ½ sec. interval.
or	IIIIIIIIIIIIIIIII	0.2 sec. tone, then 0.4 second interval.
Out of order	ꞏ ꞏ ꞏ ꞏ ꞏ	3 rising tones in 1 sec. and 1 second interval.
or		Ringing tone.

Finding Public Toilets
a.k.a. the W.C.

"When you've gotta go, you gotta go."

Public toilets in Europe, however, can be elusive, difficult to find, and cost money. When you do find one, it may be lacking such necessities as cleanliness, toilet paper, sink and soap, or even a recognizable toilet. There won't be paper toilet-seat covers, either. On the other hand, in some countries, such as Switzerland, Germany, and the countries of Scandinavia, cleanliness standards are often admirable.

All over Europe, watch for the initials "W.C.," or water closet, the Victorian invention attributed to Thomas Crapper. (Other names, including one honoring the inventor, are numerous.) A request for a "bathroom" will lead you to a bathtub, not a toilet. The phrases "restroom," "men's room," "women's room," and "comfort station" are unknown. Even in Britain, there's nothing even slightly amiss in asking for the nearest "public toilet" or, for the prudish, "public convenience."

All over Europe, women will often have to wait in line, since there aren't always enough stalls to meet the demand. Therefore, if you think you may need to use a toilet in a public place and there's no line, it's probably a short-lived fluke; use it now.

Be Prepared!

Toilets in Europe are not always free or well supplied, so plan ahead. Small coins are often necessary: 2 to 5 - 10 pfennig coins in West Germany, 1 or 2 francs in France, 100 or 200 lire in Italy, 2, 5, or 10 pence in Britain. Nominal sums, but if the stalls are coin operated, you'll usually need exact change.

Some flush handles are mere knobs you pull, push, or twist. Many are on the tops of the tanks.

Some sinks, air hand dryers, and urinals turn themselves on when you place your hands (or yourself) in the say of a beam of light.

In addition, you'll be wise to carry toilet paper or paper tissues; the more primitive toilets won't provide any. In Britain the paper you find in public conveniences may be sheets like waxed paper or tiny tissues each of which is imprinted with the town name or "Government property." In southern or Eastern Europe, you may get paper with the texture of sandpaper. Soap also may be nonexistent; you may want to carry your own or packets of disposable towelettes.

Sanitary napkins are almost never found in toilets, but are widely available at pharmacies throughout Western Europe.

If you want disposable paper toilet-seat protectors, bring your own. They are not generally available in Europe.

In some parts of southern Europe, toilets in public places often lack seats.

A new item in Europe (found in France, Germany, and the Netherlands) is the "Hygrolet," which is a toilet whose seat is covered with a strip of plastic. Just touch the button, and the plastic strip spirals around the seat, providing you with a plastic-wrapped seat untouched by human bodies.

Where to Find Toilets

Airports

Major airports usually have the cleanest and best maintained of all toilets in public facilities, and they're almost always free. They'll have toilet paper, sinks with hot and cold water, soap, and even outlets for electric shavers (though not guaranteed at 110 watt, 60 cycle current; rather more often at 220 watt, 50 cycle current).

Train and Bus Stations

Most stations have public toilets, and in major cities you will have to pay to use them. Where stalls are coin-operated, since urinals aren't in stalls, they are free. If they have an attendant (often an old dragon lady), any use will cost.

Sometimes there will be only a plate on a stand or table by the door. A coin is expected but clearly not obligatory.

The presence of an attendant, however, guarantees neither cleanliness nor adequate supplies. Again, carry some tissues with you at all times.

In middle-sized stations, the toilet will usually be free and in the building; in small stations, the toilet may be an unmarked brick or concrete outhouse 50 yards or so from the station proper. If you ask for the "W.C." spoken in some variation of "toilette," you'll be pointed in the right direction. It may be locked, in which case you'll have to ask the station master for the key.

Museums, Castles, and Historic Monuments

These attractions usually have toilets. Often inadequate in number—particularly for women—they are frequently unmarked and likely to be in the basement or near the ticket vending window. You'll probably have to ask a guard or guide for directions.

Usually there will be an attendant to collect a fee. In France and southern Europe, cleanliness, toilet paper, and soap may be lacking.

Churches and Religious Shrines

Churches and religious shrines rarely have running water, let alone toilets. There are often street-side restrooms near major tourist attractions such as Chartres, Notre Dame, and St. Paul's.

Usually monasteries such as Melk (Austria) and Fontenay (France) have toilets, well marked near entrances, and before ticket takers.

Department Stores

Large department stores almost always have toilets available to the general public. Usually they are well maintained and supplied. Some are free, and those which are pay toilets usually have an attendant.

As is usual in the United States and Canada, the toilets are on an upper floor in a back corner, often near the restaurant. Look on the store directory (usually near the escalators and elevators) or ask a sales person for directions. Most will be happy to point you in the right direction.

Hotels

Large hotels invariably have clean, well supplied free restrooms, usually on the lobby floor, often near the lounge or restaurant. The trick here is to look as if you belong. While you may have to look around, just be completely self-assured. If you look as if you aren't a guest, the doorman or desk clerk may intercept you.

For example, the Paris Ritz, though well endowed with elegant, spotless restrooms, lets no men in for any purpose without coat and tie unless they are bona fide guests.

While small hotels also have toilets, the toilets are less easy to find, and you're more likely to be questioned.

The chain hotels which cater to businessmen and tourists—names familiar to you at home—are the likeliest to be hassle free. At these hotels, you probably can ask the location of toilets from the concierge or the reception desk.

Offices

Office buildings, whether private or public, always have toilets somewhere, often available to visitors. Usually they're kept at an adequate standard of repair, cleanliness, and supply, since the patrons are local and can effectively complain. Usually the facilities are on the second or third (North American) floor.

A building with a number of different businesses is more likely to have readily accessible toilets than one occupied by a single company with a front-door receptionist.

Gas Stations

Gas stations outside central cities almost always have toilets. Some require coins, but most are free. Standards can be variable; prepare for the worst—lacking supplies, dirty, and smelly. Toilets along superhighways are usually acceptably clean in northern Europe. While your patronage of the station may be expected, you'll rarely be denied use of toilets anyway.

Check around the side, though fancier stations may have the toilets in through the lobby.

On motorways, all rest stops with gas stations also provide public toilets. While most are free, stalls in Germany may require several 10-pfennig coins to enter. (Many larger rest stops also have hot showers available for a small fee.)

Bars, Cafés, and Restaurants

Bars universally have toilets available for patrons and passersby. After all, bars dispense liquid refreshment. Bar toilets can be basic; have supplies ready. Since many bars in Europe cater mainly to men, women's toilets may not be provided, or there may be only one toilet for both sexes.

You need not purchase anything. If sensitive, go to a place with outdoor tables and pretend you're a patron.

In restaurants, practices vary. Few countries are as easy as Czechoslovakia, where many restaurants have toilets in the entry vestibule. Only a few are attended and require payment. In some other countries, the toilets are off the bar or lounge.

Street-side Toilets

Public Urinals (for men only)

Small cement street-side walk-in urinals are still found in some countries, though not as common as several years ago. They may range from doubles to eight or ten stalls. Invariably they are poorly maintained though very conveniently located.

Attended Urban Public Toilets

Major cities have public toilets, usually attended. They come in all qualities, including awful, dirty, and fragrant. They are usually clearly marked, frequently underground. There will usually be an attendant; a coin will be required. Cleanliness and supplies will vary widely. Attended public toilets almost invariably close at night.

The "Sanisette" or "Superloo"

A space-age item made in France and now being exported to Belgium, Britain, and Italy is the Sanisette. These are small oval buildings on sidewalks. When you deposit the correct coin (one Franc in France, 10 Francs in Belgium, from two to 10 pence in Britain, up to 500 lire in Italy), curved sliding door opens up a compartment. A sign outside informs you that the toilet is cleaned, sanitized, and disinfected after each and every use.

As you enter and close the door you will find abundant toilet paper, and a clean sink with soap and towels. Usually, soft music plays in the background. The entire cabin may be wet from its most recent cleaning, however.

As you leave, the toilet is pulled into the innards of the building, and the cleaning begins with the whirr of brushes and the purr of machinery.

Take note: Maximum permitted use per coin is 15 minutes. (What happens when the time is up, however, is unknown.)

Toilet Word Key

Country	*Language*
Austria	German
Belgium	French
	Flemish
Bulgaria	Bulgarian
Czechoslovakia	Czech, Slovak
Denmark	Danish
Finland	Finnish
France	French
Germany	German
Great Britain	English
Greece	Greek
Hungary	Hungarian
Ireland	English
Italy	Italian
Luxembourg	French (officially)
Netherlands	Dutch
Norway	Norwegian
Poland	Polish
Portugal	Portuguese
Romania	Romanian
Soviet Union	Russian
Spain	Spanish
Sweden	Swedish
Switzerland	German
	French
	Italian
Turkey	Turkish
Yugoslavia	Various

Toilet Word Key (continued)

Toilet	Men	Women
Toiletten, W.C.	Herren	Damen
Toilette, W.C.	Messieurs, Hommes	Femmes Dames
W.C.	Heren	Dames
Клозет (Klozet)	Мужчины (М)	Женщины (Ж)
Toaleta, W.C.	Pani, Muzi.	Damy, Zeni
Toiletter, W.C.	Herrer	Damer
Pukeutuminen, W.C.	Ihmiset, Miehet	Nainen, Naisille
Toilette, W.C.	Messieurs, Hommes	Dames, Femmes
Toiletten, W.C., 00	Herren	Damen
Toilet, Loo, W.C., Convenience	Gentlemen, Men	Ladies, Women
Τοαλέττα (Toaléta)	Ανδρών (Andrón)	Γυναικών (Ghinekón)
W.C.	Ferfi	Noi
Toilet, W.C.	Gentlemen, Men	Ladies, Women
Gabinetto, W.C.	Signori, Uomini	Signore, Donne
W.C. Toilette	Messieurs	Dames
W.C.	Heren	Dames
Toaletter, W.C.	Menn	Kvinner
Toaleta	Panovie	Panie
W.C.	Homen	Senhoras
Toaleta	Oameni	Femieile
Туалет (Tooalét)	Мужчины (М)	Женщины (Ж)
Sanitarios, W.C., Servicios	Señores, Hombres Caballeros	Señoras, Damas
Toaletter, W.C.	Herrar	Damer
Toiletten, W.C.	Herren	Damen
Toilette, W.C.	Messieurs, Hommes	Femmes, Femmes
Gabinetto, W.C.	Signori, Uomini	Signore, Donne
Tuvalet, W.C., 00	Baylara, Erkeklere	Beyanlara, Kadinlara
W.C.	Man's shoe	Woman's shoe

The Hole in the Ground (Squat) Toilet

While in northern Europe and Britain toilets will
be easily recognizable, in southern Europe and
France you will often find the squat or Turkish
toilet. This is a ceramic pan resembling a stall
shower floor with a hole in the middle and two
slightly raised foot pads (or in Turkey, an oval
ceramic bowl without foot pads) set into the floor.
If you've never used one, these instructions will
probably save you some surprises.

Walk in and turn around so that your feet are
on the foot pads, or at the edge of the oval bowl.
Drop your pants or raise your dress. Squat low.
This posture will keep your clothes clean and dry,
and is the most comfortable in the
circumstances. They are surprisingly well
designed for biological functions, in spite of your
initial state of anxiety.

When you are done, do not flush until you have
pulled your clothes back on and stepped as far
away from the toilet as possible. This is because
the flush of water completely floods the pan, and
can send odd streams and sprays all over the
compartment. Leave as soon as possible.

Be especially careful if there is no flush button,
lever, or pull chain. Some of these toilets are on
timed flushing cycles. Listen for the first gurgle
of water coming down the pipes, and prepare to
move fast to avoid getting wet.

This type of toilet, particularly at train and
bus stations, may be the worst maintained of all.
You'll almost always need your own toilet paper
or tissues in these facilities.

The Bush at the Side of the Road

Often there won't be a public toilet in the
countryside when you need it. Europeans (particularly on the continent) seem to have no reservations about using whatever fields and forests
exist. The small tufts of toilet paper scattered
behind roadside rest areas give you the idea.

Lodging
Finding a Place to Stay

Almost unlimited choices for overnight rest await
you: luxurious hotels, modest inns, pensions,
castles, bed and breakfast in private homes, rental homes, hostels, campgrounds, or just a quiet
spot by the side of the road.

Many travelers, worrying about where to stay
each night, reserve ahead. At least as many
travelers trust they'll find a place to stay as they
travel. Through the judicious use of guidebook
recommendations, hotel-finding services, and
your own intuition, you'll almost always be able
to find a place to sleep at night, even without
reservations, and without sleeping under a
bridge.

If you stay longer than a week in a single
place, you can rent an apartment or home, or
exchange your home for one over there.

If you don't even want to stay in one place for
even a single night, there are sleepers on
long-distance trains.

Hotels

Hotels range from converted palaces, chateaux,
or castles to modest home-style inns.

While large hotels and many small ones are
usually called "hotel," smaller lodgings may
carry the name "albergo," "hostaria," "pension,"
"pensione," or "Gasthof." Though in some cases

there are legal distinctions (such as whether the establishment occupies the entire building or just a single floor), the end result for you is a similar room.

When you arrive, you have every right to inspect the room before you agree to take it. Many Europeans do as a matter of course, particularly at older hotels that may not have originally built for that purpose. Desk clerks are used to this, and will either take you up or just give you the key and tell you how to find it.

If for some reason you don't like the room, ask to see another or try somewhere else. Unless you have made a reservation, you're under no obligation to stay and stay. Just say thank you, or the local equivalent, and leave.

The official, posted price for a room is called the "rack rate." This is the amount that you will pay if you walk in the door without a reservation and do not request or receive any type of discount. You shouldn't pay more than this amount; only in the case of a few festivals can these rates be exceeded.

In most European countries, the rack rate of every room must be posted either at the reception desk or in the room (usually on the inside of the door), and filed with the local tourist office and/or national tourism ministry. Local tourist offices will let you look at these summaries; many will give you copies upon request.

Hotel Classification Systems

Hotels in Europe are classified by several different entities: government agencies, independent rating services, and guidebook writers.

In most countries, in both Eastern and Western Europe, the government rates every lodging establishment. Governments tend to award hotels' stars by size, luxury, whether it has a restaurant, and the number of services provided, and to some degree, maintenance standards. Design, charm, and actual comfort aren't directly rated by governments.

In generally, the least luxurious hotels are given a one-star rank, while the most luxurious receive either five-star, or in some countries, four-star-L (for luxury) ratings. The listings in each country are only directly comparable to others with an identical rating in class in the same country; some countries' three-star hotels (such as Switzerland and France) have higher standards than other countries' three-star hotels (such as Greece or Turkey).

Most countries not only rate the hotels, but also print listings of them. These listings include lots of information: name, address, telephone, fax, and telex numbers, official star rating, number of rooms, amenities such as elevators off-street parking, and, possibly most important, rack-rate prices. You can either request listings from the national tourist office before you leave home, or refer to and request copies of local listings at tourist offices throughout Europe.

Independent rating services offer impartial assessments of most of the better hotels in Europe. Many, such as the "Star Service," are found in travel agencies at home. A good travel agent may let you browse through the listings. Hotels not meeting the minimum standards of the rating service are usually not listed.

Many guidebooks also rate hotels. These ratings can range from the extensive and anonymous inspections of the Michelin Red Guides to the rather more limited and subjective listings in many other guidebooks.

Essentially, you must use your own judgment when you compare and assess the various hotel ratings.

When reading about hotels, a "luxury" hotel means it is the best in the area, with all amenities, a multilingual concierge, on-site restaurant, swimming pool, and sometimes a business center, health center, and indoor garage.

A "tourist-class" hotel is a middle-range hotel, usually but not always with bath or shower in every room.

A "budget" hotel charges a minimum cost but offers few amenities, and simple rooms, many without private bath or shower.

How Much is the Room?

Hotels, like airlines, don't charge every person the same amount for the same room. The maximum, or rack rate, is usually posted inside the door to the room. You shouldn't pay more. You will also be able to determine from the posted card whether breakfast is included.

You can often receive discounts, but will receive them *only* if you ask for them. Discounts are usually only offered when the hotel management believes that there will be empty rooms. Discount's often aren't available during the high season, during major tourist festivals, or when large conventions take up every room for miles around.

You can never lose by asking for a discount . . . but you must ask either when you make your reservation or not later than when you check in. When you're checking out, it's too late to get *any* reduction.

Hotels discounts are often offered to the following: senior citizens, low-season travelers, long-staying guests, business travelers, and almost any other category you can imagine—but you must ask for them.

Full-Board and Half-Board (Pension) Rates

If a hotel has a restaurant, you can often arrange for "Full Board" (also known as the American Plan, or Pension), which includes your room plus three meals a day. You can also arrange for "Half Board" (also known as Modified American Plan or Demi-Pension), which includes your room plus breakfast and one other meal per day. Most board arrangements require a minimum stay of three days.

During the high season, many resorts (particularly, but not exclusively, in Italy) will only accept guests who take full board. During periods of slack demand for rooms, requirements to take lunch and dinner at the hotel are almost never encountered.

When you take this option, you usually don't choose your meal off the regular bill of fare;

instead, you choose from the pension bill of fare. Sometimes there is no choice at all.

Often these meals are prepared to avoid offending finicky palates while keeping the hotel's food costs within budgets. Therefore, you'll find few strongly-flavored, hearty regional dishes, expensive lobster, or steaks when taking "Pension."

What Your Room Includes for Your Money

Twin, Double, or Single?

Remember that in Europe, a "twin" means a room with two small beds, while a "double" means a room with a double bed. Singles are sometimes the size of a broom closet.

Baths, Showers, Sinks, and Toilets

Almost without exception, all rooms have a washbasin and mirror. At budget and tourist-class hotels, towels may be small and thin and there will rarely be a washcloth. Many small hotels don't provide soap; others give several tiny bars. When there are extras, consider taking them for future use.

You may not find a toilet, a bath, or shower in the room. A room with shower or bath and toilet will cost as much as 50% more than a similar room without them. You will find the toilet and bath or shower down the hall. If the bath or shower door is not locked from the outside with a key, there is usually no charge for its use. If the door is locked and the bath or shower isn't being used, you'll have to ask the management for the key. You will be charged a dollar or two. Many Europeans often don't consider a daily shower or bath a necessity.

Shower curtains are infrequent in France and southern Europe—don't worry too much about water splashing all over the floor (some rooms have floor drains). Many bathtubs have hand-held showers on long hoses, and if not aimed carefully inside the tub, these can drench bathroom floors.

The Bidet

Many hotel rooms, particularly in France and Italy, come with an appliance known as a bidet, which look rather like a misshapen toilet. Actually, this is meant to be used to clean yourself after you have used the toilet. Fill it up with water and sit on it facing the faucets to use it properly. (Some bidets include upward spray nozzles.)

What Floor?

In Europe, building floors are numbered differently than at home. The ground floor is always just the ground floor, while the first floor is up one flight of stairs, and floors above the first floor keep in sequence with the numbers.

On elevators, you'll see the number "0" or various names and initials for the ground floor: E (Erdgeschloss) in German, G (Ground) in Britain, RC (Rez de Chausée) in French, P or PT (Pianterreno) in Italian, and so forth.

Underground floors are preceded with a minus sign (-1, -2, etc.).

Should You Have Room Reservations or Not?

How flexible are you when you travel? How important is it to you to *know* when and where you'll stay in advance? Do you need or want the comfort of a name you know? Do you want to stay at hotels or hostels, or in sleeping compartments on trains (where you can make reservations), or look for at bed and breakfasts, tiny family-run inns, and other places where reservations are not possible?

You decide whether you need to make reservations, and where you're likely to stay.

Hotel Reservations

Hotel reservations eliminate the problems and worries of finding a place when you arrive at very town or city you visit. A reservation also guarantees a room when facilities are over-crowded, which happens in heavily touristed areas or when a large convention or two takes every bed in town.

Reservations reduce your flexibility, because you're generally obligated to stay in the hotel where your reservation is made. Many hotels require a deposit, which is not generally refundable even if you don't take the room. Exceptions exist only when you give at least a few days' notice when you change your plans.

When you have hotel reservations, take paperwork for proof: any communication from the hotel, and, at larger hotels, the confirmation number. Generally, to keep your reservation, you must check in by 6 p.m., unless you specifically get the hotel's agreement in advance to arrive later.

A confirmed reservation will include the price of the room, and you won't be able to obtain any additional discounts when you arrive.

Guaranteed Reservations

At many hotels, you can guarantee a room for the night, regardless of how late you expect to arrive. When you make a reservation (whether by your-self or through an agent), tell them you want a "guaranteed reservation." You'll have to secure this by giving your a credit or charge card, and by receiving a reservation number. Remember to ask the full names of the people you speak to, and where they're located (this can avoid problems).

If you have a guaranteed reservation, the hotel guarantees that it won't let anyone else have your room, but also guarantees that you will surely be charged for the room even if you don't ever arrive.

Reserving at Hotel Chains

Large chains of hotels—many familiar at home—have numbers of hotels in Europe. In addition, there are large European chains with repre-sentatives in North America. You can make the reservations with them yourself or ask your travel agent to do it for you. You'll probably pay the same (sometimes less) if the travel agent makes the reservation for you.

Be sure to ask at the beginning, or have your travel agent ask, for any special discount to which you may be entitled.

Should a Travel Agent Make Your Reservations?

It's often easier to let a travel agent make your reservations for you, rather than to do it yourself. In addition to the convenience, a good travel agent is familiar with the system, and can make it work for you. If you make reservations directly with a chain, you can always ask for special reductions, membership discounts, etc. When you work directly with a hotel representative group directly, you'll usually be charged rack rates (though you should ask for discounts), while a good agent can sometimes offer discounts available through agency or consortium buying volume.

Some travel agents aren't aware of special deals, may not ask for lowest applicable rate, and may not pursue the effort to get you the room best suited to your needs.

Also, many small, inexpensive, family-run hotels work on such a small margin of profit that they don't offer commissions to anyone. Unless you bring lots of other business to a travel agent, the agent may not be willing to make a reservation for you for free or even if you offer to pay.

How to Make Your Own Reservations

Most hotels will welcome reservations you make yourself. There are several ways you can do it:
- Send a letter, either by mail or (if time is short) by fax, requesting the days and type of room you want. Request confirmation and ask what (if any) is required. Many hotels will accept your personal check as a deposit, and then, when pay your bill in local currency, return it to you uncashed.

- Make a phone call—remembering the time differences. If calling directly to Europe, it's helpful to speak the local language, or at least know how to ask if anyone speaks English. Know the type of room you're looking for and exact dates you'll need the room.

When reserving, ask if a written confirmation will be sent or if a deposit is required. Be sure to ask whom you're speaking with and that person's position. Many times, you can guarantee your arrival by giving your credit-card number, but surprisingly many hotels will take your word on trust. (Remember to honor the trust, so that the next person will have the same easy time you do!)

If you have reserved a room and paid in advance for it, the management is, in many countries, under no legal or ethical obligation to return any of the deposit if you can't or won't stay in the hotel on the night you paid for.

Here are some of the places where you can reserve rooms yourself, and the main counties in which they operate:

European-Based Hotel Chains

Accor (France), (800) 221-4542; fax (914) 472-0451

CIGA (Italy), U.S. (800) 221-2340;
  Canada (800) 955-2442; fax (212) 421-5929

Crest (Great Britain), (301) 593-6440

Golden Tulip (Netherlands), (800) 344-1212

Jolly (Italy), (800) 221-2626; fax (212) 757-5061

Kempinski (Germany), (800) 426-3135;
  fax (212) 745-0899

Melia (Spain), (800) 223-0888; N.Y. (800) 522-5455

Meridien (France), (800) 543-4300, fax (212) 765-1524

Penta (Austria), U.S. (800) 225-3456;
  Canada (800) 634-3421

Romantik Hotels (Germany) (800) 826-0015

Steigenberger (Germany), (800) 223-5652;
  fax (212) 752-1937

SAS (Scandinavia), (212) 841-0108; fax (212) 319-5464

Trust House Forte (Great Britain), (800) 225-5843;
  fax (212) 686- 5054

U.S.-Based Hotel Chains with European Locations

Best Western (many in Scandinavia), (800) 528-1234;
  fax (602) 957-5695

Hilton International, (800) 445-8667

Holiday Inn, (800) 465-4329

Hyatt, (800) 223-1234; fax (312) 750-8085

Intercontinental, (800) 332-4246

Marriott, (800) 228-9290; fax (301) 791-897-5045

Ramada, U.S. (800) 272-6232; Canada (800) 228-2828,
Ont. (800) 268-8930

Westin, (800 228-3000 4206) 443-5000,
fax (206) 443-8997

Independent Hotel Representatives

Europe remains the home of many individually owned or family-run hotels. Each is too small by itself to have a sales office in North America, but is interested in inducing travelers to stay there.

In order to penetrate the market, large numbers are represented in North America by hotel representative companies. These companies, mainly but not exclusively based in New York, work to obtain guests for the hotels they represent.

Hotel representatives are widely known to travel agents; many are a specialized by area, type of lodging, etc.

Though representatives are more used to obtaining listings from travel agents, they also will accept reservations from individuals. You will usually pay rack rate when you reserve yourself through an independent hotel representative, though you should be sure to ask for discounts.

Hotel representatives work for the hotels they represent on a commission basis; their services don't usually cost you directly (they are built in to the room costs even if you call the hotel directly and pay the rack rate).

Some major hotel representative groups are:

Dial Austria, (800) 221-4980

Dial Travel (Britain) (800) 424-9822

Divy Hotels (800) 363-8484

Hungarian Hotels (800) 231-8704

HSI Reservations (800) 352-6686

Jacques de Larsay Inc. (800) 223-1510

Harry Jarvinrn (800) 421-0767

Leading Hotels of the World (800) 223-6800;
fax (212) 758-7367

Marsans (Spain and Portugal) (800) 223-6114

Selective Hotel Reservations Inc. (800) 223-6764
Utell (800) 448-8355

When You Travel Without Reservations

Many travelers prefer the freedom of traveling without advance reservations. But plans need to be made, and these hints can make the search for a place to sleep easier.

1. Find your lodging by midafternoon. Since many travelers don't arrive and start looking until late afternoon, early birds have the advantage. You won't need to worry about not finding a place if you arrive at your day's destination by late morning in cities and midafternoon in the countryside. In Eastern Europe, there is a chronic shortage of hotel rooms, so be extra early during the high (summer) season.

2. Look for hotels near a major railway station. They range from humble to at least midrange in cost and amenities. Hotels on side streets will usually be cheaper than those on main access roads.

3. Look for airport hotels. These hotels, convenient for air travelers, will usually be quite expensive, international- standard hotels geared mainly to the business traveler. Some are included right on the airport grounds.

4. Look for a room-finding service to help locate a place for you. These offices are most likely found in tourist information offices in train stations and airports. This is useful only if you arrive during business hours. You will usually be charged a small fee and may have to pay for the room right there, but you're assured of a bed for the night at a known cost. While it's a pig-in-a-poke situation, if you don't like your hotel that night, you'll be able to find another one tomorrow.
Generally airport offices are less busy and often have rooms after all the rooms listed with the train station office have been taken.

You may have to insist strongly that room-finding services keep within your price range.

4. Use a guidebook you trust. Call early in the day or even the day before you arrive.

Money-Saving Strategy: Negotiating a Price

Though hotels have posted prices, when they don't expect to be full, they have an incentive to deal: an empty hotel room produces absolutely no revenue. Therefore, when you arrive in a town without a reservation and hotels aren't full, telephone receptionists and front desk clerks often have the authority to negotiate.

The best time to negotiate is late in the day you arrive. The best way is by telephone; second best is to walk into the hotel. Establish in your mind how much you're willing to pay, and then call your chosen hotel and ask if it has a room for X amount. If it does, you're in luck. Sometimes the hotel clerk may try to negotiate, at other times may recommend a less expensive hotel. Generally, aim to pay about 50% of the posted rack rate; if your offer is too low. Then you can always ask what the lowest rate is, and go from there.

You can also try to negotiate for an upgraded room or suite at the basic posted price.

Where hotels are state-owned in Eastern Europe, there's not usually a negotiation basis, especially in East Germany and the Soviet Union where lodgings must be paid for before a visa is issued.

When There's No Room

If a hotel is full and has no room for you, what can you do? That depends. If you have a reservation (and arrive in time or have guaranteed the reservation), if there's no room for you, ask the hotel staff what they'll do for you.

Occasionally the top luxury hotels will pick up the tab for a room at another hotel, or offer you a free or reduced-stay on another visit. More often, a hotel of any class will try to find another hotel for you, and, if you have a reservation, may pick up cab fare.

If the full hotel is part of a chain, or was booked through a hotel representative service, keep track of times, dates, people you talked to, so that you can take it up with the central office when you return home.

Alternatives to Hotels

Staying on the Train

Almost every European overnight train makes special provisions for sleeping, in both first class and second class. Some travelers—especially those with railpasses and tight schedules—use trains as hotels. For only a small charge, you can reserve a sleeper "Couchette." While this arrangement may not be quite as restful or roomy as a hotel or bed and breakfast inn, it neatly combines traveling and sleeping.

There are no showers and baths aboard; however, many major European railway stations have "Day Hotels" (particularly in Italy, where they are called "Albergo Diurno") to obtain showers, baths, and even short-term room rental.

Bed and Breakfast (B&B)

The usual European bed and breakfast is very different from its North American incarnation. In North America the B&B is usually a costly, meticulously restored, antique-furnished historical monument, while the European version is down to earth and quite modest in price. There may or may not be antiques, there may or may not be elegance, and, particularly at English seaside resorts, there may or may not be peeling paint, stuffy rooms, and lumpy mattresses.

Staying at B&Bs can be one of the best ways to meet the locals, since you're often treated as an honored guest in the family home.

Your hosts will also be knowledgeable about nearby restaurants, since dinner is not usually included though, sometimes it is available at extra cost. Your hosts should also know of things to see in the neighborhood, unique adventures, and public transportation—even a nearby laundromat.

B&Bs abound in Britain, Ireland, Austria, and Germany. In France they're quite scarce; the few that do exist are mainly in the foreign-influenced vacation areas such as the Dordogne valley and Alsace.

In Eastern European nations such as Czechoslovakia and Hungary, you can often arrange such at-home lodgings on the spot through the official government tourist agencies such as Cedok and Ibusz. These lodgings are much cheaper than hotels, and will give you a far more accurate view of daily life than in the hotels open to tourists. This approach is not possible in East Germany or the Soviet Union, since all lodgings must be arranged and paid for far in advance.

British B&Bs

Almost every major town and many minor ones have Tourist Information Centres which will book you a room for a small fee (often 75p or £1). Find Tourist Information Centres by following the lower-case "i" signs. You are likely to be matched with hosts who may share your interests, or at least your age and general demeanor. Costs may begin around £10 per person per night (depending on region), including a full breakfast.

Only a few bed and breakfasts in Britain have signs, so finding them along roadsides can be difficult.

Another solution in Britain is to use the annually updated AA/BTA guide, "Guesthouses, Farmhouses, and Inns in Britain," widely available in Britain as well as in North America. (AAA and CAA members can get a members' discount when buying the book at AA offices in Britain.) You can call ahead the same day for a room or reserve well in advance.

The British Tourist Authority and regional tourist information offices publish listings of B&Bs and "FarmStay" lodgings. These booklets are free when obtained outside Great Britain, but cost up to £1.50 when obtained locally.

Irish B&Bs

You can find B&Bs throughout Ireland, and tourist information offices can call around to find you a room. Registered B&Bs can be found by looking for the Irish Tourist Board's green and white shamrock "Approved" sign. Sometimes you'll also find homemade signs on unregistered homes. Costs will begin at about 10 Irish pounds per person per night, almost invariably including a full breakfast.

Austrian and German "Fremdenzimmer" or "Zimmer Frei"

Austrian and German private homes with rooms for travelers are not usually neatly listed in a book. Local tourist offices (look for the "i" sign) can refer you, but often the best solution is to wander down a country road watching for signs reading "Fremdenzimmer" or "Zimmer Frei" (room available). The cost will be modest—often less than $15 per person, including breakfast.

These guest houses seem to be most numerous in vacation areas such as the Austrian Alps and Bavaria. Often your hillside chalet room will have geranium-filled window boxes, a view of pine-clad mountains, and the breeze-borne scent of wildflowers and new-mown hay.

Dutch Pension

When you're going to spend at least a few days in one place, you might stay at a pension, some-times known as a "Kosthuis" which is like a boarding house. For more information, follow the blue and white VVV signs to the tourist informa-tion office in the town.

Scandinavian Guesthouses

Since the tourist season is short (summer), ac-commodations are at a premium. As a result, local tourist offices usually have extensive lists of private homes providing bed and breakfast.

Breakfast

The bed is only half of the arrangement. The other half will be the breakfast.

In England and Ireland, it approximates an American or Canadian style breakfast, give or take a fried tomato or two. In fact, it can be the best meal of the day.

In Germany and Austria, it can include cheese, a boiled egg, and sometimes sliced luncheon meat, along with rolls or bread, jam butter, coffee, or pot of tea or hot chocolate. In the Netherlands, northern Belgium, and Scandinavia, it can also be substantial.

In France and southern Europe, it is almost always the continental breakfast—hard rolls (rarely croissants), butter, jam packets, and coffee (sometimes tea or hot chocolate).

Baths and Showers

Baths or showers are available at virtually all bed and breakfast establishments. In Britain, they are free and may be down the hall. On the continent, baths and showers often cost extra—a matter of a dollar or two. Ask your host about bathing arrangements. (In most European languages, the word for shower is "douche," the word for bath is "bad" in German, "bain" in French, and "bagno" in Italian.)

Staying on a Farm

Many European farm families open their homes to travelers who will stay a week or two. These arrangements usually must be made in advance.

Most areas with an established farm-stay program offer books or information brochures so that you can plan ahead.

Most farm-stay programs recommend or require a minimum one-week stay, though you can always negotiable. The summer season is the high season in all areas, since this type of holiday is popular with Europeans—most of whom take their month-long vacations in July, August, and September. The weeks usually run from Saturday afternoon to the following Saturday morning.

Costs are reasonable, approximately $10-20 per person per day for bed and breakfast. Other meals are sometimes available at added costs—and must be specially requested. Some farms rent chalets and bungalows at set prices per family, while others offer campsites at modest cost.

Many countries either offer information directly, or from their national tourist offices. You can obtain more information from:

Austria
(Mainly Tirol, Salzburger Land, and Vorarlberg.) Contact:
Austrian National Tourist Offices, ask for the brochure, "Erholung auf dem Bauernhof."

Belgium
(Mainly in the Ardennes.) Contact:
Vacances à la Ferme/Fetourag A.A.B.
rue de la Science 21, Boîte 2
1040 Bruxelles, Belgium
Tel. (02) 230 72 95

Denmark
(Mainly Jutland and Isle of Funen.) Ask for "Farm Holidays in Denmark." Contact Danish Tourist Board offices or:
Tourist Association Horsens
Det Gamle Rådhus
Søndergade 26, Postboks 184
DK-8700 Horsens, Denmark
Tel. (05) 62 31 32
Telex 61668 HSTOUR DK

Finland
Ask for "Farm Holidays in Finland" from Finnish Tourist Board offices. Contact:
Farmholidays/Suomen 4 H-Iiitto
Uudenmaankatu 24
SF 00120 Helsinki, Finland
Tel. (90) 642233
Telex 1001133 FARMHO

France
Throughout France, listed in the book, "French Farm and Village Holiday Guide," available at bookstores, or from:
Gîtes de France
35 rue Godot-de-Mauroy
75009 Paris, France
Tel. (1) 47.42.25.43, ask for "Tourisme Vert"
Telex GITRURO 211470 F

Germany (West)
Throughout West Germany, listed in the annual book, "Urlaub auf dem Bauernhof," DM 8 plus postage from:
"Deutsche Landwirtschaft Gesellschaft") - Verlag GmbH
Rüsterstrasse 13
D-6000 Frankfurt am Main 1
West Germany
Tel. (069) 716 83 41
Fax (069) 724 15 54
Telex 41318G DLG

German regional organizations:
Southwestern Germany, ask for free guide:
"Urlaub auf dem Bauernhof" from:
Urlaub auf dem Bauernhof
Freidrichstrasse 43 (in person)
Postfach 5443 (by mail)
D-7800 Freiburg
West Germany
Tel. (0761) 271 33 91

Rhineland
Ask for the free guide, "Ferien auf Bauern- und-Winzerhöfen," from:
Fremdenverkehrsverband Rheinland-Pfalz e.V.
Löhrstrasse 103-105
Postfach 1420
D-5400 Koblenz
West Germany
Tel. (0261) 3 10 79
Fax (0261) 1 83 43
Telex 862395

Great Britain
Ask British Tourist Authority offices (anywhere outside Great Britain) for the free booklet, "Stay on a Farm."

Ask the Northern Ireland Tourist Board for "Northern Ireland Farm and Country Holidays," 50 pence in Britain and free elsewhere.

Farm stays are listed in the annual book, "Farm Holidays in Britain" £4.50, from:
The Farm Holiday Bureau
National Agricultural Centre
Stoneleigh, Kenilworth
Warwickshire CV8 2LZ
England
Tel. (0203) 696969
Fax (0203) 696900
Telex 31697

or in the United States as "Britain: Country Lodgings on a Budget" for $9, postpaid from:

GHF Inc.   British Gifts
P.O. Box 1224   P.O. Box 2655
Clifton, N.J. 07012   Los Angeles, Calif. 90026
Tel. (212) 765-0898

Greece
A few regional cooperatives offer stays. For information and reservations, contact:

Women's Agricultural   Agricultural Cooperative
Tourist Cooperative of   of Petra
Ambelakia   18008 Petra-Lesvos
41000 Ambelakia   Greece
Greece   Tel. (0495)   Tel. (0253) 41238
31495

Women's Agricultural Tourist Cooperative of Chio
82102 Pyrghi-Chios
Greece
Tel. (0271) 72496

Hungary
For information and reservations, contact:
Agrotours
Dob utca 53
H-1074 Budapest
Hungary
Tel. (01) 121 4021 and 142 2950
Fax (01) 253 4144
Telex 22 2710

Ireland
Almost any country B&B qualifies. Contact Irish
Tourist Board offices outside of Ireland for infor-
mation.

Italy
National and regional Agriturist offices sell a
directory, "Guida dell'Ospitalità Rurale," 18,000
lire). For further information, contact:
Agriturist
Corso Vittorio Emmanuele 101
00186 Roma
Italy
Tel. (06) 65 12 342

Netherlands
Mainly camping on farms rather than home
stays. For further information, contact:
Central Farmers' Organization
International Secretary
19 Prinsevinkenpark
2825 HK Den Haag
The Netherlands
Tel. (070) 526666

Poland
Farm stays June through September only. For
information, contact:
Gromada
Wczasow pod gruszas
Ulica Podvale 23
00952 Warswawa
Poland
Tel. (022) 311211 through -5

Portugal
For information, contact:
Direcção Geral do Turismo
Divisão do Turismo no Espaço Rural
Ave. António Augusto de Aguiar, 86
Apartado 1929
1004 Lisboa Codex
Tel. (01) 57 50 15 and 57 50 86
Fax (01) 55 69 17
Telex 13408PORTUR P

Spain
Ask any Spanish National Tourist Office for the brochure, "Vacaciones en Casas de Labranza."

Switzerland
Farm stay or chalet rental organizations are divided by language region.

For the French-speaking region, contact:
Fédération de Tourisme de la Suisse Romande
Office du Tourisme
CH-1530 Payerne, Switzerland

For the German-speaking region, contact:
Verkehrsverein Andermatt
Bahnhofplatz
CH-6940 Andermatt, Switzerland

Yugoslavia
For farm stays in Slovenia, contact:
Zadruzna Zveza Slovenije
Miklosiceva 4/I
61000 Ljubljana, Yugoslavia
Tel. (061) 211 911

Home Exchanges

If you plan to stay in one area for an extended period, you may be able to exchange your home for a similar of period of time in Europe. This offers advantage of reducing your lodging costs often to just about nothing. Also, you can often trade the use of vehicles as well as other conveniences.

Most home-exchange services publish books or catalogues (almost all for a fee) listing homes around Europe or around the world available for exchange. You must make the arrangements yourself (marked *). Other services match you up and take care of a number of technicalities, but for a higher fee (marked +). A few offer both types of services. Screening homes and clients varies from service to service—some visit every potential listing, others list any dwelling whose owner or tenant is willing to pay the fee.

To be sure that you get a satisfactory exchange, contact the service(s) well in advance. Listings will state if the exchange includes the use of a car and/or the care of gardens or pets. If you don't want to exchange, you can sometimes rent houses listed in the exchanges.

Many Europeans are interested in visiting all areas of the United States and Canada—even those areas that on the surface you think wouldn't appeal to them.

When you exchange your home, your own insurance covers your guests. If you're renting, short-term exchanging doesn't usually affect the status of your lease or rental agreement. This is because as an exchange, you're not *renting* your home, you're welcoming guests to your hospitality if you rent or lease. Be sure, however, to carefully read your own rental contract orleast where you live regarding subletting or long-term visits by non- residents.

Home Exchange Services

Global Home Exchange & Travel Service +
P.O. Box 2015
South Burlington, Vt. 05407-2015
Tel. (802) 985-3825
Exchanges throughout Europe.

The Great Exchange Ltd. +*
438 Cambridge Ave.
P.O. Box 60147
Palo Alto, Calif. 94306
Tel. (415) 424-8455
Exchanges with Britain only.

Home Exchange International, Inc. +
22458 Ventura Blvd., Suite E
Woodland Hills, Calif. 91364
Tel. (818) 992-8990
Exchanges with Paris and Milan only.

International Home Exchange Service/Intervac USA *
Box 3975
San Francisco, Calif. 94119
Tel. (415) 435-3497
Fax (415) 956-3447
Exchanges throughout Europe.

Loan-a-Home *
2 Park Lane, 6 E
Mt. Vernon, N.Y. 10552
Tel. (914) 664-7640
Longer term (up to one year or more) exchanges, especially for academic, business, and retired people.

Vacation Exchange Club *
12006 - 111th Ave.
Youngtown, Ariz. 85363
Tel. (602) 972-2186
Exchanges throughout the world.

Worldwide Home Exchange Club *
6609 Quincy St.
Philadelphia, Penn. 19119
World Headquarters:
45 Hans Place
London, SW1X 0JZ, England
Tel. (071) 589 6055
Many exchanges in Britain, scattered listings elsewhere.

Home and Apartment Rentals

If you'd rather rent than exchange, your choices are exceedingly wide. Rentals generally are available only in Western Europe; in many parts of Eastern Europe, housing is in short supply or not considered suitable for short-term rentals.

Many frequented tourist areas in Western Europe have a wide selection of farms cottages, chalets, houses, apartments, and condominiums for short- or long-term rental. Bear in mind that amenities can vary from place to place and region to region. The minimum term is usually one week, though in some areas it is up to one month in summer. Rentals almost always begin Saturday afternoon and end Saturday morning.

For decades, Europe has had a well-organized vacation rental system, with dozens of agencies arranging rentals year after year for millions. Many of the European agencies are willing to work with United States and Canadian residents as well as Europeans.

In addition, there are almost 60 holiday rental agencies in the United States and Canada. Many are affiliated with agencies in Europe. While some have strict representation agreements for European agencies, others will represent several agencies.

The coasts of Spain and Portugal, the French and Italian Riviera, Tuscany, and the Alps have thousands of rentals, ranging from cliff side apartments above Cannes to condominiums in Spain. In other areas, you can find fully-equipped manor houses, villas, and just about anything else you can conceive.

Various agencies have different ways to select rentals. You should ask how listings are chosen, what verification has been done of amenities and surroundings, and determine exact costs. Ask about the price structure: is there a non-refundable registration? What is the agency's commission? What services do they provide?

Ask about transportation: sometimes a car is included; sometimes access to sports facilities and accommodation for children may also be included. In London, many travelers have rented flats for a period of one week or more. The cost usually includes some maid service as well as a kitchen with pots, pans, and utensils. Note that many rentals in the Britain and France do not include any services, utilities, or even linens. On the other hand, in Portuguese rentals, maids as well as cooks are sometimes included.

Generally, the entire amount of the rental is payable before you take possession.

Be sure to ask who the local representative in Europe is, and whom to contact if you're not satisfied.

Costs per person for rentals are often about two-thirds the cost a hotel of equivalent quality, partly because you're not paying for expensive hotel staff, and partly because you're freed of hotel and restaurant meals.

Dozens of agencies in the United States, Canada, and Europe are listed in the book, "A Traveler's Guide to Vacation Rentals in Europe" by Michael and Laura Murphy (1990, E.P. Dutton, New York, $10.95).

Hostels

The youth hostel system provides an inexpensive network of places to sleep in almost every country in Europe. Despite the youth hostel name, there are no age limitations except in Bavaria, where the maximum is age 30.

Most hostels are affiliated with the International Youth Hostel Federation (IYHF). To use affiliated hostels, you're supposed to have an IYHF card. Most hostels have curfews; the doors are locked at night, some as early as 10:30 p.m. and others as late as 2 a.m.

Hostels unaffiliated with the IYHF, usually only found in large cities, do not require a hostel card. These hostels, though similar, are usually less restrictive and often have no curfews.

In the United States and Canada, IYHF cards are sold with a validity of one year from the date of first use (any hostel worldwide can validate the card). In the most of Europe, hostelling cards are sold on a calendar-year basis.

In the United States, 12-month hostel cards cost $10 for individuals under 18 and over 55, $25 for all others. It is available from regional youth hostel offices and from:
American Youth Hostels, Inc.
P.O. Box 37613
Washington, D.C. 20013-7613
Tel. (202) 783-6161
Telex 384777 AYHINC UD

In Canada, 12-month IYHF cards cost $12 for individuals under 18 and $21 for all others. Family memberships are $42 per year. Cards and memberships are available in large cities from regional youth hostels or from:
The Canadian Hostelling Association
1600 James Naismith Drive, Suite 608
Gloucester, Ontario KB1 5N4
Tel. (613) 748-5638,
Fax (613) 748-5706
Telex 053-3660

Some affiliated hostels in Europe are rather casual about asking to see the card. Others will sell you a hostel card on the spot, though there may be an extra fee for this, and it will be valid for the calendar year rather than 12 months.

You can buy the International Youth Hostel Handbook, Vol. I (Europe and the Mediterranean) from the youth hostel organizations, which lists all officially recognized IYHF hostels in Europe. This is important because many of the most pleasant ones are hidden in the countryside and are hard to find. Often those in cities can be found by asking at the local tourist information offices or by following the distinctive hostel logo (a leaning pine tree and house).

Hostels do have several disadvantages. All hostels close at least the sleeping areas during the day, and often the rest of the hostel as well. This makes it inconvenient if you want a midday rest or access to your luggage.

Hostel accommodations vary from four-bed rooms to a few vast barrack-like halls with dozens of beds. The sexes are usually strictly segregated in sleeping rooms and baths.

In cities, hostels can be inconveniently located and not always close to public transit.

Perhaps the worst problem an independent traveler faces (especially in summer) is tour group reservations. Youth and elderly travel groups reserve entire hostels well in advance and then arrive in tour buses. If all beds are full, you're out of luck. Making reservations for yourself is a problem, because you must usually make your reservations directly with each hostel, stating specific dates of your stay, and make full payment with vouchers with your reservation. (The International Youth Hostel Handbook lists those hostels with this requirement.) Some hostels are linked with others by telex, and will make reservations for you upon request and payment of the telex fees.

Some hostels also have inadequate facilities, such as showers. If there are enough showers, there may not be any or enough hot water. In short, though hostels are inconsistent, most don't have the problems listed above. Though the hostel book doesn't do a complete job of telling you which ones are pleasant and which ones aren't, the book and travelers met along the way are your best hostel information.

Camping

Europeans are avid campers. A dense network of campgrounds has been created all across the continent. In Western Europe, many are privately owned, and others are owned by city and town governments.

Europeans camp somewhat differently. Many campgrounds are vacation retreats, where Europeans park trailers from year to year. More settled individual campsites include potted geranium plants and window boxes, television antennas, and occasionally a cuckoo clock.

There won't be picnic tables and barbecue pits. Open fires are usually prohibited, so all cooking must be done on portable campstoves.

Most campgrounds are simply grassy areas, and people pitch tents or park trailers wherever space can be found. Campsites vary in size; at smaller ones, you may be five or ten feet from your neighbors.

Showers may cost extra. Sometimes cold showers are free, but for hot showers you must either rent the key from the management, or drop coins every few minutes in the timer of a gas water heater.

At campgrounds, you are charged per person and per vehicle each day.

If you don't want to camp at campgrounds, in Western Europe, you are supposed to get the permission of the landowner to camp in fields and forests. In Eastern Europe, you are required to stay in official campgrounds. If you don't, you won't have the police stamps on your visa, and you may be held up at the border on your way out as the guards interrogate you about your movements.

Several camping guides exist: the Michelin camping guide of France is excellent. The most comprehensive camping guide for the entire continent, however, is the multilingual "Camping + Caravanning Europa," published in Germany and most easily obtained in Europe. The AA in Britain publishes a guide for Britain and another for the continent, obtainable in Great Britain. The "Camper's Companion to Northern Europe" and a companion guide to southern Europe are published and are available in the United States by Williamson Publishing Company (Charlotte, Vt., $13.95 each).

Most camping supplies are better and cheaper in North America. The sole item campers should get in Europe is a portable stove. They are powered by small blue cylinders of propane. Return empty cylinders for exchange at virtually every campground store and most sporting goods shops in Western Europe.

Many campgrounds require you to leave identification at the office as a guarantee of payment. Passports may be demanded unless you can offer a "Camping Carnet," which serves as identification for a whole family.

The carnet is obtainable for U.S. $23 from:

The National Campers & Hikers Association, Inc.
4804 Transit Road, Building 2
Depew, N.Y. 14043-4704
Tel. (716) 668-6242

Available in Canada from:
National Campers & Hikers Association
51 West 22nd Street
Hamilton, Ontario L9C 4N5
Tel. (416) 385-1866

Carnets are also readily available in Europe from auto clubs, camping organizations, and many campground registration offices, if they are associated with the International Federation of Camping and Caravanning (FICC).

Food and Drink

You're in for a true food feast in Europe. While at home you have to seek out special "French," "Italian," or "German" restaurants, this is not necessarily so in Europe. A "French" restaurant is just another restaurant in France, an "Italian" restaurant is just another restaurant in Italy, and so forth. A "Chinese" restaurant, however, will be so marked, as will restaurants serving another nation's food.

There are many alternatives to restaurant fare. Picnics of savory cold cuts, fresh baked bread, colorful salads, and fruit of a sweetness and flavor matched only by that you pick yourself provide a tempting and economical alternative to a restaurant lunch or dinner.

The "brötchen," " sandwich" and "pannino imbottito" are the German, French, and Italian incarnations of the sandwich. These, as well as the British "ploughman's lunch," consisting of bread, cheese, and a bit of pickle or vegetable, are usually found in cafes and pubs.

The meals are, in the day's order:

Breakfast

The Full Breakfast

In most of northern Europe you will find a breakfast resembling the familiar one at home: orange juice or grapefruit, cereal, bacon or ham, eggs, toast, and coffee or tea. (Don't expect waffles or pancakes and maple syrup—though you might get a fried tomato or sautéed mushrooms.) In these nations, breakfast is a filling, nourishing (though high-cholesterol) meal that should keep you going at least until lunch if not dinner. Breakfast is almost always included in the price of the room in these countries. In general, the smaller and more rural the establishment, the better the breakfast.

In all of France and some larger hotels in Britain, particularly in London, you will be offered the "Continental" breakfast (see below).

The Continental Breakfast

In most of southern Europe, the Continental breakfast reigns supreme, and the full breakfast is usually unknown and often unavailable even at an exorbitant price. The classic Continental breakfast consists of one or two rolls (including a croissant, if you're lucky), a pat of butter, jams and jellies in small plastic packets with peel-off covers, a single cup of coffee or a small pot of tea, or sometimes hot chocolate. If you're fortunate, you might get a small slice of cheese, or, in Eastern Europe, a slice of salami and bell pepper or cucumber.

In some countries, this modest breakfast is included in the price of the room. In others, particularly France and often Italy, it is usually a two- to nine-dollar per person add-on. Surprisingly, the most expensive hotels don't always charge the most. In France, the law states that you don't have to buy the hotel breakfast when you stay there overnight. Many innkeepers won't tell you this. Regulations vary elsewhere. Unless time and convenience are crucial, or you're a very timid traveler, try to tell the innkeeper you don't want breakfast to avoid being charged. Polite firmness at the time of registration is the best approach.

In Germany, Austria, the Netherlands, and northern Belgium, the Continental breakfast is often augmented with a hard- or soft-boiled egg and a slice of cheese. Many mid-range to luxury hotels offer a buffet breakfast. The price of breakfast is usually included in the room.

The silence in the dining room at breakfast is often broken only by the clink of spoons on china and the pouring of coffee or tea. Conversations can be even more hushed than during the sermon at church.

In modestly-priced establishments, watch out for weak or warmed over coffee, yesterday's rolls, and postage-stamp sized paper napkins.

Alternatives to the Hotel Breakfast

Cheaper and better alternatives to a hotel breakfast exist. If you crave a strong, freshly-brewed cup of coffee to wake you up, go to local cafes or bars. The bar isn't the vile smoke-filled place you might expect: it is more like a pub or cafe.

The coffee will almost always be freshly brewed for you and strong. You pay by the cup; no free refills are included. If you want another cup, you place another order and pay for it. Each cup may cost as much as a dollar or even more. You can also order tea—which usually will be an inferior tea-bag blend, often presented as a cup of hot (but not boiling) water with a tea-bag on the saucer.

Many bars and cafes have rolls or croissants to complete your Continental breakfast. Since bars and cafes depend on locals for patronage, the quality is usually far better than many hotels and much less expensive.

Even better bread and pastry than in the cafes and bars can be found in the multitude of local bakeries. These usually open at dawn or by 6 a.m., whichever comes first. You'll find bread still warm, croissants and brioche, and small batches of many kinds of pastry. You will probably not see "Danish" covered with globs of pure sugar glazing, even in Denmark. You won't find doughnuts. The bakery products will be inexpensive to downright cheap.

A baker every block or two, and at least one in each hamlet who does lots of handwork to make small quantities, may be "inefficient production" from the jaundiced eye of the economist. It is, however, an enduring pleasure to locals and travelers alike.

You can get the best of a Continental breakfast by eating it as a progressive meal—that is, progress from lodgings to a cafe or bar (where in France you'll often find workers having their morning Cognac) for coffee, or tea. Next, go to a bakery for roll or pastry, and then on to the day's events.

You can also short-circuit this approach by buying some food the day before. You can even get an electric water heater for tea or instant coffee. Either buy one in Europe or buy converter plugs for the countries you're visiting. (Most European instant coffee is very good.)

Brunch

Brunch, that wonderful meal served in the late morning, especially on Sunday, does not generally exist in Europe. Luncheon is usually served no earlier than noon.

Luncheon

The midday meal is the big meal of the day in Europe, particularly in the south. The gulped odds and ends crammed down in 15 or 20 minutes is rare. The large lunch—taking two hours or more—creates the perfect prelude to a siesta. As a result, major cities such as Rome or Madrid have four rush hours: early morning, one just before lunch and one just after, and late in the afternoon when workers head for home. On the other hand, virtually no one travels in the middle of lunch hours: it can be a real pleasure as you pass through almost empty streets.

In Britain, relatively reasonably-priced midday specials are offered by many restaurants that are far costlier at night. A few of Paris' most famous and expensive restaurants have begun to follow this custom as well.

Picnic Lunches

Lunch is the best time to have a picnic. Most of Europe has wide grassy areas along the roadside and many tranquil fields, pastures, and city park benches. But don't try to picnic in Venice's Piazza San Marco! You'll be fined 50,000 Lire if caught. The possibilities are limited only by your imagination—and by local supplies. The larder is full to overflowing throughout Western Europe. Eastern Europe presents, in contrast, cheap, excellent and widely available bread, alcoholic beverages, and sometimes little else.

East or West, you have to buy everything for your picnic before the lunch hour begins. Even many large food stores and supermarkets *may* close. Small shops and groceries almost always close. Once closed, often with the rattle of metal shutters, your only nourishment will be at an eating establishment such as a restaurant, cafe, or bar.

Buying will be an adventure: you go to the bakery for bread and pastry, to the delicatessen for meats and prepared salads, and to the general store for drink and sometimes fruit. Lines may form just before closing time. Give yourself enough time to buy everything.

Your picnic will be much more pleasant if you have a beach towel or blanket to sit on. In most European city parks, it is forbidden to be on the beautiful lush grass. If you're permitted to be on it, the grass will either be scraggly, barely surviving, or very wet. In the countryside, the lush green appearance of distant fields becomes transformed upon closer view to tough grass and sometimes dirt with a sharp pebble just where you sit down.

For a Nibble or Light Lunch

If you don't want a picnic, you can usually find a reasonably-priced snack at a cafe. This will often turn out to be the crusty equivalent of a sandwich, filled with ham, chicken, or other local products. You won't find bright yellow ballpark mustard as an everyday condiment on the table, though it is often available upon request.

The coffee shop so common in the United States and Canada is virtually unknown in Europe. When found, it is likely to be in a chain hotel, catering to the business traveler.

In major cities in Western Europe, you can also find fast food if you want it.

The Evening Meal

The evening meal served in restaurants will be the very same as the luncheon in many countries such as Italy, France, and Germany. The cost will often be the same as well. Timing will vary by country: dinners may be served beginning at 6:30 p.m. in Britain and Scandinavia, 8 p.m. in France and Italy, and almost never before 10 p.m. in Spain. (In Spain, bars serve "tapas," small appetizer plates that keep your hunger at bay until dinner.) Dinner isn't rushed: it can be even more leisurely than lunch. One and a half to two hours isn't uncommon.

When a "Menu" Isn't a Menu

When you want to know what foods a restaurant offers, in Belgium, Denmark, France, Italy, the Netherlands, Spain, and Yugoslavia, do *not* ask for a "menu" unless you want the set meal. In Britain this kind of meal is called a "table d'hôte." Many times the "menu" isn't shown on the regular bill of fare but rather on a separate sheet you may have to request.

What we call a menu is called "carte du jour" in French, "lista del giorno" in Italian, and "Speisekarte" in German. On it will be "a la carte" selections as well as the "menu(s)."

A la Carte

You compose an "a la carte" meal by choosing a procession of dishes from any of the food categories. Listings will often be broken down into appetizers, soups, pastas, meats, poultry, fish, sometimes vegetables, and desserts.

Generally you are expected to order an appetizer, one main course, and usually a dessert.

Appetizers are first: the exact content will vary by country, by region, and by the style and elegance of the restaurant. In some countries, such as Italy, the appetizers (antipasti) will be a collection of a number of pickles, cold cuts, vegetables, and salami.

If soup and pasta are on the bill of fare, do not expect to order both without getting a quizzical look from the waiter.

If there is only one meat course, it can be any meat, or even a fancy salad or an omelette. It will in most cases include a garnish of vegetables.

If there are two meat courses (very common in many countries), the first will probably be fish, and will not have vegetables.

The second main course will never be fish. It will include meat, poultry, or game, and a garnish of vegetables, potatoes, noodles, or rice.

The next course can be salad, cheese, or dessert. (In Germany and Italy, salad may be served with the main course, too.) Many European salads are simple: lettuce, tomato, or cucumber dressed with oil and vinegar. The cheese tray in France offers you as many as two dozen choices from the 400 kinds produced in that country. You can try a taste of one or of all offered for the same price.

Next will be dessert. All of the better French and Belgian restaurants take great pride in their desserts and will offer you any or all of the dozen or more on the trolley or platter—and charge for only one!

Coffee—one cup, no free refills—is rarely served until after the dessert. In fact, ordering coffee will often be taken as a signal that you have finished eating, and a call for the check with it as well.

Aside from this single circumstance, the bill is rarely brought in a restaurant until you ask for it.

The Set Meal (Menu)

If set meals (menus) are offered, they will be listed on the bill of fare at fixed prices. These are

complete meals for less money than a la carte
selections. A "menu" will at a minimum provide
an appetizer, starter, pasta or soup, followed by a
main course and dessert. Often you choose one of
the two or three items offered for each course.

The most reasonably-priced "menu" is often
called the tourist menu or *dagesnätter* in Sweden
(lunch only), *menu touristique* (France), *menu
turistico* (Italy and Spain), *table d'hôte* (Britain),
and *Tagesmenu* in Germany. In some countries,
reasonably priced two- or three-course lunches
are offered. Establishments offering these special
lunches are marked, usually by decals at the
door. In Denmark, a lunch of this type is known
as *Danmenu,* in Norway (summer only) as a
Holiday Menu, and in the Netherlands as a
Tourist Menu.

Menus, or fixed price meals, always include
tax in the price. In many, if not most, the service
charge or tip will be included, too.

Other Meals

Cream Tea

This is an especially British custom, "taken"
about four in the afternoon. It includes delicacies
such as Devonshire clotted cream, cucumber and
watercress sandwiches, biscuits and scones, and
of course, tea. It is usually found in hotels or tea
rooms rather than restaurants. Look for a sign
announcing that tea is served.

Tapas

Appetizer plates are served in Spanish bars to
ward off hunger pangs until the 10 p.m. dinner.
These "tapas" can provide enough nourishment
to serve as a light dinner by themselves.

Snacks

Pastry, ice cream, coffee, fresh fruit and
vegetables are sold almost everywhere. Cafes are
good sources of snack food. Many of the rest of

items can be bought from street vendors, kiosks, and stores.

Fast Food

For centuries, street vendors have been found all over European cities and towns. Sausage-in-a-roll vendors are still plentiful in Austria, Germany and Denmark. Belgium's favorite fast food is superb fried potatoes ("Friture" or "Frituur") served salted and with mayonnaise or mustard.

You can also find such familiar American signs as McDonalds, Burger King, Kentucky Fried Chicken, and Wendy's. McDonalds, for example, has an outlet on Paris' Champs Elysées as well as a few locations scattered throughout Western Europe. A major British fast-food chain offers the local (and very different) hamburger known as a "Wimpy." Fish and chips to go are widely available, too.

Drinks with a Meal

European customs regarding beverages at meals differ widely from familiar American or Canadian customs. Remember that there may be regional variations and even variations between next door restaurants.

Tap water

You may have to ask for tap water repeatedly, and will most likely get a small juice glass or very small carafe and a juice glass. Tap water is safe to drink except in Leningrad (U.S.S.R), Turkey, and Bulgaria.

Mineral Water

You can get mineral water virtually anywhere—it is universally available in bottles and widely accepted. You can get it fizzy or still—make your preference known. Mineral waters rarely cross national boundaries. You'll find Vichy, Perrier, and Evian in France; San Pellegrino in Italy; etc. Many mineral waters are distributed only in the region of origin, making them a local pleasure.

Milk

Few drink milk with meals. You will get very strange looks if you request it. It will probably be available after a delay since it is used almost exclusively for cooking. It will often be hot.

Coffee

Coffee is not usually served during any meal except breakfast. Otherwise, it is served only with or after dessert. When requested early at lunch or dinner, it may be considered a signal to stop the meal and bring the check immediately.

When you order coffee, you get a single cup. Refills will be brought in a new cup: you will be charged. Cream and sugar are served with coffee. Decaffeinated coffee is widely available in northern Europe, less so in southern or eastern Europe.

Since the coffee roasts and beans are different from what you're used to, be ready for different flavors. In France, you'll find "café filtre," which is brewed to order, and is strong.

In much of Europe, the most common form of coffee is espresso, which is strong and served in very small cups.

In Greece and the Balkan countries you'll be served Greek (in Greece) or Turkish coffee (in the rest of the region), which has the grounds still in it. It is so thick that a spoon can almost stand upright. It is also extremely sweet, unless you request otherwise. In some countries you'll get strong coffee with lots of hot milk such as "café au lait" in France.

Some travelers, unwilling to savor the different coffee flavors, buy a jar of instant before they leave home and drink that for their entire trip. However, instant coffee in Europe, particularly West Germany, is very good. (These travelers have to ask for the hot water.)

Tea

Tea is served at similar times as coffee, accompanied with sugar and cream, but only very rarely with lemon. Tea is usually made with tea bags, even in Britain. If you want cream or milk, ask for "white" tea.

Soft Drinks

Every country in Europe has soft drinks. Restaurants will often serve very small bottles. Coke, Pepsi, and Fanta are available most places in Western Europe. In Eastern Europe, only one or the other will be available, often in tourist hotel dining rooms. Dr. Pepper and 7-Up are not generally found in Europe.

Beer

Even in the main wine countries such as France, Italy, and Spain, beer is widely available. The acknowledged beer strongholds are Germany, Netherlands, Britain, Czechoslovakia, and Belgium. Beers, like mineral waters, rarely cross national boundaries even if they do leave their region of origin. Many beers are a localized luxury. There are light beers, dark beers, and ales.

Wine

Wine is always acceptable with meals in most countries. Entire books have been written about it, including which wine best matches certain foods. In general, you'll rarely go wrong to order red wine with red meat and cheeses, and white wine with everything else. Wine in the Soviet Union, however, is almost without exception too sweet to drink with meals.

Pre-Dinner Drinks

Before a meal, people usually order an aperitif such as vermouth, anisette, or in France a "Kir," which is white wine flavored with currant syrup. Most Europeans don't precede a meal with a hard drink; in fact, outside of major hotels and tourist oriented restaurants, a dry Martini or Scotch may be difficult to find.

After-Dinner Drinks

Europeans often drink liqueurs or distilled spirits after dessert, especially at important occasions. Nationally produced products—especially local ones—are widely available. Foreign imports such as Scotch (everywhere except Scotland) or Cognac (everywhere except France) may be limited as well as very costly. Bourbon is almost totally unknown.

Smoking in Restaurants

Europeans smoke to a much greater degree than Americans and Canadians. European cigarettes—especially in France and in Eastern Europe—can be strong. European men in some restaurants also smoke cigars with their coffee or cognac. Non-smoking sections are very rare. You're likely to have to suffer. There's usually not much you can do to avoid drifting smoke, except to move to another table.

Tipping

There are three tipping methods used in Europe, two of which include the tip in the bill.

Where a service charge is included in the price of the meal, there will be a notation on the bill of fare such as TTC, Service Compris, Servicio Incluido, Bedienungsinklusiv, etc. In this case, the price you see on the bill of fare will be the price on your bill.

In other establishments, prices do not include the tip but it is still added onto the bill. This is usually shown on the bill of fare by phrases such as the French "15% service non compris" or "15% service en sus," or equivalent phrases in other languages.

In most countries where the tip is included in the bill, it is also customary to leave a few coins, up to 5% in addition to the bill.

Where a tip is not included, the standard tip should be 10% to 15% of the total bill. Leaving more (unless truly extraordinary services have been performed) will only add to the waiter's unreasonable expectations.

(Menu key begins on next page.)

Menu Key (Simplified Menu Reader)

English	*French*
"I would like . . . "	"Je voudrais . . . "
"the set meal."	"le menu."

Appetizers (Starters)	**Hors d'oeuvres**
Soup	**Potage, bisque, soupe,** créme de . . .
First course	**Entrée**

Fish, seafood	**Poissons, crustaces**
Eels	Anguille
Trout	Truite
Pike	Brochet
Salmon	Saumon
Sole	Sole
Oysters	Huitres
Frogs' legs	Cuisses de grenouilles
Lobster	Homard
Snails	Escargots

Poultry	**Volaille**
Chicken, rooster	Poulet, coq, poussin,
capon	coquelet, poularde, chapon
Duck, duckling	Canard, caneton, canette
Goose	Oie
Turkey	Dinde, dindonneau

Meat	**Viande**
Beef	Boeuf
Steak	Entrecôte, tournedos, biftec, steak
Roast beef	Boeuf rôti
Braised beef	Boeuf braisé
Pork	Porc
Ham	Jambon
Cutlet or chop	Côte de porc
Roast pork	Porc rôtie
Veal	Veau
Cutlet	Escalope
Breaded veal cutlet	Escalope à l'anglais
Veal stew	Blanquette de veau
Liver	Foie

Menu Key (Simplified Menu Reader)

German	*Italian*
"Ich möchte . . ."	"Vorrei . . ."
	"il prezzo fisso."

Vorspeisen	**Antipasti**
Suppe	**Zuppa, Minestra,** Brodo
	Primo Piatto
Fische, Krustentiere	**Pesce**
Anguille	Anguille
Forelle	Trota
Hecht	Luccio
Lachs	Salmone
Seezunge	Sogliole
Austern	Ostriche
Froschenkel	Rane
Hummer	Aragosta, gambero
Schnecken	Lumache
Geflügel	**Pollame**
Huhn, Poularde, Kapaun	Pollo, capon
Ente, Junge Ente	Anatra
Gans	Oca
Indian, Truthahn	Tacchino, pavone
Fleisch	**Carne**
Rindfleisch	Manzo, bue
Rindschnitzel, Steak	Bistecca, filetto
Rostbraten	Arristo de manzo
Rindbraten	Stufato di manzo (bue)
Schwein	Maiale
Schinken	Prosciutto
Schweinschnitzel	Costoletto, costarello
Schweinbraten	Lombata di maiale
Kalbfleisch	Vitello
Kalbschnitzel	Costoletto, scaloppine
Wienerschnitzel	Milanesa
Goulasch	Osso buco
Kalbleber	Fegato

Lamb	Agneau
Game	Gibier
Boar	Sanglier, marcassin
Venison, deer	Chevreuil, cerf
Hare, rabbit	Lievre, lapin

Side Dishes	**Garnitures**

Starches	**Fécules**
Bread	Pain
Potatoes	Pommes (de terre)
Rice	Riz
Noodles	Nouilles
Dumplings	Quenelles
Vegetables	**Légumes**
Beans	Haricots
Cabbage	Chou
Carrots	Carottes
Mushrooms*	Champignons*

Many European mushroom varieties are considered distinct vegetables, separately named.

Onions	Oignons
Peas	Petits pois
Zucchini (marrows)	Courgettes

Salad	**Salade**
Cheese	**Fromage**

Dessert (Sweets)	**Dessert**
Crepes (Pancakes)	Crêpes
Cake	Gateau
Pastry	Pâtisserie
Fruit	Fruit
Ice cream	Glace

Drinks	**Boissons**
Tap water	Eau
Mineral water	Eau minerale
Beer	Biére
Wine (white, red)	Vin (blanc, rouge)
Milk	Lait**
Coffee	Café
Tea	Thé

**Milk is not generally served at meals.*

tip included	Service compris
Tip	Pourboire
"The check, please."	"L'addition, s'il vous plaît."

Lamm	Agnello
Wild	Caggiagione
Wildschwein	Cinghialle
Hirsch	Selvaggina
Kaninchen	Lepre, coniglio

Beilagen	**Contorni**
Brot	Pane
Kartoffeln	Patate
Reis	Riso
Teigwaren	Pasta
Knödel	Gnocchi

Gemüse	**Verdure**
Grüne Bohnen	Fagiolini
Kohl	Cavolo
Karotten	Carote
Champignons*	Funghi*

Many European mushroom varieties are considered distinct vegetables, separately named.

Zweibel	Cipolle
Erbsen	Piselli
Zucchini	Zucchini

Salat	**Insalata**
Käse	**Formaggio**

Nachtisch	**Dolci**
Pfannkuchen	Crêpes, panzerotti
Torte	Torta
Gebück	Pasticceria
Obst	Frutta
Eis	Gelato, Cassata

Getranke	**Bevande**
Trinkwasser	Acqua
Mineralwasser	Acqua minerale
Bier	Birra
Wein (rot, weiss)	Vino (bianco, rosso)
Milch**	Latte**
Kaffe	Caffè
Thee	The

**Milk is not generally served at meals.*

Bedienungsinklusiv	Servizio incluso
Trinkgeld	Mancia
"Die Rechnung, bitte,"	"Il conto, per favore."
or "Bezahlen, bitte."	

Laundry
How You Can Keep Clothes Clean While Traveling

Doing your laundry is a necessary though un-glamorous chore even at home. Keeping clothes clean while traveling in a foreign land is a special challenge. If you're constantly on the move, as many travelers are, the challenge is even greater.

There is, of course, the approach of a Midwestern couple met in Venice. "At home, we just bought extra underwear and a few other clothes, and packed them in an extra suitcase. At the end of each day, we put the dirty clothes in plastic bags in that suitcase. We'll clean it all when we get back home." Their hefty plaid extra suitcase was already stuffed with bags of dirty laundry, and they still had another week to go.

Another unique approach was taken by a California couple. They saved up all the old clothes they no longer wanted, put them in an extra duffle bag, wore them in Europe, and abandoned them when they were dirty.

There are a multitude of other approaches, of course, which fall into three main categories:

1. Using the hotel sink (a technical rule violation almost everywhere, though most guests and managements ignore the rule).

2. Finding and using a laundromat.

3. Taking the laundry (and yourself) to the cleaners. Having the staff of a plush hotel take care of the laundry is a subcategory of this (and usually even less desirable, for reasons of slowness and extra cost).

If using this option, your clothes may not be treated in accordance with suggested care instructions.

The Hotel Sink

It's a rare hotel or B&B room in Europe that doesn't have a sink with hot and cold running water, even if the toilet and bath or shower are down the hall.

If you're properly prepared, you can do an acceptable washing job. You may occasionally have to carry your clothes damp in a plastic bag, but you *will* have your clothes with you. Finish drying them at your next stop (or in your car, if you're driving).

Synthetics and synthetic/natural fiber blends dry much more quickly than 100% natural fibers. If you use this method, plan on washing every day or two.

Laundry Supply Key and Check List

Many supplies are generally available at travel stores or notions counters of large department stores in North America. Many are also available at similar locations in Western Europe.

___Sink stopper plug. Some European sinks don't have stoppers (especially in Eastern Europe). Get the kind with flexible flat flanges.

___Elastic clothes line. It should have a hook or a suction cup at each end. Many are twisted double strands you pull open to hang your clothes in.

___Clothes pins (optional). Plastic is lightweight and won't stain clothes.

___Detergent. Buy single use packets of cold-water soap, such as Woolite. You can buy detergent almost anywhere in Europe.

___Detergent container. Get a secure container to prevent powder from getting all over your possessions. A series of plastic bags, one inside the other, each sealed with a "Twist'em," a is homely but effective container.

___Hangars. Inflatable hangars are preferable for wet shirts, blouses, etc.

___Plastic bags. Much of Europe is humid. Your clothes may not dry over night. Get some before you leave. More plastic bags are available in Europe when yours give out.

___Twist 'ems or rubber bands. Get them before you leave to seal plastic bags. In Europe, twists are rarely found, and rubber bands are scarce. Take extra rubber bands: they're invaluable for lots of other purposes.

What Not to Bring

1. Liquid detergent, bleach, or fabric softener. Containers are prone to leak or break, even when sealed inside a plastic bag. If you absolutely need liquid items to do laundry, buy them in Europe. Abandon liquids before flying: not all airplane holds are fully pressurized, which could result in leakage.

2. An iron. It's bulky and the electric current is different. Most hotel desks have irons for the use of guests. If you must take an iron, be sure to get an electric converter. Permanent press clothes are a better idea.

European Laundromats

The laundromat with its sloshing machines is not always the common occurrence in Europe it is in the United States and Canada. You're especially lucky if you find one in southern or Eastern

Europe. Laundromats are more costly to use than in the United States and Canada. Some European laundromats have an attendant who actually puts the clothes in and starts the machine for you.

See below for the Hot, Warm, and Cold Water Key to help you use machines or make your washing wishes known to attendants.

How to Find Laundromats

Laundromats are scarce, have unfamiliar names, and are often in unexpected locations. Rural villages will rarely have any.

Tourist information offices are *not* good places to ask for laundromat locations. You can wander the city in search of a laundry facility, but there's a better way: the telephone book. Use the classified (Yellow) pages unless noted otherwise. Most have phones. A good map will help you find the way.

Laundromat Word Key

Austria: *Waschereien* for laundries (Look under this listing for words "Waschsalon," or "Wasch -automaten," or "Selbsbedienung" for self -service).

Belgium: French areas: *Salons-lavoirs* (Brussels Classification 7325).
Flemish areas: *Wassalons* (Brussels Classification 7325). (Check English-language Yellow Page index in other areas).

Denmark: *Møntvask.*

Finland: Finnish: *Pesulatoksia* for laundries (Look for word "Itsepalvelupesula" for self-service).
Swedish: *Tvätt-och-Strykingrättningar* for laundries ("Sjalvbetjan" means self-service).

France: *Laverie automatique—libre service.*

Germany: *Waschsalons* or *Waschereien.*

Great Britain: *Laundries—Self Service.*

Greece: *Laundries—Self Service* (in English language Blue Pages), or Αυτόματο πλυντήριο (say "Autómato Plintírio"), or Λωνδρι (say "Laundry") in the Greek classified pages.

Hungary: *Musósalon.*
Ireland: *Laundries—Self Service.*
Italy: *Lavanderie a Gettone.*
Luxembourg: *Blanchisserie* (look for words "Self-Service) in the White Pages, since there aren't any Yellow pages.
Netherlands: *Wasserette* (listed in both Yellow and White pages).
Norway: *Vaskerier og stykerier* for laundries (look for words "Selvbetjenings-vaskeri," "Launderette," "Vaskeautomat," or "Myntvaskeri" for self service).
Portugal: *Lavandaria self-service.*
Soviet Union: (Ask Intourist.)
Spain: *Lavanderia* (not listed separately from full-service laundries; watch for the words "Auto Servicio" in the name or ad). Also check the White Pages under Lavanderia followed by washing machine manufacturers' names.
Sweden: *Tvätt* for laundries (look for words "Självtvätt" or "Tvättomat" for self- service).
Switzerland: German area: *Waschsalons.* French area: Yellow Pages *Blanchisserie* (for all laundries), then look for word "Salon-Lavoir" for self-service, or look in White Pages under "Laverie automatique—libre service." Italian area: *Lavanderie.*

Self-Service Laundries

Self-service laundries are most prevalent in northern Europe, particularly Britain and Scandinavia. If you find one with American-made equipment, instructions are enamelled in English on the inside of the machine lid. Other laundromats use European equipment. There are usually instructions, but not always in English. There are a few special quirks to watch out for.

Key to Better Self-Service Laundry Results

1. Have the right coins. Change machines are rare. You may have to go to a nearby store to get change. Some machines require special tokens, available at the laundry, which require specific coins or combinations of coins. Check first.

2. Have your own detergent. You can't always count on there being any for sale. Even if there is, it will be expensive. However, in some laundries, you must use the soap provided

3. Check for a spin cycle. Not all European-made washing machines have spin cycles. When the wash and rinse are complete, your clothes will be *very* wet. An "extractor," a special machine, spins the water out of your clothes. Be sure that clothes are at the bottom of the drum, and evenly distributed. Extractors frequently remove buttons or rip clothes with buttons. A separate coin will be required.

4. Watch the dryer temperature! Many dryers are permanently set for high heat. If you have permanent press or delicate clothes, take them out before they are bone dry or immediately when the machine stops.

Attended Laundromats

Some European laundromats have attendants, especially in southern Europe. In these places, you watch as the attendant runs the machine. You can even go away and come back an hour or so later and your clothes will be all clean and dry in a basket or bin. The operator usually (but not always) includes the detergent in the price. A few simple rules...

1. Specify washing and drying temperatures or your clothes will probably get a hot treatment: hot wash, hot rinse, and hot dry.

2. Be there at the end of the cycle to hang or fold your clothes. The attendant will usually not do this for you.

3. Bring your own hangars if you need them.

4. Don't plan to do your laundry during lunch. The attendant will probably close the shop for lunch.

Hot, Warm, Cold Water Key

	Hot	*Warm*	*Cold*
Universal Color code	Red	no color	Blue
Danish	Warm	Ikkesowarmt	Cold
Dutch	Heet	Warm	Koud
Finnish	Kuuma	Lämmin	Kylmä
French	Chaud	Tiede	Froid (F)
German	Heiss	Warm	Kalt
Greek	Ζεστό (Zestó)	Ζεστό (Zestó)	Κρυο (Krió)
Hungarian	Forò	Meleg	Hideg
Italian	Caldo	Caldo	Freddo (F)
Norwegian	Het	Varm	Kald
Polish	Goracy	Ciepl	Zimny
Portuguese	Quente	Morna	Fria
Romanian	Cald	Várm	Frig
Russian	Торячая	Теплая	Холодная
Spanish	Caliente	Tepido	Frio (F)
Swedish	Het	Varm	Kall
Turkish	Sicak	Ilik	Soguk

The Full-Service Laundry

Full-service laundries are much more common than in North America. Full-service laundries charge by the piece. Some may have minimum order requirements. In almost all cases, prices will be posted. Be sure that you find out the total price of the service before you commit your clothes to them.

Your clothes will not only be washed, they will usually also be ironed (even, sometimes, casual items like blue jeans). Shirts will often be starched. If you like your clothes spotless and incredibly crisp, the full-service laundry is the way to go. Most wash clothes in boiling water. Some fabrics will shrink with this treatment. Permanent press clothes will be ironed, too, sometimes collecting new creases in the process. Give temperature and ironing instructions to avoid these problems.

Prices will far exceed any other laundry method. Shirts and trousers may cost one to two dollars each, underwear up to a dollar apiece, and socks about fifty cents to a dollar a pair.

A full-service laundry also takes time—usually two or three days. Express service may be available for a surcharge. Another drawback is that the laundry methods may not exactly follow either your recommendations or the label's.

Plush hotels will also arrange to do laundry. Often the laundry is farmed out to a local laundry, and you're charged the laundry's normal high price plus the hotel's surcharge. The hotel-arranged laundry can take the most time of all. Some hotels have quick but expensive in-house laundry service. Confirm charges and time before you entrust your clothes to the hotel staff.

Dry Cleaning

There may be one or two items in your traveling wardrobe that need dry cleaning. In a few countries, there are coin-operated dry cleaners that work like (and are often located in) coin-operated laundromats. You're likeliest to find self-service dry cleaning in Belgium, France, and West Germany.

Dry cleaning will be expensive if charged by the piece, and relatively cheap at self service operations charging by the load.

Full-service laundries also can perform dry cleaning, but it will rarely be same-day service. Hotels offer similar services at higher prices and are not necessarily quicker.

Finding Dry Cleaners

Find listings of dry cleaners in the telephone book (see the Dry Cleaner Word Key below). Tourist offices can sometimes help. Many dry cleaners are located in commercial shopping districts; you may find them during the normal course of your day.

Dry Cleaner Word Key

Austria: *Chemische Reinigung.*
Belgium: French area: *Nettoyage à sec* (Brussels classification 7335).
Flemish area: *Droogkuis* (Brussels classification 7335).
(Check index at front of Yellow Pages for classification number in other areas.)
Czechoslovakia: *Ryclo Clstiaren.*
Denmark: *Renseri* or *Kemisk rensning.*
Finland: *Kemiallisia Pesulatoksia.*
France: *Nettoyage à sec.*
Germany: *Chemische Reinigung.*
Great Britain: *Cleaners and launderers* (includes full service laundries).
Greece: Καθαριστήριο (say "Katharistírio").
Hungary: *Vegytisztìtàs.*
Ireland: *Cleaners and launderers.*
Italy: *Lavandería a secco.*
Luxembourg: *Nettoyage à sec* (in the White Pages).
Netherlands: *Stomerij.*
Norway: *Renseri.*
Poland: *Czyszczenie Chemiczne.*
Portugal: *Lavandarias a secco.*
Spain: *Tintorería.*
Sweden: *Tvätt-Kemisk.*
Switzerland:
German area: *Chemische Reinigung.*
French area: *Nettoyage à Sec.*
Italian area: *Lavandería a secco.*
(No Yellow Pages, check in the White Pages.)
Turkey: *Kuru temizleme.*
Yugoslavia: *Hemisjsko cišcenje.*

Security

Guarding Against Loss and Theft
(and What to Do if It Occurs)

You, as a traveler, are an easy target. Your possessions are a desirable target to thieves since you are rich enough to travel and probably have your valuables with you. Foiling thieves consists mainly of traveling unostentatiously and keeping valuables hidden—and not taking irreplaceable valuables.

Keep all of your identification and valuables with you at all times. Don't put them in checked luggage on airplanes and trains. Don't leave them in hotel rooms; lock them in hotel safety-deposit boxes provided free to guests.

In some countries you may have to leave your passport at the hotel or campground desk for a few hours while the police make their routine checks. This is normal procedure in many countries (especially in Eastern Europe) and nothing to worry about. But don't forget to recover your passport.

Keeping a packet of papers and money on you can be difficult if you don't prepare. A number of systems to help you exist: money belts, purses, and pouches.

Many people use money belts worn under clothing. They are safe and satisfy many people, but money belts have some disadvantages: they are uncomfortable, some don't hold passports and travelers checks, and most important, the contents can be difficult to get at when you need them at border crossings, banks, etc.

Many Europeans (especially men) use pouches hung around their necks and under their shirt to keep their valuables safe. An excellent rip-stop nylon pouch with Velcro closures called the Field Office, made by the Madden Company, 2400 Central Avenue, Boulder, Colorado 80301, Tel. (303) 442-5828. It has pockets the exact size of passports and travelers checks. You can find them in bicycle shops carrying Madden bicycle touring luggage, or you can contact the company directly. It is available only in North America. Various other pouches also exist, but are not as handy for the traveler. Another way to hide valuable documents is a shoulder holster, also worn under your clothes, and sold at travel supply shops.

Many women prefer purses, which are more exposed than either of the above possibilities. See the Clothing chapter for a thorough discussion of what makes a good travel purse. If you use a purse for your valuables, wear it bandolier-style and keep it under your arm like a football, especially in crowds. In Italy (especially Naples and Rome), Spain (especially Malaga and Valencia), and other large cities throughout Europe, try not to walk on the street side of sidewalks unless you keep the purse away from the street.

Avoid keeping all of your valuables and identification all together. This way if some are lost or stolen, you aren't entirely without money or identification. For example, keep a copy of the identification page of your passport and travelers check receipt in your luggage.

Swindles and Cons

Tourists are considered fair game and a rich prize for a variety of swindles and cons. Some of them can cost you your valuables, your money, and your common sense. (Don't end up thinking, "How could I have been so dumb?")

Some of the most common thievery methods are listed below. To a great degree, being a victim very much depends on odds and luck. You can improve the odds in your favor by being aware of them and watching out for them.

The Gypsy Kid Con

Roving groups of pathetic Gypsy children come begging for coins. While some tug at your clothes, others pick your pocket or rifle your purse. Your best defense is to try to ignore them, not to let them get too close, and to keep your eyes peeled. This con is most common in Italy, southern Spain, and Paris, but can be found elsewhere in southern and Eastern Europe, too.

If they keep approaching, the best defense is to start yelling at them (in any language) something like "Get Away!" They usually leave, since unwelcome attention from bystanders and local residents is the last thing they want to attract.

The Loaded Drink Scam

If a debonaire stranger offers a drink, especially on a train, let him or her sample it first. Once in a while sleeping drugs are included—and you'll be robbed while you sleep.

The "Helpful Stranger" Con

If someone offers you a helping hand or free information, consider his or her motives. Are they being a shill for someone? Are they acting in a company of thieves? Treat these offers carefully—some people are genuinely friendly but many have ulterior motives.

Foiling Pickpockets

Put a new thick rubber band snugly around your wallet. New rubber bands won't slide easily, and the pickpocket runs a greater risk of being discovered when your wallet won't slide easily.

Don't keep your wallet in a rear hip pocket: not only is it all too apparent to thieves, it is out of your sight. Front hip pockets are better, an inside coat pocket is better yet.

Preventing Luggage Theft

Don't take the most expensive designer luggage! (Why shout about how rich you are?) Lock the luggage or tape it shut.

Put distinctive markings on all your luggage—such as ribbons, tape wrapped around it, travel stickers, even bright lavender paint. Don't make it easy for someone to mistake your luggage for theirs. Watch for luggage switches, especially at airports.

Put clear, permanent identification on the outside and have another set inside, too. You may even want to sew it into soft and semi-soft luggage. Identification should have your name and phone number. If you can use a post office box instead of a street address, it will not give potential thieves a clue that your home might be unoccupied.

Keep your luggage in sight at all times, or check it into a locker or baggage check, or with a hotel reception clerk. Watch your luggage on trains and keep your valuables with you.

If you travel on a sleeping car on a train, lock your luggage and put it between you and the wall. In this way, potential thieves will think twice before rifling through it looking for valuables, and risking awakening you, the intended victim. Some travelers have even locked their luggage to the seats or luggage racks using a cable lock.

Don't entrust your luggage to strangers, no matter how tempting the prospect.

Avoid taking more luggage than you can carry.

Securing Your Room

In many European countries, you are expected to leave room keys at the desk when you are out during the day. However, sometimes, you may wish to take the keys (and their almost invariably large handles) along with you.

Other ideas are to turn on the television or a radio, and put a "Do Not Disturb" sign outside of the door. This way any thieves may believe the room is occupied and try another one.

You should, in any case, not leave easily portable valuables on night tables or the bed. Put your camera and other small valuables in your suitcase if not taking them along. Lock the suitcase, then put the suitcase in the closet or armoire. Bear in mind that many hotel door locks have see-through keyholes and are easily picked. Don't leave your valuables in view to tempt a thief.

Remember that all hotels have a safe for small valuables. Once you hand over the valuables and obtain a receipt for them, the management is legally responsible for them. Larger hotels often have safety-deposit boxes for the use of guests.

Preventing Car Theft

In cities, consider parking your car at parking garages attended 24 hours a day (though thefts can even occur there), or taking your car to the suburbs, where theives aren't as likely to be on the prowl.

Take all valuables (especially cameras) and luggage with you, or at least make sure that nothing of value is visible. Put the valuable items in the trunk. While it is true that thieves can break into trunks, they are unlikely to do so without a clear knowledge that valuables lie inside.

Visible empty food shopping bags and newspapers don't cause that acquisitive urge to the same degree as cameras and luggage. However, it is wiser to hide them, too.

Leave the glove compartment door open with nothing visible. Then potential thieves know that there are no valuables there, and may try another car instead. Note that Italy and parts of Spain are particularly noted for thefts from vehicles with foreign licence plates.

Money Exchange Problems

When you change money, know in advance how much you're supposed to receive. Count it at the counter before you turn to leave—even if the clerk or cashier counted it out in front of you. Don't be in a hurry; even banks in Switzerland have been known to make "mistakes."

Avoid buying money on the street from someone offering a great bargain. Note that in Eastern Europe the black market is illegal, and if you're caught, penalties can be severe: long jail terms, confiscation of all your valuables, and worse. In Western Europe, there's generally no advantage to changing money on the street, but there are serious risks. Make sure you're not being given obsolete bills, play money, a single cleverly folded high-value bill covering low-value ones or plain paper, or are being set up for a mugging. If you insist on this type of dealing, keep your eyes open and count theirs before you hand over your cash. Best of all, don't deal with these types.

Overcharges and Shopping Cons

What is This Charge For?

Sometimes, for some reason especially in Italy, charges are added for items you haven't had. Ask for explanations when you need them. When caught, the clerk or waiter will gracefully shrug, and take it off the bill.

The Addition Error in the Bill

When you get a bill, add it up carefully. If you're not used to the change of currency from country to country, take a pocket calculator along. In an obvious but not obnoxious way, add the bill up and make sure it's right. If you can't read the bill, ask for a detailed explanation of every charge before paying.

Count your change, even if you aren't sure its right. (The vendor may not know that and will make it right.) Of course, sometimes it could also be an honest mistake: sometimes the error is in *your* favor.

Tax Refund Cons

When shopping and you want your Value-Added Tax refund, you must get all the paperwork then and there. Don't believe it when they say, "Everything is taken care of at the _____" (fill in airport, train station, ferry port, etc.).

Street Vendors: What Are They Really Doing?

Watch out for swindling "something-for- nothing" cons from street vendors. Be especially suspicious if you're approached on the street rather than at a market.

You give them your something (usually money) and get nothing (or worthless items) back as they quickly vanish.

If "the deal" seems too good to be true, it usually is.

Buying "Genuine" Antiquities

Occasionally you will be offered a "genuine antique," such as a Greek bronze statue, various Roman remains, and so on. In spite of the appearance of being antique, few actually are. If you buy the item, buy it for its decorative value, not its supposed antique value.

If the item really is an antique, its export is usually illegal without special government permits. Many countries, particularly in Eastern Europe, Greece, and Turkey, are especially harsh on those who try to take antiques out of the country without permission. (Sometimes the dealers have turned in the traveler!) They keep your money and receive a reward from the police as well.

Preventing Camera Theft

You can reduce the chances of losing or having your camera stolen with a few precautions. First and foremost, label the camera, its case, and camera bag with your name, address, and phone number.

It is a good idea to have a second tag where you can write down your local address—such as a hotel, campground, etc.

Learn to consider it as part of your clothing. Keep the camera strap on you at all times, especially in buses, subways, and trains. When you sit down at a restaurant or other place, put the camera on the table, or at least on your chair—preferably in your way when you get up. Better, keep it in a nondescript day pack unless actually taking a picture.

If you have a variety of camera equipment, you may wish to purchase special coats in place of a leather or metal camera case. Though heavy when full of equipment, they are less likely to be forgotten or stolen by thieves. One such coat created especially for photographers is the Domke jacket, which has lots of places for photographic equipment. It is available through camera stores in the United States and Canada.

Preventing Purse Theft

Purses are prime targets for thieves. Full of valuables, compact, and portable, purses are easy to snatch if not carefully guarded.

When walking, be sure that you hold on to the purse; if possible put it over your shoulder. Avoid clutch bags.

Be especially careful at airports, train and subway stations, museums, and in crowds.

In sidewalk cafés and restaurants, keep it in your view. Make it impossible to leave without remembering it.

In any case, keep some money and identification in a place other than your purse, so that if it is stolen or lost, you're not totally destitute.

A Note on Honesty

Most people are very honest throughout Europe, and will try to return items you accidentally leave. You can help these well-meaning people promptly return anything you have forgotten if you label your possessions with a local address (such as a hotel), however temporary. This would cause many losses to become lost *and* found-and-returned items instead.

Remember! A little prudence can go a long way.

Don't let fear ruin your travels. After all, Europe is generally safer than large United States cities, and no more hazardous than large Canadian cities.

When Loss or Theft Occurs . . .

If you lose some or all of your possessions, you obviously will try to recover or replace them. Notify anyone who can help or can limit your losses, and then try to continue.

If you lose some of your possessions, immediately call or return to the place you last had them. Surprisingly often, the item or items will be waiting for you. (This is the case even with valuable, unmarked items such as cameras, purses, coats, etc.)

If your items are stolen, report it to the police and get a report. It is true that in some places (Paris, Rome, Seville, and Madrid are reputed to be some) you will spend lots of time reporting it to officers uninterested in assisting you to recover anything. But this will not happen most of the time. If the theft occurred in a hotel room, report it to the management . . . but remember that the management is not usually legally liable for thefts from a room.

If you are mugged, the police will usually be more interested: you will still have to give statements and watch while a report is made out.

If your passport and travelers checks are stolen, take the police report to the embassy along with the photocopy of the passport page you should have, and to the travelers check replacement office. It will provide a guarantee of authenticity to your claim.

If you don't speak the language, it will often be worth while contacting the consular services division of the nearest consulate or embassy first. (Thefts are so frequent in Rome, among other cities, the United States Embassy gives theft victims a six-page handout to explain reporting procedures including instructions on what to do and where to report.) The consular staff should be able to explain the procedures to make your report to the police.

Your Embassy
How Can It Help You?

"Call the embassy!" may be one of your first thoughts in an emergency. The consular staff of your embassy can be of some help in protecting and assisting its own citizens abroad.

You should know the limits of an embassy's powers and services. For example, an appeal to an embassy will not get you out of any legal problems that occur—but will give you a list of qualified local attorneys and ensure that you're not being treated any worse than the locals.

The embassy's consular staff will render different services and provide different levels of help, depending on the subject and circumstances.

Consular officials do not provide the services of travel agents, tour guides, or bankers.

For emergency help to United States citizens, there's the State Department's Citizens' Emergency Center 24-hour response lines in Washington, D.C. The address is:

Citizens Emergency Center

Department of State

2201 C Street N.W., Room 4811

Washington, D.C. 20520

Tel. (202) 647-5225; if no answer, call the central switchboard at (202) 634-3600 and ask the operator for the "overseas citizens' services duty officer" or "O.C.S."

Missing Passports

If your passport is lost or stolen, contact the nearest embassy or consulate (see lists below for the United States and Canada).

Before you actually go, first call to find out how to file a missing passport report. Take the photocopy of the identifying front pages of your passport you should have put elsewhere in your belongings. This photocopy will dramatically speed the passport replacement process.

You are actually applying for a new passport and are required to pay the full fee. In addition, you must complete and sign a "Declaration of Lost Passport" form, and provide information about that passport to the consular official. Required information includes the passport number and date and place of issuance.

If you have the required information, your passport can often be replaced within a day or two. If you don't have this information, the renewal may take longer, since an inquiry will have to be sent to either Washington or Ottawa for a records search.

Visas

While consular officials issue visas to foreigners coming to the United States and Canada, they do not issue visas for foreign countries. They will usually be able to tell you about current visa requirements of foreign countries, however, and tell you where visas can be obtained.

The visa requirements of foreign governments for United States citizens are summarized in the brochure, "Foreign Visa Requirements," given away or available for reference at passport agencies and other places where passport applications are taken, or available for 50 cents from:

Consumer Information Center, Dept. 438T
Pueblo, Colorado 81009

Legal Problems

Laws in foreign countries can differ greatly from those of your own. While in another country, you are fully subject to its laws. The Bill of Rights and legal philosophy of "innocent until proven guilty" often does not apply. Actually, in most nations, if you come to the attention of the police, you must disprove the legal presumption of guilt.

If detained, do not expect to be informed of your rights, and do not say anything. Most, if not all, of your statements can be used against you. Avoid signing any papers, especially if they are not written in a language you know.

If you run afoul of the law, you are subject to the same laws and jails as the local residents. The embassy's consular officials will, in most countries, be contacted by the government as the result of a consular agreement. However, you should ask the police to notify the nearest consular office of your arrest. You will be visited by a consular representative. He or she will try to ensure that you're not being treated any differently than anyone else. (In some countries, this will be small consolation.) If your life and health are endangered in jail, United States citizens are able to receive a government loan for diet supplements and medical care under the Emergency Medical and Dietary Assistance Program. (In some countries, prisoners must buy most food, blankets, and clothing.)

The consular official will not give legal advice, but will give you a list of local attorneys. You will have to hire and pay for your own lawyer. Do not expect (or hope for) release as a result of the embassy's knowledge of your plight. The embassy will, however, contact your family or other persons you designate.

Medical Problems

Your embassy can provide a limited amount of help with medical problems. It will, upon request, give you a list of English-speaking doctors or dentists, listed by specialty. It will not pay for any services or medicines, however.

Travel Advisories (United States)

The Department of State issues advisories about various parts of the world to warn travelers about risks or dangers. Many advise travelers to avoid particular places because of potential dangers such as civil unrest, natural disasters, or to be aware of risks such as prevalent diseases or epidemics. Travel advisories are available for reference at all United States embassies and consulates, U.S. Passport Agencies, and are also available from the Department of State (tel. (202) 647-5225.)

In addition, the Department of State issues Travel Notices, which advise about inconveniences such as conventions booking all hotels in a city, etc. Travel Notices are available from U.S. Passport Agencies, the State Department Bureau of Consular Affairs, and from many travel agencies.

Disorders and Disasters

If you find yourself in the midst of disorders, such as a revolution or civil war, or a disaster, such as an major earthquake, contact the nearest embassy as soon as possible. The staff will give you the best available advice. In some situations, the staff will also assist with evacuations.

Notary Service

Embassy consular officers can notarize many types of documents which require this service. Generally, your passport is required for proof of identity.

Death

In case of a death abroad, the embassy staff can provide advice. Staff members can also contact the next of kin.

In some circumstances, the consular staff can also be the conservator of possessions or an estate. However, you or your relatives must pay for funeral costs.

Taking bodies home can be the subject of great amounts of difficulty and large expense—much more than merely crossing the border when alive.

Registration

If you plan to stay in any country for an extended period, or are in a country where there is public disorder or any reason that you feel you could have problems, you can and are advised to register at the nearest embassy or consulate. You can register in person or by mail or phone. Registration in person when you have your passport with you also provides proof of citizenship in case your passport is lost or stolen.

Absentee Voting (United States citizens only)

If you wish to vote while abroad, contact the nearest consular office and request information about voting. You must complete a Federal Post Card Application to register and/or request an absentee ballot from your United States jurisdiction of residence.

National Holidays

Embassies and consulates are closed on all national holidays—both of the country you're visiting and of your own country. On Independence Day and Dominion Day, most embassies and some consulates hold parties or receptions as part of their national celebration. If interested, check beforehand to find out if there will be an event open to citizens.

Mail Service

Canadian consulates and embassies will accept and hold letters (but not parcels) for pick up. Mail sent to an embassy or consulate will not be forwarded. Mail can even be sent directly or in care of the embassy or consulate through the Ministry of External Affairs in Ottawa. However, in most of Europe, having mail sent to American Express offices or Post Restante (General Delivery) at post offices will prove more convenient.

Embassies Are Not Travel Agencies

If your hotel reservation isn't honored, you need your airplane flight changed, or want tickets to a sold-out concert, do *not* contact the embassy. It will generally do no more to help you than to refer you somewhere else.

Likewise, if your baggage is mangled on the plane, or you were cheated in the flea market, or you need to cash a check, the embassy won't do much more than say, "Sorry!" and head you in another direction.

Money

When you run out of money, do not apply for a loan at the embassy or consulate. In general, it will not give you a loan, or cash a check. Rather, if you're in need, it will make (collect) calls to family, friends, or others who may be able to send money. The staff will also arrange for its transfer and payment to you.

If all of your possessions are stolen, small interim loans can also be made until money from home is received.

If you have a real emergency, are destitute, and have no one who will aid you, you may qualify for a "repatriation loan." The Repatriated American Program and its Canadian equivalent is a little-known, under-funded program that provides a loan for your direct return home. Your passport is endorsed to prevent its future use (or have another one issued) until the loan is repaid in full. In general, repatriation loans, when granted, are given to destitutes, mental patients, or seriously ill individuals with no known relatives or others willing to handle their affairs. The consular staff makes the decision about whether you qualify for a repatriation loan, and the decision generally cannot be appealed.

United States Embassies and Consulates in Europe

Embassies are usually in capital cities. Consulates are located in other cities and function as branch offices. These are offices of the United States' diplomatic representatives to other countries. The consular sections provide services to Americans.

In some countries, consular affairs are handled in a separate building with a different address.

Austria

American Embassy
Vienna
Boltzmanngasse 16
A-1091 Wien
Consular section:
Gartenbaupromenade 2,
4th Floor
A-1010 Wien
Tel. (0222) 31-55-11
Fax (0222) 370 84 86
and -7   Telex 114634

American Consulate
Giselakai 51
A-5020 *Salzburg*
Tel. (0662) 28-6-01
Telex 633164

Belgium

American Consulate
Antwerp
Rubens Center
Nationalestraat 5
B-2000, Antwerpen
Tel. (03) 225- 00-71
Fax (03) 242-06-96
Telex 31966

American Embassy
Brussels
27 boulevard du Regént
B-1000 Bruxelles
Tel. (02) 513- 38-30
Fax (02) 511-27-25
Telex 846-21336

Bulgaria

American Embassy
1 A Stamboliski Blvd.
Sofia
Tel. (02) 88-48-01
through -05
Telex 22690 BG

Американское
Посольство
1 А Стамболийский
Бульвард

Czechoslovakia

American Embassy
Prague
Trziste 15
12548 Praha
Tel. (02) 53-66-41
through -49
Telex 121196 AMEMBC

Denmark
American Embassy
Copenhagen
Dag Hammarskjölds
Alle 24
2100 København 0
Tel. (31) 42-31-44
Fax (31) 43 02 23
Telex 22216 AMEMB DK

Finland
American Embassy
Itainen Puistotie 14A
00100 *Helsinki*
Tel. (90) 171 931
Fax (90) 174 681
Telex 121644 USEMB SF

France
American Consulate
22 cours du Maréchal
Foch
33080 *Bordeaux* Cedex
Tel. 56.52.65.95
Telex 540918 USCSUL

American Consulate
7 quai Général Sarrail
69454 *Lyon* Cedex 3
Tel. 78.24.68.49
Telex 380597 USCSUL

American Consulate
12 boulevard Paul
Peytral
13286 *Marseille* Cedex
Tel. 91.54.92.00
Telex 430597

American Embassy
2 avenue Gabriel
75382 *Paris* Cedex 08
Tel. 42.96.12.02
Telex 650221 AMEMB

American Consulate
15 avenue d'Alsace
67082 *Strasbourg* Cedex
Tel. 88.35.31.04/-06
Telex 870907 AMERCON

Germany, East (GDR)
American Embassy
Neustädtische Kirchstrasse 4/5
DDR-1080 *Berlin*
Tel. (02) 220 2741
Telex 112479 USEMB DD

Germany, West (BRD)
American Embassy
Deichmannsaue
5300 *Bonn* 2
Tel. (0228) 3 39 1
Telex 885452

American Mission
Clayallee 170
1000 *Berlin* 33 (Dahlem)
Tel. (030) 8 32 40 87
Telex 183701 USBER D

American Commercial
Office
Emmanuel-Letuz-Str 18
4000 *Düsseldorf* 11
Tel. (0211) 59 67 90
Felex 8584246 FCS

American Consulate
Siesmayerstrasse 21
6000 *Frankfurt*
Tel. (069) 75 30 50, or
75 30 5-500 after hours.
Fax (069) 74 89 38
Telex 412589 USCON D

American Consulate
Alsterufer 27/28
2000 *Hamburg 36*
Tel. (040) 41 17 10
Fax (040) 44 30 04
Telex 213777

American Consulate
Munich
Königinstrasse 5
8000 München 22
Tel. (089) 2 30 11
Fax (089) 23 80 47
Telex 522697 ACGM D

American Consulate
Urbanstrasse 7
7000 *Stuttgart*
Tel. (0711) 21 02 21
Fax (0711) 24 1046
Telex 07-22945

Great Britain
American Consulate
Queen's House
14 Queen St.
Belfast BT1 6EQ
Tel. (0232) 228-239
Telex 747512

American Consulate
3 Regent Terrace
Edinburgh EH7 5BW
Tel. (031) 556-8315
Telex 727303

American Embassy
24/31 Grosvenor Square
London W1A 1AE
Tel. (071) 499-9000; Fax (071) 409-1637
Telex 266777

Greece
American Embassy
Athens
Vassilisis Sophias Bl. 91
10160 Athenai
Πρεοζεια Αμεριχανιδα
ςασσιλισιζ Σοφιαζ 91
Tel. (01) 721-2951 or
721-8401
Fax (01) 722-6724
Telex 215548

American Consulate
Leoforos Nikis 59
54622 *Thessaloniki*
Αμερικἀνικη Πρεσβἐια
Λεωφὀρος Νἰκιζ 59
Tel. (031) 266-121

Hungary
American Embassy
V. Szabadsag Ter 12
H-1054 *Budapest*
Tel. (01) 112 6450
Fax (01) 132-8934
Telex 18048 224-222

Ireland
American Embassy
42 Elgin Rd.,
Ballsbridge *Dublin*
Tel. (01) 687-122
Fax (01) 689-946
Telex 93684

Italy
American Consulate
Florence
Lungarno Amerigo
Vespucci 38
501233 Firenze
Tel. (055) 298-276
Fax (055) 284-088
Telex 570577 AMCOFI I

American Consulate
Genoa
Edificio Banca
d'America e d'Italia
Piazza Portello 6
16124 Genova
Tel. (010) 282-741/5
Telex 270324 AMCOGE I

American Consulate
Milan
Via Principe Amedeo
2/10
20121 Milano
Tel. (02) 655-7533 -6
Telex 330208

American Consulate
Naples
Piazza della Repubblica
80122 Napoli
Tel. (081) 761- 43036
Telex ICA NAPLES
720441 ICANA

American Consulate
Via Vaccarini 1
90143 *Palermo*
Tel. (091) 343-532
Telex 910313 USACON I

American Embassy
Rome
Via Veneto 119/A
00187 Roma
Tel. (06) 46741
Telex 622322 AMBRMA

Luxembourg
American Embassy
22 Blvd. Emmanuel-
Servais
2535 *Luxembourg*
Tel. 460123
Telex 461401

Malta
American Embassy
2nd Floor, Development
House,
St. Anne St., *Floriana,*
P.O. Box 535, Valletta
Tel. 623653 and 629424

Netherlands

American Consulate
Museumplein 19
Amsterdam
Tel. (020) 79 03 21
or 64 56 61
Telex 044-16176
CGUSA NL

American Embassy
The Hague
Lange Voorhout 102
Den Haag
Tel. (070) 62 49 11
Telex 044-31016

Norway

American Embassy
Drammensveien 18
0244 *Oslo* 2
Tel. (02) 44-85-50
Telex 78470

Poland

American Consulate
Ulica Stolarska 9
31043 *Krakow*
Tel. (012) 229-764
and 221-400
Telex 0325350

American Consulate
Ulica Chopina 4
Poznan
Tel. (061) 529-586/7
and 529-874
Telex 0413474 USA PL

American Embassy
Warsaw
Aleje Ujazdowskie 29/31
Warszawa
Tel. (022) 283-041 through -049
Telex 813304 AMEMB PL

Portugal

American Embassy
Lisbon
Avenida das Forças
Armadas
1607 Lisboa Codex
Tel. (01) 726-66-00
and 725-66-59
Fax (01) 726-88-14
Telex 12528 AMEMB

American Consulate
Apartado No. 88
Rua Julio Dinis 826, 3rd
Floor
4000 *Oporto*
Tel. (02) 6-3094/6
Fax (02) 62737
Telex 24905 AMCOM P

Romania

American Embassy
Bucharest
Strada Tudor Arghezi 7-9
Bucuresti
Tel. (0) 10-40-40; Telex 11416

Soviet Union

American Consulate
Ulitsa Petra Lavrova 15
Leningrad
Tel. (812) 274-8235
Telex 64-121527
AMCONSUL SU

Американское Консульство
Улица Петра Лаврова 15

American Embassy
Ulitsa Chaykovskogo
19/21/23
Moscow
Tel. (096) 252-2451/9
Telex 413160 USGSO SU

Американское Посольство
Улица Чайковского 19/21/23

Spain

American Consulate
Via Layetana 33
08000 *Barcelona*
Tel. (93) 319-9550
Telex 52672

American Consulate
Avenida del Ejercito 11,
3. piso
48014 *Bilbao*
Tel. (94) 435-8300
Telex 32589

American Embassy
Serrano 75
28006 Madrid
Tel. (91) 276-3400/-3600
Fax (91) 564-1652
Telex 27763

Sweden

American Consulate
Sodra Hamngatan 2
41106 *Göteborg*
Tel. (031) 100 590
Telex 21054 AMCON S

American Embassy
Strandvagen 101
11527 *Stockholm*
Tel. (08) 783 53 00
Fax (08) 661 1964
Telex 12060 AMEMB S

Switzerland

American Embassy
Jubilaeumstrasse 93
CH-3005 *Bern*
Tel. (031) 43 70 11
Fax (031) 43 73 44
Telex 845-912603

Embassy Branch Office
Geneva
11 Route de Pregny
CH-1292 Chambesy/
Genève
Tel. (022) 738 76 13 and
738 50 95
Telex 22103 USMIO CH

American Consulate
Zollikerstrasse 141
CH-8008 *Zurich*
Tel. (01) 55 25 66
Telex 0045-816830

Turkey

American Consulate
Ataturk Caddesi
Adana
Tel. (071) 139-106,
142-145 and 143-774

American Embassy
110 Ataturk Blvd.
Ankara
Tel. (04) 126-54-70
Telex 43144 USIA TR

American Consulate
Istanbul
104-108 Mesrutiyet
Caddesi
Tepabasi
Tel. (01) 151-36-02
Telex 24077 ATOT-TR

American Consulate
92 Ataturk Caddesi
Izmir
Tel. (051) 149-426
and 131-369

Yugoslavia

American Embassy
Belgrade
Kneza Milosa 50
11000 Beograd
Tel. (011) 645-655
Fax (011) 645-221
Telex 11529 AMEMBA
YU

American Consulate
(Americki General
Konzulat)
Brace Kavurica 2
Zagreb
Tel. (041) 444 800
Telex 21180 UY AMCON

Canadian Embassies, High Commissions, and Consulates in Europe

Canadian embassies and high commissions (similar to embassies, but in Commonwealth nations) are the offices of the chief Canadian representatives to another country. Consulates are like branch offices of the embassy.

If you need help, ask to speak to the Consular Officer.

No passports are issued at consulates marked with an asterisk (*).

Austria
Canadian Embassy
Vienna
Dr. Karl Lüger-Ring
A-1010 Wien
Tel. (0222) 63-66-26 and
63-36-91

Belgium
Canadian Embassy
Brussels
2 avenue de Tervuren
1040 Bruxelles
Tel. (02) 735-60-40

Czechoslovakia
Canadian Embassy
Prague
Mickiweiczova 6
Praha 6
Tel. (02) 32-69-41

Denmark
Canadian Embassy
Copenhagen
Kr. Bernikowsgade 1
1105 København
Tel. (01) 12-22-99

Finland
Canadian Embassy
Pohjois Esplanadi 25B, P.O. Box 779
0100 *Helsinki* 10
Tel. (90) 171 141

France
Canadian Consulate
Edifice Ponnel, 3ième
etage,   Part-Dieu,
Coin Bonnel et Garibaldi
74 rue de Bonnel,
69003 *Lyon*
Tel. 72.61.15.25

Canadian Embassy
Consular Section
35 avenue Montaigne
75008 *Paris*
Tel. 47.23.01.01

Germany, West (FRG)
Canadian Consulate
Europa-Center
1000 *Berlin* 30
Tel. (030) 2 61 11 61/2

Canadian Embassy
Consular Section
Godesberger Allee 119
5300 *Bonn* 2
Tel. (0228) 81 00 60

Canadian Consulate
Immermannstrasse 3
Postfach 4729
4000 *Düsseldorf* 1
Tel. (0211) 35 34 71

Canadian Consulate
Munich
Maximilianplatz 9
8000 München 2
Tel. (089) 55 85 31

Great Britain
Canadian Consulate*
Mackay, Murray &
Spens
151 St. Vincent St.
Glasgow G2 5NJ
Scotland
Tel. (041) 248 5011

Canadian High
Commission
Macdonald House
1 Grosvenor Square
London W1X 0AB
Tel. (01) 629-9492

Greece
Canadian Embassy
Athens
4 Ioannou Ghennadiou
St.
Athenai 140
Πρεοζεια Καεαδοζ
4 Ιωαννον Γενναδιον
Tel. (021) 739-511/19

Hungary
Canadian Embassy
Budakeszi Utca 32
H-1021 *Budapest*
Tel. (01) 138-7312 and
138-7711/2

Ireland
Canadian Embassy
65 St. Stephens Green
Dublin 2
Tel. (01) 781-988

Italy
Canadian Consulate
Milan
Via Vittor Pisani 19
20124 Milano
Tel. (02) 669-8060
and 669-7451/5

Canadian Embassy
Rome
Consular Section
Via Zara 30
00198 Roma
Tel. (06) 844-1841/5

Malta
Canadian Consulate*
103 Archbishop St.
Valletta
Tel. 233121/6

Netherlands
Canadian Embassy
The Hague
Sophialaan 7
2514 JP Den Haag
Tel. (070) 61 41 11

Norway
Canadian Embassy
Oscar's Gate 20
Oslo 3
Tel. (02) 46-69-55/9

Poland
Canadian Embassy
Warsaw
Ulica Matejki 1/5
00481 Warszawa
Tel. (022) 29-80-51

Romania
Canadian Embassy
Bucharest
36 Nicolae Iorga (in
person)
Post Office 22, Box 2966
(mail)
71118 Bucuresti
Tel. (0) 50-62-90
and 50-63-30

Portugal
Canadian Embassy
Lisbon
Rua Rosa Araujo 2, 6th
Floor
1200 Lisboa 2
Tel. (01) 56-38-21

Soviet Union
Canadian Embassy
23 Starokonyushenny
Pereulok
Moscow, U.S.S.R.
Tel. (096) 241-9155,
241-3067, and 241-5070
Канадское Посольство
23 Староконюшенный
переулок

Spain
Canadian Consulate*
Via Augusta 125 08006
Barcelona
Tel. (93) 209-0634

Canadian Embassy
Edificio Goya Calle
Nuñez de Balboa 35 (in
person)
Apartado Postal 587
(mail) *Madrid*
Tel. (91) 431-4300

Canadian Consulate*
Edificio Horizonte
Plaza de la Malagueta 3
(in person)
Apartado Postal 99
(mail)
29016 *Malaga*
Tel. (952) 22 33 46

Canadian Consulate*
Seville
Avenida de la
Constitución 24
3 Centro Pasaje de los
Seises
41001 Sevilla
Tel. (945) 22 94 13

Sweden
Canadian Embassy
Tegelbacken 4, 7th Floor (in person)
P.O. Box 16129
S-10323 *Stockholm* 16
Tel. (08) 23-79-20

Switzerland
Canadian Embassy
88 Kirchenfeldstrasse
P.O. Box 3000
CH-3006 *Bern*
Tel. (031) 44-63-81/5

Canadian Mission
Geneva
Consular Section
10A Avenue de Budé
CH-1201 Genéve
Tel. (022) 33-90-00

Turkey
Canadian Embassy
Nenehatun Caddesi 75
Gaziosmanpasa,
Ankara
Tel. 27-58-03 through -05

Canadian Consulate*
Büyükdere Caddesi
107/3
Begün Han Gayrettepe
Istanbul
Tel. (1) 172-5174

Yugoslavia
Canadian Embassy
Belgrade
Kneza Milosa 75
11000 Beograd
Tel. (011) 644 666

Open and Closed
Business Hours, Weekends, and Holidays

Business hours in many European countries are radically different from those in the United States and Canada; furthermore, they differ widely between countries as well, reflecting different histories, cultures, and attitudes.

The country-by-country key below provides details. However, several general rules are worth stating at the beginning.

Sundays

Sunday is a day of rest in most of Europe. As such, some things are virtually impossible to do on Sunday. For example, banks, post offices, many shops and even food stores and restaurants are tightly closed every Sunday.

Frequently flea markets take place on Sunday, when there are few other entertainments.

However, Monday is the usual closing day in much of France.

National Holidays

National holidays can be a delight, often providing unexpected parades and pageantry. Holidays can also difficult for travelers, because trains and hotels are full to capacity, and sometimes more.

Religious holidays, particularly Christmas, are celebrated in most countries. When a country is part Catholic and part Protestant, such as West Germany, some religious holidays may be observed only in some sections of the country.

Some countries have lots of holidays, while Britain and Ireland have so few traditional holidays that they have declared Bank Holidays, when the whole country goes on long weekend vacations.

Common religious holidays found in more than one country are:

January 6: Epiphany

Maundy Thursday (Thursday before Easter)

Good Friday (Friday before Easter)

Easter Monday (Monday after Easter)

Ascension Day (five weeks after Easter during the week)

Eighth Sunday and Monday after Easter (Whit Monday; Corpus Christi)

August 15: Assumption Day (the biggest holiday of the year: try to avoid travel or finding lodgings immediately before or on this day)

November 1: All Saints' Day

Immaculate Conception Day (early December)

December 25: Christmas

December 26: Boxing Day or St. Stephen's Day.

Common holidays not of religious origin:

January 1: New Year's Day

May 1: Labor Day

Daily Business Hours

The climate as well as the culture determine when businesses, banks, and restaurants are open. For example, in Yugoslavia, most businesses are closed from noon until 4 or 5 in the afternoon.

In contrast, in Norway, businesses are open during the day, but often close relatively early.

When climates and cultures differ widely in a single country, there may be several different patterns.

Usually, banks are open for less of the day than other businesses.

Government offices, including post offices, are often on different schedules from shops or banks.

Department stores and sometimes supermarkets often remain open during lunch, when almost all other stores are closed.

Daylight Saving Time

In summer, most of Europe goes onto Daylight Saving Time. However, remember that each country starts on a different day in the spring and ends on a different day in the fall.

Strikes

Europe has its share of strikes. In some countries, such as Germany, Switzerland, and Scandinavia, the likelihood of being inconvenienced by strikes is small to nonexistent. In others, such as Belgium, strikes are rarely a problem to travelers.

In still other countries, primarily Italy, Britain, Spain, and France, strikes can affect public transportation. In Britain, strikes are usually for the duration of the dispute; in Portugal, Spain and France, strikes usually last for 24 hours.

Special Notes for Italy

Sometimes in Italy, strikes—particularly on railways—last only for one hour, or one day. It is rather a surprise to come to a halt in the middle of nowhere, while the train crews get off the train and joke among themselves. At the end of the hour, they all climb aboard, and the train is one hour late along the rest of the route.

Italian hotel and restaurant workers are also unionized, and as liable to one-day strikes as transport workers. When this happens, almost all middle-size and large hotels and restaurants are affected. In hotels, this means that you make the beds and that the bathrooms aren't cleaned. In restaurants, this means that they stay closed.

Small family-run operations, since they are nonunion, remain open during strikes.

Business Hours & Holidays Key

Albania

Daily Business Hours
Banks: Open all day, 7 days per week. (You'll probably use Albtourist service desks in hotels.)
Government Offices: Post offices: 8 a.m.—10 p.m. 7 days per week.
Sundays: Many shops and offices are open.
National Holidays: January 1, 2, 11 (Republic Proclamation Day), May 1, November 28 (Independence Day), November 29 (Liberation Day).

Austria

Daily Business Hours
Shops: 8 a.m.—6 p.m. Monday through Friday, and Saturday morning; smaller shops often close noon—2 p.m.
Banks: 8 a.m.—12:30 p.m. and 1:30—3:30 p.m., often open until 5:30 p.m. on Thursdays.
Government Offices: 8 a.m.—4 p.m.
Sundays: Almost everything is closed except for hotels, some restaurants, and cafes.
National Holidays: January 1, 6, Easter Monday, May 1, Ascension Day (five weeks after Easter), Whit Monday (eight weeks after Easter), August 15, October 26 (National Day), November 1, December 8 (Immaculate Conception Day), 25, 26.
Special Information: Many shops are open on Saturdays only until noon.

Belgium

Daily Business Hours
Shops: 9 a.m.—noon and 2—6 p.m. Monday through Saturday. In the Flemish (northern) part of Belgium, hours may vary slightly in the after-

noon, from 1—5 p.m. Supermarkets are open until 8 p.m. Monday through Saturday.

Banks: 9 a.m.—12:30 p.m. and 1:30—4:30 p.m. (or sometimes 4 p.m.) Monday through Friday; a few are open Saturday 9 a.m.—12:30 p.m.

Government Offices: 8:30 a.m.—noon and 2—5 p.m. Monday through Friday.

Sundays: Most shops and all offices are closed, except for hotels and most restaurants.

National Holidays: January 1, Easter Monday, Ascension Day, Whit Monday, May 1, July 21 (National Day), August 15, November 1, November 11 (Armistice Day), 15 (Dynasty Day—government offices only), December 25 (and informally December 26).

Bulgaria

Daily Business Hours

Shops: 9 a.m.—1 p.m. and 2.p.m.—7 p.m. Monday through Saturday.

Banks: 8 a.m.—noon Monday through Friday.

Government Offices: 8:30 a.m.—5:30 p.m. Monday through Friday.

Sundays: All shops are closed except for a few in resort areas. Hotels and most restaurants are open.

National Holidays: January 1, March 3 (Liberation Day), 8 (Women's Day), May 1, 2 (Labor Day), 24 (Culture Day), September 9, 10 (National Day), November 7 (Soviet Revolution Day).

Czechoslovakia

Daily Business Hours

Shops: 9 a.m.—6 p.m. Monday through Friday; some shops close noon—2 p.m. Some shops close at noon Saturday, the rest are closed all day Saturday.

Banks: 8 a.m.—2 p.m. Monday through Friday and 8 a.m.—noon on Saturday.

Government Offices: 8:30 a.m.—5:15 p.m. Monday through Friday.

Sundays: Almost everything is closed except hotels and restaurants.

National Holidays: January 1, Easter Monday, May 1, 9 (National Day), December 25, 26.

Denmark

Daily Business Hours

Shops: 9 a.m.—5:30 p.m. Monday through Saturday (all close at noon on Saturday).

Banks: 9:30 a.m.—4 p.m. Monday through Friday, and until 6 p.m. on Thursday.

Government Offices: 8 a.m.—4 p.m. Monday through Friday.

Sundays: Virtually everything is closed except restaurants, hotels, and entertainments.

National Holidays: January 1, Maundy Thursday, Good Friday, Monday after Easter, two weeks after Easter (Common Prayers Day), May 1 (afternoon only), Ascension Day, Whit Monday, June 5 (Constitution Day), December 24 (afternoon only), 25, 26, and 31 (afternoon only).

Finland

Daily Business Hours

Shops: 9 a.m.—5 p.m., but 8 p.m. on Monday and Friday and 2 p.m. on Saturday.

Banks: 9 a.m.—4 p.m., Monday through Friday.

Government Offices: 8:30 a.m.—4 or 4:30 p.m. Monday through Friday.

Sundays: Almost all shops closed; hotels and restaurants are usually open.

National Holidays: January 1, Epiphany, Good Friday, Easter Monday, May Day Eve and and May 1, Ascension Day, Whitsun (Saturday and Sunday), Midsummer Eve and Midsummer Day, All Saints' Day, December 6 (Independence Day), 24, 25, 26.

France

Daily Business Hours
Shops: 9 a.m.—12:15 p.m. (food stores and bakeries 6 or 7 a.m.—12:15 p.m.) and 2—6:30 p.m. Monday through Saturday. Many shops are closed on Monday, especially in the provinces, but are sometimes open on Sunday.
Banks: 9 a.m.—noon or 12:30 p.m.; 2 or 2:30—4 or 4:30 p.m. (varies regionally), Monday through Friday, and some on Saturday 9 a.m.—1 p.m.
Government Offices: 8 a.m.—noon and 2—5 p.m., Monday through Friday.
Sundays: Many food stores and, in the provinces, other types of shops are open on Sunday but closed on Monday.
National Holidays: January 1, Easter Monday, May 1, 8 (Victory Day), Ascension Day, Whit Monday, July 14 (Bastille Day), August 15, November 1, 11 (Armistice Day), December 25.
Special Information: August is a holiday month: many businesses and shops are closed, and government offices are minimally staffed. The better restaurants in major cities are often closed as well.

Germany, East (GDR)

Daily Business Hours
Shops: Variable but generally 10 a.m.—7 p.m. in Berlin and 9 a.m.—6 p.m. elsewhere. Late closings on Thursdays (8 p.m.), Only large shops are open on Saturdays, and everything is closed on Sundays.
Banks: 8—11 a.m. Monday through Friday.
Government Offices: 8 a.m.—4 p.m. Monday through Friday.
Sundays: Everything is closed except hotels and restaurants.
National Holidays: January 1, Good Friday, Whit Monday, May 1, October 7 (German Democratic Republic Day), December 25, 26.

Germany, West

Daily Business Hours

Shops: 8 a.m.—noon and 1 or 1:30 p.m.—6 or 6:30 p.m., and 8 a.m.—2 p.m. on Saturdays. Large department stores stay open during lunch hours.

Banks: 8:30 a.m.—1 p.m. and 2—4 p.m. Monday through Friday, and until 5:30 on Thursday.

Government Offices: 8 a.m.—5 p.m. Monday through Friday.

Sundays: Virtually everything is closed on Sunday except hotels, restaurants, and a few shops in main railway stations, and autobahn rest stops.

National Holidays: January 1, Good Friday, Easter Monday, May 1, Ascension Day, Whit Monday, June 17 (German Unity Day), Prayer Day (mid November), December 25, 26.

Regional Holidays: November 1 (in Catholic areas only).

Great Britain

Daily Business Hours

Shops: 9 a.m.—5:30 p.m. Monday through Saturday.

Banks: 9:30 a.m.—3:30 p.m. Monday through Friday (closed 12:30—1:30 p.m. in Scotland).

Government Offices: 9 a.m.—5 p.m. Monday through Friday.

Sundays: Virtually everything is closed except hotels, restaurants, and some small corner-store groceries. Some of the large open-air flea markets and street markets are open only on Sundays.

National Holidays: January 1, Good Friday, Easter Monday, first Monday in May (May Day), last Monday in May (Spring Bank Holiday), first Monday (Scotland only) or last Monday in August (rest of Great Britain—Summer Bank Holiday), December 25, 26.

Regional Holidays: January 2 (Scotland only), March 1 (St. David's Day—Wales only).

Special Information: Early Closing (EC): In most towns (but not cities), all shops close early one day per week, usually at noon. Several of the hotel and restaurant guides list Early Closing days in each town listing.

Greece

Daily Business Hours
Shops: 8 a.m.—2:30 p.m. Monday, Wednesday, and Saturday and 8 a.m.—1:30 p.m. and 5:30—8:30 p.m. Tuesday, Thursday, and Friday.
Banks: 8 a.m.—2 p.m. Monday through Friday. (A few are also open on Saturday for foreign exchange only.)
Government Offices: 8 a.m.—3 p.m. Monday through Friday.
Sundays: Many shops are closed, but restaurants and tavernas are open. The flea market in Athens is open on Sunday mornings.
National Holidays: January 1, 6, Shrove Monday (Monday before Lent), March 25 (Independence Day), May 1, Good Friday, Easter Monday, August 15, October 28 (National Day), December 25, 26.
Regional Holidays: A number of festivals take place before Lent as part of Carnival. Navy Week, at the end of June and beginning of July, is a waterfront festival, especially on some of the Aegean islands.

Hungary

Daily Business Hours
Shops: 10 a.m.—6 p.m. Monday through Friday and 10 a.m.—3 p.m. on Saturday. Smaller shops often close during lunch. Food stores are open 6:30 a.m.—7 p.m. Some stores are open Thursday until 8 p.m.
Banks: 8:30 a.m.—3 p.m. Monday through Friday.
Government Offices: 8 a.m.—4:30 or 5 p.m. Monday through Friday.
Sundays: Virtually everything is closed except restaurants, hotels, and places of entertainment.
National Holidays: January 1, March 15, April 4 (Liberation Day), May 1 (Labor Day), Easter

Monday, August 20 (Constitution Day), December 25, 26.

Ireland

Daily Business Hours
Shops: 9 a.m.—5:30 p.m. Monday through Saturday.
Banks: 10 a.m.—12:30 p.m. and 1:30—3 p.m. Monday through Friday (5 p.m. Thursday).
Government Offices: 9:30 a.m.—5:30 p.m. Monday through Friday.
Sundays: Virtually everything is closed except hotels and restaurants, and some tourist attractions in summer.
National Holidays: January 1, March 17 (St. Patrick's Day), Good Friday, Easter Monday, first Monday in June (June Bank Holiday), first Monday in August (August Bank Holiday), last Monday of October (Halloween), December 25, 26.
Special Information: Early Closing (EC): Most Irish towns have Early Closing Day one day a week, usually Thursday or Wednesday, but occasionally Monday or Tuesday. On this day, most shops in town close about 1 p.m.

Italy

Daily Business Hours (Note: Shorter lunch closings in the north than in the south.)
Shops: 9 a.m.—1 p.m. and 3:30 or 4 p.m.—7:30 or 8 p.m. Monday through Fridays and Saturday mornings.
Banks: 8:30 a.m.—1:30 p.m. Monday through Friday. and 3 p.m.—4 to 4:30 p.m. (variable).
Government Offices: 8:30 a.m.—1:45 p.m.; post offices and SIP telephone offices also open 3—5:30 p.m.
Sundays: Virtually everything is closed except hotels, restaurants, entertainments, and outdoor vendors and flea markets.
National Holidays: January 1, 6 (Epiphany), Easter Monday, April 25 (Liberation Day), May 1, August 15, November 1, December 8 (Immaculate Conception Day), 25, 26.

Special Information: In many but not all towns, everything is closed one week day (Closing Day) except restaurants and hotels. Some hotel and restaurant guides state which day.

Luxembourg

Daily Business Hours
Shops: 9 a.m.—noon and 2—6 p.m. Monday through Saturday.
Banks: 8:30 a.m.—noon and 1:30—4:30 p.m. Monday through Friday (some remain open 9 a.m—4 p.m.).
Government Offices: 9 a.m.—noon and 2—5 p.m. Monday through Friday.
Sundays: Almost everything is closed except restaurants and hotels.
National Holidays: January 1, Shrove Tuesday, Easter Monday, Ascension Day, Whit Monday, May 1, June 23 (Grand Duke's Birthday), August 15 (Assumption Day), November 1, 2, December 25, 26.
Regional Holiday: Schobermess, the Luxembourg Fair (variable, but twice a year in spring and fall).

Netherlands

Daily Business Hours
Shops: 8:30 or 9 a.m.—5 or 5:30 p.m. Monday through Saturday. Many shops are closed Monday morning. Some shops remain open until 9 p.m. Thursday or Friday (depends on city).
Banks: 9 a.m.—4 p.m. Monday through Friday.
Government Offices: 8:30 a.m.—5:30 p.m. Monday through Friday.
Sundays: Virtually everything is closed except hotels and restaurants.
National Holidays: January 1, Good Friday, Easter Monday, April 30 (Queen's Day), Ascension Day, Whit Monday, December 25, 26.
Special Information: Many stores stay open at least part of Good Friday.

Norway

Daily Business Hours
Shops: 9 a.m.—5 p.m. Monday through Friday and 9 a.m.—1 or 2 p.m. Saturday.
Banks: 8:15 a.m.—3 p.m. Monday through Friday, and until 5 p.m. on Thursday.
Government Offices: 9 a.m.—4 p.m. Monday through Friday.
Sundays: Almost everything is closed except hotels and restaurants.
National Holidays: January 1, Maundy Thursday, Good Friday, Easter Monday, May 1, 17 (Independence Day), Ascension Day, Whit Monday, December 24 (afternoon only), December 25, 26, December 31 (afternoon only).

Poland

Daily Business Hours
Shops: 9 a.m. (sometimes 11 a.m.)—7 p.m. Monday through Saturday, food stores 5 a.m.—7 p.m., department stores 11 a.m.—7 p.m.
Banks: 9 a.m.—noon or 2 p.m. Monday through Saturday.
Government Offices: 8 a.m.—3 p.m. Monday through Friday and 8 a.m.—1:30 p.m. Saturday.
Sundays: Almost everything is closed except restaurants and hotels.
National Holidays: January 1, Easter Monday, May 1, 9 (Victory Day), Corpus Christi (Thursday date varies), July 22 (National Day), November 1, December 25, 26.

Portugal

Daily Business Hours
Shops: 9 a.m.—1 p.m. and 3—7 p.m. Monday through Friday, and Saturday 9 a.m.—1 p.m. Shopping centers are open daily (including Sunday) 10 a.m.—midnight.
Banks: 8:30—3 p.m. Monday through Friday.

Government Offices: 9 a.m.—1 p.m. and 3—5 p.m. Monday through Friday (occasional variations outside of Lisbon and Oporto).
Sundays: Most shops closed.
National Holidays: January 1, Shrove Tuesday, Good Friday, April 25 (Liberty Day), May 1, June 10 (National Day), August 15, October 5 (Proclamation of the Republic), November 1, December 1 (Independence Day), 8 (Immaculate Conception Day), 24, 25.
Regional Holidays: Lisbon: June 13 (St. Anthony's Day), Oporto: June 24 (St. John's Day).

Romania

Daily Business Hours
Shops: 8 a.m.—noon and 4—8 p.m. Monday through Saturday, and sometimes Sunday mornings.
Banks: 9 a.m.—noon and 1—3 p.m. Monday through Friday and Saturday morning.
Government Offices: 8 a.m.—4 p.m. Monday through Saturday, but 8 a.m.—1 p.m. Friday.
Sundays: Most shops and restaurants are open, especially in resort areas.
National Holidays: January 1, 2, May 1, 2, August 23, 24 (National Days). Informally, also December 25, though most shops remain open.

Soviet Union, U.S.S.R.

Daily Business Hours
Shops: 9 a.m.—7 p.m., closed one hour during lunch (often 2—3 p.m.). Large department stores stay open during lunch. Food shops and bakeries are usually open 7 a.m.—7 p.m.
Banks: 9 or 10 a.m.—5 or 6 p.m. (closed one hour during lunch).
Government Offices: 9 or 10 a.m.—5 or 6 p.m. (closed one hour during lunch).
Sundays: Most shops and many restaurants are closed.

National Holidays: January 1, 2, May 1, 2, May 9 (Victory Day), November 7, 8 (Days of the Revolution), December 5 (Constitution Day).

Special Information: Many shops may not have much to sell; if there's a long line, it may have something of value to Soviets only.

Spain

Daily Business Hours

Shops: 9 or 10 a.m.—1 p.m. and 4—7 p.m. (winter) or 5 p.m.—8 p.m. (summer) Monday through Friday and Saturday mornings.

Banks: 9 a.m.—2 or 3 p.m. (1:30 or 2:30 p.m. in summer) Monday through Friday and 9 a.m.—12:30 p.m. Saturday.

Government Offices: 9 a.m.—1:30 p.m. and 4 p.m.—7 p.m. Monday through Friday.

Sundays: Many shops are closed but flea markets and public amusements and many restaurants are open.

National Holidays: January 1, 6, March 19 (St. Joseph's Day), Maundy Thursday, Good Friday, May 1, Corpus Christi (date is variable), July 25 (St. James' Day), August 15, October 12 (Columbus Day), December 8 (Immaculate Conception Day), 25.

Regional Holidays: Each city has a patron saint: during the patron saint's festival, all work comes to a halt for several days.

Special Information: 1. Evening meals don't begin until 10 p.m. and most restaurants don't open for dinner until 7:30 p.m. or later.

2. When holidays come during midweek, they often stretch to include the nearest weekend. (Please see Food & Drink chapter.)

Sweden

Daily Business Hours

Shops: 9:30 a.m.—6 p.m. Monday through Friday and 9 a.m.—1 p.m. (sometimes 4 p.m.) Saturday. Some stores (Närbutiker) are open 7 a.m.—10 or 11 p.m. Monday through Saturday in cities and towns.

Banks: 9:30 a.m.—3 p.m. Monday through Friday and also 4—5:30 p.m. Thursday.
Government Offices: 9 a.m.—5 p.m. Monday through Friday.
Sundays: While most shops are closed, some bakeries, florists, and vendors are open, as are most restaurants.
National Holidays: January 1, 6, Good Friday, Easter Monday, May 1, 28 (Ascension Day), Whit Monday, June near but not usually on the solstice (Midsummer Day), October 31 (All Saints' Day), December 25, 26.

Switzerland

Daily Business Hours
Shops: 8 a.m.—12:15 p.m. and 1:30—6:30 p.m. Monday through Friday and 9 a.m.—4 p.m. Saturday. Large department stores stay open during lunch.
Banks: 8:30 a.m.—4:30 p.m. Monday through Friday.
Government Offices: 8 a.m.—noon and 2 p.m.—6 p.m. Monday through Friday.
Sundays: Almost everything is closed, except for hotels, restaurants, and gas stations.
National Holidays: January 1, 2, Good Friday, Easter Monday, Ascension Day, Whit Monday, August 1 (Independence Day), December 25, 26.
Regional Holidays: Almost every canton has at least one local holiday during the year.

Turkey

Daily Business Hours
Shops: 9 a.m.—1 p.m. and 2:30—7 p.m. Monday through Friday and 9 a.m.—1 p.m. and 1:30—8 p.m. Saturday.
Banks: 9 a.m.—noon and 2—5 p.m. Monday through Friday.
Government Offices: 9 a.m.—noon and 2—5 p.m. Monday through Friday.
Sundays: Many but not all shops are closed.
National Holidays: April 23 (National Day), May 19 (Youth Day), August 30 (Victory Day),

October 29, 30 (Declaration of the Republic Days).

Special Information: Ramadan is the ninth month of the Muslim calendar, and lasts 30 days. During Ramadan, little food or drink is served from dawn to sunset.

Yugoslavia

Daily Business Hours

Shops:

Winter: 8 a.m.—1 p.m. and 4—7 p.m. Monday through Saturday.

Summer: 7 a.m.—noon and 5—8 p.m. Monday through Saturday.

Banks:

Winter: 8 a.m.—noon and 4—7 p.m. Monday through Friday.

Summer: 7—11 a.m. and 5—8 p.m. Monday through Friday.

Government Offices: 7 a.m.—2 p.m. Monday through Saturday.

Sundays: Most shops are closed, but some self-service food stores in cities are open.

National Holidays: January 1, 2, May 1, 2, July 4 (Partisan Day), November 29, 30 (Republic Days).

Regional Holidays: Bosnia-Herzegovina and Croatia, July 27; Macedonia, August 2 and October 11; Montenegro, July 13; Serbia, July 7; Slovenia, July 22, 23.

Religious Holidays: Easter and Christmas are unofficially celebrated in the northern Christian republics; Ramadan is unofficially celebrated in the southern Muslim republics.

Special Information: Business hours vary slightly from region to region.

Shopping
What are the Good Buys?

You can find a world of things to buy in Europe. Each country has its specialties, which are widely available locally, though often unknown or very expensive elsewhere. Some items, particularly crafts, are regional. Sometimes the regions are very small. For example, in Provence near Arles, gnarled olive wood trunks are carved into freeform fruit bowls of exceptional beauty. But 50 miles or farther away, you'll never find them.

If you find items you want because they are unique, or you won't have the time to come back and get them, buy them because you may never see them again. (Of course, you may see something better later, but that is a matter of chance and not likely.)

Prices vary greatly, but often prices within a country are fixed, regardless of the store of purchase. This is particularly true for well-known trademarked items such as Baccarat crystal or Lladró porcelain. Whether the price is less than near your home depends very much on the product. Be sure to price things you may want to buy at home before you go, because in many cases there are no savings at all.

There is a wealth of art and antiques. However, while there is generally no restriction on purchase, you must get export licences for art in many countries.

In Eastern Europe, virtually anything older than 1950 is considered an antique, which requires a rarely given export license.

Fine Arts and Antiques

Export of old fine arts such as painting and sculpture is carefully regulated in Britain, France, Greece, Italy, Spain, and Turkey.

In France, you apply for an export permit from the Customs office if the item is valued over 100,000 francs. The items then must be approved by Customs and an official of the National Museums of France. In Spain, the process is similar: the curator is from the Prado Museum. Italy also requires approval from the ministries of culture, education, interior, plus a national museum curator.

In Italy and Spain, if the permit is denied, the museum can purchase the work—at a valuation it decides on. In France, permission can be denied without any desire to purchase. In these countries, you should insist that the sale is "contingent upon issuance of an export permit."

In Britain, export permits are required for art, antiques, and collectors' items and motor vehicles over 50 years old valued at more than £16,000. Lesser limits apply in some cases: photographs more than 60 years old (£400), representations of British historical personages (£4000), all archaeological items recovered in Britain, and architectural and engineering drawings made by hand. If a museum wants the art, it will have to buy it for the amount you paid for it. Otherwise you will be granted the export permit.

Details and step-by-step procedures of the export permit process for Britain, France, and Germany are found in "Manston's Flea Markets" guides for those countries.

For further information about purchases and removal of fine art and antiques contact:

France
Direction Générale des
Douanes et Droits
Indirects
182 rue Saint-Honoré
75001 Paris
Tel. (1) 42.60.35.90

Great Britain
Department of Trade
and Industry—Export
Licensing Branch
Millbank Tower
London SW1P 4QU
Tel. (071) 211-4620

Greece
Ministry of Culture
Supervisor of Prehistoric
and Classical
Antiquities
Museum Section
Aristidou 14
101 86 Athens
Υπουργείο Πολιτισμού
Δ/νση Προιστ. & Κλ.
Αρχ/Των.
Τμήμα Μουσείων
Αριστείδου 14
101 86 Αθήναι
Tel. (01) 324 3015/133

Italy
Ministero dei Beni
Culturali ed Ambientali
Ufficio Esportazione
Opere d'Arte
Via Cernaia 1
00185 Roma
Tel. (06) 461457

Spain
Ministerio de Cultura
Paseo de la Castellana 39
Madrid 16
Tel. (91) 455 5000

There are few if any problems in the export of art from Belgium, the Netherlands, West Germany, or Switzerland. In these countries, if you buy it, you can generally take it. In all cases, you must be able to provide a "Declaration of Exportation" if requested to Customs when you leave the nation of purchase.

Aside from antiques and fine arts, every country in Europe has specialties you can buy and take home. Here a few specialties, listed by country.

Shopping Specialties Key

Austria: Jaeger outfits for men and women, jewelry, down pillows, quilts, and comforters.

Belgium: Diamonds, chocolate, lacework.

Bulgaria: Folk art, such as painted and carved wooden plates, embroidered tablecloths, leather goods.

Czechoslovakia: Crystal, hand woven carpets. (If you buy crystal elsewhere than a Tuzex shop, you may have to pay a 100% export duty when you leave Czechoslovakia, however, inspection is spotty.)

Denmark: Fine-design jewelry, silver, stainless steel, porcelain, furniture, furs, smoking pipes and tobacco products, women's furs.

Finland: Furs, Marimekko designs, wood products.

France: Perfume, crystal, Limoges porcelain, fashions, kitchenware.

(West) Germany: Sensible kitchen gadgets, cuckoo clocks, mechanical products, motor vehicles.

Great Britain: Woolens, raincoats, Wedgwood and other porcelain, books.

Greece: Copperware, enamelware, ouzo, furs (in Kastoria). (Be sure that the furs you buy aren't on the U.S. or Canadian endangered species list, however.)

Hungary: Folk art such as handwoven carpets and embroideries, Herend porcelain, paprika.

Ireland: Aran hand-knit sweaters, Waterford crystal, Belleek porcelain.

Italy: Leather goods, gold jewelry, faience pottery.

Monaco: Postage stamps.

Netherlands: Diamonds, wooden shoes, Delft ware.

Norway: Ski sweaters.

Poland: Folk art, vodka.

Portugal: Hand-painted tiles, woven goods, straw, and pottery.

Romania: Folk embroidery.

Spain: Toledo metalware, leather goods.

Sweden: Crystal, furnishings.

Switzerland: Knives, linens, watches, chocolate.

Turkey: Rugs, copperware, onyx, brass, leather goods.

Yugoslavia: Folk art such as weaving, carved wooden plates, wickerwork, wine barrels, crystal, etc.

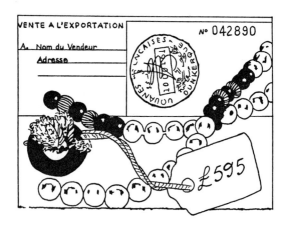

Value-Added Tax Refunds

The price you pay for nearly everything you buy in most of Western European countries includes the "value-added tax" (VAT), a sort of national sales tax. VAT raises a large proportion of government revenue and can be as high as 35% in some countries. The tax is usually hidden in the stated price rather than added on to the actual price.

The value-added tax is not collected in Switzerland (though there is a somewhat equivalent turnover tax), Andorra, or the Eastern European countries, except Hungary and Yugoslavia.

These tax rates vary (sometimes wildly) over time as well as by country. They also can change between categories of products: "luxuries" are usually taxed at a rate higher than "necessities." The legal distinctions between "necessities" and "luxuries" are not always clear to the traveler—but the higher tax rate is.

Refunds on Purchases of Goods

You can often get a refund on all or part of this tax on merchandise you take out of the country of purchase, whether you ship it home or take it with you. You cannot generally receive a refund on goods and services you can't take with you, such as hotel rooms, car rentals, or meals.

If the seller ships the purchase directly, the tax will be deducted then and there, and you won't pay it in the first place. Instead, you will pay shipping and insurance, which often amounts to about the same price as the tax.

Refunds are usually made only as a courtesy; no store or shop is required to refund the tax (except in Italy). Many do not.

Special and more restrictive rules apply if you purchase an item in the Common Market (EC) and live in an EC country. Contact the Customs and Excise office in your home country for exact procedures.

Some stores have been known to say that the tax is refundable but not complete the paperwork. If you don't have the paperwork completed when you leave the store, you will not get a refund from that establishment.

When you go shopping, either have your passport or passport number, since it is almost always required to receive a refund.

Many countries have minimum purchases per item, or more usually per store in order to collect a refund. In addition, stores are free to impose additional requirements.

Each country's procedures for refunds are a bit different. They are very precise, and failure to follow them exactly will usually result in failure to receive the refund you expected.

Refunds on Services and Consumed Items

Tourist Travel

You cannot generally receive a refund on goods and services you can't take with you such as hotel rooms, car rentals, or meals.

Deductions for Business Trips

If you visit the Common Market (EC) countries and the European Free Trade Association (EFTA) countries of Austria, Finland, Norway, and

Sweden, at least in part for a business purpose (such as attending a trade show, meeting with a prospective business associate, or looking for certain types of merchandise for resale), you may be able to reclaim some or all of the value-added tax paid for travel expenses and services, including hotels, meals, transportation, and trade-show exhibits.

Each country has its own complex and different rules: for example, in Germany, you must submit the original receipts with your forms; in Britain, if you dine with a British counterpart, you must ask for separate checks, since your meal qualifies for a refund but your counterpart's meal does not; in Italy, repairs to diesel-powered vehicles are eligible for reimbursement but repairs to gasoline-powered vehicles are not.

Some countries, such as France, now have specialized companies whose main business is to process these claims for a percentage of the refund.

Information about these rules can be obtained from each country's government office for collecting the tax.

General Procedures for Reimbursement

Each country's procedures for refunds are a bit different. They are very precise, and failure to follow them exactly will usually result in failure to receive the refund you expected.

In general, a three- or four-part form must be filled out by the store at the time of your purchase. Be sure you have the business name, address, and phone number, and sales person's name either on the form or elsewhere.

When you leave that particular country (not Europe as a whole), you must be ready to show the goods to customs and must have customs stamp the forms. You will keep a copy yourself. Another must be mailed by customs back to the store, and one or two more are kept for customs' use.

Refunds are usually mailed to your home address by check. Sometimes the refund is credited through your bank into your checking, savings, or credit-card account. Be sure you have the following banking information with you: your bank's name and address and your account number. The routing code (the computer readable numbers at the bottom of your check) contains much of this information.

Expect to wait up to three months for refunds to arrive. Inform your bank to watch for these credits to your account.

European bank checks are occasionally written in United States or Canadian dollars. Avoid this if at all possible, since these are very difficult to cash. You will need to find a North American branch of the European bank to cash it.

More commonly, you will receive a European check drawn in the European currency. If you get this kind of check and your bank will not cash it or wants to charge a large commission (as much as $15!), you can also send or take it one of several foreign currency dealers:

Ruesch International Inc.
1140 - 19th Street N.W.
Washington, D.C. 20036
Tel. (202) 887-0990, or
(800) 424-2923
Fax (202) 872-0527
Telex 89435

Ruesch International, Inc.
3 First National Plaza
Suite 2020
Chicago, Ill. 60602
Tel. (312) 332 5900
Fax (312) 332-5901

Ruesch International, Inc.
450   Park Ave.
Suite   2301
New York, N.Y. 10022
Tel. (212) 421-7100
Fax (212) 421-6487

Ruesch International, Inc.
1925 Century Park East.
Suite 240
Los Angeles, Calif. 90067
Tel. (213) 277-7800
Fax (213) 277-0832

You must sign and endorse each check, then write "Payable to Ruesch International," and your signature as payee. This company charges a $2 service fee per check, and in about 10 days to return a check to you in U.S. dollars.

Another organization that performs similar services is:

New York Foreign Exchange, Inc.
26 Broadway Suite 767
New York, N.Y. 10004
Tel. (212) 248-4700 or (800) 346-3924, telex 3767022
and
New York Foreign Exchange of N.J.
591 Summit Ave.
Jersey CIty, N.J. 07306

This company charges a no more than a $2 service fee for each check. In addition, it will charge any European currency into Canadian dollars for the same charges.

Payments are sent out the same day they are received.

Deak International, with offices in major cities in the United States and Canada, will cash foreign-denominated checks as well, usually at walk-in offices. For information call:
(800) 421-8391 (U.S. except California)
(800) 424-1186 (California)
(800) 268-8155 (Canada)

In other cases, if the store participates in a "Tax-Free" plan (look for the "Tax-Free Shopping for Tourists" logo, you get a check at the store with the amount of refund on it. It becomes valid when stamped by Customs; then it can be cashed at exchange booths or banks at borders, or later through an exchange service.

Value-Added Tax Refund Key

Austria

Tax name: Mehrwertsteuer (Initials MWST).
Tax rates: Minimum: 20%, or 16.66% of the sales price.
    Maximum: 32%, or 24.24% of the sales price.
How to determine in advance if a store gives tax refunds: The Austrian National Tourist Office has a booklet about Tax-Free Shopping. Some stores have a sign reading "Tax-Free Shopping." In any case, you can ask at the store if there is no other marking.

Minimum Purchase: 1001 Austrian schillings (AS) at each store.

Procedures at the store:

1. When purchasing, ask for refund.
2. Store clerk must fill out form U-34, "Ausfuhrbescheinigung für Umsatzsteuerszwecke."
3. You will have to present your passport.
4. Clerk will retain one copy, give you remaining ones, with envelope to return stamped papers to store.

Procedures when leaving Austria:

1. Stop at Austrian customs (Zollamt) on your way out.
2. Present form U-34 with receipt attached.
3. Have goods ready for inspection. (They should not have been used.)
4. Austrian customs will stamp all copies of the form.
5. Give store's return envelope to Customs officer. It will be returned to the store. (Be sure it has postage on it.)
5 Alternative. Mail the original stamped copy back to the store yourself, after you have left Austria. (Be sure to keep a copy of everything you mail.)

You can receive cash refunds when leaving, at ÖAMTC offices (the Austrian Auto Club) at main international road frontier crossings. To receive this refund, the form U-34 must have the Club's blue imprint. For a small fee (sliding scale 10%-4%, minimum AS 40), the Club frontier office will give you a cash refund. Customs officers cannot refund money. In addition to road crossings, the ÖAMTC has offices at the Vienna airport and Salzburg and Kufstein railway stations.

You can receive a refund if you are unable to follow procedures when leaving Austria. If you aren't able to obtain a customs stamp when leaving by train, mail the form U-34 to Bundesministerium für Finanzen, Abteilung III/2, Himmelpfortgasse 4-8, Postfach 2, A-1015 Wien, Austria with a letter explaining when you left Austria (train number, day), and a confirmation from your home country's Customs that you imported the goods.

You will receive the refund as cash at the border from ÖAMTC, as a credit to your checking or savings account (be sure the paperwork includes your bank and account number), international money order sent to your home, or an Austrian check drawn in schillings.

Belgium

Tax name: *French:* Taxe sur la Valeur Ajoutée (TVA); *Flemish:* Belasting Toegevoegde Waarde (BTW).

Tax rates: Maximum: 25% for "luxury" items, plus 8% non-refundable "luxury tax," but most items are 19%.

Minimum purchase requirement: 3000 Belgian francs in one store.

How to determine if a store gives tax refunds: Ask the store staff.

Procedures at the store:

1. Complete the refund form.

2. The merchant will keep one copy and give you the rest.

3. Be sure you get a self-addressed envelope from the store. (Buy stamps for it if the store doesn't put them on.)

Procedures when leaving Belgium:

1. Submit filled-out form to Belgian customs for signature and stamp. Be prepared to show the items you bought.

2. Give stamped envelope to Customs to mail, or mail it yourself.

3. Wait a month or two for the refund to arrive.

You cannot receive cash refunds when leaving Belgium.

Tax cannot be refunded if you are unable to follow procedures when leaving Belgium.

If you are leaving Belgium by train, there are usually no customs officers on the train. You may have to check your luggage and have the station customs officials stamp the forms.

If you leave by plane or ferry, there are customs officials at the airport or docks.

If you drive across the border, there are customs offices at main road border crossings.

You will usually receive the refund as a check in Belgian francs.

Denmark

Tax name: Mer Omdaetnings Afgift (MOMS).
Tax rate: 22% (or 18.03% of selling price including tax).
How to determine if a store gives tax refunds: Often stores have a clearly visible red and white sign reading "Danish Tax-Free Shopping."
Minimum purchase requirement: 600 Danish kroner (including tax) at one store.
Procedures at the store:
A. If merchandise is sent home (outside of the Common Market or Scandinavia), or delivered to Kastrup airport, fill out paperwork at store. No tax will be charged, but you will have to pay any shipping charges.
B. 1. Fill out the refund form at the store. Most stores catering to tourists or with the Danish Tax Free Shopping sign have the form.
2. The store will charge a 3% service fee to process the refund (maximum 350 Dkr).
Procedures when leaving Denmark:
1. Declare goods at border, ferry landing, or airport and get each copy of the form(s) stamped by customs officers.
2. Give an addressed envelope and all except one copy of the form to the Customs officer or mail it back to the store yourself.
You cannot receive cash refunds at the border when leaving Denmark, except at Kastrup Airport near Copenhagen.
The tax cannot be refunded if you are unable to follow procedures when leaving.
Your refund will be as a check sent to you in Danish kroner, dollars, or as a direct deposit made to your bank account.

Finland

Tax name: Liikevaihtovero (LVV).
Tax rates: 16% on most purchases, but refund is 11% of purchase price.
Minimum purchase requirement: 200 Finnish marks (FIM).
How to determine if a store offers tax refunds: The store will usually have the "Fin-

land Tax-Free Shopping" logo displayed. If not, ask a clerk.

Procedures at the store:
1. Tell the store you want a "Tax-Free" refund when you buy.
2. You must present your passport, proving that you live outside of Scandinavia.
3. The store staff will fill out the Tax-Free Export Receipt and Shopping Cheque.

Procedures when leaving Finland:
1. Take the tax-refund form and merchandise to the Tax-Free Service Office found at airports in Helsinki, Turku, Mariehamm, Vaasa, or Rovaniemi, road crossings to Sweden, Norway, and the Soviet Union, and on some ferries (check before you board).
2. Show the receipt, present the cheque, and be ready to show the merchandise. (Do not open the package until you receive your refund.)
3. You will receive your refund in cash on the spot in Finnish marks, even if you charged the purchase on a credit card.

You cannot get the refund if you are unable to follow procedures when you leave Finland.

France

Tax name: Taxe sur la Valeur Ajoutée (TVA)
Tax rate: 18.6% on most items, 33% on luxuries.
Minimum purchase requirement: 1200 French francs in one store, though some stores may require a higher amount.
How to determine if a store gives tax refunds: Ask if the store offers "détaxe." Many but not all stores in Paris offer tax refunds, but fewer stores in the provinces refund tax.
Procedures at the store:
1. Make it clear you want refund (ask for "détaxe" and be sure you receive a "Fiche de Douanes").
2. A four-part form called "Vente a l'exportation" must be filled out in the store.
3. You will have to present your passport or give the passport number.
4. Pay full amount, including tax.

5. Get stamped envelope preaddressed to the store.

Procedures when leaving France:

A. *Normal procedure:* refund to your home or account.

1. Take all your forms and purchased merchandise to customs (Douane) officers. Note: If leaving by train (except to Britain), take care of this before you board. Get a customs official in the baggage area to stamp the forms. You will probably be required to check the luggage containing the goods. No on-train customs officers will stamp the forms.

2. At night, you may have to rouse an official.

3. Have each copy stamped and initialed by customs.

4. Customs official will keep white and pink copies.

5. Give customs official the return envelope.

6. Keep the completed green copy.

B. *For refund in cash* (only available at Charles de Gaulle, Orly, and Nice international airports during airport bank branch hours):

Follow steps 1, 2, and 3 immediately above. At this point, have customs give you a "Bon de Remboursement Aéroport," which you must take to the bank in the airport to cash.

Note: Be sure to allow plenty of extra time if you use this procedure, since these offices are usually understaffed. Your refund must be made before you leave, since the "Bon" is only good at the airport bank.

C. *Use a credit card.*

Follow steps 1, 2, and 3 above. When you pay, have separate charge slips made up for the price of goods and for the amount of tax. Some shops will make the second charge slip a credit to be processed when your customs-stamped paperwork is returned to them. Others will make the TVA an additional charge that will not be made if the customs-stamped paperwork is returned to them in a reasonable time.

Tax cannot usually be refunded if you are unable to follow procedures when leaving France, but you can try by returning the form by registered mail to the store when you arrive in the U.S. or Canada.

You can receive the refund as a U.S. dollar check drawn on either an American bank or French bank, a French franc check drawn on a French bank, a credit to your bank account (give them the name of your bank and account number), or a credit to your charge or credit card.

Germany, West

Tax name: Mehrwertsteuer (MWST).
Tax rate: Minimum: 7% (books and groceries); Maximum: 14% (almost everything else)
Minimum purchase requirement: set by each store; a small service charge may be levied.
How to determine if a store gives tax refunds: Ask the store staff, though a few stores have a "Tax-Free" sign or sticker at the door.
Procedures at the store:
1. Present your passport.
2. Clerk will fill out an Export and Buyer's Certificate (Ausfuhr- und Abnehmerbescheinigung), including a description of the merchandise and its price.
3. Obtain a stamped and addressed envelope.
4. Give the seller your bank's address and account number.
Procedures when leaving West Germany:
1. Be sure you have a copy of the certificate to keep; make a photocopy if necessary.
2. Take the form to the Customs office (Zollamt), or find a customs officer when you leave. Have the purchases available for inspection.
3. Customs officer will stamp all copies of the form, and take the preaddressed, stamped envelope and mail it to the store.
You cannot receive cash refunds when leaving West Germany.
You can receive a tax refund if you aren't able to follow procedures when leaving if you take the certificate and merchandise to the nearest German consulate. The staff will sign and stamp the certificate, which you will have to mail to the store.
You will receive the refund as a direct deposit made to your bank account or, rarely, a credit to a charge or credit-card account, or a check in Deutsche marks.

Great Britain

Tax name: Value-Added Tax (VAT).
Tax rate: 15% on most items.
No minimum purchase requirement, though many stores impose their own. Stores are permitted to levy a service charge. (Example: Harrods has a minimum £70 purchase, and charges £2 for processing the refund.)
How to determine if VAT refunds are offered: ask the sales person, or look for the "Tax-Free Shopping" sticker near the door.
Procedures at the store:
1. The store staff must fill out the "Value-Added Tax Retail Export Scheme" form.
2. You must show your passport.
3. Sign the "Declaration by the Customer" on the form.
4. Get pre-addressed (and usually stamped) envelope.
Procedures when leaving Great Britain:
1. Take form and merchandise to H.M. Customs and Excise counter or office at the airport or ferry terminal.
2. Customs officials may view merchandise and will stamp papers. Give official the return envelope to send to the store.
3. Get the customer's copy of the form for your records.
Note for air travelers: Due to the way Heathrow and Gatwick airports are laid out, you must check luggage before you can have your paperwork stamped. Carry your purchases in your hand luggage or hope the official doesn't want to see anything you've checked in your luggage. Check the computerized display board at Gatwick for exact location of the office.
You cannot receive cash refunds at the airport or ferry terminal when leaving Britain.
If you fail to get British customs to stamp your paperwork before you leave Britain, you can still get a refund if you have the refund form.
Procedure:
1. Get a United States or Canadian customs duty receipt or a copy of your customs declaration, or United States or Canadian customs stamp on the refund form.

2. You can also get a United States or Canadian Customs officer, chief of police, or notary public to stamp Box B of each copy of the VAT form. This certifies that the goods were exported from Britain.

3. Mail the stamped and signed forms (except the customer's copy) to the seller as in the normal procedure.

You will receive the refund in the form of either a cheque drawn in pounds sterling or a credit to your credit card (if originally charged).

Ireland

Tax name: Value-Added Tax (VAT).

Tax rates: Minimum: 10% (clothing), though almost everything else is 23%.

No minimum purchase requirement, though many stores set a minimum purchase of about £50. Stores may charge a service fee (about £2) for processing the refund.

How to determine if VAT refunds are offered: Ask the store staff; stores are not required to offer refunds.

Procedures at the store:

1. Obtain an invoice which includes your name, address, describes the merchandise, and shows the amount of VAT paid.

2. Before leaving Ireland, make a copy of the invoice if you don't have one made by the store.

Procedures when leaving Ireland:

1. At customs (whether airport or ferry slip), present the invoice to Customs for stamping and initialing. Also, ask them to stamp the copy you keep.

2. Mail the original stamped and initialed invoice back to the store, or a central value-added tax refund clearing house (address on the invoice).

You cannot receive cash refunds at ferry terminals when leaving Ireland, but you can receive cash refunds in Irish pounds at Shannon and Dublin airports. Look for the "Cashback" office.

You can receive a refund if you are unable to follow procedures when leaving Ireland. Get any Customs officer or notary public outside the

Common Market to stamp the form and return the stamped form to Ireland.

You will receive the refund either as a check (usually in Irish pounds), a money order, a credit to a credit-card account, or cash at Shannon airport. If you pay in cash, the credit can still be in the form of a credit-card credit if you leave the account number with the merchant.

Italy

Tax name: Imposta Valore Aggiunto (IVA).

Tax rate: 18% to 30%, depending on the item, but refund is 13%.

Minimum purchase requirement: 250,000 lire for each single item or set. Some stores will combine all items as a "set"; others will not.

How to determine if a store gives tax refunds: Every store is legally required to offer tax refunds. (Legal Authority: Art. 38-quater— Sgravio dell'imposta per i viaggiatore stranieri, 16 D.P.R. 30-12-1981.) Some stores have a "Tax-Free Italia" or "Euro-Free Tax" sign or sticker on the door.

Procedures at the store:

1. Obtain an invoice, which includes your name, address, passport number, and a description of the purchase. Be sure to get two copies, and the export forms. If you are to receive credit on your credit card, be sure that a credit slip is imprinted.

2. If the store uses a Tax-Free system, it will fill out the approved form, along with instructions for how to redeem it.

Procedures when leaving Italy:

1. Show both copies of the invoice or Tax-Free statement and the merchandise to Italian customs at the "Ufficio della Dogana" when you leave Italy. (There is no special tax-refund office.)

2. Italian customs will stamp the invoice and return it to you.

3. Send the original stamped invoice to the store or Tax-Free company by registered mail (to guarantee it is received).

4. The store must receive the invoice by mail within three months of the purchase or you will not receive a refund.

5. The store is required to send the refund within 15 days of the day it receives the stamped invoice.

You cannot receive cash refunds when leaving Italy.

The IVA tax cannot be refunded if you are unable to follow procedures when leaving Italy.

Your refund will be most often an Italian check in lire, bank draft, or, in rare occurrences, a credit to your VISA, MasterCard, or American Express account.

Note: Due to the slow and erratic state of the Italian mails, you should allow a good deal of time to receive your refund.

Luxembourg

Tax name: Taxe sur la valeur ajoutée (TVA).

Tax rates: 3%, (mainly food), 6% (mainly food and books), and 12% (almost everything else).

Minimum purchase requirement: 3,000 francs.

How to determine if a store offers refunds: Ask the store staff whether tax refunds ("détaxation") are offered.

Procedures at the store:

1. The store will give you an special Tax-Free refund form, describing the purchase and amount of TVA tax.

2. Be sure to get a copy of the form for your records.

Procedures when leaving Luxembourg:

1. Present the form to the customs officer (at the Bureau des Douanes) when you leave Luxembourg, Belgium, or the Netherlands. You will have to show your passport and may be asked to show the purchases.

2. Mail the stamped invoice to the store.

3. If you are leaving by train from Luxembourg City, take the invoice and goods to the customs office (Bureau des Douanes) at the right side of the Gare Centrale station. They will stamp the invoice, and will refund the money on the spot.

You cannot receive a TVA tax refund if you are unable to follow procedures when leaving.

You will the receive the refund as a credit to your credit-card account, or credited to your checking account at home, unless you receive an immediate refund before you leave (see #3 above).

Netherlands

Tax name: Belasting Toegevoegde Waarde (BTW).

Tax rates: Minimum: 6% (only on food), maximum: 25%, plus luxury tax, only on cars.

Minimum purchase requirement: 300 guilders in one store.

How to determine if a store gives tax refunds: Ask the store staff, or look for "Tax-Free for Tourists" sticker.

Procedures at the store:

1. The store staff will complete a form, listing the item, price, and your name, address, and passport number, or sometimes give you a check with the refund amount. The check becomes valid when stamped by customs.

2. Be sure you get an envelope addressed to the store as well, or the refund service agency.

Procedures when leaving the Netherlands:

1. Dutch Customs officers must sign and stamp all copies of the form. Sometimes when leaving by train, there will not be any Customs officers on the train, especially when going into Belgium. In this case, check your bags and get the stamps at the station.

2. Send the form back to the store from another country.

You can get cash refunds when leaving at Schiphol airport and major road border crossing with "Grenswisselkantoren" banks if you have a check. You'll be given a voucher by Customs to exchange at the airport bank.

The BTW tax cannot be refunded if you are unable to follow procedures when leaving.

You will usually receive the refund as a check, usually payable in guilders, or in money at borders.

Norway

Tax name: MOMS.
Tax rates: Minimum: 16.67%
Minimum purchase requirement: 1000 kroner in one store.
How to determine if a store offers tax refunds: The store will usually have the Norway Tax-Free logo displayed, either as a decal at the door or as a placard or poster. If it is not shown not, ask a clerk.
Procedures at the store:
1. Tell the store you want a "Tax-Free" refund when you buy.
2. You must present your passport, proving that you live outside of Scandinavia.
3. The store staff will fill out the Tax-Free Export Receipt and an attached Shopping Cheque.
Procedures when leaving Norway:
1. Take the tax-refund form and merchandise to the Tax-Free Service Office found at ports, airports, and on some ships, and at Kastrup Airport in Copenhagen, Denmark.
2. Show the forms and be ready to show the merchandise.
3. You will receive your refund in cash on the spot in Norwegian kroner, even if you charged the purchase on a credit card.
You cannot get the refund if you are unable to follow procedures when you leave Norway.

Spain

Tax name: Impuesto de Valór Añadido (IVA).
Tax rates: 7% to 33%, depending on type of merchandise.
Minimum purchase requirement: 25,000 pesetas at one store.
How to determine if a store offers tax refunds: Ask the store staff. You can only apply for a refund if you take the goods with you. If you have the store ship the goods to your home, tax is not charged.
Procedures at the store:
1. The store staff must complete the form, "Desgravación Fiscal a la Exportación de Mer-

cancias Adquiridas por Residentes en el extranjero." You must present your passport.

2. Be sure you have the form and return envelope when you leave the store.

Procedures when leaving Spain:

1. Take the form to the window or office marked "Desgravación Fiscal" or the Customs office at the frontier.

2. Customs officers will stamp your forms, mail the blue copy back to the store in the provided envelope, give you the yellow copy, and keep the other copies. (At Madrid's Barajas airport, the window is on the concourse of the departures level. Allow about a half hour to take care of this before check-in.)

You cannot receive cash refunds when leaving Spain.

The tax can be refunded if you aren't able to follow procedures when leaving Spain. You must mail the blue copy of the completed form back to the store from the U.S. or Canada. (An official postmark should be stamped in the box reserved for the Customs stamp to provide proof of exportation.)

You will usually receive the refund as a Spanish check in pesetas.

Sweden

Tax name: MOMS.

Tax rate: 23.46%, but refund is 14%.

Minimum purchase requirement: None, but most stores require a purchase of at least 200 Swedish kronor.

How to determine if a store offers tax refunds: The store will usually have the Swedish "Tax-Free" logo displayed as a decal near the door or a poster. If not, ask a clerk.

Procedures at the store:

1. Tell the store you want a "Tax-Free" refund when you buy.

2. You must present your passport, proving that you live outside of Scandinavia.

3. The store staff will fill out the Tax-Free Export Receipt and a Shopping Cheque.

Procedures when leaving Sweden:
1. Take the tax-refund form and merchandise to the Tax-Free Service Office found at ports, airports, and on some ships. (At Arlanda airport, the counter is on the check-in level, another is in the transit hall. Refunds are only given in the transit hall. Allow up to an extra hour for this chore.)
2. Show the forms and be ready to show the merchandise.
3. You will receive your refund in cash on the spot in Swedish kroner, even if you charged the purchase on a credit card.
You cannot receive the refund if you are unable to follow procedures when you leave Sweden, except at Kastrup Airport in Copenhagen, Denmark. Make your purchases within seven days of your departure from Sweden, to guarantee your refund. (While reasonable allowances over seven days can be made, refunds are not guaranteed.)

Switzerland

Merchandise Turnover Tax:
German: Warenumsatzteuer (WUST).
French: Impôt sur le chiffre d'affaires.
Italian: Imposta sulla ciffra d'affari.
Tax rates: 5.6% to 8.4% (food, newspapers, livestock, and utility service are tax free).
Minimum purchase: 500 Swiss francs in one store.
How to determine if tax refunds are offered: Ask the store staff.
Procedures at the store: Store staff will complete the paperwork, and give you forms, a receipt, and further instructions.
The refund will usually be a Swiss franc bank check, or a credit to your credit-card or bank account.

Flea Markets and Street Markets

You can find almost anything at Europe's street markets and flea markets. Hidden amidst the junk are more than a few jewels.

Flea markets range from indoor collections of private shops to rowdy street scenes offering everything from antiques to old clothes, tools, and other used items.

Street markets offer fresh produce, shoddy new clothes, cheap kitchen gadgets, entertainment, and sometimes even live chickens and farm animals.

Many markets overlap in their offerings, including fruit, vegetables, and clothes as well as junk.

Almost every city, town, and many villages have street markets, usually on one or two days of the week. Most people in town know which days are market days and where they are located.

Another easy way to find out is to watch the "No Parking" signs in squares and on wide streets for prohibitions from about 6 a.m. to 2 to 4 p.m. on specific days. During those times, the area becomes a street or flea market.

On market day in some towns, such as Sarlat-le-Canéda in the Dordogne valley of southwestern France, virtually the entire center of town becomes a market, one of the most exciting in one of the most beautiful settings in Europe.

Larger cities have more than one market, each with its own specialty. Often city markets are held daily.

Know what you're looking for or you may not get good buys. For example, there are sometimes solid silver pieces mixed in with the silver plate—but if you don't know European silver hallmarks, you may get stuck with virtually worthless plated ware at sterling prices. At a flea market, you are most likely to find solid silver cheaply if the hallmark is from another country than the one you're in. Judge other specialty items with the same knowledge.

Of course, if you just *like* the item, buy it and enjoy it!

At any street market, the local currency's cash is the only welcome medium of exchange.

Bargaining—Prices at the Flea Market

Bargaining is expected in all flea markets, except those selling food and new items. Generally, you'll fare better by offering about half the asking price, and expect to pay about two thirds to three quarters. You can try walking away—the sellers may concede and call you back just as you pass out of earshot. But don't let the game keep you from your purchase. You may never see it again if you don't return.

Flea Market Key: Locations and Times

The following Flea Market Key is just a sampling of the flea and street markets of Europe. (For more information, including shipping, antiques export and customs regulations, as well as hundreds of flea markets, antique fairs, and auctions, please see "Manston's Flea Markets" for Britain, France, and Germany.)

Austria

Vienna. Flea market (Flohmarkt) at Naschmarkt, near Mariahilferstrasse, west of the Opera house. Saturday mornings. Especially good during the summer.

Belgium

Antwerp. Flea market (Vogelmarkt, literally bird market) at Oudevaartplaats, near the Nationale Bank building in the city center. A large flea market, food market, and flower market, plus animals and birds. Sunday mornings.

Antwerp. Auction (Vrijdagmarkt, literally Friday market), an outdoor antique and used furniture auction at Vridagmarkt, near the Plantin-Moretus Museum in central Antwerp. Wednesday and Friday mornings. One of the most interesting in Europe.

Antwerp. Antique market at Lijnwaadmarkt, Saturdays from about 10 a.m. to 6 p.m.

Brussels. Flea market (marché aux puces) at Place du Grand Sablon, near the Art Museum (Musèe d'Art). Antiques, including silver, paintings, and old arms (such as swords and crossbows). Saturdays from 9 a.m. to 3 p.m. and Sundays from 9 a.m. to 1 p.m.

Brussels. Daily flea and street market at Place de Jeu de Balle, on rue Blaes (south of Grand Sablon). A junkier flea and street market. Daily from 8 a.m. to about 1 p.m., best on Wednesday and Saturday.

Brussels. Huge Sunday morning produce, and clothes, and used items market all around the Gare du Midi (Zuidstation). Used bicycles are sold in the median of the Boulevard du Midi.

Ghent (Gand). Food and produce market at St. Michaelsplein. Sunday mornings.

Liège. Flea and street market (La Batte) on the left bank of the Meuse between Place Cockerill and Pont Maghin. Saturdays from 9 a.m. to 2 p.m. Possibly the best single market in Belgium.

Denmark

Copenhagen. Israels Plads flea market, near the Norrepost S-tog station and botanical gardens. Saturdays from May through September from 8 a.m. to 2 p.m.

Copenhagen. Flea market behind the Fredericksberg Rådhus near the Fredericksberg S-tog station. Summer Saturday mornings, early, but no set opening time.

Copenhagen. Frelsens Haer indoor antique market, at Høhusgade 5. Lots of booths and small shops. Tuesdays, Wednesdays, and Thursdays, 1 p.m. to 5 p.m., Fridays, 1 p.m. to 6 p.m., Saturdays 9 a.m. to 1 p.m.

Finland

Helsinki. Street market in the central market square. Food and souvenirs but few antiques. Daily 7 a.m. to 2 p.m. except Sundays. Also 3:30 to 8 p.m. in summer.

France

Aix-en-Provence. Flea, antique, and street market at the place de Verdun in the city center. One of the most picturesque markets in France. Tuesday, Thursday, and Saturday from 8 a.m. to about 1 p.m.

Dijon. Food market in the old market hall in place du Marché in the old town. The hall is reminiscent of famous the old Les Halles market in the center of Paris. Clothes and other items around; antiques on the adjoining place de la Banque. Tuesdays and Saturdays from 6 a.m. to about 12:30 p.m.

Lyon. Flea market (marché aux puces) on rue Tita Coîs in the northeast suburb of Vulx-en-Velin. Take Metro to Cosset and walk. Saturday and Sunday mornings.

Lyon. Flea market (marché aux puces de la Feyssine) along the Rhône. Antiques and collectables are inside the oval building. Saturday and Sunday mornings.

Lyon. Brocante Stalingrad. Lyon's antique trades center, where the Parisian dealers buy, on boulevard Stalingrad in the Villeurbanne district. Thursday, Saturday, and Sunday.

Paris. Flea market (marché aux puces) at Porte de St. Ouen and Porte de Clignancourt, near the Metro stops of the same names. This market is huge, probably the largest in Europe. Thousands of small shops and booths, street tables, with junk, clothes, antiques. Know what you're buying and bargain or don't pay much. These people are wise to tourists! Sunday is the best day. Saturdays, Sundays, and Mondays from dawn to dusk. The best pickings are just before dawn from the street stands.

Paris. Smaller flea market at Porte de Vanves near the Metro station of the same name. More relaxed, less sophisticated, delightful tree-shaded setting. Saturdays and Sundays, dawn to 7 p.m.

Paris. Flea market at Porte de Montreuil, near the Metro station of the same name. Large, open, dusty, and windblown. The best antiques and collectables are along the west fence; kitchenware, clothes, and odds and ends towards the east. Saturdays, Sundays, and Mondays from 7 a.m. to 7 p.m.

Paris. Smaller flea market in a poor neighborhood at place d'Aligre, near the Ledru Rollin Metro station. Poor selection, low prices. Every day.

Paris. Le Village Suisse, a modern several-story gallery of several hundred tiny, elegant antique shops southeast of the Eiffel tower. Open 10 a.m. to 7 p.m., closed Tuesdays and Wednesdays.

Paris. Flower market. Retail flowers at the place Louis-Lépine, Île de la Cité, Daily 8:45 a.m. to 6 p.m.

Paris. Bird market at place Louis-Lépine, Île de la Cité, Sundays morning through mid-afternoon. Note that without a permit you may not bring birds back to the United States or Canada. Contact the U.S.D.A. or Agriculture Canada for more information.

Paris. Book market. Bookstalls along the Quais des Seine, from the Louvre to near Notre Dame. Lots of prints and old books. Prices are negotiable, but still often more expensive than Britain or New York. Daily, mornings through afternoons.

Paris. Rungis-Les Halles. The wholesale food market for the Paris region that was moved from the colorful but cramped 19th-century cast-iron marvels at Les Halles in the center of Paris. Go on Autoroute A6 to the Rungis-Les Halles exit just north of Orly airport. When you drive in, you must pay an entrance fee equivalent to several dollars. Clean, organized, architecturally undistinguished, but the products are the show. Hundreds of acres of fresh fruit and vegetables (such as matchstick-size string beans laid parallel in the crates), football-field size halls of flowers, hundreds of hanging sides of beef and other meats, rows of cheeses, and warehouses of wines and spirits. Wholesale only: you need a wholesalers' permit to buy. Often you sample free cheeses and wines. 11 p.m.—8 a.m. You will not meet many tourists here!

Sarlat-le-Canéda. Street market in village center. Virtually the entire village becomes a marketplace of food, clothes, junk, and gadgets. Saturdays, dawn to afternoon.

Tours. Flea market at place des Victoires, between the Halles food market (open daily) and the Pont Napoleon. Neighborhood is partly urban renewal, partly broken-down, partly impeccably restored antique homes. Wednesdays and Saturdays from early morning to midafternoon.

Note: for a complete listing of flea markets in France, please see "Manston's Flea Markets, Antiques Fairs, and Auctions of France."

Germany (West)

Frankfurt. Flea market (Flohmarkt) at the Schlachthof on the south bank of the Main River east of the Sachsenhausen district. Saturdays from 8 a.m. to about 3 p.m. (Also see Offenbach.)

Hamburg. Fish market (Fischmarkt), a huge flea market and food and miscellaneous market along the Alster river in the St.-Pauli district (S- and U-Bahn: St.-Pauli Landungsbrücke). Sunday mornings from 5:30 a.m. to about 1 p.m.

Munich. Flea and antique market and carnival (Auer dult), a huge selling festival on Mariahilfplatz, across the river Isar from the Frauenhoferstrasse U-Bahn station. The last week in April and July and the first week in October, all day.

Offenbach. Flea market (Flohmarkt) along the bank of the Main. Best market in the Frankfurt region, on a delightful tree-shaded riverside promenade. Lots of brass, glass, some furniture.

Note: for a complete description and listing of markets in Germany, please see "Manston's Flea Markets, Antique Fairs, and Auctions of Germany."

Great Britain

Birmingham. Flea market every Tuesday, Thursday, and Saturday at St. Martin's Market, immediately across the street from Bull Ring Centre in the city center. Occasional huge Wednesday antique markets as well.

Brighton. Flea market, on Upper Gardiner Street the railway station, Saturday mornings. Brighton is one of the centers of the antiques trade in Britain, and there are dozens of antique shops in the area.

London. Few cities can rival London in the number of its street and flea markets. There is one somewhere every day of the week.
London. Monday through Friday. Leadenhall Street, near Bank underground (subway) station. General street market. Dawn to afternoon.
London. Monday through Saturday. Camden Passage near Angel underground station. Street and flea market (antiques and junk especially on

Wednesday), plus scores of exclusive antique shops. Dawn to dusk.

London. Saturday and Sunday. Camden Lock. Street musicians, jugglers, food makers, and craftspeople in a delightful canal side setting. Nearby, The Stables, north along Chalk Farm Road, are packed with stall-sized shops offering used merchandise of all types, including one of the best selections of collectables in Britain, especially strong in Art Deco.

London. Monday through Saturday. Portobello Road, near Ladbroke Grove and Notting Hill Gate underground stations. Street and flea market (antiques and junk especially on Saturday). Lots of small shops as well as street stalls, high-priced junk as well as high-priced antiques; well picked over. Though a few gems may lurk, it is a tourist attraction as much as a market, with prices to match. Know what you're buying, and watch out for pickpockets!

London. Tuesday, Thursday, Friday, and especially Saturday. Greenwich Antiques Market, nearest to Elephant & Castle underground station.

London. Friday only. New Caledonian (also called Bermondsey), nearest to London Bridge underground station. Flea market possibly with London's best collection of antiques. Treasures lurk here. Dealers predominate as buyers as well as sellers until 7 a.m. Dawn to afternoon.

London. Sunday only. Petticoat Lane, which during the rest of the week is Middlesex Street, near Aldgate underground station. The quintessential London street market, with lots of cheap new junk, sleazy toys, clothes, food, and music. 7 a.m. to mid-afternoon.

London. Sunday only. Chapel Market, Islington, near Angel underground station. Street market with a bit of junk thrown in.

Note: for a complete listing of markets in Britain, please see "Manston's Flea Markets, Antiques Fairs, and Auctions of Britain."

Greece

Athens. Flea market at the east end of the Plaka district. Especially lively on Sunday mornings.

Italy

Arezzo (Tuscany). Antique market (Mostra mercato dell' antiquariato) takes place in the arcaded medieval Piazza Grande and surrounding streets and alleys. The first weekend of every month. Saturdays and Sundays, dawn to late afternoon.

Milan. Flea market (Fiera di Sinigaglia) on Via Catalafini. Saturdays from 8 a.m. to dusk. A long, narrow paved strip in a neighborhood of drab apartment buildings.

Rome. Flea market at Porta Portese. Clothes, antiques, junk, tourist souvenirs, and almost anything else you can think of. Antiques are about one kilometer south of the entrance gate. Chaotically crowded; beware of pickpockets, particularly groups of Gypsy children. Sundays from dawn to about 1 p.m.

Turin. Flea market ("Il Balôn") at Porta Palazzo (also called Piazza della Repubblica). Every Saturday morning. All types of antiques, old clothes, and odds and ends are offered at this large market, which during the rest of the week is a regular street market with food, clothes, and gadgets.

Netherlands

Amsterdam. Flea market and street market at Waterloopleinmarket on Rapenburgerstraat, near where the Amstel and Nieuwe Herengracht meet. Some stands are old railroad cars. Daily from about 7 a.m.

Rotterdam. Flea market and street market on the square under the Blaak Station, across from the public library. Wednesday and Saturday mornings.

Portugal

Barcelos (about 30 miles north of Oporto). A street and craft market at the Campo da Fiera, a quarter-mile square in the center of town graced by a beautiful fountain. Lots of handicrafts, such as the famous Portuguese roosters, embroidered lace and copperware; a food market; live poultry; and assorted odds and ends. Thursdays from 7 a.m. until midafternoon.

Lisbon. Flea market (Fiero da Ladra) behind the S. Vicente de Fora church. Know what you're buying and be prepared to bargain. Tuesdays and Saturdays, early morning until about noon.

Spain

Madrid. Huge flea market (El Rastro) along the Ribera de Curtidores and the alleys and streets around it. Street market Sunday mornings, though dealers' shops and indoor covered galleries are open during the week. Everything from genuine antiques to used electric appliances, clothes, books, records, and junk of every type. Know what you're buying and watch out for pickpockets (especially Gypsies).
Madrid. Stamp market. Plaza Mayor, Sunday mornings until about noon.

Switzerland

Basel. Flea market at Petersplatz. One of Switzerland's best markets. Sundays, April—November, starts about 6:30 a.m.

Geneva. Flea market at Plain de Plain Palais. Get there early—the good stuff goes fast. Wednesdays and Saturdays promptly at 6 a.m.

Zurich. Flea market at Burkliplatz, where Bahnhofstrasse meets the lake. Saturdays May through October from 7 a.m. to midafternoon.

Turkey

Istanbul. Flea Market at Beyazit square. Sunday mornings from dawn to about 1 p.m.

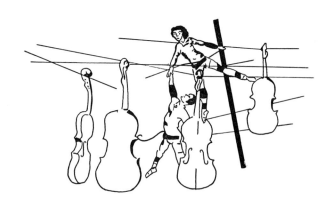

Cultural Pursuits

Performing Arts

Europe offers you an exciting and varied array of symphony, opera, and theatre. You'll also find everything from singers and guitarists in the subways of Paris, to the magnificent circuses of Eastern Europe.

London Theatre

London is famous for its thriving year-round theatre. The theatre district is centered on Shaftesbury Avenue near Piccadilly Circus. Other theatres are throughout the city.

Ticket costs depend on the play and the seat. Musicals cost between £7 and £20 for large productions, while less extravagant theatres offering plays may charge between £4 and £10. Theatre box offices sell tickets at cost, and are usually open about 10 a.m. Tickets can also be obtained from ticket agencies, listed in the phone book under Theatre Booking Agents. In Britain, many agencies charge the price of the ticket plus 21%.

Curtain time is as early as 7 p.m. for evening performances, so be sure you ask for exact information when buying your tickets.

Tickets to smash hits (also called "bombs")
may be difficult to obtain at the last minute.
Some tickets are returned to the box office, and
any unsold special house seats are sold just
before the play at the original cost to anyone
waiting. For hit plays, the lines (queues) form
hours in advance. However, scalpers, known as
"ticket touts" also hover around just before the
play begins.

If you know what you want to see, and when
you'll be there to see it, you can either deal
directly with a ticket agent or the theatre box
office in Britain (ask for the British Tourist
Authority's publications about theatre in
Britain).

You can also order in the United States and
Canada for actual ticket cost plus a booking fee
from:

Edwards & Edwards
1 Times Square Plaza
New York, N. Y. 10036
Tel. (212) 944-0290
or (800) 223-6108
(Fee: ticket + $6 to $15)

Keith Prowse Ltd.
U.S.A.
234 West 44th Street
New York, N.Y. 10036
Tel. (212) 398-1430 or
(800) 223-4446
(Fee: ticket + 21% + $5)

Half-Price Tickets

The Half-Price Ticket Booth in Leicester Square,
in the theatre district, offers tickets valued at
more than £5 or more at half price plus a £1
service charge. Tickets are sold only on the same
day as the performance. (You won't get a seat to
a smash hit here.) The office is open from noon to
2 p.m. for matinee tickets and 2:30 to 6 p.m. for
evening tickets.

Theatre on the Continent

Theatre is as prevalent in major continental
cities as in London. However, English-language
performances are rare, except in Vienna, where
the English Theatre mounts frequent English-
language productions, and in Amsterdam, where
many London productions go on the road.

Information is best obtained on the spot from tourist information offices, from weekly or monthly programs put out by cultural affairs offices, and from newspapers.

Opera

Opera has long been a European favorite. La Scala of Milan is world famous, as are the opera companies of Paris, Vienna, and Berlin, among many others.

Most European opera houses are relatively small, and tickets may be difficult to obtain at the last minute. In this case, you can often purchase standing room tickets an hour or two before the performance. The price of standee tickets may be just a dollar or two, though the comfort level will be low and the sight lines less than ideal.

You can rent opera glasses at opera houses.

Music

Most European countries give great emphasis and often large subsidies to music. It has been said that Austria spends more on music than on the armed forces! The capitals and large cities of almost every country support at least one symphony orchestra, as well as innumerable chamber groups and ensembles.

Obtaining current information is difficult from a distance. Many tourist information offices have free schedules of musical events and can advise you about getting tickets.

Tickets usually must be paid for in cash and are sold at the box office. Some cities have ticket agents. Computerized ticket-purchasing services are rare.

Ticket prices are generally lower than in North America. They are especially low in Eastern Europe, where music is highly subsidized. However, tickets to the most popular cultural events, such as the Bolshoi Ballet, must usually be obtained through the government tourist office, and reserved well in advance.

Movies

Movie theatres are found throughout Europe. Though the highest concentration of movie houses is found in Paris, other large cities are not too far behind.

The films shown run from the current American and European films to retrospectives and Third World film festivals.

Many films in France and Germany are presented in their original language with subtitles for translations. In Italy, most but not all films are dubbed.

Usually films in the original language with subtitles are called the equivalents of "original voice."

In most theatres you'll be escorted to your seat by an usher, who expects a small tip.

Evensong—Church Concerts

Anglican churches in England, particularly in large cities, offer a rare opportunity to enjoy religious music at the daily evensong. Check in churches for the schedule.

Also, many churches offer daytime organ recitals. St. Paul's in London has recitals on a regular schedule.

On the continent, there are also performances in churches, but most of them are in conjunction with church services. Look for posters at churches and elsewhere around town advertising special concerts in churches.

If you're lucky, you will occasionally come across the organist practicing early in the morning or early in the afternoon. However, this is rare in churches where there are significant numbers of tours, which seem to take precedence over music.

Season and the Summer

Most European concert and opera seasons run from late September or early October through May. During the summer, there are many other places to enjoy music: chamber performances and, especially, summer festivals.

The European Association of Music Festivals functions as an information center for these festivals. Its main office is:

Association Européenne des Festivals de Musique
122 rue de Lausanne
CH-1211 Genève 21, Switzerland
Tel. (02) 732 28 03
Fax (02) 738 40 12
Telex 412585 AEFM CH

A free schedule of festivals is put out each year by the Association, listing the major music festivals, and is available from the above address. Tickets and information can be obtained from each festival organizer.

Schedules and ticket information can also be obtained from:

North America	*Great Britain*
Dailey-Thorp Travel Inc.	Specialised Travel Ltd.
315 W. 57th Street	12-15 Hanger Green
New York, N.Y. 10019	London W5 3EL
Tel. (212) 307-1555	Tel. 081-998 1761
Telex 666210 DAITHO	Telex 887863 STPR G

A list of official agents in other countries is available from the Association.

Museums and Museum Passes

Europe's museums range from the well-known riches of the Vatican, Louvre, and the Tate Gallery to small, less known museums focusing on local artists and history. Most standard guidebooks list the museums.

Many museums throughout Europe are closed on Mondays. Often admission prices are reduced on Sundays or one day during the week.

Note: Pickpockets frequently work crowded museums, particularly on free or reduced-price admission days. Guard your valuables carefully.

Passes

Some countries offer special passes that, for a one-time charge, will give you unlimited entry to dozens of museums, estates, and other cultural sites, and sometimes free or reduced price transportation.

Denmark

The Copenhagen Card. This card provides free transportation in the Copenhagen area and free admission to almost all museums and the Tivoli Gardens. Validity is from 1 to 3 days. Contact the Danish Tourist Board for information. This card is sold widely in Copenhagen at tourist information and transit information offices.

France

La Carte. This card provides free or reduced-price admission to over 60 national and municipal museums in Paris and the surrounding region, including the Louvre, Centre Pompidou, Musée d'Orsay, and Versailles. The card costs 100 francs, and is sold at all participating museums and Paris regional offices of the Credit Agricole (CA) bank.

Great Britain

Great Britain has four different and partially overlapping cards.

The Great British Heritage Pass. This card gives you free entry to more than 500 historic houses, castles, and gardens. When you get the card, you also get a map folder showing where you can use it. The card is valid for 15 days or one month. Do not date the card until you first use it.

Buy the card in Great Britain from:

Tourist Information	British Travel Centre
Centre Victoria Station	Lower Regent Street
Forecourt	Piccadilly Circus
London SW1	London W1
or	

London Tourist Information Offices.

Buy the card in North America from British Airways offices or most travel agents, and the British Bookshop (Clifton, N.J. or Los Angeles, Calif.)

On the European continent, ask the British Tourist Authority for local vendors.

Historic Buildings and Monuments Commission for England Card. This one-year card provides free entry to all monuments and sites of the Historic Buildings and Monuments Commission, such as Hampton Court and the Tower of London, as well as some castles in Scotland and Wales.

Buy the card at the ticket office of the first site you visit. The ticket is half price for children and senior citizens.

National Trust Card This one year membership card provides free entry to all National Trust of England, Wales, and Northern Ireland, and National Trust for Scotland sites. There are individuals, family, junior, and life memberships.

The card is available at ticket offices at National Trust properties and from:

The National Trust	The National Trust
Membership	36 Queen Anne's Gate
Department	London SW1H 9AS
P.O. Box 39	Tel. 071-222 9251
Bromley, Kent BR1 1NH	Fax 071-222 6619
Tel. 081-464 1111	

The National Trust also has a United States affiliate, the Royal Oak Foundation, Inc. Membership cards from this foundation provide the same benefits as the National Trust Card. For further information contact:

The Royal Oak Foundation, Inc.
285 West Broadway
New York, N.Y. 10013
Tel. (212) 966-6565
Fax (212) 966-6619

The less expensive (particularly for families) *National Trust for Scotland Card* offering identical privileges in England, Wales, and Northern Ireland as well as Scotland is available from:

The National Trust for Scotland	The National Trust for Scotland
5 Charlotte Square	12 Sherwood St.
Edinburgh EH2 4DU	London W1V 7RD
Tel. 031-226 5922	Tel. 071-437 1012
Telex 272955	

The National Trust for Scotland also has a United States affiliate, Scottish Heritage U.S.A. Membership cards from this organization provide the same benefits as the National Trust for Scotland Card. For further information contact:

Scottish Heritage U.S.A.
Razook Building
P.O. Box 457
Pinehurst, N.C. 28374
Tel. (919) 295-4448

Historic Houses Association Card. This one-year card provides free entry to about 250 privately owned historic houses, including some of those in the Great British Heritage Pass program. This card is available from:

Historic Houses	or P.O. Box 21
Association	Letchworth,
38 Ebury Street	Hertfordshire SG6 4ET
London SW1W 0LU	Tel. 071-730 9419

Italy

There is no nationwide museum pass, but people under 18 and over 65 from Italy and large number of countries (including Canada but not the United States) get free admission to most sites run by the Ministero de Beni Culturali ed Ambientali. Some sites run by regional governments and local let all students and persons over 65 in free; be sure to ask.

The Netherlands

National Museum Card. This annual card (January 1—December 31) gives you free entry to about 400 museums in the Netherlands, including Amsterdam's Rijksmuseum. The card is available in the Netherlands from all local tourist offices (VVV). It is not available outside the Netherlands. The price 21 guilders, but is lower for those under 25 (18.50 guilders) and senior citizens (13.50 guilders).

Holland Culture Card. This annual card (U.S. $20, Canadian $25) looks like a credit card, and a provides free Museum Card (see above). In addition, it also provides entry to artists' studios, and a 50% discount on first-class train tickets inside the Netherlands. You can also use it to obtain tickets for concerts and other performances using the KLM Airlines computer without a service charge. The Holland Culture Card is available only in the United States, Canada, and in Australia, Japan, and New Zealand from KLM airline or Netherlands National Tourist Offices.

Holland Leisure Card. This annual card (U.S. $10, Canadian $13) includes 55% discounts on first class train tickets, 25% discounts on Avis rental cars, and 30% discount on Dutch domestic flights. It is available through the Netherlands Board of Tourism offices outside of the Netherlands.

Sweden

Three cities—Gothenborg, Malmö, and Stockholm—issue transport and tourist cards.
Göteborgskortet. This 3-day card provides free entry to most museums, the Liseburg park, and a free sightseeing tour of the city. Buy it at the Tourist Information Office at Kungsportsplaatsen 2. Reductions are offered for children.
Malmökortet. This 3- or 7-day card gives free public transportation, free entry to most museums, and various other discounts. Buy it at the Tourist Information Office at Hamngatan 1, near the railway station.
Stockholmskortet. This card provides free entry to most Stockholm museums as well as free public transportation. Buy it at the Tourist Office at Hamngatan 27.

Reading in Europe
**Finding English Language Books,
Magazines, and Newspapers**

Looking for the day's news, a novel, or reference
book on the continent of Europe?

You'll have to look harder than in Britain,
Ireland, or at home. When you find an
English-language book or periodical to buy, you
will often pay much more for it than you're
accustomed to.

You can, however, find enough
English-language reading in most countries if
you know where to look. This chapter includes
city-by-city and country-by-country listings with
locations of English-language libraries,
bookstores, and newspapers.

Newspapers and Magazines

English-language newspapers can be found at
street newsstands in major cities and tourist
areas throughout Western Europe. Most of them
are either British or locally produced. British
papers are often one day old, and are widely
available. Locally produced papers are often
oriented to the tourist and expatriate community.

The International Herald Tribune is a 20- to
30-page American-style weekday newspaper sold

on newsstands throughout Western Europe. This Paris-based newspaper for the American community in Europe is jointly owned by the New York Times and the Washington Post. It is the only paper where you'll find American sports news and comic strips. It also carries American and New York stock market quotations. The cost is approximately one dollar per issue, listed in local currency equivalents at the top of the front page. Be sure it is the current day's issue, however: news vendors have been known to slip an old issue to an unsuspecting buyer.

The Wall Street Journal also has a European edition available, published every business day. It is harder to find, but is carried by newsstands of major hotels catering to American business travelers. It is similar to the United States edition but has fewer pages and carries more European business news. Complete stock market quotations are included in every issue.

USA Today is also widely available in most large European cities.

Newsweek and Time European editions are also available reasonably widely in Europe. Like the International Herald Tribune, they are relatively expensive: the prices in each country where they are widely sold are printed on the covers.

McLeans is not generally found.

News in Eastern Europe is quite different. Western publications are often unavailable many Eastern European countries. When available, they will be found at the newsstands inside the hotels reserved for foreigners, and can be up to two weeks old. The only current English-language newspapers and magazines are likely to be those issued in the country you're in, though this is likely to change. Sometimes the local papers are left in stacks in the foreigners' hotel lobbies, and are free for the taking. These Eastern newspapers are very different than those you're used to, both in the type of the stories and their slant. There is much less advertising, if any.

Books

English-language books are much harder to find than newspapers and magazines. In general, you are more likely to find English-language books in the small countries of northern Europe such as the Netherlands and Scandinavian nations. There are also a few bookstores thinly scattered in large cities in the rest of Europe as well.

Finding English-language books to buy in the Eastern Bloc will be difficult and the selection limited.

English-language books, whether new or used, are almost always more expensive than at home, in part because costs of import are high and the volume is low.

English-Language Libraries

The United States Information Service of the United States government maintains a network of English language libraries in most major cities of Europe. While primarily designed for local residents (who are able to check out books), they also welcome travelers. They resemble a small-town public library, with standard reference works, nonfiction and fiction sections, and a limited selection of periodicals. These libraries are marked (USIS) in the listings.

Great Britain also has a network of English language libraries operated by the British Council, a quasi-governmental nonprofit agency. They have British books and periodicals. Many have both nonfiction and some particularly good fiction sections. These libraries are marked (BC) in the listings.

All USIS and all British Council libraries are open to anyone for reading room and reference use. If you will be staying in one location for an extended period, you can qualify for a library card to obtain check-out privileges at either or both of these libraries. Sometimes a small card fee is charged at the British Council libraries.

In addition, public libraries are scattered around, particularly in northern Europe. Some of them have English-language sections, particularly at universities

Key to English-Language Libraries, Bookstores, and Some Newspapers in Europe

Austria

Vienna
Libraries

Amerika Haus
Bibliothek (USIS)
Friedrich Schmidt-Platz
2 (behind the Rathaus at
the American consular
offices)
A-1010 Wien
Tel. 31 55 11

British Council Library
(BC)
Schenkenstrasse 4
(behind the Burgtheater)
A-1010 Wien
Tel. 533 26 16
Fax 533 25 16 85
Telex 132521 BC VIE A

Bookstores

The British Bookshop
Weihburggasse 8
A-1010 Wien
Tel. 512 19 45

Wilhelm Frick
Buchhandlung
Graben 27
A-1010 Wien
Tel. 533 99 14 and
533 99 15

Leopold Heidrich
English Bookshop
Plankengasse 7
Tel. 522 72 87

Shakespeare &
Company, Booksellers
Sterngasse 2
A-1010 Wien
Tel. 535 50 53
Fax 535 50 54
Telex 75312509 SHAK A

Belgium

Brussels
Libraries

The American Library
(USIS)
Square du Bastion 1-C
(at the Porte de Namur
Pre-Metro stop)
1050 Bruxelles
Tel. (02) 512 21 29

British Council Library
(BC)
Brittania House
Rue Joseph II 30
1040 Bruxelles
Tel. (02) 219 36 00
Fax (02) 217 58 11
Telex 24743 BCBEL B

Bookstores

W.H. Smith   71-79
boulevard Adolphe Max
(near de Broukere
Metro)
1001 Bruxelles
Tel. (02) 219 27 08

La Route de Jade Travel
Bookstore
rue de Stassert 116
1050 Bruxelles
Tel. (02) 572 96 54
Many guidebooks in
English, lots of maps.

The Strathmore
Bookshop
131 rue St. Lambert
(behind shopping center)
1200 Bruxelles
Tel. (02) 771 92 00
Fax (02) 771 21 55
Metro: Roodebeek, then
through shopping center.

House of Paperbacks
813 Chausée de
Waterloo
1180 Bruxelles
Tel. (02) 343 1122
(tram 90 + 23 to
Churchill)

The English Shop (Le Magazin Anglais)
1384 Chausée de Waterloo
Uccle, 1180 Bruxelles
Tel. (02) 374 9839

Czechoslovakia

Prague
Library
British Council Library (BC)
British Embassy
Jungmannova 30
110 00 Prague 1
Tel. 22 45 01, 22 45 50; Telex 122097 BCCZC

Denmark

Copenhagen
Libraries

American Library(USIS)
Dag Hammerskjølds Alle
24 (also the U.S.
Embassy)
DK 2100 København
(Open 12-5 p.m., 12-6:30
on Monday)
Tel. 33 42 31 44

British Council Library
Møntergade 1 (near the
east end of the Strøget)
1116 København K
(Open 9:30—4:30)
Tel. 33 11 20 44
Telex REF BCO023
265451 MONREF G

Bookstores

Boghallen
Rådhusplads 37
1585 København V
Tel. 33 11 85 11

Arnold Busck
International Boghandel
Købmagergade 49
DK-1150 København K
Tel. 33 12 24 53
Fax 33 03 44 90

Magasin du Nord
Kongens Nytorv 13
1095 København K
Tel. 33 11 44 33
(books on fourth floor)

Illums
Østergade 52
Tel. 33 14 40 02
(book department on
ground floor)

Norisk Boghandel
Østergade 16
DK-1100 København K
Tel. 33 14 07 07
Fax 33 93 44 90

Erik Paludan Boghandel
Fiolstr. 10
Tel. 33 15 06 75

Magazine
Copenhagen This Week (published monthly!) Free four-
color glossy with information about cultural events in
the center pages, and street and transit maps. Widely
available in Copenhagen.

Finland

Helsinki
Libraries
America Center Library
(USIS)
Kaivokatu 10A
00101 Helsinki 10
Tel. 176599

British Council Library
(BC)
Erottajankatu 7B
00130 Helsinki 13
Tel. 640505
Fax 603820
Telex 123936 BCHEL SF

Bookstores
Akateeminen
Kirjakauppa
Keskuskatu 1
00100 Helsinki
Tel. 121 41
Fax 121 4441
Telex 125080 AKAHE

Suomalainen
Kirjakauppa
Branches throughout
Helsinki; central tel.
65155

France

Bordeaux
Library
British Council Library
(BC)
c/o British Consulate
General
15 cours de Verdun
33000 Bordeaux Cedex
Tel. 56.52.28.35

Lille
Library
British Council Library
(BC)
c/o British Consulate
General
24 square de Tilleul
59019 Lille
Tel. 20.52.87.90

Lyon
Library
British Council Library
(BC)
c/o British Consulate
General
24 rue Childebert
69288 Lyon Cedex 1
Tel. 78.37.59.67

Marseille
Library
British House
24 avenue du Prado
13000 Marseille
Tel. 91.54.29.43
or 91.33.48.02

Paris
Libraries
British Council Library
(BC)
9 rue de Constantine
75007 Paris
Tel. (1) 45.55.95.95
Fax (1) 47 05 77 02
Telex 250912 BRICOUN

Centre de Docu-
mentation Benjamin
Franklin (USIS)
2 rue St. Florentin
75001 Paris
Tel. (1) 42.22.22.70

Bookstores
Brentano's
37 ave. de l'Opéra / 8
rue Danielle Casanova
75002 Paris
Tel. (1) 42.61.52.50
Metro: Opéra

Shakespeare & Co.
37 rue de la Bûcherie
75005 Paris
Metro: St. Michel
Used books only; no
phone

Galignani
224 rue de Rivoli
75001 Paris
Tel. (1) 42.60.76.07
Fax (1) 42.86.09.31
Metro: Tuileries

W.H. Smith
The English Bookshop
248 rue de Rivoli
75001 Paris
Tel. (1) 42.60.37.97
Metro: Concorde

NQL International -
Nouveau Quartier Latin
78 blvd. St. Michel
Tel. (1) 43.26.42.70
Fax (1) 47.35.53.27
Telex 202650 F
Metro: Luxembourg

Village Voice
6 rue Princesse
75006 Paris
Tel. (1) 46.33.36.47

Toulouse
Bookstore
The Bookshop—Librairie Anglo-Saxonne
17 rue Lakanal (near place du Capitole)
31000 Toulouse
Tel. 61.22.99.92

Germany East (DDR)

Berlin
Library
British Council Library (BC)
Unter den Linden 32/34
DDR-Berlin 1080
Tel. 220 2431. Fax 312 1064. Telex 113171 GBBER DD

Germany, West (BRD)

Berlin
Libraries
Amerika Haus Berlin
(USIS)
Hardenbergstrasse 22-24
D-1000 Berlin 12
Tel. 8 19 79 05
Fax 31 79 45

British Council Library
(BC)
Hardenbergstrasse 20
D-1000 Berlin 12
Tel. 31 19 99
Fax 310 1099 20
Telex 185814 BCGB D

Bookstores
Buchexpress
Habelschwerater Alle 4
Tel. 8 31 40 04

Marga Schoeller
Bucherstube GmbH
Knesebekstrasse 33
D1000 Berlin 12
Tel. 881 11 12, 881 11 22

Bonn
Library (USIS)
American Embassy
Deichmannsaue 29
D-5300 Bonn 2
Tel. 33 91 (central number)

Cologne (Köln)

Libraries

Amerika Haus Köln
(USIS)
Apostelnkloster 13/15
D-5000 Köln 1
Tel. 209 01 47   Fax
24 45 43

British Council Library
(BC)
Hahnenstrasse 6
D-5000 Köln 1
Tel. 20 64 40
Fax 2064455
Telex 888 1147 BCGK D

Frankfurt
Library

Amerika Haus
Frankfurt (USIS)
Staufenstrasse 1
D-6000 Frankfurt 1
Tel. 72 33 37
Fax 72 02 05

Bookstore

The British Bookshop
GmbH
Börsenstrasse 17
D-6000 Frankfurt 1
Tel. 28 04 92

Freiburg
Library

Carl-Schurz-Haus
German-American Institute
Kaiser Joseph Strasse 266
D-7800 Freiburg
Tel. 3 16 46

Hamburg
Libraries

Amerika Haus Hamburg
(USIS)
Tesdorpfstrasse 1
D-2000 Hamburg 13
Tel. 44 46 30
Fax 44 47 05

British Council Library
(BC)
Rothenbaumchausee 34
D-2000 Hamburg 13
Tel. 44 60 57
Fax 47 11 4
Telex 2162557 BCHB D

Hannover

Library
Amerika Haus
Hanover (USIS)
Prinzenstrasse 9
D-3000 Hannover 1
Tel. 32 72 86
Fax 32 16 34

Heidelberg

Library
German-American
Institute
Sophienstrasse 12
D-6900 Heidelberg 1
Tel. 2 47 71

Munich (München)

Libraries
Amerika Haus München
(USIS)
Karolinenplatz 3
D-8000 München 2
Tel. 59 53 67
Fax 55 35 78

British Council Library
(BC)
Bruderstrasse 7/111
D-8000 München 22
Tel. 22 33 26
Fax 9 57 45
Telex 528446 BCGM D

Bookstore
Anglia English Bookstore
Schellingstrasse 3
D-8000 München 40
Tel. 28 36 42

Nürnberg

Library
German-American
Institute
Gleissbühlstrasse 13
D-8500 Nürnberg 1
Tel. 20 33 27

Saarbrücken

Library
German-American
Institute
Berliner Promenade 15
D-6600 Saarbrücken
Tel. 3 11 60

Stuttgart

Library
Amerika Haus Stuttgart
(USIS)
Friedrichstrasse 23A
D-7000 Stuttgart 1
Tel. 229 33 17
Fax 229 83 39

Tübingen

Library
German-American
Institute
Karlstrasse 3
D-7400 Tübingen
Tel. 3 40 71

Great Britain

Public libraries
Britain has an excellent public library system. A library can be found in almost every medium size town or city. Check the telephone book and look under libraries, or ask at the local tourist information office.

Bookstores
There are so many bookstores in London that you can buy books about them. Many are on Charing Cross Road. In the rest of Britain, bookstores abound, particularly in university towns such as Oxford and Cambridge.

Newspapers
A wide variety of newspapers is sold in every city, town, and almost every village. Almost all of the London newspapers also have national distribution throughout Britain.

Magazines
The weekly magazines Time Out and What's On, £1 each, are probably the best source to find out about London's current entertainment and cultural events. You can buy them at every newsstand in London.

Greece

Athens
Libraries

American Library (USIS)
22 Massalias Street (at right angles to Akademius)
22 Μασσαλίας
10 144 Athens
Tel. 77 89 407

British Council Library (BC)
17 Plateia Philikis Etairias
Kolonaki Square
17 Πλατέια Φιλικῆξ Εταιρίαξ
(Πλατέια Κολωνακίου)
10673 Athens
P.O. Box 3488
10 210 Athens
Tel. 36 33 211
Fax 36 34 769
Telex 218 799 BRIC GR

Bookstores

Eleftheroudakis
4 Nikis (near Syntygma
Square)   105 63 Athens
Ελευθεροδάκης
Νίκης 4
Tel. 32 21 255
Fax 32 39 821
Telex 219410

Pantelides
11 Amerikis (near the
Academy)
Παντελίδης
Αμερικής 11
Tel. 64 48 547

Reymondo's International Bookstore
18 Voukourestiou (near Syntygma)
Tel. 36 48 188
18 Βουκουρεστίου

Newspapers
The Athens News and the Athens Daily Post, published
daily. Sold at news kiosks and hotels. Also, The Week
in Athens, published weekly, is found at tourist information offices and main hotels. Lists current cultural
events and a useful hodgepodge of information, including a map of central Athens inside the back cover. The
Athenian magazine is monthly, 250 drachmas.

Thessaloniki (Salonika)
Libraries

American Center
Library (USIS)
34 Metropoleos Street
34 Μητροπολέως

British Centre Library
(BC)
9 Ethnikis Aminis
(corner of Tsimiski)
54 013 Saloniki
P.O. Box 50007
Εθνικής Αμύνις 9
Tel. 235 236
and   285 570
Fax 282 490
Telex 412974 BCSLGR

Hungary

Budapest
Library
British Council Library (BC)
Harmincad Utca 6
Budapest V
Tel. 118 28 88
Fax 117 17 40
Telex 224527 BRIT H

Newspaper
The Daily News/Neueste Nachricten. This bilingual (English-German) daily newspaper publishes local news. It can be found in some news kiosks, but is sometimes free in the lobbies of the foreigners' hotels (such as the Intercontinental, Hilton, and Gellert). The main Western-oriented hotels newspaper stands sometimes have the London Times, International Herald Tribune, and other Western newspapers.

Italy

Florence
Library
Biblioteca dell' Instituto Britannico
Palazzo Lanfredini
Lungarno Guicciardini 9
50010 Firenze
Tel. 228 40 31

Bookstores
BM Bookshop
Borgognissanti 4r
50123 Firenze
Tel. and Fax 29 45 75
All English language.

Feltrinelli
Via Cavour 12/20
50129 Firenze
Tel. 29 21 96 and 21 95 24
Large English-language section.

G.P.L. Librerie Marzocco
Via Martelli 22r
50129 Firenze
Tel. 28 22 73
Fax 21 58 12
Has large English section.

Paperback Exchange
Via Fiesolana 31r
Tel. and fax 247 81 54
Almost all English-language and will trade.

Milan (Milano)

Libraries

Biblioteca Americana
(USIS)
Via Bigli 11/A
20121 Milano
Tel. 79 50 51 -5

British Council Library
(BC)
Via Manzoni 38
20121 Milano
Tel. 782018, 782016,
781749
Fax 78 11 19
Telex 311084 BRICON I

Bookstores

American Bookstore
via Camperio 16 at
Largo Cairoli
20123 Milano
(Metro: Cairoli)
Tel. 870944
All English language

English Bookshop
via Mascheroni 12
20123 Milano
(Metro: Conciliazione)
Tel. 4694468

Hoepli
via Hoepli 5
20121 Milano
(Metro: Duomo or San Babila)
Tel. 865446

Naples (Napoli)

Library British
Council Library (BC)
Palazzo d'Avalos
via dei Mille 48
80121 Napoli
Tel. 414876 and 421321
Telex 710460 BRICON I

Bookstore
Universal Books
Rione Sirignano 1
80124 Napoli
Tel. (081) 663217

Rome (Roma)

Libraries

Biblioteca Americana
(USIS)
Via Veneto 119a
00187 Roma
Tel. 46 742

British Council Library
(BC)
(Biblioteca Britannica)
Palazzo del Drago
Via delle Quattro
Fontane 20
00184 Roma
Tel. 475 66 41
Fax 475 4296
Telex 622231 BRICON I

Bookstores

Anglo-American
Bookshop
Via delle Vite 57
00187 Roma
Tel. 679 52 22

Economy Book & Video
Center
Via Torino 136
00184 Roma
Tel. 474 6877
Fax 48 36 61
Many used books—they
will trade!

The Lion Bookshop
Via del Babuino 181
(near the Spanish steps)
00187 Roma
Tel. 322 58 37
Fax 322 47 27

Open Door Bookshop
via della Lungaretta 25
00179 Roma
Tel. 589 64 78

Newspapers
International Daily News, sold at newsstands in
tourist-frequented areas. This Week in Rome lists
entertainment and tourist-oriented and cultural
events. Get it at tourist information offices and some
newsstands.

Turin
Bookstore
Libreria Luxemburg
via Cesare Battisti 7
10123 Torino
Tel. (011) 597621

Luxembourg
Bookstore
The English Shop (Le Magasin Anglais)
Allée Sheffer 19
L-2520 Luxembourg
Tel. 2 49 25
Newspaper
Luxembourg News Digest, weekly; sold at some
newstands (80 F) or free in major hotels. Strictly local
and expatriate news. Tel. 97 00 52

Malta

Valetta
American Center Library (USIS)
Development House, Floor 3
St. Ann Street, Floriana
P.O. Box 510, Valetta

Netherlands

Amsterdam
Library
British Council Library (BC)
Keizersgracht 343
1016 EH Amsterdam
Tel. 22 36 44 Telex 16599 BCAMS NL

Bookstores
Allert de Lange
Boekhandel B.V.
Damrak 60-62
1012 LM Amsterdam
Tel. 246744

American Discount Book
Centers
Kalverstraat 185
1012 XC Amsterdam
Tel. 25 55 37
and 23 53 36
Fax 24 80 42

English Book Shop
Lauriergracht 71
1016 Amsterdam
Tel. 26 42 30

Athenaeum Boekhandel
Spui 14-16
1012 XA Amsterdam
Tel. 22 62 48

Scheltema Holkema
Vermeulen B.V.
Koningsplein 20
1017 BB Amsterdam
Tel. 26 72 12

Robert Premsela
 van Baerlestraat 78
1071 BB Amsterdam
Tel. 6624266

Haarlem
Athenaeum Boekhandel
B.V.
Gedempte Oude Gracht
70
2011 GT Haarlem
Tel. 31 87 55

The Hague

Library
American
Documentation Center
(USIS)
Korte Voorhout 2
2521 EK Den Haag

Bookstore
American Discount Book
Centers
Spuistraat 72
2511 BE Den Haag
Tel. 364 27 42
Fax 335 65 57

Norway

Oslo

Libraries
U. S. Reference Center
(USIS)
Drammensveien 18
0255 Oslo 2
Tel. 44-20-63

British Council Library
(BC)
Fridtjof Nansens Plass 5
0160 Oslo 1
Tel. 42 68 48
Fax 55 10 41
Telex 79421 BRICO N

Bookstores
Tanum-Karl Johan
Karl Johans gate 43
0162 Oslo 1
Tel. 42 93 10
Fax 33 32 75

Olaf Norlis Bokhandel
Universitetsgaten 18-24
0162 Oslo 1
Tel. 42 91 35
Fax 11 10 22
Telex 79265 NORLI N

Poland

Krakow

Library
Biblioteka Amerykanski
(USIS)
Konsulate Stanow
Zjednoczonych Ameryki
Ulica Stolarska 9 (in the
U.S. consulate)
31043 Krakow
Tel. 229400

Poznan

Library
Biblioteka Amerykanski
(USIS)
Konsulate Stanow
Zjednoczonych Ameryki
Ulica Chopina 4
Tel. 59586

Warsaw
Libraries

British Council Library
(BC) Al Jerozolimskie
59 (in the British
Embassy)
00697 Warszawa
Tel. 287401/3
Telex 812555 BRIN PL

Biblioteka Amerykanski
(USIS)
Ambasada Stanow
Zjednoczonych Ameryki
Aleje Ujadowskie 29/31
(in the U.S. embassy)
Tel. 229-764

Portugal

Coimbra
Library

Casa de Inglatera (BC)
Rua do Tomar 4
3000 Coimbra
Tel. 39 23549, 39 33437, 39 36705
Telex 29297 BRITCO P

Lisbon
Libraries

The British Institute
(BC)
Rua Rua de São Marçal
1294 Lisboa
Tel. 347 5141
Fax 347 61 52
Telex 42544 BRITCO P

Biblioteca Americana
(USIS)
Avenida das Forças
Armadas
Apartado 4258
1507 Lisboa
(in the U.S. Embassy)
Tel. 726 66 00

Bookstores

Livraria Britannica
Rua de São Marçal 83
1200 Lisboa
Tel. 32 84 72

Also, several bookshops
on Rua Garrett have
some English-language
books.

Newspaper

Anglo-Portuguese News, published the second and
fourth Thursday each month, has news, entertainment
listings, and ads. Available at newsstands.

Porto

Library British Council
Library (BC)
Rua de Breyner 155
4000 Porto
Tel. 317321 and 384762
Telex 29297 BRIOPO P

Bookstore   Livraria
Britanica
Rua Jos Falcão 184
4000 Porto
Tel. 323930
Telex 27247 ESCOL P

Romania

Bucharest

Libraries
Biblioteca Americana
(USIS)
Strada Alexandru Sahia
7-9
Bucuresti 70201

British Council Library
(BC)
Strada Jules Michelet
24
Bucuresti
Tel. 11 1634/6
Telex 11295 PRODM R

Soviet Union

Moscow

Library (BC)
Naberezhnaya Morisa
Toreza 14
Moscow 109072
Tel. 2318511 (Embassy)
2334507 (Cultural
Section)
Fax 2333563
Telex 413341 BEMOS
SU

Bookstore
Bookstore
U.S. Bookstore
Ulitsa Checkhova 16
103006 Moscow
Telex MK 41160
(Behind Sovincentr, at
Zone 4A, Exhibition
Complex) Accepts hard
currency only.

Британское Посольство
(Библиотека)
Набережная Мориса Тереза
14
109072 МОСКВА

СШ А Книжный магазин
Улица Чехова 15
103006 МОСКВА

Spain

Barcelona
Libraries

British Council Library
(BC)
Calle Amigo 83
08021 Barcelona
Tel. 209 13 64
Fax 202 31 68
Telex 50512 BINB E

Centro de Referencias y
Bibliografia
Via Augusta 123
08006 Barcelona

Madrid
Libraries

Biblioteca Washington
Irving (USIS)
Centro Cultural de los
Estados Unidos
Marques de Villamagna
8
28001 Madrid
Tel. 447 19 00

British Council Library
(BC)
Calle Almagro 5
28010 Madrid
Tel. 419 12 50
Fax 410 46 15
Telex 42769 INSBR E

Bookstore
Turner English Bookshop
Calle Génova 3
28004 Madrid
Tel. 410 43 59 and 410 29 15
Fax 419 39 30
Telex 41884 TEBSA E

Newspapers
Iberia Daily, sold at newsstands and hotels. Also,
Guidepost Magazine, a weekly magazine, lists enter-
tainment and cultural events.

Seville
Library

British Council Library
(BC)
Plaza Neuva 8 DPDO
41001 Seville
Tel. 22 88 73
Telex 72107

Valencia
Library

The British Institute
(BC)
General San Martín 7
46004 Valencia
Tel. 351 88 18, 352 98
74
Fax 352 867 88
Telex 63281 INBV E

Sweden

Stockholm
Libraries
American Reference
Center (USIS)
Strandvagen 101
S-11350 Stockholm
Tel. 783 53 00

British Council Library
(BC) Skarpögatan 6
S-115-27 Stockholm
Tel. 667 01 40
Fax 6637271
Telex 19340 BRITEMB S

Bookstores
Almqvist & Wiksell
Bokhandel AB
G Brogade 26
Tel. 23 79 90

English Book Centre
Sorbrunnsgatan 51
Tel. 30 14 47

Fritzes Horbokhandel
AB
Regeringsgade 12
Tel. 23 89 00

Hedengrens Bokhandel
Stureplan 4
S114 35 Stockholm
Tel. 611 51 28 and
611 51 32
Fax 611 51 38

Switzerland

Zurich
Bookstores
Buchhandlung Friedrich
Däniker
In Gassen 11
Tel. 211 27 04

Buchhandlung Kurt
Stäheli & Co.
Bahnhofstrasse 70
8021 Zurich
Tel. 211 33 02
Fax 202 55 52
Telex 813771 STAE CH

Turkey
Ankara
Libraries
British Council Library
BC
Kirlangic Sokak 9
Gazi Osman Pasa
Ankara 06700
Fax 143 76 82
Telex 42049 IBIK TR

Amerikan Kutuphanese
(USIS)
Cinnah Caddesi 20
Kavaklidere, Ankara

Istanbul

Libraries
Amerikan Kutuphanesi
(USIS)
104-108 Mesrutiyet
Caddesi (in the
American Conslulate)
Tepebasi
Tel. 1436200/09

British Council Library
(BC)
Cumhuriyet Caddesi
22-24   PK436
Beyoglu
Ege Han K2   Elmadag
80074 Istanbul
Tel. 1467125/6, 1463073
Telex 23283 IKIK TR

Bookstore
Redhouse Kitabevi
Rizapasa Yokusu 50 (district near the Misir Carsisi)
Tel. 5223905

Newspaper
The Turkish Daily News and Dateline Turkey (week-ly), are available at some newsstands and hotels.

Yugoslavia

Belgrade

Libraries
Americki Centar (USIS)
Cika Ljubina 19
11000 Beograd

British Council Library
Generala Zdanova 34,
mezanin   Post Fah 248
11011 Beograd
Tel. 332 441, 327 910
Telex 11032 BRIBEL YU

Ljubljana

Library
Ameriški Center (USIS)
Cankarjeva 11
61000 Ljubljana
Tel. 210 910

Sarajevo

Library
Americki Centar (USIS)
Omladinska broj 1
71000 Sarajevo
Tel. 16 079 and 25 997

Skopje

Library
Amerikanski Centar
(USIS)
Grandski Zid, blok IV
91000 Skopje

Titograd

Library
Americki Centar (USIS)
Bulevar Oktobarske
Revolucije 100
81000 Titograd

Zagreb

Libraries
Americki Centar (USIS)
Zrinjevac 13
41000 Zagreb

British Centre (BC)
Ilica 12/1
41001 Zagreb
Tel. 425 244
Telex 22533 BRIZAG YU

Returning Home
Airports and Customs

Returning home requires some planning. You'll have to pack your belongings, get to the airport or dock, arrange for value-added tax refunds if your purchases qualify, and check in.

In either the United States or Canada, you'll have to face customs and immigration officials on arrival. Advance planning and knowledge can make the task easier.

Packing

You should pack your declarable items where they're easily available for United States or Canadian customs inspection. If you plan to ask for value-added tax refunds, you may be required to show the purchases made before the European customs officer stamps your refund forms, which is usually necessary to receive a refund.

Getting to the Airport

Major airports are relatively easy to get to by public transit. A London subway line, for example, goes to Heathrow. Quick, frequent, inexpensive trains go to airports in London (Gatwick), Brussels, Frankfurt, Amsterdam, and Zurich, among others. The rest, such as Charles de Gaulle and Orly in Paris, Schwechat in Vienna, and most of the airports in Eastern Europe are linked to their cities by frequent shuttle buses traveling from city or airline terminals.

In most cases the public transit alternatives are much cheaper and quicker than taxis. Likewise subways and trains can be quicker than a private car, too.

See the Public Transit chapter for details.

Check-in and Security Checks

You must pass through security and passport control after check-in. This will take about an hour and a half, on the average. While check-in is about the same the world over, security varies country by country and airport by airport, and, also, by the level of terrorist activity in the previous few weeks. Several inspection systems can be used. At some airports, all checked-in passengers must pass through a single inspection station. At others, such as Frankfurt, you are inspected by security only as you actually board the plane. (The second system is preferable for the passenger, since it means your plane is less likely to take off without you as you squeeze and jostle passengers on all other flights.)

Occasionally, every piece of your baggage will inspected by hand in your presence after check-in but before you board the plane—a very time-consuming event.

You can ask for film to be hand inspected but the request will not always be honored.

Value-Added Tax Refund

When you leave, if you want to have your value-added tax money refunded, you must have all the paperwork stamped. Be prepared to show your receipts and the merchandise. In some countries, these offices are before the security check (and before check-in). Others, particularly in Britain, have them after check-in. You have to ask specifically for the office—otherwise you cannot, in most cases, receive your refund. The office name to ask for varies from country to country. Allow an extra hour or two to take care of this task. It may not take this long, but then again, it might.

Note: you can only be "de-taxed" for items purchased in the country you're leaving. See the Value-Added Tax Refunds chapter for detailed information.
Some of the customs office names are:

Austria: Zollamt

France: Bureau de la Douane—Détaxe

Italy: Ufficio della Dogana

West Germany: Zollamt

Great Britain: Her Majesty's Customs and Excise Office The windows are after check-in and security check at Heathrow. At Gatwick, be sure to visit the Customs office before check-in.

Spain: Oficina de Aduana, usually called "Oficina de Desgravaciónes Fiscales." The window at Madrid's Barajas airport is before check-in and security on the main departure level.

Duty-Free Shops

Virtually every airport has one or more "duty-free" or "tax-free" shops. You'll encounter them after you have passed the point of no return. These shops can amount to small shopping centers, such as at Amsterdam, Copenhagen, Frankfurt, and Shannon (Ireland).
    Duty-free doesn't mean you may not have to pay customs duty at the other end of the flight. Duty-free means only that you don't have to pay any national value-added tax or tariff in the country of purchase.
    Compare prices carefully, and know what the items cost outside, since you may find that prices at duty-free shops are no bargain. In fact, at many airports, the only duty-free items are liquor and tobacco products. Often you can pay

less in town if you can get the value added-tax refunded. Some in-city stores will even deliver the goods to the airport for pickup. (This may save you from the paperwork of the value-added tax refund process.) Some items are even cheaper at home than at the duty-free shops.

Duty-Free Allowances for United States Residents

If you live in the United States, you are permitted to bring in $400 of merchandise duty free every 30 days, as long as it is only for personal use. Those traveling together may pool their allowances.

If you bring in more, the next $1,000 worth is taxable at 10% of the purchase price. If you bring in more than $1,400 worth the duty on the additional amount is calculated according to the tariff handbook (Tariff Schedule of the United States of America). Duty varies from item to item, and by country of origin, in a complicated and complex code.

The items with the highest duty are supposed to be included in the duty-free allowance.

Some items such as art (but not new frames) and items originating in Third World countries are not subject to payment of duty.

You are also permitted to bring in one liter of alcohol into the United States without payment of tax. Some states you land in permit you to bring in more, while some (such as California) limit the amount to the single liter. If permitted to bring more, you may have to pay tax on all alcohol except the single tax-free liter.

Duty-Free Allowances for Canadian Residents

You can bring in purchases of up to $300 Canadian per person once per calendar year. You must remain out of Canada for at least seven days to claim this exemption. Allowances cannot be pooled among families or others traveling together. You will have to complete a written declaration upon your return.

If you have already taken your $300 yearly exemption (even though you didn't use it all up), you can also bring in purchases worth up to $100 each calendar quarter if you remain outside of Canada for at least seven days. In order to receive this exemption, you *must* give your written declaration to the customs inspector.

You are permitted to bring in 1.1 litres (an imperial quart) of wine or hard liquor if you meet the provincial age limit where you enter Canada. Instead of wine or spirits, you could bring in up to one case (8.2 litres) of beer or ale. Duty will be charged on amounts over this allowance.

Customs During Your Return

Every passenger approaching the United States or Canada from Europe whether on an airplane or ship, receives a customs declaration form (for the United States, Customs Form 6059B). You have to complete it in detail, particularly if you are bringing in more than the $400 (or $300 for Canada) per person exemption.

You should have the items you purchased while abroad available for inspection. You should have any fruit or vegetables available, too. Note that importation of many, but not all, are forbidden. (Pineapples and bananas are admitted, though the customs inspector may have to refer to the regulations manual.) Also, all pork products (except canned ones), including salami and sausages, are forbidden. Other forbidden items include switchblade knives (except by one-armed amputees), illicit drugs, liqueur-filled chocolates, and items made from endangered species.

Trademarked Items

If you buy trademarked items (such as cameras, perfumes, designer clothes, etc.) while abroad, you can usually bring in at least one of each trademarked item (even if it is counterfeit).

Trademarks are owned by the manufacturers. The manufacturer can set the allowable number of items (over one) and customs will enforce the allowance. If you wish to bring in more, you may have to remove the trademark from all of the surplus items, whether counterfeit or original.

Special rules are enforced for copyrighted material such as computer programs.

If you exceed the permitted quantity of trademarked items, you may be permitted to pay a bond and later bring the items to a customs office to prove you have removed the marks and reclaim the bond. At other times, you may have to remove them there on the spot, which can be awkward.

Materials in violation of copyright law can be refused entry completely.

Potential problems can be eliminated by obtaining the brochure, "U.S. Customs Service Trademark Information for Travelers," or contacting any customs office. You can also contact commercial officers in Canadian or United States embassies.

Immigration and Customs

You can be subjected to any one of several customs and immigration clearance systems. In some, you must first show your passport at the immigration counter and then retrieve your luggage and let customs inspect it at another counter. In others, the passport and baggage inspection are done at the same time by the same officer.

Sometimes you show your passport and then reclaim your baggage and face the "Red-Green" option: go to the Red counters if you have something to declare and Green if you don't. (Random checks are made of people using the Green line, too.)

If you have something to declare, or have bought over the $400 (or $300) limit, go to the Red line. Otherwise, go to the Green nothing-to-declare line.

Registering Imported Items at Home

If you take expensive imported items (such as bicycles, cameras, computers, Swiss watches, etc.) with you which you had at home in North America, you should register your items before you leave. You can do this at any time prior to leaving the United States or Canada. You will usually have to take the item(s) to the nearest customs office, where you will receive a small form proving that you already own the item. These forms include brand name and serial number or description. Keep the form with your passport and valuable travel papers. The Customs form for United States residents is Certificate of Registration for Personal Effects Taken Abroad, Customs Form 4457. The Customs form for Canadian residents is Customs Form Y38.

You need only to do this once as long as you still own the item.

Paying Customs Duty

If you have to pay Customs duty, you will be given a tag to take to the cashier, just past the customs inspection booth. You will have to pay, with either cash, travelers check, or a personal check.

At some major international airports in the United States (including New York, Los Angeles, Chicago, Dulles, Baltimore-Washington, San Francisco, and Seattle; more to be added), VISA and MasterCards are also accepted.

All payments to the United States Customs must be made in U.S. dollars.

Payments to the Canadian Customs and Excise must be made in Canadian dollars.

Inspection Note

United States Customs officers performing a customs or immigration inspection are the only law enforcement officers who are not required to advise you of your rights if you're under suspicion, and are not required to have a search warrant to search either you or your baggage for contraband.

Index

English-language
  library in 441
U.S. embassy in 366
Bookstores
  English-language
    in Europe 436-455
  for background infor-
    mation 9-10
  specializing in travel 9-10
Bordeaux
  English-language library
    440
  U.S. consulate in 366
Breakfast
BRD (see West Germany)
  alternative to hotel
    325-326
  at bed & breakfasts
    307-310
  Continental
    324-325
  English 310, 323-324
  full 323, 324
Brighton (England), flea
  market in 421
British Council libraries
  436-455
British Travel Centre 430
BritFrance RailPass 113
BritRail pass 118-120
Brunch 326
Brussels
  Canadian embassy in 372
  English-language
    bookstores 438
  English-language libraries
    437
  flea markets 417
  obtaining Eastern
    European visas in 39
  public transport in
    135-137
  U.S. embassy in 365
BTW tax
  Belgium 402
  Netherlands 411
Bucharest
  Canadian embassy in 374
  English-language libraries
    in 452
  U.S. embassy in 369
Bucket shops (discount
  air fares) 46, 49
Budapest
  Canadian embassy in 373
  English-language library
    in 445
  English-language news-
    paper in 446
  U.S. embassy in 368

Bulgaria
  business hours 380
  embassy and consulate
    in Canada 38
  embassy in U.S. 36
  emergency road service
    187
  fuel coupons 124
  holidays 380
  shopping 395
  telephones 225-226
  tourist office in Canada 18
  tourist office in U.S. 12
  U.S. embassy in 365
  visas 41
Bundes Netzkarte (West
  Germany) 117
Bundesnetzkarte (Austria)
  114
Bureaux de Change 76
Business hours 376-391
  Albania 379
  Austria 379
  Bank Holidays 377-378
    Great Britain 383
    Ireland 385
  Belgium 379-380
  Bulgaria 380
  Czechoslovakia 380-381
  Denmark 381
  early closing 383-384, 385
  Finland 381
  France 382
  Germany, East 382
  Germany, West 383
  Great Britain 383-384
  Greece 384
  Hungary 384-385
  Ireland 385
  Italy 385-386
  Luxembourg 386
  Netherlands 386
  Norway 387
  Poland 387
  Portugal 387-388
  Romania 388
  Soviet Union 388-389
  Spain 389
  Sweden 389-390
  Switzerland 390
  Turkey 390-391
  Yugoslavia 391
Buses
  intercity 100, 126, 127
  local (see city names)
  long distance 126-127
  postal 126
CAA (Canadian Automobile
  Association)
  International Driver
    Permits at 170

Will You Help?

Time passes. Things change. Almost as soon as this book was sent to the printer, a few things became out of date. You can help, because you'll make discoveries about how to get things done. Future readers can benefit from your experiences and learn need to know about the changes you've found. Please fill in the blanks and send us the form. Use additional (and larger) sheets of paper if you need more space.

Thank you!

Peter Manston, Travel Keys

Country:

Chapter:

What did you find different?

How did you solve the problem?

Are there any tricks for success or pitfalls to avoid?

What else did you find?

Thank you very much! Your help is appreciated not only by us but also by next year's readers.
(See over)

Send your comments to us at:

Travel Keys
TKE Next Edition
P.O. Box 160691
Sacramento, California 95816
U.S.A.

If you'd like, let us know your:

Name·

Address

Telephone

Order Form

We'll ship your order postpaid as soon as we receive it. We welcome checks, money orders, and Visa, Access, Carte Bleu, and MasterCards. Also available from better booksellers.

Title	Unit Price	Total Price
Manston's Europe (annual editions) $11.95		_____
Manston's Travel Key Britain $9.95		_____
Manston's Flea Markets of Britain $9.95		_____
Manston's Flea Markets of France $9.95		_____
Manston's Flea Markets of Germany $9.95		_____
Manston's Before You Leave on Your Vacation $6.95	_____	
Manston's Italy $10.95		_____
Californians please add sales tax		_____
Postage and handling		*included*
(Airmail outside U.S. please add $5.20 per book.)	_____	
Total		$_____

Make payments to *Travel Keys*.

Include the mailing address with your order. Please include adaytime telephone number.

If your check is not drawn on a U.S. bank, please send the equivalent on your check, and add the equivalent of U.S. $4.

Please do not send checks in U.S. dollars unless payable at a U.S. bank (except from Canada.)

Send your order to:
Travel Keys
P.O. Box 160691
Sacramento, California 95816 U.S.A.
Telephone (24 hours) (916) 452-5200.

Payment may also be made by VISA and Master-Card.

___ Visa

___ MasterCard

Card number _____ _____ _____ _____

Expiration date _____

Today's date _____

Your signature _____

Daytime telephone number (_____) _____

This order should be sent to the following address:

Order Form

We'll ship your order postpaid as soon as we receive it. We welcome checks, money orders, and Visa, Access, Carte Bleu, and MasterCards. Also available from better booksellers.

Title	Unit Price	Total Price
Manston's Europe (annual editions) $11.95		_____
Manston's Travel Key Britain $9.95		_____
Manston's Flea Markets of Britain $9.95		_____
Manston's Flea Markets of France $9.95		_____
Manston's Flea Markets of Germany $9.95		_____
Manston's Before You Leave on Your Vacation $6.95		_____
Manston's Italy $10.95		_____
Californians please add sales tax		_____
Postage and handling		*included*
(Airmail outside U.S. please add $5.20 per book.)		_____
Total		$_____

Make payments to *Travel Keys.*

Include the mailing address with your order. Please include adaytime telephone number.

If your check is not drawn on a U.S. bank, please send the equivalent on your check, and add the equivalent of U.S. $4.

Please do not send checks in U.S. dollars unless payable at a U.S. bank (except from Canada.)

Send your order to:
Travel Keys
P.O. Box 160691
Sacramento, California 95816 U.S.A.
Telephone (24 hours) (916) 452-5200.

Payment may also be made by VISA and Master-Card.

___ Visa

___ MasterCard

Card number _____ _____ _____ _____

Expiration date _____

Today's date _____

Your signature _____

Daytime telephone number (_____) _____

This order should be sent to the following address:

Find the jewels among the junk . . .

- where to look
- how to bargain
- how to get your treasures home

Widely acclaimed, authoritative handy-size "field guides" for the collector, the dealer, the traveler.

Manston's Flea Markets, Antique Fairs, and Auctions of Britain

Manston's Flea Markets, Antique Fairs, and Auctions of France

Manston's Flea Markets, Antique Fairs, and Auctions of Germany

by Peter B. Manston

Each $9.95 (U.S.)
Illustrated with maps and line drawings

Leave Home Worry-Free

Manston's Before You Leave On Your Vacation . . .

by Robert C. Bynum and Paula R. Mazuski

Shows you how to protect your home, valuables, pets, and plants from theft and neglect. A workbook section you fill in creates your "House Book" of where things are and how emergencies should be handled when you are a-way—invaluable for your house or pet sitter or anyone watching your home while you're gone.

128 pages, $5.95 (U.S.), paperback.
ISBN 0-931367-13-1. LC No. 88-12349.
5-1/2 x 8-1/4 inches (154 x 231 mm)
Illustrated with line drawings. Indexed.

Enjoy your travels more with

Manston's Travel Key Britain

by Peter B. Manston

Become familiar with its history, kings and queens (both England and Scotland), and architecture. Learn about everyday Britain—the food, telephones, transportation, and the "English" language.

A page from the unique Time-Line to help you identify ages of structures and see their historical context and reigning monarch of each period.

288 pages, paperback, $9.95 (U.S.)
ISBN 0-931367-11-5
3-3/4 x 7-1/2 inches (95 x 190 mm)

Illustrated with line drawings, diagrams, and maps

Weights

Metric:

1 Gram = Weight (Mass) of 1 Cubic Centimeter of water

1000 Grams = 10 Decagrams = 1 Kilogram
1000 Kilograms = 1 Metric Ton

1000 Cubic Centimeters = 1 Liter

English:

16 Ounces = 1 Pound = 453 Grams
14 Pounds = 1 Stone = 6.35 Kilograms

2000 Pounds = 1 Short Ton
2240 Pounds = 1 Long Ton

Fluid Measures

United States:

16 Fluid Ounces = 1 Pint
32 Fluid Ounces = 1 Quart = .94 Liters
1 8 Fluid Ounces = 4 Quarts = 1 Gallon = 3.78 L.

Imperial (U.K. and Canada):

16 ounces = 1 pound = 453 Grams

16 Fluid Ounces = 1 Pint
32 Fluid Ounces = 1 Quart = 1.12 Liters
128 Fluid Ounces = 1 Imperial Gallon = 4.54 L.

Note: 1 U.S. Pint, Quart, or Gallon =
0.83 Imperial Pint, Quart, or Gallon.

Measures

Centimeters and Inches: (right)
2.54 Centimeters = 1 Inch.

30.5 Centimeters = 1 Foot

91.5 Centimeters = 1 Yard

100 Centimeters = 1 Meter

39 Inches = 1 Meter

English:

12 Inches = 1 Foot
3 Feet = 1 Yard
5,280 Feet = 1 Statute (Land) Mile

Metric:

1000 Millimeters (mm) =
100 Centimeters (cm) =
1 Meter

1000 Meters = 1 Kilometer (KM)
1.6 Kilometers = 1 Mile

Speed:

KM/hour	Miles/hour
10	6
16	10
20	12
30	18
32	20
50	30
100	62
160	100
200	124

About the Author:

Peter Manston has been traveling in Europe since he was a child. He has seen Europe by car, train, plane, bus, boat, bicycle, and on foot.

His fascination for how things work is clearly evident in his detailed coverage of subjects as diverse as public transportation, toilets, and visas.

He has haunted flea markets, book stalls, and antiques stores searching for the "jewels among the junk" he talks about in this and his other books.

His love of fine food has taken him to many restaurants, both famous and unknown, along the way. He's also spent early mornings at street markets, bakeries, and the many other shops for which Europe is renowned.

He has organized this book for both the seasoned traveler and the first-time traveler, whether wise in the ways of other lands or cautiously off for an exciting first venture. He wants you to enjoy traveling as much as he does.

Bon Voyage!
Buon Viaggio!
Gute Reise!